HAITI'S PAPER WAR

AMERICA AND THE LONG 19TH CENTURY
General Editors: David Kazanjian, Elizabeth McHenry, and Priscilla Wald

Black Frankenstein: The Making of an American Metaphor
Elizabeth Young

Neither Fugitive nor Free: Atlantic Slavery, Freedom Suits, and the Legal Culture of Travel
Edlie L. Wong

Shadowing the White Man's Burden: U.S. Imperialism and the Problem of the Color Line
Gretchen Murphy

Bodies of Reform: The Rhetoric of Character in Gilded-Age America
James B. Salazar

Empire's Proxy: American Literature and U.S. Imperialism in the Philippines
Meg Wesling

Sites Unseen: Architecture, Race, and American Literature
William A. Gleason

Racial Innocence: Performing American Childhood from Slavery to Civil Rights
Robin Bernstein

American Arabesque: Arabs and Islam in the Nineteenth Century Imaginary
Jacob Rama Berman

Racial Indigestion: Eating Bodies in the Nineteenth Century
Kyla Wazana Tompkins

Idle Threats: Men and the Limits of Productivity in Nineteenth-Century America
Andrew Lyndon Knighton

Tomorrow's Parties: Sex and the Untimely in Nineteenth-Century America
Peter M. Coviello

Bonds of Citizenship: Law and the Labors of Emancipation
Hoang Gia Phan

The Traumatic Colonel: The Founding Fathers, Slavery, and the Phantasmatic Aaron Burr
Michael J. Drexler and Ed White

Unsettled States: Nineteenth-Century American Literary Studies
Edited by Dana Luciano and Ivy G. Wilson

Sitting in Darkness: Mark Twain's Asia and Comparative Racialization
Hsuan L. Hsu

Picture Freedom: Remaking Black Visuality in the Early Nineteenth Century
Jasmine Nichole Cobb

Stella
Émeric Bergeaud
Translated by Lesley Curtis and Christen Mucher

Racial Reconstruction: Black Inclusion, Chinese Exclusion, and the Fictions of Citizenship
Edlie L. Wong

Ethnology and Empire: Languages, Literature, and the Making of the North American Borderlands
Robert Lawrence Gunn

The Black Radical Tragic: Performance, Aesthetics, and the Unfinished Haitian Revolution
Jeremy Matthew Glick

Undisciplined: Science, Ethnography, and Personhood in the Americas, 1830–1940
Nihad M. Farooq

The Latino Nineteenth Century
Edited by Rodrigo Lazo and Jesse Alemán

Fugitive Science: Empiricism and Freedom in Early African American Culture
Britt Rusert

Before Chicano: Citizenship and the Making of Mexican American Manhood, 1848–1959
Alberto Varon

Emergent Worlds: Alternative States in Nineteenth-Century American Culture
Edward Sugden

Haiti's Paper War: Post-Independence Writing, Civil War, and the Making of the Republic, 1804–1954
Chelsea Stieber

Haiti's Paper War

*Post-Independence Writing,
Civil War, and the Making
of the Republic, 1804–1954*

Chelsea Stieber

NEW YORK UNIVERSITY PRESS
New York

NEW YORK UNIVERSITY PRESS
New York
www.nyupress.org

© 2020 by New York University
All rights reserved

A portion of chapter 4 previously appeared in Chelsea Stieber, "The Myths of the Haitian Republic." In Remembering Early-Modern Revolutions, ed. Edward Vallance. London: Routledge, 2018. Portions of chapter 7 previously appeared in Chelsea Stieber, "'Camelots du roi ou rouges': Radicalism in Early Twentieth-Century Haitian Periodicals." Contemporary French Civilization 45, no. 1 (2020): 47–69; and "The Northern Récit Paysan: Regional Variations of the Modern Peasant Novel in Haiti." French Studies 70, no. 1 (2016): 44–60. All are used with permission.

References to Internet websites (URLs) were accurate at the time of writing. Neither the author nor New York University Press is responsible for URLs that may have expired or changed since the manuscript was prepared.

Library of Congress Cataloging-in-Publication Data
Names: Stieber, Chelsea, author.
Title: Haiti's paper war : post-Independence writing, civil war, and the making of the republic, 1804–1954 / Chelsea Stieber.
Description: New York : New York University Press, [2020] | Series: America and the long 19th century | Includes bibliographical references and index.
Identifiers: LCCN 2019041463 | ISBN 9781479802135 (cloth) | ISBN 9781479802159 (paperback) | ISBN 9781479802166 (ebook) | ISBN 9781479802173 (ebook)
Subjects: LCSH: Haitian literature—19th century—History and criticism. | Radicalism in literature. | Blacks—Haiti—Intellectual life—19th century. | Haiti—Intellectual life—19th century. | Haiti—Politics and government—1804–
Classification: LCC PQ3948.5.H2 S75 2020 | DDC 840.9/97294—dc23
LC record available at https://lccn.loc.gov/2019041463

New York University Press books are printed on acid-free paper, and their binding materials are chosen for strength and durability. We strive to use environmentally responsible suppliers and materials to the greatest extent possible in publishing our books.

Manufactured in the United States of America

10 9 8 7 6 5 4 3 2 1

Also available as an ebook

In memory of Michael Dash
And for Stella, his light.

CONTENTS

Note on Translation	xi
Introduction	1
1. Dessalines's Empire of Liberty	21
2. Civil War, *Guerre de Plume*	60
3. Southern Republic of Letters	91
4. The Myth of the Universal Haitian Republic, or *Deux Nations dans la Nation*	128
5. The Second Empire of Haiti and the Exiled Republic	163
6. Nationals and Liberals, 1904/1906	201
7. Haiti's National Revolution	227
Epilogue	255
Acknowledgments	261
Notes	265
Bibliography	327
Index	347
About the Author	367

NOTE ON TRANSLATION

In the interest of making these Haitian texts available to the widest audience, I have chosen to present them in translation here. Translations are my own unless otherwise indicated. Given the importance of language, especially in early post-independence Dessalinean writing, I have included the original text in an endnote. In some cases, where I have determined that a term, phrase, sentence, or full passage is noteworthy (either for its originality, its nuance, or its intertextuality), I have included the original in the body of the text alongside the translation. My hope is that this method, though it may distract some, will allow for substantive engagement with the original materials by both Anglophone and Francophone readers.

Introduction

This book begins where so many others conclude: 1804. On January 1, 1804, Jean-Jacques Dessalines, general of the Armée Indigène, proclaimed the independent state of Haiti, marking the triumphant end to thirteen years of revolutionary fighting and over three centuries of colonial rule. The year 1804 also marked the end of the redemptive possibilities of a utopian revolution and the beginning of the fraught project of postcolonial, antislavery statehood.[1] Recent scholarship has begun to explore the challenges that Atlantic world powers posed to Haitian sovereignty and legitimacy during the Age of Revolution,[2] but there existed an equally important *internal* challenge to Haiti's post-independence sovereignty: a civil war between those who envisioned an anticolonial, antislavery empire and those who wished to establish a liberal republic. Yet this post-1804 context of empire and civil war remains shrouded, silenced in North Atlantic scholarship on Haiti in part because of what we *desire* 1804 to be: a radical, liberal, universal revolution.[3] The authoritarian nature of the post-1804 state troubles that narrative from its very first moments, acts, words, and texts.

I argue that this civil war context is central to understanding Haiti's long postcolonial nineteenth century: the foundational political, intellectual, and regional tensions that constitute Haiti's fundamental plurality.[4] Considerable work has been dedicated to unearthing the uneven and unequal production of historical narratives about Haiti in the wake of Michel-Rolph Trouillot's groundbreaking *Silencing the Past*, but many more narratives—namely, those produced from *within* Haitian historiography and literary history—remain to be questioned and deconstructed. In this book, I unearth and continually probe the conceptually generative possibilities of Haiti's postrevolutionary divisions, something the current historiographic framework on Haiti's long postcolonial nineteenth century fails to fully apprehend. Through close readings of original print sources (pamphlets, newspapers, literary magazines, geographies, histories, poems, and novels), I shed light on the internal realities, tensions, and pluralities that shaped the aftermath of the Haitian Revolution to reveal the process of contestation, mutual definition, and continual (re)inscription of Haiti's meaning throughout its long nineteenth century.

* * *

We need only consider the persistent slippage in North Atlantic scholarship between 1804 and 1806, between the foundation of an anticolonial, antislavery state and the foundation of a republic, to see the need for such a study. Historians regularly mislabel 1804 as a republican revolution when in fact it ushered in a postcolonial state, then empire.[5] Not only that: the secretaries and military leaders behind the textual performance of Haitian independence in the nation's foundational documents did their best to *avoid* referring to the events of 1804 as a "revolution" altogether. It was the 1806 assassination of Jean-Jacques Dessalines and overthrow of his empire, orchestrated by a faction of pro-republican military leaders, that cast itself as the *true* republican revolution. A similar clarification is in order for Haiti's label as the "first black republic": the problematic part of this formulation is not "first black," but "republic." Haiti was incontestably the first independent anticolonial black state in the hemisphere, but it was also a self-proclaimed empire. Civil war between republicans and Christophean monarchists divided the independent nation from 1807 to 1820, until Haiti finally unified under a republican form of government. Even then, the republic was far from inevitable: for nearly a century it remained embroiled in civil war, secessionist regimes, and the threat—and briefly, reality—of a return to empire.

To begin to make sense of the unrelenting obscurity in the naming and meaning of one of the decisive world historical events of Western modernity, we must start at the beginning of the postcolonial state: its civil war, ideological inscriptions, and partisan narrative constructions that were ultimately emplotted into the myth of the inevitable republic after 1820. My exploration of the discursive "making" of the Haitian Republic and its myth(s)—the stories that get told about it and the beliefs that result from them—is in no way intended to dim the project of Haitian independence and the very real material, political, and embodied transformations that the Haitian Revolution brought about. Instead, I take aim at the received notions and teleological narratives that lead us to confound the republicanism of 1806 with the radical anticolonial gesture of 1804, which belonged to a different set of political beliefs. That is: North Atlantic scholars' conflation of 1804 and 1806 is not a repeated slip-up, but the result of a blind spot created by the myth of the inevitable republic. The problem of 1804/1806, of empire/republic, reveals something profound about the way scholars read, write, and ultimately (mis)understand Haitian history: a failure to account for the foundational tensions at work in the postrevolutionary civil war and their reverberations throughout Haiti's long nineteenth century.

I begin this work by disentangling the multiple meanings of *liberté* in contestation—and mutual constitution—at work in Haiti's post-independence civil wars between the nation's foundational, oppositional ideological factions: republicans and Dessalineans. Through a close reading of the print production of each, I reveal two very different conceptions of Haiti's place within the progressive universalist claims of the Enlightenment—conceptions in tension that shaped the politics and writing of Haiti's long nineteenth century. Writing and, indeed, the very meaning of literature were central to the political contests that unfolded between these two factions. Literature and literariness were concepts self-consciously and politically deployed—and resisted—in the *guerre de plume*, or paper war,[6] in post-independence Haiti. Paper itself became the battleground upon which the civil war was waged.

While this book destabilizes the monolithic or homogeneous idea of Haiti through a long-view immersion in its archive, the discoveries I unlock in the process have consequences for a much wider set of fields, including Francophone and world literary studies, studies of the postcolonial Global South, and black radical studies. My reading of post-independence Haitian writing reveals key insights into the nature of literature, its relation to freedom and politics, and how fraught and politically loaded the concepts of "literature" and "civilization" really are. The competing ideas of *liberté*, writing, and civilization at work in postcolonial Haiti have consequences for the way we think about Haiti's role—as an idea and a discursive interlocutor—in the elaboration of black radicalism and black Atlantic, anticolonial, and decolonial thought. For what could be more transparent than the idea of liberty in the context of the Haitian Revolution? Yet once we look past the idea of Haiti and embrace its plurality, we begin to grasp the plurality of the seemingly monolithic, self-evident concept of *liberté*.

The Many Meanings of Liberty: Dessalinean Critique of Western Episteme

In early post-independence Haitian writing, we see two drastically different versions of postcolonial statehood vying for hegemony: possible futures for an abolitionist black state that differed precisely according to their conceptions of *liberté*. To be sure, the leading political factions of the period—Dessalineans and republicans—agreed that *liberté* meant freedom from chattel slavery. They nevertheless differed on the meaning of *liberté* as it related to rights, especially individual rights, and on the best political program for the future postcolonial state. Did *liberté* mean independence from colonial rule, or did it mean freedom from arbitrary government and the guarantee of individual rights? What differed—indeed, what was fundamentally at odds between the two—were the intellectual and philosophical bases upon which this conception of *liberté* was constructed and performed. In many ways they were mutually exclusive, constituted in dialogic opposition in the civil war and *guerre de plume* in the first two decades of independence (1804–1820). These very different conceptions of *liberté* were crucial to each faction's self-imagining and self-representation within Haiti and the wider revolutionary Atlantic.

Republicans wanted *liberté* to encompass the meaning associated with political liberalism and Enlightenment universalism. *Liberté* meant individual rights, political equality, and the active contestation of any arbitrary government (though it often fell short of these ideals in practice). Haitian republicans embraced the revolutionary language of France's short-lived First Republic, and saw an opportunity to make independent Haiti into the last remaining site of liberal republicanism after it faltered in France. For republicans, humanity—universal equality—was guaranteed by the philosophy of Enlightenment liberalism taken to its most radical, egalitarian conclusion. Conversely, Dessalineans meant *liberté* primarily as independence from colonial rule and not as a guarantee of individual rights, very much akin to the *liberté générale* maintained by Toussaint Louverture.[7] Dessalines's state-turned-empire placed anticolonial independence above all else, such that individual liberties had to be sacrificed to the greater cause of sovereign statehood. Dessalineans flexed their radical anticolonialism and actively worked to put that political agenda out into the Atlantic world. Thus, theirs was an antiliberal *liberté,* in the sense that they directly questioned the utility of political liberalism in their fledgling anticolonial, antislavery state and challenged the putative universalism of the Enlightenment. For Dessalineans, humanity was guaranteed through their own act of self-liberation, wresting it from those who purported to grant it by defining it through their own words, acts, and terms.

By insisting on these internal tensions at work in Haiti's early post-independence intellectual and political project, I aim to add further complexity and precision to the vital question of Haiti's Enlightenment critique.[8] In her superb conception of Black Atlantic humanism, Marlene Daut theorizes a Haitian intellectual project that worked to "disrupt the Enlightenment philosophies that undergirded colonial slavery and colonial racism" by countering the European discourses of black dehumanization that underwrote slavery.[9] She casts Haitian independence and the foundational texts that narrated it as a radical assertion of black humanity and a critique of the systems of oppression that underwrote Enlightenment humanism. Crucially, however, I argue that this radical critique was achieved by a faction of Haitian post-independence writers and thinkers—Dessalineans—who elaborated it as much in opposition to the republican faction within Haiti as to the larger Atlantic world. I am insisting that we see a more complex and complicated picture of factionalism and intellectual formation in tension: between a republican faction that performed itself as the purest and most radical instantiation of Enlightenment humanism (colorblind, antislavery, pro-equality) in the Western Hemisphere, and a Dessalinean faction whose members *critiqued* Enlightenment universalism because they saw it as fundamentally flawed. By foregrounding these internal tensions, I reveal civil war factionalism as generative for the Dessalinean critique of the Western tradition, and of the republican performance of its purest instantiation. That is: the black humanistic tradition that Daut defines was born out of these two strands of Haitian thought—the critique of Western Enlightenment liberalism and the embrace of its most radical possibilities—that were mutually constituted *in opposition*. What is more, these tensions around Enlightenment thought (the meaning of humanity, civilization, liberty) produced conversation and conflict throughout Haiti's long nineteenth century, with various intellectual and political factions continuing to evoke, repurpose, and deploy them within a larger set of Atlantic connections. In many ways, my book traces the long postrevolutionary history of what Lyonel Trouillot has termed the "modèle Dessalines": the continual return by various political regimes and intellectual projects to the radical heritage of Dessalinean critique cut short in 1806.[10]

My book's emphasis on the specifically Dessalinean contours of Haiti's Enlightenment critique has important consequences for the study of black radical political and intellectual thought.[11] If, as Anthony Bogues has argued, black radical thought serves as a "counterpoint" to the "progressive universalist claims" of modernity, Dessalinean thought goes a step further.[12] As Grégory Pierrot has recently argued, Dessalinean political thought was "a bold attempt at lighting a beacon beyond the confines of white Western thoughts."[13] Dessalinean thought challenged—*critiqued*—the progressive universalist claims of the Enlightenment *in real time*, as they were being put into practice in the revolutionary Atlantic. Dessalinean thought instantiated an anticolonial, antislavery state and a people that challenged the Enlightenment's putatively universal self-framing by positing—and living—alternative epistemologies and ontologies. We find a critical, negative idea of French republican liberty at work in the Dessalinean 1804 Acte de l'indépendance. We see a similar critique of Enlightenment universalism in Article 14 of Dessalines's 1805 imperial constitution, which proclaimed all Haitians under the general denomination "Noirs."[14] Sibylle Fischer has argued that Article 14 "both asserts egalitarian and universalist intuitions and puts them to a test."[15] By insisting on color, Dessalines's imperial constitution rejected the notion of color-blind republicanism born, at least in part, out of the fight for equality among lettered, propertied free men of color in Saint-Domingue. We might go further still: Dessalines's imperial constitution recognized the limits—perhaps even the trap—of Enlightenment universalism for black, unlettered, and unpropertied men in the Atlantic world. This critique was not limited to Dessalines's short-lived government, but found purchase under those who took up his ideological mantle. This book thus unearths the obscured intellectual tradition that troubles republicanism and the putative universalism of Enlightenment liberalism throughout Haiti's long nineteenth century.

Dessalineans founded an anticolonial, antislavery state, and then an empire, all the while resisting the only other viable anticolonial state formation in the hemisphere: the republic. It nevertheless bears repeating: Dessalineans challenged and resisted Enlightenment universalism not because they were "premodern," "uncivilized," or any other teleological term that has been retroactively applied to the imperial state and its aberrance within the liberal order. Dessalineans challenged and critiqued the liberal bourgeois order—political liberalism, republicanism, and Enlightenment humanism—*because* of its basis in chattel slavery. It was always already flawed: its exclusionary conception of white, European normativity placed clear limits on a black polity. Dessalineans initiated—and embodied—what Anthony Bogues calls the "heresy" of the black radical intellectual: "becoming human" by "overturning white/ European normativity."[16] Following both Daut's powerful notion of a genealogy of Black Atlantic humanism and Deborah Jenson's presentation of "Dessalines's documents" as a "dialogic foundation in a longer chain of radical African diasporan thinkers," the archive of Dessalinean counterhegemonic texts offers one—though certainly not singular—discursive origin point of radical black thought.[17] The textual and discursive practices of vindication and refutation, key aspects of black radical writing, are already instantiated in Dessalinean writing, as we shall see in this book.[18] The spirit of Dessalinean critique of Western episteme translated and traveled to contexts outside Haiti, as we can see in the form, style, and rhetoric of many radical black thinkers.[19]

By placing Dessalinean thought within the context of black radical thought, I aim to clarify the notion that early Haitian intellectual thought "anticipates" or should be seen as "prophetic" of the postmodern condition.[20] Dessalinean thought and political action constituted a radical critique that revealed the abstractions upon which Enlightenment thought relied, and how these abstractions denied the forms of oppression the project itself depended upon.[21] As a scholar firmly ensconced in a system of valuation and legibility dictated by Western episteme, I have often found myself reaching for Derrida or Butler as a useful shorthand (and a "valuable," legible one in the Western academy) to index a praxis and a political project that Haitian writers had already established.[22] Dessalinean thought unmasked, deconstructed, and decentered the Western tradition *in formation* at the turn of the nineteenth century. Indeed, I would argue that this is why the *idea* of Haiti is so useful and its revolution such a central event for artistic reimagining in black radical thought: as a subject, it carries with it the full weight of its Enlightenment critique. Haiti's very existence questioned Western episteme: the first Haitian words, the first Haitian acts pointed out the system's fundamental structural flaws. From the very beginning, Haiti resisted organizing itself according to Western principles.[23] Perversely, it is for these same reasons that Haiti is *also* a near-obsession for nativists and white supremacists throughout the world who instrumentalize Haiti's "failed state" status as proof of the impossibility of a nonwhite, non-Western black state.[24]

It is also because of its challenge to Western episteme that radical Dessalinean thought was rendered "unthinkable" in Haitian national history, internally by those Haitians committed to casting the nation within the dominant Western norms of civilization and humanism, and externally by those foreign powers whose own systems of oppression depended upon silencing Haiti's radical critique of the West. As Bogues argues, black radical intellectual production is unthinkable only insofar as it challenges "the epistemic limits established by the Western intellectual tradition."[25] In the case of the revolution, scholars have overlooked or been unable to assimilate Dessalinean critique precisely because of the extent to which it challenges and refuses Western political modernity.[26] In contrast, republicans did not fundamentally change the terms of the debate set out by Enlightenment universalism—they did not refute Western episteme, but rather sought to perform their revolution within the hegemonic terms of Western Enlightenment: individual reason, autonomy, civilization, perfectibility. Thus, the republican elements are "seeable," thinkable, and able to be recuperated within a Western paradigm. In these terms, we see why scholars and histories have privileged the republican faction, pushing the Dessalinean faction to the margins of history. Dessalineans questioned the terms of the debate set out by Enlightenment universalism, and insisted on a system of thought that could hold both their fundamental blackness and their fundamental humanity. This set them upon a different path, working to subvert and deconstruct the dominant Western paradigm with the creation of a black antislavery empire. There is also a logic in this choice of state formation: to serve a majority-illiterate population of former slaves, recalling the traditions of African kingdoms and performative, symbolic public power made a lot of sense.[27] The choice made more sense, in many ways, than republicanism, which by 1804 was an embattled ideology in the Atlantic world and would remain so for much of the nineteenth century. But once we recognize and move beyond the limiting, silencing domain of the Western tradition, Haiti's long nineteenth-century heritage of Dessalinean critique becomes legible once more. As we shall see in this book, Haitian writers like Emile Nau defined Haitians' humanity and civilization not by their ability to measure up to Atlantic standards, but by their act of resistance—of reclaiming their human rights through violence against an inherently violent world system. Louis Joseph Janvier returned to Dessalinean critiques to point out the forms of oppression that were always at work in putatively liberal systems, and to define an idea of Haitian civilization that was forged in concert with, in opposition to, and as a constant *challenge* to the ideals of Enlightenment liberalism.

The stakes of what I'm proposing here are high. Let me address them head-on by returning to scholars' "desire" to see Haiti as a utopian or redemptive republic that I mentioned in my opening gambit. What does it mean to assert that a faction—perhaps a majority—of Haitian intellectual and political thought engages in an antiliberal critique of the Enlightenment? What difficult, thorny questions does this bring up for our own investment in the universal Enlightenment and in Western political modernity? What does it mean to give full due to the discomfiting realities of violent antislavery anticolonialism in Dessalines's independence, which privileged an imperial government that assured freedom from chattel slavery but eschewed any sense of individual rights? In my work, this has meant confronting the specter of anti-Enlightenment integral nationalism and fascism *within* Haiti. It raises with it the very real histories of Haitian intellectuals' alignment with the anti-Enlightenment thought that gained prominence in the late nineteenth and early twentieth centuries in Europe (especially in Francophone spheres of influence), and ultimately, the Duvalier dictatorship, which co-opted the long heritage of Dessalinean critique of Western episteme into the service of a fascist, anti-Enlightenment political regime. Here, I am offering an alternative to what Robert Fatton has labeled Haiti's "authoritarian habitus" to explain the roots of the Duvalier dictatorship in Haiti.²⁸ In my analysis, there is something much more complex, and indeed tragic, at work in Haiti's 150 years of political and intellectual history. The tragedy, it seems to me, is how Duvalier co-opted and converted Haiti's radical Enlightenment critique in the service of his fascist dictatorship. Duvalier marshalled the pathbreaking, radical, brilliant critiques of racism and systems of oppression instantiated in Haiti's anticolonial independence, and used them to systematically oppress, terrorize, and dehumanize his own people for a generation.

Beyond the Bourgeois Public Sphere

The concept of "literature" is equally bound up in the transformations of the eighteenth and early nineteenth centuries that shaped Haiti's divergent meanings of *liberté*. Once we evoke the radical critique of Enlightenment liberalism, we can no longer assume the category of "literature" itself to be static or politically neutral. Raymond Williams has long cautioned us against taking "literature" naïvely at face value. In his woefully underutilized socio-historicization of the concept, Williams reminds us that literature is a "specific sociohistorical development of writing," a process of development that engages "a powerful and often forbidding system of abstraction, in which the concept of 'literature' becomes actively ideological."²⁹ Prior to the Enlightenment era, the term *literature* simply denoted "a condition of reading: of being able to read and of having read."³⁰ During the eighteenth century the concept of "literature" developed from its previous, broader meaning of "literacy," toward the more specialized—and exclusive—notion of "'creative' or 'imaginative' works" of quality that were distinct from utilitarian or nonimaginative writing.³¹ The concept of "criticism" emerged alongside this modern form of "literature" to mean "the conscious exercise of 'taste,' 'sensibility,' and 'discrimination.'"³²

Writers and actors *at the time* were making these distinctions and engaging with the emergent concepts of literature and criticism. When we disentangle our contemporary definitions and valuations of the concept of literature and actually historicize it, we see how invested it is in the transformations of the period and the political work it does as a category. My reflection here builds on recent scholarship that directly addresses this question of literature and authorship in early Haitian writing, particularly Chris Bongie's vital critique of Francophone postcolonial literary criticism.[33] Yet where previous scholars have endeavored to recuperate early Haitian writing as literary, my work makes no such claims.[34] Instead, I prefer to point out the problem with this kind of "question" in the first place, which is bound up in the practice of literary criticism and the bourgeois public sphere.[35] Put otherwise, if cultural studies theory has come to terms with the limits and possibilities of Jürgen Habermas's bourgeois conception of the public sphere, the notion of an all-encompassing rational, "modern," yet narrowly defined bourgeois public sphere nevertheless remains unchecked and unmarked in our literary critical praxis. Let me first rehearse briefly Habermas's arguments about the structural transformations of the public sphere and bourgeois society before engaging some recent debates in world literature and hermeneutics that reveal the limits of the Habermasian modern literary paradigm.[36]

Habermas establishes the putative rupture between "premodern" (pre-Enlightenment) and "modern" (post-eighteenth-century) practices of textual production and consumption. The Enlightenment-era emergence of a bourgeois public sphere broke with what he deemed the "monarchical" and "feudal" (but also religious) practices of textual production and hermeneutics based in performance, memorization, recitation, symbolic representation, and the mystique of authority.[37] The emergence of a literary public sphere, based in individual reason, judgment, critical reflection, and debate between private citizens, made possible the emergence of a political public sphere. Habermas's autonomous subject exercised private reason, critique, and judgment with other such private individuals to make meaning and create a shared opinion, which led to the self-reflection of an individual's role in society and the emergence of rationally constituted public opinion that challenged the authority of the state.

Critical interrogations of Habermas's concept of the public sphere have long insisted on the exclusions of this white, male, propertied sphere as well as the myth of its singularity.[38] Despite the nonbourgeois "alternative" counterpublics that various post-Habermasian critics have highlighted, few, if any, have attended to counterpublics that reject the liberal, putatively modern practices of textual production and hermeneutics that Habermas establishes as dominant.[39] Here, we can look to some recent critical engagements with world literature and hermeneutics questioning this narrow conceptualization of reading and writing practices that obscures many other uses of texts.[40] Specialists in non-Western literatures reveal the degree to which "literature" as concept is never neutral, casting in its shadow "textual forms and modes of experience no longer thinkable in a modern literary paradigm."[41] From this perspective, what Pascale Casanova has identified as the "world republic of letters" begins to look quite reductive for its privileging of a bourgeois, liberal conception of secular, autonomous, reasoned critical reading practices to the exclusion of many other kinds of texts and readings. If indeed the practice of literary criticism and bourgeois liberal modernity are mutually constitutive, then these scholars' call for alternative hermeneutics is especially urgent.

Put in these terms, we begin to see the problem of applying Williams's "abstract retrospective concept" of literature, devoid of its context or its ideological content, to early post-independence Haitian writing that emerged precisely during the period in which *literature, liberalism,* and even *liberty* itself were highly contested and debated terms *within* post-independence Haiti. Building on these post-Habermasian critiques, I am interested here in the way that a faction of Haiti's print sphere was elaborated precisely in critique and refusal of the bourgeois literary public sphere and its "modern" praxis of textual production and hermeneutics. That is, I am working against the notion of some Habermasian rupture that accompanied Haiti's revolution in the practice and politics of writing (from a putatively "premodern" symbolic or performative writing to a putatively "modern," rational, liberal, autonomous notion of textual creation and hermeneutics). Quite the opposite: these conceptions and uses of writing remained hotly contested in both civil war and paper war between a republican, bourgeois faction (which touted individual reason, private subjectivity, and communicative rationality) and a monarchical state that relied upon symbolic representation, public performance, collective textual production, and the mystique of authority to define its political project within Haiti and the larger Atlantic sphere.

Let us see the bourgeois public sphere and its limits at work in early post-independence Haitian writing. In colonial Saint-Domingue, free men of color enjoyed some access to the emergent spaces of private deliberation and critical discourse in the early part of the eighteenth century, and then were excluded as the colonial state worked to create a unified white colonial public in the 1760s and 1770s.[42] It was precisely because of these race-based exclusionary tactics that free men of color in the colony led the fight for equality during the early years of the French Revolution. In many ways, they constituted the Habermasian bourgeois public sphere in the colony *par excellence*: they engaged in reasoned, critical debate of the colonial state and its exclusionary policies, and were foundational to the emergence of public opinion for the equality of men of color as citizens of the republic. As we shall see in this book, post-independence Haitian republican writing constituted itself very much in the heritage of this bourgeois public sphere, writing within a nascent Francophone lettered sphere and performing the fruits of liberal republicanism to a wider Atlantic audience.

While this Habermasian bourgeois public sphere continued among a certain political faction in early post-independence Haiti, it was not the *only* sphere to emerge during the period. There was a sphere of writing, print, and critique that emerged in early post-independence Haiti that was highly critical of political liberalism and the bourgeois liberal order. We might call this the "Dessalinean sphere," which dominated late-revolutionary Haiti and the first years of independence. Dessalinean and later Christophean writing was first and foremost a weapon of antislavery, anticolonial resistance. It was writing based on utility and defense: the performance of violent anticolonialism or the refutation of pro-colonial discourse from France through the publication of written texts. The print production in this sphere was decidedly antiliberal and antibourgeois: it was not the private, autonomous, liberal bourgeois reason that existed apart from the state, but a collective, collaborative textual production from a militarized secretarial corps that swore an oath to defend the monarchy. Indeed, the Dessalinean sphere embraced—and performed—many of the practices that Habermas considered "premodern": public symbolic representation, the mystique of power, memorization and recitation, all in service of the state. Crucially, Dessalinean textual production and consumption encompassed decidedly more

Haitian voices outside the narrow, property-owning, literate, educated sphere of the republicans. As we shall see in this book, Dessalinean and Christophean spheres insisted on the public practice of textual creation and performance and gave voice to those who otherwise lacked the "right" or the ability to enter into print: insurgent slaves, illiterate or uneducated free men of color, and even the dead.

Having demonstrated the overdetermined, abstract retrospective concept of "literature," I would like to describe my approach to generic, formal, and discursive structures that coded the Dessalinean and later Christophean sphere—beyond the bourgeois public sphere. I am basing my approach on a few basic assumptions. First, I assume that the process of writing is always citational and intertextual; it draws upon already existing language and structures in a process of citation and iteration that is *never* new. I thereby distance my approach from the either/or proposition of radical newness or colonial borrowing, derivativeness or "imitation" (which are bound up in anachronistic judgments of value that have much less to do with the textual production of the period itself) and move toward a more thorough accounting of the norms, practices, and mechanisms of print culture in early post-independence Haiti. Second, I approach published writing (that is, writing that actively sought a *public*) as determined by a set of implicit and sometimes explicit codes, language, syntax, and forms that determine a text's legibility and meaning in a given time.[43] This involves a considerable amount of modeling, adapting, and (re)iterating existing genres, forms, and language.[44] What is more, the Haitian writing of independence was produced *literally* on the ground, often in the fog of war, by men (alas, no women!) with varying degrees of French-language schooling *and* in an entirely multilingual context: French, Kreyòl, which was the lingua franca, and Niger-Congo languages among the insurgent slaves. Dessalines's 1804 Acte de l'indépendance provides a prime example of these codes and structures. While the radical, anticolonial gesture of 1804 was performed by other means and in other mediums (the symbolic naming of "Ayti," the burning of plantations, and the massacre of the remaining French *colons* on the island), Haitians nevertheless instantiated their radical newness in the French language, in the textual act of a declaration of independence. They wrote in French to render legible—and legitimate—their radical claims to statehood and independence in an Atlantic public sphere hell-bent on not recognizing those claims. It is *both* radically new and entirely the same, through a process of modeling, adaptation, and iteration.

Finally, my approach to early post-independence writing emphasizes the performativity at work in the production of text, and more specifically the performative speech acts by which formerly colonial subjects and the enslaved seized the means to (re)define themselves as human, independent, postcolonial, black writing and publishing subjects.[45] I understand this form of performativity in early post-independence Haitian writing as related to a specific generic form: printed polemics, or pamphlets. The form and practice of polemical pamphleteering are central to questions of legitimacy, subjectivity, authority, authorship, and authorization; pamphlets were consecratory speech acts that created space for legitimatizing speech that was not otherwise "legally" granted to them. As Katie LaPorta's research on early modern anti-absolutist pamphlets shows, writers contested authority and staked a claim to the public sphere even as they lacked the "right" to do so, and deployed the written word against established power in order to forge new subjectivities and construct new publics.[46] Thus the notion of performativity we see theorized in Derrida's "performative speech acts" and Butler's "political performativity" is, as LaPorta points out, endogenous to the early modern sphere of political pamphleteering—despite the fact that we assume it to be a contemporary theoretical term.[47]

I would argue that we can trace Dessalinean and Christophean performative pamphleteering, as well as Faustin Souloque's later use of portraiture, to a longer tradition of reformist and anti-absolutist pamphlet writing of the early modern period. Indeed, we must consider their claims to sovereignty, legitimacy, and humanity via the pamphlet form as part of a longer early modern context of challenging absolutist and statist discourses and claiming authority and subjectivity. In the spirit of sixteenth-century Protestant Monarchomach pamphlets, seventeenth-century anti-absolutist "bad books" (*mauvais livres*), and eighteenth-century *pasquinades* and *libelles*, Dessalinean and Christophean writing challenged the legitimacy of colonialist and pro-slavery discourses by performing its own authority in print. What is more, its activation of this polemical form repairs—and renders moot—Habermas's putative rupture between "premodern" and "modern" writing. To be sure, I consider performativity across the civil war divide, and reveal the extent to which bourgeois liberal texts in Haiti's southern republic were themselves performing a political project to an Atlantic world audience. Their new literary and political journals (*revues*) were performing their own political liberalism, individual reason, and private and autonomous subjectivity in opposition to what they deemed the premodern, politically complicit texts of Dessalinean and Christophean monarchism.

Civil War and the Myth(s) of the Republic

My interest in the myth of Haitian republicanism is grounded in deeper reflections on the French republican myth and its paradoxes.[48] I have found Jean-Clément Martin's historiographic method in his work on revolution and counterrevolution in France of particular use. Martin works against the teleology of republicanism, or "against historiographic memory," by focusing on the internal tensions and specifically the "semantic struggles" of different factions vying for discursive hegemony in the revolutionary period. Ultimately, Martin argues that revolution and counterrevolution must be considered mutually constitutive: fed by their "shared source" and exacerbated by their rivalry against one another, they participated in the cultural and political process that created the nation.[49] David Armitage's recent shift in thinking about civil war in the Age of Revolution offers additional clarity on new methodologies beyond revolution. Armitage shows how civil war is "paradoxically fertile": highly destructive but also "conceptually generative," a process that polarizes groups as they seek to define and claim legitimacy over concepts of freedom, authority, or sovereignty, which themselves become sites of "ferocious contestation."[50] I adapt Martin and Armitage's approach to trouble the republican teleology at work in the historiographic memory of Haiti's early post-independence history, focusing on the ideologies in tension during the Haitian civil war and their mutually constitutive role in creating the Haitian nation. Through close readings of fiction and nonfiction texts, I endeavor to emphasize the narrative constructions and discursive "making" at work in the production of Haitian history from within, while recognizing the stakes these local histories had for the larger Atlantic story that would be told. Republican historiography sought to nationalize the republican narrative of the revolution, papering over the imperial and military authoritarian nature of Haiti's revolutionary foundation. Such writing has shaped the way that scholars, both within and outside Haiti, have conceptualized the goals of the Haitian Revolution and the agendas at play in the post-independence civil war.

While I performed considerable archival research and work with original sources, readers will note that I privilege one work of Haitian historiography: Thomas Madiou's eight-volume *Histoire d'Haïti* (1847–1848; 1989).[51] Simply put, for want of a chronological guide to the events of the revolution and early post-independence period, I determined Madiou's history to be more neutral than the other possibilities in early Haitian historiography: Baron de Vastey, Hérard Dumesle, Beaubrun Ardouin, and Joseph Saint-Rémy.[52] Ardouin in particular is highly ideological in his account of the early post-independence civil war, despite his reliance on a greater amount of archival and documentary evidence. Of particular importance for me is Madiou's method, which relied on oral testimonies from revolutionaries and insurgent slaves who had lived through the early post-independence civil war. Here, I follow Colin Dayan's incisive assessment of Madiou's utility: "Madiou's interest in preserving the stories told by those who had not been educated in French, who did not share in the mastery of the text, results in those contradictions for which he has been condemned, but which help us to get closer to a history shot through with ambiguity."[53]

In order to foreground regional factionalism and civil war in Haiti, I privilege locally produced Haitian texts, which maintain the regional detail, the internal tensions, and the complexities of civil war that tend to get flattened by Atlantic world scholarship.[54] I draw specifically on printed matter (including visual culture) published on the ground, by Haitian presses, which I argue offers access to a discursive self-fashioning and performance of statehood that are less mediated than writing published in Paris or other capitals of the world republic of letters.[55] My focus on marginal writers and less-studied texts is not, however, an attempt to redeem forgotten heroes or write a redemptive counternarrative. This book has no heroes, to borrow a phrase from Michel-Rolph Trouillot.[56] Rather, I am recovering marginalized texts in order to explain precisely why they have been overlooked in historiography and literary histories of Haiti. They are texts that are marginal and illegible to the world republic of letters because they actively wrote against the dominant, normative concepts of "civilization" and "literature."[57]

While my corpus of locally produced Haitian print culture reveals the discursively bounded debates about the meaning of liberty between Dessalineans and republicans, these textual debates must be seen in contrast to the embodied practice of *liberté* that a multitude of other Haitian political factions fought for.[58] My corpus reveals much about the competing ideas for how best to self-fashion post-independence Haitian politics, identity, and culture, but cannot give voice to those factions that did not engage in (or have access to) the same self-representative print practices. The northern insurgent slaves who rallied around Sans Souci and Macaya, or the former slaves in the Grand Doco mountains led by Goman (Jean-Baptiste Perrier), produced little in the way of print and are therefore only briefly accounted for in my book. Moreover, nineteenth- and early twentieth-century Haitian print was controlled by literate men and those illiterate men who had the power to command them. Many other ideological camps operated throughout Haiti's long nineteenth century while existing between the lines of print—namely, the peasantry and women.[59]

Finally, I take plurality as a guiding principle to unlock deeper discoveries about Haitian agency and political ideology in postcolonial Haiti. In order to reach a more capacious and inclusive understanding of Haiti in all of its iterations, I embraced a specific understanding of "regionalism" that stands apart from its customary use in Caribbean studies. Because Caribbean populations have been defined, since their inception, in relation to a European metropole, their "marginal" status makes them always already "regional" in the larger Euro-Atlantic context. The Caribbean as marginal to the metropole thus masks or obscures the complex realities within this vast, diverse "region." How, then, to address the local realities of connections, circulations, and (im)mobilities within and across national, linguistic, and geographic boundaries, on the margins of the margin, as it were?[60] My new regionalism allows us to acknowledge—and disabuse ourselves of—the tendency to allow Caribbean capital port cities to stand in for the entirety of the island nation. In the case of Haiti, it was only really in the mid-twentieth century that the capital city became the Republic of Port-au-Prince (Repiblik Pòtoprens): a highly centralized state bureaucratic machine that reached its completion under the Duvalier dictatorship.[61] By privileging the diversity and plurality of Haiti's regional existence, my work provides a more fulsome accounting of the rich history of Haiti's long nineteenth century and its writing from the margins of the world republic of letters. Indeed, the foundational regional tensions in early post-independence Haiti are central to understanding the continued civil war, secessionist regimes, and regional conflicts that persisted in nineteenth- and twentieth-century Haiti, and even to the present day. More important for our purposes here, the revolutionary and post-independence civil wars provide crucial context for making sense of the battles over national identity and cultural legitimacy that have marked Haitian writing since independence. For, while I place great importance on the historical and political context here, my book is ultimately about *writing*, how it became the primary battleground upon which the internal conflict and *guerres de plume* were waged, and the heritage of these regional and ideological tensions in Haiti's long nineteenth century, the Duvalier dictatorship, and even today. Through a sustained synchronic and diachronic engagement with the plurality of Haiti's textual existence since 1804, we grasp the internal battle over the nature of freedom, civilization, and the meaning of literature that fundamentally shaped Haiti from its founding to our present day.

1

Dessalines's Empire of Liberty

Il faut par un dernier acte d'autorité nationale, assurer à jamais l'empire de la liberté dans le pays qui nous a vu[s] naître; il faut ravir au gouvernement inhumain qui tient depuis long-tems nos esprits dans la torpeur la plus humiliante, tout espoir de nous réasservir; il faut enfin vivre independans ou mourir.

(We must, in one final act of national authority, forever ensure the supremacy of liberty in the country where we were born; we must take away all hope of reenslaving us from the dehumanizing government that has kept our minds in the most humiliating torpor; we must, at last, live free or die.)
—Acte de l'indépendance

The Haitian Republic was not founded in 1804. In fact, the secretaries and military leaders behind the textual performance of Haitian independence did their best to *avoid* referring to the events of 1804 as a "revolution" or the state a "republic" in the nation's foundational documents.[1] The first declaration of independence, proclaimed on November 29, 1803, by Jean-Jacques Dessalines, Henry Christophe, and Augustin Clerveaux, notably refers to "disturbances" (*désordres*), "excesses" (*excès*), "turbulent times" (*temps orageux*), and a "terrible war" (*guerre affreuse*), but avoids calling the proclamation of Haitians' humanity, rights, and anticolonial independence a *révolution*. Although contemporary American English translations of the November 29 declaration do use the term "revolution," *within* Haiti it was not until 1810, under Christophe, that writers would consistently begin to refer to the events of 1791–1804 as a revolution: "the birth of our revolution," "our immortal revolution," "the phases of the revolution," "the tormented revolutionaries," and so on.² Further still, Dessalines's January 1, 1804, declaration encouraged Haitian citizens and countrymen *not* to export the events of Haitian independence to neighboring colonies in the Caribbean. He uses the term "revolution" only to refer to what independent Haitians should not be—revolutionary incendiaries or firebrands (*boutes-feu*): "Let us not, as revolutionary firebrands, declare ourselves the lawmakers of the Caribbean and let our glory consist in troubling the peace of our neighboring islands."³ The orchestrators of the 1806 overthrow and assassination of Dessalines, on the other hand, billed their actions explicitly as a republican revolution. The republican opposition self-consciously deemed themselves "révolutionnaires" engaged in a Haitian campaign "against tyranny" (*contre la tyrannie*)—inscribing their liberal revolution in the heritage of 1789 and even casting Haiti as the lone remaining instantiation of the values of Enlightenment liberalism and republicanism that metropolitan France had failed to secure.

If 1804 often gets confused for the 1806 foundation of a republican state, it is worth considering the aftermath of Haiti's radical anticolonial gesture in further detail. What happened in the first years after Haitian independence? As we shall see, the early post-independence period is marked not by national or political unity, but rather by tension between those who wanted a republic and those who wanted a military authoritarian state, and by many other actors outside the print public sphere who envisioned other iterations of post-independence Haiti. This simple fact, all too often overlooked in scholarship, raises a number of questions. How and why did newly independent Haitians become divided between supporters of Dessalines's authoritarian state and the republican opposition? How did this foundational tension shape the Empire of Hayti and the 1805 imperial constitution? Why did men like Juste Chanlatte and Louis Félix Mathurin Boisrond Tonnerre rally around Dessalines? Why did they want to proclaim an empire? And finally, how did these early divisions spill into the 1807–1820 civil war between North and South?⁴

To begin to answer these questions, we must first understand the political and rhetorical strategies that defined Dessalineanism. Dessalineans believed that the best—perhaps the only—way to secure freedom from slavery and independence from French colonial rule was through violence: the performance of violence in written and spoken rhetoric, and the act of violence in the sanctioned massacre of French colonists from February to April 1804. These writers, thinkers, and military men embodied the principle of Haitian independence: their freedom was conditioned on the negation of French colonial power, accomplished via the same weapons the French had wielded against them; they were, in Thomas Madiou's words, "barbarians against colonial barbarity."[5] Thus, Dessalineans did not just reverse "the terms of the colonialist binary of civilization and savagery," they engaged in a radical, violent anticolonialism—a zero-sum game whose ultimate aim was to annihilate the very premise that the wayward island could be retaken.[6]

In addition to battling an external enemy—France and other European colonial powers—Dessalineans also constantly negotiated an internal threat: the republic. While we are not yet witnessing the full-blown civil war *guerre de plume* that we will see in later chapters, this early period offers an important prelude to later divisions. I am aware that this is not the way we are used to thinking about early post-independence Haiti. Yet what I want to suggest here is that our assumptions about this period—namely, of an internal unity set against the threat of an inhospitable, external Atlantic sphere—have made it difficult for us to see the political fault lines that fractured early post-independence writing.[7] What I am suggesting here is that the political and ideological divisions that shaped Haiti's long nineteenth century of post-independence writing *were already present* in the 1804–1806 period, which, I will argue, was marked by a constant internal tension between Dessalineans and republicans,[8] with each group vying to define the post-independence future of Haiti according to its own ideology and political agency, which performed for the dominant Atlantic world powers in starkly different ways.

Although the various factions in revolutionary Saint-Domingue united in the war for independence under the banner of Dessalines's Armée Indigène, as soon as the war was over, the newly independent state of Haiti divided again along the same lines of disagreements, antagonisms, and suspicions that were present during the revolutionary period. The republicans were primarily former Rigaudins from the South who had fought against Toussaint in the War of Knives, among them Alexandre Pétion, Nicolas Geffrard, Laurent Férou, Jean-Louis François, Elie Gérin, Guy Joseph Bonnet, Bruno Blanchet, David Troy, Yayou, and Guillaume

Vaval. According to Thomas Madiou, the republicans (or "constitutionalistes," as he refers to them) were especially concerned with the title of "gouverneur-général" assigned to Dessalines and the murmurings of monarchy, fearing that they were participating in a process of "legalizing despotism."[9] They expected Dessalines's title to be changed once the new government was structured, preferring that he be named president accompanied by a democratic constitution. Among the Dessalineans, the important work of organizing the new state was undertaken by Louis Félix Mathurin Boisrond Tonnerre, Louis Laurent Bazelais, Jean-J. Dominique Diaquoi (Diaquoi Aîné), and Carbonne; Juste Chanlatte served as "secrétaire générale du gouvernement," alongside secretaries Alexis Dupuy, Carbonne, and Jean-Jacques Charéron, who with Diaquoi Aîné made up the emperor's "counseil privé."[10] Other leading Dessalineans included Joseph Balthazar Inginac, François Capois (Cappoix), Corneille Brelle, and later Etienne Victor Mentor and Charles Victor Rouanez. According to Madiou, the Dessalineans were less concerned with the form the government took, so long as Dessalines remained leader: "It mattered little that the head of state call himself king, emperor, or president."[11]

This chapter traces the print culture of the immediate post-independence period leading up to Dessalines's assassination on October 17, 1806, recasting Haiti's earliest post-independence writing within the context of political and ideological divisions that shaped the period. Dessalines's empire of liberty was a military government with a single powerful executive, committed to order, discipline, and duty as the only way to ensure lasting independence from French colonial rule. Under Dessalineanism, individual rights and liberties had to be sacrificed to the greater cause of sovereign statehood. The republicans disagreed: they sought to found a state according to liberal Enlightenment ideals, embracing the revolutionary language of individual liberties and radical democracy that characterized France's short-lived First Republic. They wanted to talk about virtue, talents, the rights of man, laws and a constitution, citizens and sharing of power, but were overpowered by the Dessalinean faction—until 1806, when they would revolt against the "tyrannie" of Dessalines's arbitrary rule and found the southern republic. I begin by focusing on how Dessalineans consolidated and codified Haitian anticolonial independence through writing, which asserted itself externally as an anticolonial weapon and internally as a force of unity against the enemy within. Next, we consider the republican opposition's mobilization of the language, ideals, and symbolism of French republicanism to overthrow Dessalines's empire and their subsequent disavowal of this foundational act of parricide-regicide.

Dessalinean Writing: *Une Arme Anticoloniale*

Kreyòl pale, kreyòl konprann.
—Haitian proverb

Dessalines formed the intellectual core of his empire by bringing writers, intellectuals, and generals together in a secretarial corps—a key branch of his Armée Indigène. He began assembling his secretarial corps in the summer of 1803, when it became clear that the French were likely to lose the war.[12] While Dessalines had not wanted for soldiers, he needed men of letters to transition to an independent state that was legible—and legitimate—in a wider Atlantic sphere. There were many fewer men of letters in the country; most had left during the revolutionary tumult of the 1790s. Dessalines thus began methodically recruiting talented writers and thinkers into his service. The corps was a heterogeneous group: from North and South, of black and mixed-race parentage, from the army and from planting backgrounds, of wealthy and modest means. He started by courting Boisrond Tonnerre, a native of Les Cayes from a wealthy and well-connected planting family, who had spent time in France during the revolution before returning to the colony.[13] Boisrond Tonnerre was working as a secretary to the commander of the South, Nicolas Geffrard, when Dessalines selected him to be part of his growing "secretariat" in July 1803.[14] Dessalines soon extended his reach outside revolutionary Saint-Domingue to find lettered men to join his cause, most notably Juste Chanlatte and Etienne Mentor. Both Chanlatte and Mentor had been living outside Saint-Domingue during the revolutionary tumult and made plans to return in 1803 to join Dessalines. Mentor had been in France since 1797, having accompanied the French commissioner Sonthonax into exile after Toussaint expelled him.[15] Yet news of the success of the Armée Indigène drew him back to the island, much as it did for Chanlatte.[16]

It is important to note here that while Chanlatte and Mentor answered Dessalines's call, many other exiled Saint-Dominguans did not. The most staunch Rigaudins, supporters of French republican rule in the colony, remained in exile in France or joined revolutionary movements in neighboring Caribbean territories before finally returning to the island in 1815–1816 (see chapter 3).

Dessalines's focus on amassing an army of secretaries and lettered men over the course of 1803 and 1804 reveals the importance of discourse and the printed word to the Dessalinean independence project. Writing was a weapon of anticolonial independence. Just as Dessalines brought together his fiercest, most trusted generals to secure and preserve Haitian independence, he assembled a secretarial corps to wage that battle on the discursive front. And just as he armed his soldiers with weapons to disassemble the mechanisms of the colonial machine, he armed his secretaries with rhetoric and printing presses.[17] Indeed, Dessalines's secretarial corps collaborated with military leaders in support of their common goal. Deborah Jenson has pointed to the process of "technological and lettristic partnering" in early post-independence writing between military leaders and secretaries, involving "dictation, discussion, and editing and refinement of the product," which was common practice among print publics throughout Europe and North America.[18] I would add further that this collaborative, collective nature of textual practice extended to the secretarial corps itself: its members shared text, language, and talking points to create a fascinating discursive, citational network that we can trace through all of the documentation from the period. Collectively, they established the lines of argumentation, key phrases, and tone of the text.

In this sense, I am not considering Dessalines's role within post-independence writing as "author" but rather as general: he was in charge, he chose the strategy (in conversation with his trusted counselors), and he gave orders—in Kreyòl—to be executed by his generals and his secretarial corps.[19] I want to stress that I am not eschewing concepts of authorship or literature because I think Dessalinean writing is unworthy of such denominations. On the contrary, Dessalinean writing is brilliant, complex, and innovative. Rather, I am attending to precisely what this writing intended to do: to perform Haiti's anticolonialism legibly in an Atlantic world. As Jenson rightly puts it, Dessalinean writing formulated "an anticolonial poetics in the service of the representation of former slaves' experience and subjective claims, leading to or protecting the establishment of their subversive dominance over colonial authority."[20] As I argued in the introduction, the mechanism through which Dessalineans achieved this anticolonialism is radically new in the colonial context. At the same time, Dessalinean writing draws upon the strategies of vindicationism and refutation—at work in the French print sphere as early as the sixteenth century and widespread in eighteenth-century revolutionary pamphlets—in order to displace and destabilize the authority of French colonial discourse through reiterative speech acts. Dessalinean writing relied upon taking existing language and generic forms from the former colonizer, and making them its own through a process of citation, iteration, and ultimately, deconstruction.[21]

The point of entry into Dessalinean anticolonial writing is the January 1, 1804, Acte de l'indépendance: a three-part text that includes Dessalines's proclamation of independence, the act and oath of independence, and the official nomination of Dessalines as "Gouverneur-Général, à vie, d'Hayti."[22] Therein, we find all of the ideas, metaphors, and vocabulary that furnish early Dessalinean writing: the importance placed on language; the need for violence to expiate the horrors of French colonialism and protect Haitian independence (that is, antislavery *liberté*); and the danger of the enemy within. First and foremost, we note the centrality of discourse and the power of the word to the performance of anticolonial independence. As the Acte makes clear, words matter. It was not merely force of arms that kept the enslaved from achieving independence, but the deceptive *words* of France's colonial agents: the enslaved had been "victims of our own gullibility and our own leniency for fourteen years; vanquished not by French forces, but by the deceptive eloquence [*pipeuse éloquence*] of their agents' proclamations."[23] The deceptive, dishonest, or misleading eloquence with which the French colonists and administrators—like Pierre Victor Malouet—wrote in defense of slavery and the colonial system was designed to obscure the inhumane, barbaric treatment of the enslaved.[24]

I insist here on the meaning of the French *pipeuse* (deceptive, dishonest, misleading) because recent scholars have assumed that the term is a misprint or misreading of the more common *piteuse* (sad, pitiful). Such an assumption fails to account for the power and significance of the term *pipeuse* and the Dessalinean strategy it deploys: to portray European colonial discourse as masking truth, veiling insidious motives, and covering with flowers the abyss of slavery[25]—in short, to call out Western civilization for its hypocrisy. I would like to expound briefly here on the problem of the assumption of "misprinting," which fails to see the radical *critique* at work in Dessalines's original text.[26] Or rather, it is because of the assumption that Dessalinean language was operating squarely within Western episteme that scholars have assumed that the word was a misprint or a *mistake*. Critics assume that Dessalinean writers were trying to embarrass or heckle French colonists by making literary judgments on the quality of French writers' eloquence: it was *bad* eloquence, pitiful, sad, not worthy. This takes us back to my discussion in the introduction of the anachronistic assignment of the bourgeois liberal codes of "literariness" (taste, finely wrought style) to the period, when indeed Dessalinean writing was actively resisting these codes. When we recognize that Dessalinean writers were operating in a different sphere, the critical assumption of misprinting appears quite problematic. Critics are literally imposing a bourgeois literary hermeneutic back *onto* a Dessalinean text that was actively challenging it. The assumption of a misprint becomes even more tenuous when we consider that the second letter *p* in *pipeuse* is clearly printed in each version of the document and that the term itself was in common usage in the eighteenth century. If we take my proposition that Dessalinean writing was a weapon of anticolonial independence, then Dessalinean secretaries and printers treated it as a priceless resource—as they would the arms and gunpowder that they used to fight the enemy.[27] What is more, by putting this term into its rightful context—the Dessalinean sphere—we see a much clearer strategy at work, and its lasting heritage in Haitian discourse throughout the long nineteenth century to our present day. The Dessalinean denunciation of "pipeuse éloquence" is at the origin of the proverb "Kreyòl pale, Kreyòl konprann," which is translated literally as "Kreyòl spoken, Kreyòl understood" but is used to indicate honesty and candor: "Speak plainly and do not deceive" or "Speak honestly and be understood."

If the deceptive treachery of French colonial discourse—French words—had the power to enslave and dehumanize the inhabitants of Saint-Domingue, then Dessalinean writing deployed French words to equally powerful ends. Dessalinean writers sharpened, wielded, and deployed discourse to claim their own freedom by force in the Atlantic print public sphere. Dessalinean writing is a way for independent subjects to fight back and correct their own naïveté ("victims of their own credulity")—an inward-looking focus that sought to rally Haitians by placing their fate in their own hands.[28] In order to neutralize France's colonial discourse and to protect against European nations' desire for dominance over other human beings, Dessalineans argued that it was not sufficient merely to expel the French colonial army from Haiti's shores. The Dessalinean rhetoric of Haitian independence sought to render Haiti un-colonizable by "stealing" or "robbing" (*ravir à*) France of the idea, the hope, that it could ever resubjugate the Haitian people, as cited in the epigraph at the beginning of the chapter (*il faut ravir au gouvernement inhumain*).[29] The only way to achieve this goal, to become human subjects of their own, was to strike fear into the French and other nations through an act of violent, blood-filled vengeance: "Know that you will have accomplished nothing if you do not show the nations a fearsome, but just, example of the vengeance that a people, proud of having regained their liberty and intent upon maintaining it, must exercise; let us terrify all those who would dare try to steal [ravir] it away from us again."[30] The repetition of "ravir" here is quintessentially Dessalinean writing: highly constructed, but also playing with language. Haiti's foundational national act is to steal away the idea of reenslaving Haitians, and to strike fear into any country that might try to "steal" Haiti's just, legitimate independence.[31] In this sense, I see Dessalines's foundational act of anticolonial vengeance—the massacre of French planters and soldiers—and his strategy of discursive or rhetorical violence that I have been sifting out here as different implementations of the same strategy, one of Haiti's "first acts of sovereignty."[32] It was a multi-front political strategy to maintain antislavery, anticolonial independence at all costs. Moreover, the memory of French imperial violence remained fresh: Leclerc's expeditionary forces had engaged in spectacular violence during the War of Independence, and the general had even called for the extermination of all black men, women, and children over the age of twelve in the colony.[33] Further, David Geggus has pointed out that the massacre of the former colonists was understood as a message to Haiti's would-be foes: "A 'terrible but just' act of retribution would send a message to France and the outside world that the Haitians would not surrender the freedom they had won."[34] Dessalinean writing was thus an anticolonial weapon on two levels: a discursive sabre rattling to keep France and other would-be colonizers at bay, and a disarming or defusing of textual weaponry the French might use in retaking the island.

Haiti's act of anticolonial vengeance is written into the foundational documents of independence. The act of stealing away the idea of reenslavement through violence (the massacre of the French) and terror (the fear of violence) is a necessary precondition to the creation of an "empire of liberty" in Haiti. Though the Empire of Haiti would not be proclaimed until many months later (as I discuss below), it is worth considering briefly here Dessalines's use of the phrase "empire of liberty" (*empire de la liberté*) in the foundational document of Haitian independence. First, though the phrasing might seem like the soldering together of two seemingly discordant concepts—empire and freedom— Dessalines defined *liberté* as antislavery independence from colonial rule and *not* the guarantee of individual rights. Indeed, as I translated it in the epigraph above, the phrase "empire de la liberté" in the Acte de l'indépendance does not refer to a specific government form, but rather ensures the supremacy of freedom—from chattel slavery and from colonial rule (*l'empire de la liberté dans le pays qui nous a vu[s] naître*). Dessalines's anticolonial, antislavery state was just that: an independent authority that ensured Haiti's control of its own liberty, independence from colonial rule, and eternal freedom from chattel slavery through the act of vengeance/self-liberation. Second, I believe that there is a good argument to be made for Dessalines's use of the phrase as an iteration and adaptation of Thomas Jefferson's earlier use of the phrase "empire of liberty" (as early as 1779) in his republican, expansionist project to create new liberal subjects and spaces of liberty.[35] Scholars of Jefferson argue that he used the phrase in order to create a productive tension between the two terms of the comparison: the unlikely joining of the idea of *imperium* with the idea of individual liberties that the republican leader valued above all else.

Dessalines's "empire of liberty" understood *imperium* as the means to reclaim, secure, and protect the *freedom* and humanity denied to the colonial enslaved. What is more, it did not seek expansion: its principles of non-intervention, and thus non-expansion, were made explicit in the Acte. Independent Haiti did not seek to embody Jefferson's phrase, but rather to critique it. According to these same Dessalinean principles of adaptation and iteration, it performed the Jeffersonian idea of "empire of liberty" to delegitimize and subvert it. Anthony Bogues has shown how black radical critique reveals the paradox of Jefferson's universal Enlightenment idea. Jefferson's "empire of liberty" was based on the refusal of freedom to slaves and to Native American tribes, "a project in which the possibility of total domination was the horizon."[36] Here again, Dessalinean thought provides a useful origin point for black radical critique of the paradoxes—and hypocrisy—of Enlightenment liberalism. By claiming the legitimacy of an empire of freedom—one that performed the opposite of Jefferson's expansionist project *and* proclaimed radical antislavery—independent Haiti laid bare the paradoxes at the core of Jeffersonian ideals of liberty. Haiti's claiming of the empire of liberty is yet another example of Dessalinean rhetoric: rescripting dominant terms that circulated in the eighteenth-century Atlantic print public sphere to perform and legitimize Haitian statehood while simultaneously calling into question the putative legitimacy of those dominant systems.

Is it so strange to think that Dessalineans intended to create an empire from the start? Scholars' desire for a redemptive revolution has translated into a lack of engagement with Dessalines's discomfiting empire. What little analysis there is of Dessalinean *imperium* places it within the paradigm of Napoleonic imperialism.[37] But the empire in Haiti was also designed to safeguard against the political faction that challenged Dessalineans' hold on power: republicanism. Dessalines warned that Haitians would not truly be free until they rid themselves of the "mark of the French" (*empreinte française*), which in the Acte de l'indépendance is linked directly to a republican form of government: "The French name still haunts our lands. Everything here revives the memory of the cruelties of this barbaric people; our laws, our customs, our cities, everything still bears the mark of the French; nay, there are still Frenchmen on our island and you believe yourself free and independent of that Republic that fought all nations, it is true, but that never defeated those who wanted to be free."[38] Here again, as before, Dessalines contrasts the putative liberalism of France's revolutionary republicanism and Haiti's radical, anticolonial self-liberation. Dessalineans also sought to counter the threat of liberal republicanism from within Haiti—the claims to equality and individual rights, but not necessarily a strong anticolonial, antislavery stance—by establishing an anticolonial, antislavery empire.

The Enemy Within

At the very end of Dessalines's address to the independent people of Haiti, he calls upon his generals to join in the oath that will eternalize their glory and their independence: to die rather than live under France's domination. He also issues an important warning: "If there be a tepid heart among us, may he stand back and tremble to utter the oath that will unite us."[39] And once more after the oath is repeated, he warns his generals: "And if ever you were to refuse or begrudgingly receive the laws dictated to me by the spirit[40] who watches over your future and your happiness, you would deserve the fate of ungrateful people."[41] These threats are far from veiled, taking aim not only at those who would refuse his orders, but also at the lukewarm generals who might grumble under their breath instead of vehemently proclaiming their desire to renounce the French. Those who dissent, those who are only halfhearted in their support—they will receive the treatment reserved for the ungrateful. Dessalines concludes his address by saying, "But be it far from me this terrible idea," which serves both to expose and threaten his internal dissenters, gesturing to the dreadful idea of what might befall those who moderated their support of their leader.[42]

It would be useful here to imagine the effect of this address on the revolutionary generals assembled in Gonaïves. Dessalines was publicly calling out those who disagreed with his designs for the post-independence Haitian state. Did they look to their allies, recognizing the threat against them? Did they look to the ground, hoping not to catch the attention of the Dessalineans? And who were these lukewarm, grumbling resisters? Dessalines was targeting primarily, and perhaps only, his remaining source of opposition after 1804: the republicans. Indeed, Madiou notes that while republican generals such as Pétion, Gérin, and Bonnet signed the proclamation elevating Dessalines to "Gouverneur Général à vie," they expressed concern for the way other members of the independence movement were speaking about power, government form, violence, and vengeance.[43] Recall from the introduction that during the War of Independence, northern insurgents such as Jean-Baptiste Sans Souci and Macaya were a great source of internal dissension for Dessalines—what Michel-Rolph Trouillot calls the "war within the war."[44] Dessalines largely quashed that threat by having Christophe and other northern generals assassinate the insurgents, consolidating his power and unifying the North under the Armée Indigène. While followers of Sans Souci, Macaya, and others continued to foment uprisings in the North, the main power centers in post-independence Haiti were held by Dessalineans and republicans. These divisions played out along geographic lines: Dessalines's power was strongest in the first division of the West, but also in the North in Gonaïves and Cap-Haïtien. The South remained mostly out of his reach: he negotiated power there primarily through the southern generals, and, as Madiou has noted, generals like Elie Gérin operated autonomously most of the time.

In many ways, tension with the republicans and the potential for civil war was a constant through line from the earliest days of the revolutionary tumult in the colony. Even with pro-republican André Rigaud's loss and exile after the War of the South, the southern peninsula—a bastion of pro-French republicanism—continued to operate autonomously from Dessalines's Armée Indigène, only capitulating to his rule in July 1803. And the role of the pro-republican faction within the Armée Indigène was not seamless: in September 1803, Dessalines criticized Geffrard in the South for being too accommodating to the French, openly trading with them in the port of Les Cayes and treating them with a "moderation" that Dessalines disapproved of.[45] The transition from the November 29, 1803, proclamation of independence by Christophe, Dessalines, and Clervaux to the official, ceremonial Acte de l'indépendance of January 1, 1804, reveals these factional divides within the revolutionary government and the very different futures these groups envisioned. During the intervening month, the politics of Dessalineanism, and the language and imagery through which it would be communicated, were decided among Dessalines's generals and his secretarial corps. The January 1 document reveals their choice: that violent anticolonialism coupled with a military authoritarian state enforcing order, unity, and obedience was the best strategy to move forward as an independent black abolitionist state in the Atlantic world.

Madiou notes that the secretarial corps set out collectively to draft the text of the official Acte de l'indépendance that would put forth Haiti's politics into the world.[46] The well-known, possibly apocryphal story that Dessalines rejected a first attempt at the Acte de l'indépendance by Charéron, a French-educated member of his secretarial corps, in favor of the unbridled violence of Boisrond Tonnerre's version is not wrong, so much as it is incomplete.[47] That Dessalines would reject versions lacking the requisite tone and imagery is entirely consistent with his view of writing as an anticolonial weapon. But Charéron's version may also have been too in line with the republican faction, especially if he modeled it on the US Declaration of Independence. What is noticeably absent from the January 1, 1804, proclamation is the language of individual rights and the idea of *liberté* associated with those rights, the pursuit of happiness, talents, virtue, parliamentarism or the sharing of power, democracy, or a constitution.[48] The fact that the final and ultimate version of the proclamation so clearly refuses these elements suggests that Dessalines commanded a document that more fully embodied the spirit of anticolonial independence *and* addressed the internal threat of republicanism.

Juste Chanlatte performed a similar anti-republican anticolonialism in his Dessalinean writing.[49] His first published text in independent Haiti was his "Hymne haytiène," performed on January 21, 1804, which included the signature "Ch . . ." found in many of Chanlatte's other texts.[50] The identification of the author only by the two letters of his last name affirm that Dessalinean writing was a collective and performative endeavor: it was not meant to glorify the individual author or praise his lyric genius, but to glorify Dessalines, the great military hero of Haitian independence, and to unify *under* him in order to preserve Haitian order and liberty. Chanlatte participates in the multi-generic, multi-platform promotion of Dessalinean anticolonial antislavery, in proclamations, pamphlets, broadsides, poems, and songs. Chanlatte's hymn rehearses the same themes, imagery, and political positions as the Acte, but through a different form: the ceremonial song of praise. Such poems commonly accompanied ceremonial occasions, and also appear in the pages of Dessalines's official government paper, the *Gazette politique et commerciale*, published in Cap-Haïtien in 1804. These poems were sung and performed aloud for an audience—in the case of Chanlatte's "Hymne haytiène," reiterating and anchoring in oral performance the content of the Acte de l'indépendance.

I want to look closely at Chanlatte's song because he constructs it as a complement to the Acte de l'indépendance and specifically its anti-republicanism and the threat of the enemy within, made evident in the first lines of Chanlatte's hymn. He addresses the lukewarm Haitians whom Dessalines called out, asking incredulously why anyone would remain silent in the face of Dessalines's glorious proclamation: "What? You are staying silent, Indigenous People? / When a Hero, by his feats, / Avenging your name, breaking your chains / Has forever ensured your rights?"[51] Given the radical anti-French and anti-republican tenor of the Acte, it is notable that Chanlatte's "Hymne" is directed to be sung to the tune of "Allons enfants de la patrie" as a parody or contrafactum.[52] Chanlatte is pointing here of course to Rouget de Lisle's "Chant de guerre pour l'Armée du Rhin," which later became known as the "Hymne des Marseillais," and was declared the French Republic's national anthem on July 14, 1795.[53] But why pen a contrafactum to this particular tune, one of the many symbols of French republicanism? In the spirit and rhetoric of Dessalinean writing, Chanlatte's hymn highlights and critiques the paradox of French republican *liberté* enshrined in this foundational text of the French First Republic. More than thumbing his nose at a French readership or listening public, though, I believe, Chanlatte's contrafactum also had an internal Haitian audience in mind: the pro-republican faction. Chanlatte's parodic hymn was aimed at those Haitians who had wished to create a republic, and who continued to grumble from the southern peninsula while buying themselves time to make independent Haiti into the radical instantiation of French *liberté* that they believed it should be: Gérin, Pétion, Yayou, Vaval, Bonnet, and many others, who would eventually overthrow the empire and assassinate the emperor in 1806.

Let us look briefly at the two songs together, to see how Chanlatte cites and adapts the French original, ultimately subverting the republican ideal of *liberté* it promoted. Chanlatte's hymn follows the same organization of fourteen-line stanzas, each composed of nine lines (with the fourth and fifth lines repeating), followed by a shorter five-line refrain that repeats in each stanza. Here are the first stanzas of each:

Allons enfants de la Patrie,
Le jour de gloire est arrivé!
Contre nous de la tyrannie,
L'étendard sanglant est levé, (*bis*)
Entendez-vous dans les campagnes
Mugir ces féroces soldats?
Ils viennent jusque dans vos bras
Egorger vos fils, vos compagnes!
Aux armes, citoyens,
Formez vos bataillons,
Marchons, marchons!
Qu'un sang impur
Abreuve nos sillons![54]

Quoi? tu te tais Peuple Indigène!
Quand un Héros, par ses exploits,
Vengeant ton nom, brisant ta chaine,
A jamais assure tes droits? (*bis*)
Honneur à sa valeur guerrière!
Gloire à ses efforts triomphants!
Offrons-lui nos cœurs, notre encens;
Chantons d'une voix mâle et fière,
Sous ce bon Père unis,
A jamais réunis
Vivons, mourons,
Ses vrais Enfants, (*bis*)
Libres, indépendants.

(Arise children of the Fatherland,
The day of glory has arrived!
Against us tyranny's
Bloody flag is raised! (*twice*)
Do you hear in the countryside,
The roar of those ferocious soldiers?
They're coming right into your arms
To cut the throats of your sons, your companions!!
To arms, citizens,
Form your battalions,
Let's march, let's march!
Let impure blood
Water our furrows!)

(What? you keep silent, Native People!
When a Hero, with his feats,
Avenging your name, breaking your chains
Forever ensures your rights? (*twice*)
Honor to his military might!
Glory to his triumphant efforts!
Let us offer him our hearts, our heady praise;
Let us sing strongly and proudly,
United under this good Father,
Forever joined together,
We live, we die,
His true Children, (*twice*)
Free, independent.)

If we ignore Chanlatte's second indication to repeat the lines in the refrain ("Vivons, mourons, ses vrais Enfants, / Libres, indépendants"), the rhythm and disposition of syllables, caesurae, and rhyme follow exactly the refrain in Rouget de Lisle: "Marchons, marchons! / Qu'un sang impur / abreuve nos sillons!" with even the third-person imperative "-ons" ending matching up in the refrains. Chanlatte's hymn also draws on many of the same images and terms from de Lisle's original, remaking them in the service of the Dessalinean imagery established in the Acte de l'indépendance. For example, where de Lisle calls upon "children of the fatherland" (*enfants de la patrie*), Chanlatte calls upon independent Haitians to live and die as Dessalines's "true Children" (*vrais Enfants*), replacing the republican fatherland in France with the imperial father of independent Haiti. The poignant image in de Lisle's refrain of the invaders' blood irrigating France's fields is taken up later by Chanlatte, again infused with Haitian revolutionary *and* Vodou imagery: "With the blood of a cruel horde, / Yes, when you water their bones, / These words can be heard, / Deep from within the land of the dead" (*Du sang d'une horde cruelle, / Oui, quand vous arrosez leurs os, / Elles font entendre ces mots, / Du sein de la nuit éternelle*).⁵⁵ The blood of the "cruel horde," here taken to mean the French expeditionary army and the other colonists massacred after independence, irrigates the bones of "victims"—those earlier inhabitants of the island who perished under slavery and at the hands of the French forces, but also the much longer heritage of Amerindian victims of colonial dominance—a key element in the justification of Dessalines's foundational act of vengeance. Just as the Acte evoked the bones of the enslaved ancestors and the need to avenge their spirits, Chanlatte evokes the act of watering these ancestors' bones with blood to allow them to speak. The words voiced by these ancestors—Amerindian and African—are a reprisal of the refrain "Vivons, mourons, ses vrais Enfants" (quoted above), this time transformed from the first-person imperative, "nous," to the second-person imperative, "vous" command: "Vivez, mourez, ses vrais Enfants" (Live, die, his true Children).⁵⁶ Here, we have the voices of the island's dead—slaves, Amerindians—commanding their progeny to rally under Dessalines and avenge their death. The act of giving voice to the voiceless victims of slavery, African and Amerindian is a central part of the Dessalinean anticolonial critique of Enlightenment universalism and with deep ties to Vodou mythology. We mistake and misrepresent these critiques when we assume that Dessalinean writers like Chanlatte are operating purely within Western episteme.[57]

The terror of metaphoric slavery—slavery to arbitrary rule—abounds in Rouget de Lisle's hymn, which he describes using the language of chattel slavery.[58] He rallies the French revolutionary army to fight against an enemy that threatened to "reenslave" them by depicting the soldiers of Prussia, Austria, and other European armies as a "horde of slaves" (*horde d'esclaves*) because they are subjects of arbitrary rule. By contrast, he describes the French soldiers' resistance to "vile chains" (*ignobles entraves*) and "irons" that other European countries were preparing for them: "It is us that they dare plan / To return to ancient slavery [*l'antique esclavage*]!" Elsewhere, de Lisle warns that the French will labor under the yoke of another master: "By chained hands / Under the yoke [*sous le joug*] our brows would bend! / Vile despots would become / The Masters of our future!" How can Haitian revolutionaries have heard this, the French Republic's official anthem, and not seized upon the deafening silence on the actual practice of African, chattel slavery? Again, Chanlatte's choice of tune for his contrafactum is a significant one: he evokes the paradox of "slavery" in French revolutionary republican discourse and its ultimate failure to ensure the universal project of liberty from chattel slavery. Here again, we are at the heart of Dessalinean critique and the paradox of the Enlightenment idea of *liberté*. Where Rouget de Lisle's hymn is a collective song to rally troops, Chanlatte's hymn is closer to a religious song of worship and thanks to the great liberator of the slaves, who will ensure the Haitian people's collective future and continued freedom from chattel slavery and French colonial rule. Where de Lisle offers the hypothetical possibility of metaphoric, political reenslavement if the French republican army does not fight European monarchs ("Under the yoke our brows would bend!"), Chanlatte uses a similar phrasing to describe Dessalines's actual, historical liberation of Saint-Domingue's enslaved masses. It is Dessalines the African eagle who materializes from the sky (echoing his proclamation in the Acte "I sacrificed everything to fly to your defense"), to lift Haitians from their subjection and rid the island of the French: "To lift up our weary brows / Jacque appears, they vanish."[59] Where there is a collective element to the French Republic's fight against tyranny in de Lisle's hymn, in Chanlatte's there is a clear glorification of Dessalines and his role in the liberation and humanization of the colony's enslaved, and thus a call to unity under the great liberator.

The penultimate stanza returns to the indignant, aggressive nature of the first, and rehearses the full weight of Dessalines's warning about internal discord and the enemy within:

> Quel est cet indigne Insulaire,
> Ce lâche cœur, ce vil soldat
> Qui, désormais sous sa bannière
> N'affronterait point le trépas? (*bis*)
> Qu'il parle; au défaut du Tonnerre,
> Pour expier cet attentat,
> Nos bras levés contre l'ingrat,
> Sauront le réduire en poussière.
>
> (Who is this unworthy Islander,
> This cowardly heart, this worthless soldier
> Who, henceforth under his banner
> Would not face death? (*twice*)
> May he speak; in the absence of a Thunderbolt,[60]
> To atone for this attack,
> Our arms raised against the ingrate,
> Will reduce him to dust.)

Here, like the Acte de l'indépendance, Chanlatte's song seeks to identify those who do not commit fully to Dessalines's anticolonial independence. The stanza serves as an open call to ferret out the "unworthy Islander" (*indigne Insulaire*) who shuns his duty to renounce the French and live and die under Dessalines's paternal authority. The assonance in the letter *i* links the "indigne Insulaire" with the adjective "ingrat," in a direct reference to the Acte, which warned those who refused or begrudgingly received Dessalines's orders (*tu mériterais le sort des peuples ingrats*). The internal dissenter is all of these things (an unworthy islander, an ingrate), but he is surely not a Haitian—not worthy of this name that Dessalines chose to symbolize Haiti's Amerindian ancestors and their brave fight to the death against the conquistadores. It is more than simply being an islander (*insulaire*) that makes one Haitian: one must be committed to Dessalines's radical regime. Chanlatte demands that this ingrate (*ce lâche cœur, ce vil soldat,* here linking back to the *cœur tiède* of the Acte) make himself known. He asks: who is this dissenter who shies away from confronting death, from taking the oath that Dessalines delivered—to live free and independent, to choose death for all those who would seek to reenslave Haiti? May he speak ("Qu'il parle") and may a thunderbolt strike him down right then. Only if this divine intervention does not come will his own brothers strike him down, reducing him to dust (an image that picks up on the image of ashes in both Rouget de Lisle's original and the Haitian Acte).

The song ends on a note of religious worship that serves to transform the revolutionary fervor of 1802–1804 into a consolidation of the empire and Dessalines's imperial rule. Chanlatte takes the famous rallying cry of the Armée Indigène, "Liberté ou la mort," and transforms it into a kind of prayer to Jacques, the patron saint of the emancipated: "Henceforth, Jacque is the Patron / Of those who reject slavery."[61] United under this saintly father figure, Chanlatte invites his fellow Haitians, "Under this good Father, united / Forever joined together / Let us live, let us die, his true Children / Free, independent."[62] Chanlatte's hymn pivots independent Haiti's motto toward something that further codifies Dessalines's power as leader. While "Liberté ou la mort" captured the revolutionary fervor of the Armée Indigène, "Vivons, mourons, ses vrais Enfants" commits the Haitian people to swear fidelity to Dessalines; it takes the revolutionary notion of living independent or dying and transforms it into life and death as subjects of their great military leader. The "enfants" in his song are not the children of a collective "patrie" as in the French republican anthem, but of a singular "bon Père," the great man to whom they owe their liberation and their collective identity as Haitians. The song is a hymn in praise of Jacques "le Patron"—patron saint of all who have fought off the chains of enslavement.

The need for such a hymn of praise and devotion to "Papa Desalin" suggests the degree to which post-independence Haiti was fractured and full of dissent. The pivot toward greater investment in Dessalines's singular power was undoubtedly to the great dismay of republicans, who still wished to see a different form of government. And if they were frustrated with the tenor of the Acte de l'indépendance and the rhetoric of worship in Chanlatte's hymn, one can only imagine how they reacted when they learned that the Dessalineans planned to proclaim Haiti an empire.

Dessalines's Empire of Hayti

The specific details surrounding the proclamation of the Empire of Hayti are opaque—surrounded by doubt, questions of forged signatures, secret plans, and backdated documents. I argue here that the decision to proclaim Dessalines as Jacques I, emperor of Haiti, was a codification of the same political strategy and statecraft that informed the empire of liberty: order, discipline, and duty under a single imperious ruler were the only way to secure the radical anticolonialism and human rights the government had seized in 1804. It was also at odds with the democratic, constitutional government that the republican faction was agitating for. The petition Chanlatte and Boisrond Tonnerre drew up nominating Dessalines as emperor makes their stance quite clear: "convinced that there is no sharing supreme authority" and that "a people can only be suitably governed by one," in order to assure the security of Haiti's inhabitants, they needed to have a singular head of state with "an august and sacred title that concentrated in his person the forces of the state."[63]

Dessalines's nomination consists of a short two-page "Nomination de l'Empereur d'Hayti, J. J. Dessalines," prepared by the generals of his army, followed by Dessalines's official acceptance. As Madiou's documentary research shows, however, the decision to proclaim Dessalines emperor was not taken up until August 1804—after Haitian administrators had learned of Napoléon Bonaparte's nomination to emperor and the plans for a *sacre* by Pope Pius VII later that same year.[64] It appears that all of the documents related to the nomination and proclamation of Dessalines as emperor, including a pamphlet from Juste Chanlatte addressing his fellow Haitians, *A mes concitoyens*, were printed in bulk on September 2,[65] but the official printed versions meant for distribution carry the dates January 25, 1804, for the official signed nomination, and February 15, 1804, for Dessalines's address accepting the nomination. Madiou maintains that upon learning of Napoléon's nomination, Chanlatte, Boisrond Tonnerre, and his principal officers immediately began laying groundwork, coming up with the idea of a petition that the generals would sign. Madiou's evidence also shows that Dessalines and his counselors attempted to keep this effort a secret from his republican generals, mostly those in the South and West. For example, Dessalines told them of Napoléon's elevation to emperor on August 8, 1804, but did not say that he and his counselors were considering doing the same in Haiti. Instead, he told them that Napoléon's power was now even greater than during the Leclerc expedition because he was virtually unopposed, and that Haitians needed to be even more committed to anticolonial independence. He made similar claims in a letter to Pétion, appealing to Pétion's republicanism by addressing him as "citoyen général" (not something Dessalines did for everyone) and asking him to accelerate work on the fortifications and defense structures in place. He gave no indication of plans to proclaim Haiti an empire.[66]

Those Dessalineans who were preparing the empire were aware of the delicate nature of the decision, evinced in a letter Dessalines had delivered to Pétion just a few days later, along with the petition appointing Dessalines emperor of Haiti. The tone of the letter is deferential—Dessalines is careful to again appeal to Pétion's "democratic sentiments" (*sentimens démocratiques*).[67] He asks Pétion to sign the petition only if he judged it appropriate ("si vous le jugez à propos") and to have it signed by the other generals and chiefs of his division, l'Ouest. The letter lays out a serpentine relay system by which Pétion would send aides-de-camp further out into the southern peninsula until each of the officers had signed the petition—a testament to the continued autonomy of the region. Dessalines seems to acknowledge the complicated nature of his request, which would have been made much easier by simply calling an assembly of the "officiers généraux," by arguing that he needed his officers to remain in their command posts, working on his diverse fortification projects.[68] Surely this was a pretense to keep the southern generals at bay and to avoid an immediate confrontation. Dessalines's letter gave Pétion only ten days from the original date of the cover letter (August 11) to receive all of the signatures, a challenging time frame. Nevertheless, Madiou notes that the petition returned to Dessalines at the end of August "covered in signatures" (*revêtue de signatures*), though it is unclear how many of the southern generals had actually signed it.[69]

Then suddenly, on September 2, Dessalines was proclaimed emperor effective immediately, though perhaps this was always the plan in order to avoid an uprising among the republican faction. The official nomination document was signed only by the officers stationed in Marchand that day, those most faithful to the Dessalinean cause, while the rest, according to Madiou, were forged.[70] Furthermore, the document that was prepared for printing listed all of the officers' names together indiscriminately, despite the fact that most had never signed the original. The speedy nomination and appointment of Dessalines as emperor was effective: there was no coup, and his official coronation was celebrated as planned, on October 8, 1804. Madiou includes an account of his celebration in Cap-Haïtien, with the parish priest Corneille Brelle (who would later join the Christophean faction) presiding, and César Télémaque (who would later join the republican faction) and others presenting sung couplets in honor of His Majesty, Jacques I.[71] In theory, Dessalines's October 8 coronation was celebrated throughout the North, West, and South, though it is almost certain that the South abstained.

The proclamation of empire occasioned a shift in Dessalinean rhetoric: a softening of anticolonial violence for the Atlantic audience, and a hardening of the threat to the republican enemy within. We can see this shift in Chanlatte's pamphlet *A mes concitoyens*, which accompanied the nomination documents.[72] Given the backdating scheme, it is possible that Chanlatte penned the pamphlet in early 1804 and that Dessalineans selected it to accompany the nomination documents: it contains the same signature, "Ch . . . ," that he used in the earlier "Hymne haytiène," and refers to Dessalines as the "Gouverneur-Général." It is equally plausible that Chanlatte simply penned the pamphlet as part of the nomination scheme. In either case, the pamphlet is a reissue in a new generic form of the images, vocabulary, and rhetoric of existing Dessalinean texts: the Acte de l'indépendance, his "Hymne haytiène," and Dessalines's April 28, 1804, proclamation, which Chanlatte had penned. *A mes concitoyens* reiterates Dessalines's foreign policy commitment to non-intervention by insisting on the principle of neutrality among neighboring colonies. The pamphlet also performs the same discursive show of force aimed at would-be colonizers (noting arms, ammunition, and willing soldiers) and at Haiti's internal dissenters, the enemy within. But the pamphlet also pivots decidedly from the violent anticolonialist rhetoric of independence toward a softer, more diplomatic touch for a foreign audience, particularly British abolitionists.[73] Indeed, Chanlatte addresses the fact of his audience directly in the pamphlet, acknowledging that the events surrounding Haitian independence were without precedent. As a result, he argues, all eyes are now on Haiti, waiting to see what it will do: "It is going to focus the attention of the Old World on the New."[74] With the acknowledgment of this foreign gaze, the main goal of the text becomes propagandistic, concerned with promoting a certain image of the Haitian nation in order to forge new alliances in the Atlantic world as Haiti officially branded itself an empire. Here, Chanlatte does not write out or disavow Haiti's foundational act of anticolonial violence so much as transform it into metaphors and euphemisms. Chanlatte casts the Armée Indigène as inspired by natural law. He argues that self-preservation is an innate human right and that the "right of revolution" (*la résistance à l'oppression*[75]) is a "natural obligation" (*devoir naturel*). He cites forces of nature as having "put weapons in our hands" (*nous ont mis les armes à la main*), which deftly distances Haitian soldiers from the violent imagery of slave insurrection. Haitians were victorious not because of rebel soldiers plunging their "blood-stained arms, avengers of perfidy and betrayal, into the breasts of" their French adversaries (to quote an earlier text of Chanlatte's), but rather by the grace of God: "Thanks to the Supreme Being who does not wish the innocent to perish, our executioners disappeared before the Indigenous Phalanxes, like an impure haze vanishing in the sunlight."[76] It is an almost mystical image, without bloodshed, in which the Armée Indigène emerges victorious over the French.

Yet if Chanlatte's pamphlet softened its anticolonial violence and played up its religious tone to target an Atlantic world abolitionist audience, it also doubled down on threatening the enemy within, assuring the readership of the order and unity that prevailed under Dessalines. The pamphlet reiterates and strengthens Chanlatte's earlier appeals to Dessalines's internal authority and the need to maintain order. It rallies Haitians to assume their rightful place under their great leader: "faithful above all to the laws of discipline and subordination, let us live and die under the command of our intrepid, precious leader that the heavens intended for us."[77] With freedom achieved, Chanlatte pivots to an oath based in the military vow to follow one's commander into battle, a post-independence stance that he describes as "ordered by necessity, the most imperious of laws" (*commandée par la nécessité, la plus impérieuse des lois*).[78] Chanlatte's use of the adjective "impérieuse" here warrants note: while he is not describing Dessalines as the emperor, he is saying that necessity—the need to survive, to maintain independence—demands that Haitians submit to him. It is in this context that Chanlatte advances his threat to the enemy within, rendering it more vehement and violent than in previous texts. He warns: "Woe to the madman who would try to trouble the whole and the harmony that reigns among us! may he be immediately eradicated from society, as one uses a machete to uproot a parasitic and venomous plant."[79] May the enemy and his spirit of discord and division, silently plotting to take down the state, be cast out of independent Haiti so that the state may hold: "Go far from these premises this spirit of discord and division that silently prepares and finally carries out the fall of even the most unified governments!"[80] Chanlatte's use of local imagery—a machete uprooting a venomous, parasitic plant that saps nutrients from the host—confirms his attack against local, internal actors. His use of the verbs "extirper" and "déraciner" is particularly noteworthy: he wants to remove these internal agents of dissent by uprooting them, leaving them unable to regenerate, so that sovereignty and autonomy can be maintained. It reveals the long history of political uprooting (*déchoukaj*) in Haiti.

* * *

The news of Dessalines's sudden elevation to emperor in September 1804 undoubtedly agitated the pro-republican faction in Haiti, particularly when accompanied by Chanlatte's pamphlet intensifying his language and attacks against them. Still, it wasn't until mid-1805 that the republican opposition to the Dessalineans began to gain momentum, after Dessalines's failed military expedition to take back the eastern part of the island from the French, who had remained there since the revolution.[81] Dessalines's prolonged absence and ultimate failure in the East may have been enough to move the opposition from a state of resistance to full-blown revolution. Indeed, Madiou notes that a sustained, vast conspiracy formed in the South in the summer of 1805, and was the first of many.[82] It is within this context of mounting pressure against his rule that I would like to briefly consider the 1805 imperial constitution (composed in early 1805, during Dessalines's campaign in the East). I am less interested in the text of the constitution itself, which has been analyzed in detail by historians and literary critics, but rather the written and oral delivery of this constitutional material in an increasingly fraught political atmosphere.[83] More specifically, I am interested in the account of a June 16, 1805, ceremony organized in Marchand to present the imperial constitution, in which Dessalines's secretaries read documents and made speeches that attempted to placate republican dissenters and even address some of their concerns. The ceremony is as interesting for its performative, symbolic gestures as for its discursive content: it shows how texts were disseminated to a larger illiterate public through oral readings, ceremonial grandeur, and political symbolism, but also offers an example of how political participation might have looked during the early post-independence period. For example, the text of the ceremony indicates that troops from Port-au-Prince as well as the Polish and German battalions were called to Marchand to assist in the ceremony, and were put on display for the wider viewing public.[84] What is more, the ceremony reveals how Dessalines's secretaries worked together to perform their roles. Chanlatte's duty was to read the text of the constitution aloud, while Diaquoi Aîné, "chef d'escadron," read the military penal code, and Bazelais, "chef de l'état major général," read a speech encouraging the people "to submit themselves to the laws and to devote themselves to upholding the Constitution," swearing eternal hatred to the French for good measure.[85] Boisrond Tonnerre played the role of Dessalines himself: Madiou notes that "His Majesty by the organ of Boisrond Tonnerre pronounced the following speech" to the people of Haiti.[86] Their division of labor gives us a more nuanced understanding of the different roles in Dessalines's secretarial corps: Chanlatte read the text that he had a lead role in producing; Diaquoi Aîné spoke about military discipline, which he actively oversaw; Bazelais urged the people to maintain order, which he was responsible for maintaining; and Boisrond Tonnerre read Dessalines's own words in French.

More significant is the content of the speech that Boisrond Tonnerre read, and what it reveals about Dessalineans' attempts to address the concerns of republicans (not to mention what it reveals about the shared lexicon and writing practices of Dessalinean secretaries). First, the speech incorporates the turn initiated by Chanlatte's earlier *A mes concitoyens* pamphlet, from spectacular, anticolonial violence toward metaphor and euphemism. Dessalines's speech goes further still in its attempts to performatively transform revolutionary violence into the stability of a constitutional empire: "While your victorious weapons were fertilizing this soil saturated with a salubrious and expiatory dew, your eyes were turned toward a constitution that secured your rights on solid ground, and placed you among the ranks of civilized nations."[87] The speech transubstantiates the blood of the French into water: blood that previously fertilized the bones of Haiti's ancestors is now a forgiving (expiatory) and beneficial dew. What is more, it collapses the chronology of events, insisting—retrospectively—on the primacy of laws and rights and codifying them in a constitution at the very same moment ("en même temps") that Dessalines's army carried out the massacres of the French. The speech further stresses the language of civility, morals, politics, laws—words that, up to this point, had not been used by Dessalineans in relation to rights, but rather to the maintenance of order and discipline. Dessalines concludes the speech by remarking that June 16, 1805, was the beautiful day when he witnessed law, liberty, and independence triumph. Dessalines's speech further transforms the role of his secretarial corps, embracing the figure of the warrior-secretary who achieves his goals first by the point of his sword, and then by the point of his pen: "Honor to the generals who did not forget to stipulate the people's interests with their pens, after having seized them at the point of the sword."[88] The seamless transition from sword to pen here symbolizes the transition that the speech attempts to enact: from revolution to legislation, from violence to order. Crucially, this image of the sword and the pen will serve as a constant point of return for much of Haitian writing in the nineteenth century: in Christophe's secretarial corps, whose heraldry depicts a sword crossed with a pen (see chapter 2), in Louis Joseph Janvier's writing (see chapter 6), and in the Haitian proverb "Konstitisyon se papye, bayonet se fè" (Constitutions are made of paper, but swords are made of steel).

Dessalines's June 16, 1805, speech is thus a performative act that attempts to pivot away from the violence and disorder of revolution toward an orderly imperial regime. He asks the same of the Haitian people, that they submit to the "brake" of law and order: "Glory to the people who ... submit themselves to the brake [*frein*] of laws and discipline."[89]

The word *frein* here points to a key idea voiced in the republican resistance to Dessalineanism: the belief that laws, constitutions, parliament, and other government checks act as a brake on tyrannical power. Perhaps Boisrond Tonnerre even wrote the speech with the idea of directly addressing these republican critiques of unchecked power, paying service to them, though not fully assimilating them. If Dessalines did not accept a brake on his own power, as the republicans would have liked, he did seem to accept the need for an end to the violent unrest that accompanied the War of Independence and the post-independence massacre of the French. He does so in the closing to his speech, by once more reshaping the oath of independence, to live free or die. He presents it as a final act, a complement to the first oath of Haitian independence, *liberté ou la mort*. It is telling that at this moment, Dessalines finally utters the word "revolution"—in a proclamation that seeks to distance his empire from its tumult and put an end to the Haitian Revolution. He reflects on his first oath to "live free or die" and the time that passed "since I have been journeying the circle of ups and downs into which the revolutionary activity threw me; this oath is my stopping point."[90] Dessalines declared that the 1805 constitution marked the end of the revolutionary cycle of change, pivoting toward state power based in law and order. He also intended his speech act to put an end to the revolutionary agitations among the republican faction—a strategy that would ultimately prove unsuccessful.

The 1806 Republican Revolution

Here they are, revealed, these secrets full of horrors.
—Letter from the Army of the South to General Christophe, describing Dessalines's rumored orders to massacre all men of mixed race[91]

On October 16, 1806, Haiti's second "revolution" took place: the republican faction sought to found the nation anew by overthrowing the empire and establishing a new government in its place. Southern insurgents had proclaimed the "Haitian campaign against tyranny" (*campagne haïtienne contre la tyrannie*) and staged an uprising in the southern town of Les Cayes.[92] Dessalines departed from Marchand to quell the insurrection, leaving Vernet, his finance minister, in his stead (assisted by none other than the young Jean Louis Vastey, future Baron de Vastey), and was accompanied by Generals Mentor, Bazelais, Dupuy, and Boisrond Tonnerre, as well as Colonels Roux and Charlotin Marcadieux, and other superior officers.[93] On October 17, 1806, the insurgency ambushed and assassinated Jean-Jacques Dessalines, Jacques I, first emperor of Haiti, at Pont Rouge. The leaders of the insurrection—Pétion, Gérin, Yayou, Vaval, and Bonnet—proclaimed that their movement would abolish tyranny forever and "revive liberty" (*faire renaître la liberté*).[94] The fact of the assassination is itself shocking: the greatest hero of Haitian independence, the great liberator, the African eagle, was brought down by his own countrymen in an ambush. But at the time, the revolutionaries believed that they were achieving *true* revolution, *true* liberty, and that it was necessary to sacrifice Dessalines to their righteous cause. The aftershocks of their decision reverberate throughout Haiti's history.

While Dessalines's assassination has been the subject of many creative (mostly theatrical) works that cast it as the effort to defeat one man whose ambitions had grown too large for the Haitian state, few have cast it as a political, revolutionary battle between republicanism and Dessalineanism.[95] The fact that Dessalines's assassination is more commonly recounted in theater, song, proverbs, and Vodou than in historical monographs gets to the heart of Haiti's unsettled postrevolutionary tensions, and the unresolved trauma of this foundational act.[96] For many years his memory existed outside of the state. While Christophe's state-turned-monarchy remembered Dessalines as a liberator and hero of national independence, the northern leader also distanced himself from the emperor's shortcomings as a head of state, particularly concerning matters of diplomacy and trade.[97] Republicans, on the other hand, cast Dessalines as a dangerous tyrant whom they were duty-bound to remove. Much of the work of subsequent chapters in this book will be to trace the various attempts to re-sound the trauma and the violence of the republicans' assassination of Haiti's liberator and first head of state. To begin to further illuminate this foundational act in Haiti's history, I argue that it is essential to see the events of 1806 as a republican revolution, and specifically what the southern republicans cast as the *true* Haitian Revolution. Indeed, the republican faction self-consciously referred to its movement as a revolution more consistently and purposefully than the Dessalineans ever did. In my discussion of this final phase of Dessalinean rule, I analyze the revolutionaries' mobilization of the language, ideals, and symbolism of French republicanism to overthrow Dessalines's empire, as well as their subsequent disavowal of this foundational act of parricide-regicide.

Republican resistance had been growing since the summer of 1805, and after the January 1, 1806, Independence Day celebrations, the question of ending Dessalineanism was not a matter of *if*, but *when*.[98] As we saw above, Dessalineans were keenly aware of this. Nevertheless, neither their threats against the internal dissenter nor their attempts to pivot to a more constitutionally based government quelled the republican opposition. External factors also exacerbated the pressure on Dessalines's regime: on February 28, 1806, Thomas Jefferson signed the Logan bill, which suspended US commerce with Haiti. It is unclear what Dessalines could have done to stop this bill. James Dun argues that it was much more about the making of a postrevolutionary US identity than it was about Haiti: the making of the *idea* of Haiti as a non-nation, a pariah "brigand state," and an aberration.[99] Nevertheless, the blow still hastened Dessalines's overthrow. The republicans' revolutionary manifesto of October 16, 1806, bemoaned that commerce was languishing under "this stupid man," an apathetic, uneducated Dessalines.[100]

The ultimate conspiracy against Dessalines originated in Les Cayes among the supporters of Elie Gérin, who had been operating outside Dessalines's authority for some time. Dessalines's push to verify property titles in the South, his decision to rescind land grants made to free men of color by the French colonial government, and even burning wood that southern loggers had illegally cut down for export—all of this further stoked southerners' commitment to overthrowing his "tyrannical" rule.[101] According to Madiou, Dessalines referred to the southern peninsula, and Les Cayes in particular, by the familiar term "the lower Coast," and berated inhabitants of the South as "bad Haitians" (*mauvais indigènes*) because they sacrificed all else to their own individual interests—a clear indictment of their liberalism.[102] The shared disdain for one another is evident in these factions' statements leading up to and during the republican revolution, and so is their fundamental disagreement on the meaning of *liberté*: republicans believed that Dessalines had usurped his authority and was infringing upon the rights of planters and traders in the southern peninsula, and Dessalineans believed that the southerners were self-interested, unwilling to sacrifice their own rights to ensure lasting antislavery, anticolonial independence.

The degree to which liberal republican ideology scripted Dessaliness's assassination and the overthrow of Dessalineanism is unmistakable. When Gérin led the final southern insurgency against Dessalines, he cast his role in terms of republicanism in a letter to the northern general Henry Christophe on October 12, 1806: "But liberty, good God! is a vain word in this country, we don't dare utter it openly, though it sits atop declarations; it exists there alone."[103] Referring to the new constitutional regime that Dessalines made so much of in his 1805 proclamation, Gérin maintained that he "tramples upon it every day" (*foule aux pieds chaque jour*).[104] The southern insurgents' cause was aided by a rumor that Dessalines planned to massacre all of Haiti's former *anciens libres*, no matter their color—almost certainly a fabrication by the southern revolutionaries, something actors on both sides of the civil war acknowledged.[105] What is most fascinating about the southern generals' accusation is that their phrasing "Here they are, revealed, these secrets full of horrors" borrows from Pierre Victor Malouet's infamous pro-colonial text, his *Mémoires sur les colonies, et particulièrement sur Saint-Domingue*. In the 1802 introduction, Malouet writes of the aftermath of the slave uprising in Saint-Domingue: "*Here it is, revealed, this secret full of horror. Liberty for the blacks: Domination for them! Whites massacred or enslaved.*"[106] The republicans' use of Malouet's language in their accusation of Dessaliness's rumored massacre of free men of color reactivated the memory of Dessaliness's violence against the French in order to persuade—by association—that he would extend it to his own countrymen. The republican revolutionaries were aware that this allusion would resonate with both their supporters and their adversaries, which suggests that Malouet's text was foundational not only to later Christophean writers (as Chris Bongie has incisively pointed out) but to the discourse of Haitian independence more broadly.[107]

Another crucial text to the republican revolution is their manifesto, "Résistance à l'oppression,"[108] dated October 16, 1806—the day before Dessaliness's assassination at Pont Rouge (signed by Gérin, Pétion, Yayou, Vaval, Bonnet, and many others).[109] There is no reason to believe they had not already drawn up their plans to assassinate Dessalines, and so their manifesto reads like a justification for future acts, in the clear, methodical language of Enlightenment liberalism and classical republicanism: laws, rights, the pursuit of happiness, protection of individual interests, and constitutionalism. What is more, the title of their manifesto places their ideology squarely within the French revolutionary heritage of 1789: the second article of the Declaration des droits de l'homme et du citoyen states that among the natural and inalienable ("imprescrible") rights of all men are "liberty, property, security, and resistance to oppression" (*la liberté, la propriété, la sûreté, et la résistance à l'oppression*).[110] Southern Haitian republicans saw their movement as the sole remaining instantiation of the values that revolutionary France had inaugurated in 1789 and made manifest in 1793 in Saint-Domingue, and had ceded to Napoléon Bonaparte in 1799.[111] They were working to save the liberal revolution in Haiti after it had failed elsewhere.

The "Résistance à l'oppression" manifesto is constructed around the metaphor of the brake or the wall, which became a contested image between opposing factions (recall that Dessalineans had lauded the "brake" of law and order in their presentation of the 1805 imperial constitution). Conversely, the republicans liken their movement to a brake on the unchecked power of Dessalines, who is described alternately as a levee-busting flood ("le torrent dévastateur") and a savage, bloodthirsty beast: "No brake [*frein*] was going to stop the savagery of this tiger thirsting for the blood of his fellow men."[112] By equating Dessalines to an unbridled force of nature, republicans argued that laws were futile in the face of his savage power.[113] Moreover, they describe Dessalines's interests as purely linked to his own power, not the interests of individual citizens, arguing that what laws he did impose he never respected: "No law was able to protect the people from the sovereign's barbarity; his supreme will."[114] As such, republicans concluded, the regime had to fall; it was the only way to stop the destructive force of his power.

The republicans' language was aimed at delegitimizing Dessalines and promoting the meaning of *liberté* that they would pursue in their post-independence state. It was perhaps also intended to resonate with liberal republicans throughout the Atlantic world. James Dun notes that one of the few times the phrase "Revolution in Hayti" was used in the US press during the 1791–1806 period was in reference to the assassination plot against Dessalines, which newspapers presented as validation of Jefferson's decision to suspend trade.[115] Dun notes that "by the end of 1806, most reports on Haiti described the nation in terms that fleshed out the brigand state's shape"; for example, the authors of the 1805 constitution were considered "lowly," illiterate, and rash.[116] Newspapers derided Dessalines as "a 'tiger' who had risen through the ranks since 1791 solely because of his inveterate hatred of white people."[117] Crucially, the language that Dun attributes to a US racialist discursive creation is the very language Haitian republicans used to delegitimize Dessalines's empire and justify their revolution. To what degree did US and Haitian republican discourse draw upon one another, or from the same well of language, ideology, and imagery? At the very least, we must acknowledge that the language with which the United States vilified Dessalines and his Haitian state was part of a complex network of anti-despotic writing that circulated among a faction of Haitians and in the Atlantic world.

The republicans' program sought to make possible the *liberté* that they envisioned for Haiti. Pétion, Gérin, and the southern revolutionaries wanted *liberté* through a government based on "the rights and duties of all," a promise that they announced in their manifesto.[118] Defining theirs as "true liberty" (*la vraie liberté*), they signed their manifesto by indicating a new revolutionary calendar, "year 3 of independence, and of true liberty the first" (*an 3 de l'indépendance, et de la vraie liberté le premier*).[119] That the republicans deemed it necessary to distinguish between the anticolonial, authoritarian *liberté* of Dessalineanism and the *vraie liberté* of republicanism is a testament to the critical importance of this word and its many meanings in revolutionary Saint-Domingue/Haiti. Importantly, and tellingly of their project, the republican revolutionary leaders effaced their own role in the uprising against Dessalines, which they attributed to "the people" of Haiti: "The people, as well as the army, weary of the unbearable yoke imposed upon them, calling upon their courage and their energy, finally and by spontaneous movement, broke free. Yes, we have thrown off our chains!"[120] Along the same lines, they presented Dessalines's hatred of the republicans as part of his hatred of Enlightenment and reason. They connected the rumored massacre of free men of color to Dessalines's putative hatred of men who wished to manifest principles of true liberty: "men likely to think, those ultimately capable of ensuring the sublime principles of true liberty" (*les hommes susceptible de penser, ceux capables enfin de faire triompher les sublimes principes de la vraie liberté*).[121]

If the leaders of the republican revolution were vociferous in their critique of Dessalines's tyranny, they were equally critical of Dessalinean secretaries because they were learned and literate—recipients of the fruits of Enlightenment liberalism—and yet had turned their backs on the republican cause. They depicted Dessalinean secretaries as inauthentic turncoats: they were men who just yesterday had fought to ensure the "sublime principles" of true liberty, but who refused their duty after independence.[122] Worse still, they saw men like Inginac, Mentor, and Boisrond Tonnerre using their intellectual ability and individual genius as enablers of Dessalines's imperial state. This is undoubtedly why Pétion and Gérin would later work so hard to woo Chanlatte to their side after Dessalines's assassination: he was the brightest example of what a thinking man could be for the republic. The ideas of individual will, self-liberation, and intellectual ability and those men capable of bringing liberal Enlightenment principles to fruition—these are the elements that the republican revolutionaries believed must be embodied and performed by intellectuals in the liberal republican state.

The Dessalinean Counter-Revolution, or *Venger l'Empereur ou Mourir*

The republicans felled Dessalines, but were unable to consolidate power over the entirety of his former empire. There remained a significant faction of loyal Dessalineans who believed that the independent nation would be best served by a monarchy. Although it is little studied, there was an important counterrevolutionary movement among Dessalines's closest generals, counselors, and secretaries. Gaétan Mentor's original documentary research into this—mostly in the form of personal correspondence between key republicans and Dessalineans—sheds important light on the political aftermath of the republican revolution and the eventual civil war between Christophe and Pétion. The day following the assassination, a core group of Dessalineans refused to accept the republican revolution, including Chanlatte, Dupuy, Boisrond Tonnerre, Cappoix, Diaquoi Aîné, Inginac, Magny, and Goman (who led his own insurrection against the republic in the mountains of the extreme Southwest, proclaiming himself "Dessalines's avenger").[123] In a final symbolic transformation of Dessalines's original oath "Liberté ou la mort," they solemnly vowed to "Avenge the emperor or die" (*Venger l'empereur ou mourir*), reactivating the image of vengeance that was a foundational piece of Dessalinean anticolonial, antislavery independence and reclaiming Dessalines's title as "the avenger and the liberator" (*le vengeur et le libérateur*).[124] They responded to the republican revolution's claims in kind, reversing the idea of a republican "campaign against tyranny" by proclaiming it the "tyranny of parricides" (*tyrannie des parricides*).[125] The Dessalineans proclaimed their counterrevolutionary response in a document signed October 18, 1806 (written from Sarthe, just north of Port-au-Prince). Chanlatte, Diaquoi, Inginac, Dupuy, Vernet, and Boisrond Tonnerre signed the document, in which they also swore to give Dessalines the funeral services he merited, even if only symbolically.[126]

By declaring themselves a counterrevolutionary movement, the Dessalineans made themselves targets for reprisal, and those who remained in the South and West had to go into hiding. Boisrond Tonnerre and Etienne Mentor were jailed and then assassinated in their cell in Port-au-Prince on October 23, 1806. Many others fled to the North, out of the reach of Pétion and Gérin, and later became part of Christophe's government during the civil war: Toussaint Daut (eventually the Prince de Saint-Marc); Etienne Magny (eventually the Duc de Plaisance); Alexis Dupuy (eventually the Baron de Dupuy); Goman/Jean-Baptiste Perrier (eventually the Comte de Jérémie, who never moved north but maintained an opposition insurrection and independent state in the South until 1819); even Corneille Brelle, who was eventually named préfet d'Hayti under Christophe. And, of course, Juste Chanlatte, eventually the Comte de Rosiers, who had by far the most interesting post-Dessalinean trajectory.

Chanlatte managed to evade capture, likely owing to his family connections among the republican revolutionaries, though he was far from safe. Pétion wrote him a letter urging him to seek cover, and to reconsider the sincerity that guided the leaders of the republican revolution.[127] Indeed, Pétion and Bonnet each appealed to Chanlatte to join the republicans, referencing past personal interactions and demonstrating an intimate familiarity with his writing to make their case. Pétion reminded Chanlatte of his commitment to *liberté*, though he failed to acknowledge the chasm that separated republicans' notion of "vraie liberté" from the anticolonial, antislavery independence that Chanlatte had pursued with Dessalines: "You always said and I wish to repeat back to you, that a People's first possession, the first condition of civil society, is liberty."[128] Pétion makes a curious closing statement to Chanlatte, arguing that he is "better steeped in republican virtues than us" (*mieux imbu que nous des vertus républicaines*) and for that reason, must have suffered greatly, as Pétion did, under Dessalines.[129] To what is Pétion referring here? Chanlatte's education? His family background? I would argue that Pétion is pointing to Chanlatte's writing, his *esprit*, when he says that Chanlatte is more steeped in republican values than the southern revolutionaries themselves. Pétion saw Chanlatte as the man most capable of making manifest the Enlightenment principle of "vraie liberté." He asks Chanlatte, "How many of us didn't remain faithful to your ideas, your opinions, how many of us weren't influenced by your thinking, your language?"[130] Pétion thus appeals directly to Chanlatte's influential use of language and the printed word, and his invaluable service as a wordsmith in the post-independence period. Indeed, with Boisrond Tonnerre's assassination, Chanlatte was the most powerful and prolific Haitian writer still living—a fact Pétion made clear in his letter.

Chanlatte was unmoved. He rebuffed the republicans' attempts to bring him to their side, despite the fact that members of his own family remained in the South.[131] What attached Chanlatte to Dessalines, and to the counterrevolutionary cause? Was it an attachment to ideology? Or anger at the assassination of his venerated leader, Haiti's great liberator? In his letters following the assassination, Chanlatte expresses a sentiment of duty to serve Dessalines even after his death, and of resignation to a life of resentment and uncertainty. In a letter to Dessalines's widow, for example, he speaks of the "great friendship" between them (which developed, ostensibly, only over the three years following Chanlatte's return to Haiti) and their collective fight "for the most noble ideals."[132] He maintains his commitment to honoring Dessalines's memory: "his venerable memory," "the grandiose dreams that he nurtured for his brothers, and which cost him his life."[133] His reaction to Pétion saving his life is perhaps even more telling: he admits that Pétion's actions only further entrenched his determination to avenge Dessalines: "Far from leading me to change my mind, they only serve to harden my resolve. I remain up in arms, vowing to die [*disparaître*] rather than endorse such an appalling crime."[134] The crime that Chanlatte points to here, the reason for his refusal to follow the republicans—and the motor behind much of his later writing from Christophe's northern regime—was the crime of parricide. Was the republicans' claim of "résistance à l'oppression" justifiable? Haitian historians, intellectuals, and statesmen have debated this fundamental question under various layers of metaphor, performance, and disavowal for over two hundred years.

* * *

The Dessalinean counterrevolutionary faction would continue its fight from the North, though not unchanged, under Henry Christophe's state-turned-monarchy, as we shall see in the next chapter. This raises the question: where was Henry Christophe during Dessalines's assassination, and what role did he play in it? We might contrast his position to that of Goman, who took up the banner of Dessalines's avenger immediately following the news of Pont Rouge, and remained in his anti-Pétion, anti-republican separatist state for more than fifteen years. Christophe, on the other hand, stayed out of the way during the republican revolution and did not actively participate in the plans to assassinate Dessalines. Instead, he moved to consolidate his own power in the North, orchestrating the assassination of General Cappoix (Capois), who Madiou argues posed a threat to the unity of Christophean support among generals and inhabitants of the northern region. Christophe also accepted when the republicans appointed him "chef provisoire" of the Haitian government in their October 16, 1806, manifesto, but shrewdly chose to remain in Cap-Haïtien instead of immediately assuming his position in Port-au-Prince.[135] He played both sides in the chaos that followed Dessalines's assassination, but it quickly became evident to Christophe and his supporters in the North that the republicans planned to work independently of his authority.

Christophe made his position clear in a November 2 proclamation from the North: as provisional leader, he wanted discipline, obedience, and military rule.[136] He addressed military men directly first, reminding them that the survival of the state, of their families, and of Haitian citizens depended on their strict obedience to their superiors. He next reminded agricultural laborers (*cultivateurs* and *habitans*) that their happiness (*bonheur*) was in their work (*travaux*), and the "steadiness" of their conduct and their continued productivity were essential for the government to function.[137] He implored both groups to accept "the necessity of a rigorous obedience to the laws," and, in Dessalinean fashion, demanded that they ferret out the enemy within: "If there are agitators or agents of our enemies [*stipendiés*] among you, . . . know who they are."[138] His emphasis on military order and obedience set him at odds, already, with the republican faction's lofty discussions of the constitutional rights of man, democratic government, and equality. According to Madiou, Christophe sent his November 2 proclamation to Pétion and the Constituent Assembly in the South along with a request that his agent, General Jean-Baptiste Dartiguenave, advocate for greater executive power in the new constitution. Pétion roundly rejected Christophe's vision for the future state, threatening to fight against anyone who dared support it: "The people want liberty, and I will assist them with all my efforts."[139]

Tellingly, Christophe never left the North during his deliberations with the southern revolutionaries. According to Madiou, as soon as Christophe received confirmation that the new constitution gave him no power, he declared Pétion, Bonnet, Boyer, and other members of the new republican Senate outlaws (*hors-la-loi*).[140] On December 24, 1806, he declared that he would march on "Port-aux-Crimes" against these traitors to take back the capital, and the government, by force.[141] The language he uses in his declaration of civil war reveals both its connection to Dessalinean writing and the tenor that would take shape in Christophean writing over the next decade and a half. Of particular interest here is the metaphor of unmasking, which we will see mobilized again and again by both sides of the civil war: these "villains" (*scélérats*) "just lifted their masks; they brought their plans to light. . . . They want to establish a Constitution that will put power in their hands."[142]

After vanquishing Pétion in the Battle of Sibert, just north of Port-au-Prince, Christophe laid siege to Port-au-Prince over the day and night of January 6, 1807, to no avail. He retreated to the North, via Marchand, and proclaimed his territory "l'Etat d'Hayti," which claimed authority over lands north of the Artibonite River, including Saint-Marc, or what constitutes today the departments of the Centre, Artibonite, Nord-Est, Nord, and Nord-Ouest. Soon after, Pétion accepted the Senate's nomination to serve as president of the "République d'Haïti," which covered the

South and parts of the West. Was there ever a legitimate, uncontested republic in the first decades of Haitian independence? Not one that was not mired in accusations of rebellion and illegal usurpation of power. It would not be until 1820 that the unified and (mostly) uncontested Republic of Haiti, the Haitian Republic, the first black republic, became a reality.

In the decade and a half that followed Dessalines's assassination, the newly independent nation was mired in a civil war that contested the very meaning of the Haitian Revolution and the form of government that the state should take. As we shall see over the next two chapters, this war was fought not only with weapons, but with words.

2

Civil War, *Guerre de Plume*

Konstitisyon se papye, bayonet se fè.
—Haitian proverb

When the Senate announced Alexandre Pétion's nomination as president of the republic on March 9, 1807, to the sound of seventeen cannon blasts, was Juste Chanlatte listening? Though Pétion and other leading republicans had tried to bring Chanlatte over to their side, to take advantage of the wordsmith (and avoid being on the receiving end of his textual weaponry), Chanlatte had refused. Recall from the previous chapter that Chanlatte was one of Dessalines's most prolific and powerful secretaries; during the civil war, he would play a similar role in Christophe's northern state. He served as editor in chief of the official northern *Gazette* and published searing indictments of Pétion and his new republican government. Thus the tension that had simmered under the surface between Dessalineans and republicans during the first years after independence—the threats against internal dissent, the push and pull over the true meaning of *liberté*, and the form of government that post-independence Haiti should take—became a full-blown civil war between North and South after Dessalines's assassination (1807–1820).

The symbolic inaugural events of Pétion's republic—the seventeen cannon blasts to mark the victorious day of Dessalines's assassination—inform Chanlatte's first pamphlet written from Christophe's northern government in May 1807, *Réflexions sur le prétendu Sénat de Port-au-Prince*.[1] The pamphlet is a fierce critique of Pétion and his republican government, one of the first texts of the North-South *guerre de plume* that reaffirmed Chanlatte's commitment to avenge Dessalines and exact retribution for the crimes committed by Gérin, Pétion and the republican revolutionaries that we saw in the previous chapter. He addresses the pamphlet directly to southern republicans—his "concitoyens" in the South.[2] His stated purpose in the pamphlet is to draw attention to the illegitimacy of the southern Senate in particular: "To correct the opinion of my fellow citizens or enlighten them to the illegitimate existence of this Senate, its illegal composition, and its unjust usurpations, here is the precious subject of this document."[3] Thus, Chanlatte writes to reveal the *illiberal* nature of the republican institution and its purported values of shared power, equality, and democracy, deriding the institution as "the Senate of Port-aux-Crimes or, Pétion's Senate, of which he is simultaneously the leader, the regulator, the president, and demigod."[4] Importantly, such critiques leveled by Chanlatte and other Christophean writers were well known to Pétion. The republican president made attempts to address them: his inauguration speech stressed his emphasis on transparency and he even opened up the Senate proceedings to the public as a show of good faith and commitment to these democratic principles. Pétion's attempts at transparency set the "stage" for Chanlatte's pamphlet: the northern writer pens the text from the point of view of the gallery above the Senate floor, gazing down upon the stage of republican parliamentary democracy that Chanlatte seeks to expose as mere theater.[5]

In addition to polemic and theater, Chanlatte incorporates a variety of genres and intertexts into his pamphlet. His mastery of the tone and style of these various genres is a testament to his personal talent and wit, at the same time that it reflects the richness of the Atlantic world print discourse upon which he drew. The text begins as a traditional eighteenth-century–style refutation pamphlet: in the first-person singular, Chanlatte sets out to refute "by compelling arguments" the assertion from the republicans that the Senate was a lawful institution. He begins with the premise ("principe incontestable") that sovereignty resides only in those who have been invested with this power by the people—a reference to Dessalines's popular support as the great liberator and hero of the Haitian Revolution.[6] The Senate, he argues, was illegally constituted, it was incompetent, and its members immoral, uninterested in the rights of the people, and diametrically opposed "to the great work of regeneration."[7]

After refuting the legitimacy of the republican Senate, Chanlatte shifts to a different mode: that of a *physiologie*, or a written portrait that inventories social types according to their appearance and *milieu*.[8] Chanlatte pens a series of portraits, depicting each republican senator, from

Blanchet to David Trois, using their distinctive physical characteristics. The names of these men should come as no surprise given Chanlatte's stated motives: they are the men who participated in Pétion and Gérin's "campaign against tyranny," facilitating Dessalines's assassination and supporting the republican revolutionaries when they took power during the transition to Christophe. In this way, Chanlatte brilliantly subverts Pétion's efforts at transparency by situating his narrator in the observation gallery of the Senate, from a point of view perched above the men below. We can almost picture Chanlatte leaning against the balustrade, identifying each man and taking aim with his weapon—his pen—to expose them for the frauds, traitors, and enemies that he believes them to be, and to humiliate them in a public fashion. He situates his targets with relation to one another in space, scanning the room from one man to the next. He addresses his reader directly, drawing him into the fray with interrogative phrases full of alliteration and puns. For example, next to Daumec the "tartuffe" he spots Télémaque: "Don't you recognize the deceitful ingrate [*ingrat*] Télémaque by his opulence and his rotundity?"[9] Next to the treasonous general Lamothe Aigron he spies the prideful David Trois, "former satellite of the kinglet Rigaud."[10] He spies Louis Barlatier the composer, old Simon, Lys, Théodat Trichet, and on and on. With each portrait, Chanlatte further populates the room, filling it with the sights and sounds until it resembles the bustling of a parliamentary chamber.

Having set the stage with his humorous, biting portraits of his republican enemies, Chanlatte's essay takes a dramatic turn. The final pages of the text shift into the mode of Greek tragedy. We will recall from the previous chapter that Chanlatte was already steeped in the genre of theater and performance; his earlier Dessalinean texts embraced the practice of performativity in order to communicate the political goals of the state and to reach a desired audience—strategies that he would continue to develop under Christophe, and especially in his later theatrical works. To mark the transition from physiological description to the tragic mode, the narrator describes a transformation in the chamber: a hush comes over the senators. They rise and the narrator realizes what is about to happen: "Have no doubt; it is he, the infernal Pétion, who approaches."[11] He describes Pétion as he enters the sanctum and then delivers a speech to the senators, calling each man out by name and assigning him the sinister, underhanded tasks that he wants them to carry out. As Pétion goes to take his seat on the dais, he is seized by some force and transformed: "a violent contraction of nerves stopped him suddenly; his features turned, a wild fury glimmered in his eyes."[12] The sanctum is thus transformed into an amphitheater, as the senators become spectators themselves to the gruesome spectacle that unfolds. Pétion waves a bloody knife around with one hand, and grabs a torch with the other, confused and staggering. His mind transports him back to Pont Rouge, as the narrator describes Pétion muttering to himself in a hushed voice: "Wasn't this the scene [*en ces lieux*] where the furies of hell made their horrible serpents hiss above my head? . . . Yes, it was here; I see, I recognize this miry swamp [*marais fangeux*]."[13] Pétion calls out the names of Greek gods: the Euménidies, gods of vengeance, and Tisiphone, who punishes fratricide. Then a spectral figure, called back from the grave by Tisiphone, enters the scene: it is Dessalines. He warns Pétion that his day of vengeance is not far. Pétion flees the Senate room racked with sobs, and the other senators rush out of the room, cursing the moment they decided to join him. In the final paragraph of the text, Chanlatte returns to the pamphlet genre, telling his readership that he hopes his "feeble efforts" to expose the "so-called Senate in Port-au-Prince" were successful, and that they too will confirm "the public opinion of righteous indignation [*la juste indignation*]."[14]

Chanlatte's essay is a fierce, biting critique of the republicans: Pétion, Gérin, and their allies committed the ultimate crime against the nation by assassinating Dessalines, the great liberator. For Chanlatte, this was the Achilles' heel of the republican project: they did not establish their "democratic" state on popular will, but rather on their own ideological superiority and belief that they were the men meant to lead. What is notable about Chanlatte's piece is its effort to keep the brutal realities of Dessalines's assassination at the fore; he shines a spotlight on the events of Pont Rouge and the treason of Dessalines's assassination with theatricality and gusto. As we will see in subsequent chapters, republicans systematically disavowed Dessalines's role as a post-independence leader in the years following his assassination with increasing effectiveness. Indeed, the disavowal of Dessalines, the thorny subject of his assassination, and the inability to come to terms with his legacy will haunt subsequent governments and historical narratives of Haiti—a possibility

Chanlatte presciently grasped in his analysis of the southern republic. Chanlatte's attacks on the merits of Pétion's putative liberal republicanism proved to be prescient in other ways, too: after only a few months in office, Pétion suspended the Senate from July 1807 to January 1808, citing the civil war with the North as justification to grant him absolute powers.[15] Though the Senate resumed its powers in 1808, Pétion had slowly begun to chip away at its authority—he, more than anyone, knew that the 1806 constitution gave far too little power to the executive.[16]

Chanlatte's pamphlet was an opening shot, the first volley in a paper war between the North and South that would last for nearly fifteen years. The columns of the North and South's respective government newspapers became trenches, from which writers would trade fire. This chapter is the first of two that trace the distinctive cultures of writing in the North and South that emerged during this civil war period. In the present chapter, I begin with an analysis of the print culture of the civil war by comparing each government's press operations. Next, I focus on a particularly fraught moment in the North-South civil war with the French Restoration government's threat to retake the former colony. Here, I make the case for a specific Christophean form that emerged during this period, the "refutation pamphlet," based in the disassembling, unweaving, or piercing through of a political opponent's text— deployed first against the French Restoration government, and then against Pétion's southern republic. The Christophean writing that I present in this chapter stands in stark contrast to the southern liberal republican writing that we will study in chapter 3, which positioned literary writing as central to the task of illustrating and performing the successes of the liberal republican model. Taken together, these two chapters reveal Haitian writing during the civil war to be mutually constituted—in tension and in opposition—between a performative, polemical notion of writing in the Christophean sphere, and the emergent "literary" sense of writing in Pétion's republican sphere.

The Print Culture of Civil War

In the official proclamations, constitutions, and print operations that organized the southern republic and the northern state, we observe the stark difference—and differentiation—in the political and ideological objectives of each separatist state. The republic built itself on the reversal of Dessalines and the disavowal of his militant antislavery and anticolonial state-turned-empire. Pétion's government codified in 1806 what the republicans had intended in 1804: the republic. Their staunch republicanism is apparent not only in their language of revolution, as we saw in the previous chapter, and the 1806 constitution, but in the national holidays that the republic inaugurated: May 1 was the fête de l'Agriculture; July 5 was the fête de la Constitution; October 17 was celebrated as the fête de la Liberté, the "memorable day of the last tyrant's death"; and January 1, the fête de l'Indépendance.[17] Pétion transformed Haiti's administrative territorial organization from the colonial (and ancien régime) parish system to "communes," exactly as the Constituent Assembly had done in France. He ordered liberty trees planted throughout these communes to celebrate the republican revolution's victory over Dessalines's empire, and thus, liberal republicanism's triumphant overcoming. That the date of Dessalines's assassination, October 17, was celebrated as a national holiday, the fête de la Liberté, makes clear the degree to which the republic constructed itself discursively and symbolically in opposition to Dessalines and Dessalineanism. Pétion's acceptance of his nomination to the presidency of Haiti on March 9, 1807, to the sound of seventeen cannon blasts only served to confirm this point.[18]

For their part, Christophists wasted no time in putting together their own set of national holidays, though these were traditional, Catholic, and anti-republican in nature: the fête de l'Annonciation on March 25, Christmas on December 25, and on August 15 the "Fête-Dieu, celle de l'Assomption de la Vierge, de l'Ascension, de la Toussaint, de la Saint Jean, de saint Henry, de sainte Louise."[19] In matters of state, Christophists promulgated the Constitution de l'Etat d'Haïti on February 17, 1807, codifying a military authoritarian regime, with Christophe named "Président et Généralissme des forces de terre et de mer d'Haïti." Many of the men who had been committed Dessalineans signed the northern constitution: Toussaint Daut, Etienne Magny, Corneille Brelle, André Vernet, Paul Romain, Martial Besse, and José Campos Tavares (Thabares), among others.[20]

The dueling symbolism of the North-South civil war was played out, importantly, in each government's press operations.[21] First, it is important to note that while there were presses in the North and South during the colonial regime, Cap Français was the undisputed center of printing and print culture in colonial Saint-Domingue. Moreover, post-independence Cap-Haïtien had remained a crucial center of power in Dessalines's state-turned-empire. Although he officially based the seat of power and the capital in the town of Dessalines (Marchand), he maintained a printing base in the northern city of Cap-Haïtien. Pierre Roux was indispensable in this effort; he was the printer who oversaw the transition from the colonial paper the *Gazette officielle de Saint-Domingue* (which ended around November 1803, coinciding with the French defeat at Vertières) to the independent Haitian paper the *Gazette politique et commerciale d'Haïti*, which reappeared a year later on November 1, 1804, and which listed Roux's new title as "Imprimeur de l'Empereur" in Cap-Haïtien. Roux survived the 1806 republican revolution and remained committed to his northern print operation under Christophe. He transitioned Dessalines's government paper the *Gazette politique et commerciale* to Christophe's *Gazette officielle de l'Etat d'Hayti* (1807–1811, where Roux is listed as "Imprimeur de l'Etat" in Cap-Haïtien) and its successor, the *Gazette royale d'Hayti* (1811–1820, where Roux is listed as "Imprimeur du Roi" in Cap-Henry through August 1816). The newspapers published in the North under Roux can be considered more or less a single publication that stopped and restarted with the transitions in government, changing only slightly in name and in format (the typeface, two-column layout, and masthead remain quite similar) over the course of the nearly twenty years of revolutionary and post-independence movements, or at least until 1817, when Christophe moved the capital of his kingdom to Sans Souci and installed the royal printing press there on site—run by a certain Buon.[22]

While in the North we see a flourishing press with remarkable continuity, consistency, quality, and reliability under Roux from 1804 to 1816, it took the southern republic considerably longer to establish a sustained, regular government paper. Christophe's government controlled most of the printing presses, had in its employ the most talented and experienced printer, Roux, and counted a host of secretaries and intellectuals in its secretarial corps, including Chanlatte. The South had comparatively less technological knowledge of printing and fewer seasoned secretaries in its employ and had little capacity for building it

(Numéro 1.)

GAZETTE
POLITIQUE ET COMMERCIALE D'HAÏTI.

Du Jeudi 15 Novembre 1804, l'an premier de l'indépendance.

Figure 2.1. Masthead of Dessalines's official newspaper, *Gazette politique et commerciale d'Haïti* (Cap-Haïtien), November 15, 1804. Courtesy of the New York Public Library.

(Numéro 39.)

GAZETTE OFFICIELLE
DE
L'ÉTAT D'HAYTI,

Du Jeudi 28 Septembre 1809, l'an sixième de l'indépendance.

Figure 2.2. Masthead of Christophe's first official newspaper, *Gazette officielle de l'Etat d'Hayti* (Cap-Haïtien), September 28, 1809. Courtesy of Yale University Library.

out in the first years of the civil war. There are many fewer copies in existence of the republic's first official newspapers,[23] suggesting that not as many copies were published, or that there were gaps in production, something that is common during times of war and instability. The republic remained locked in battle against Goman's armed insurgency in the far Southwest and against Christophe in the North. In addition, for a yearlong period from 1810 to 1811, Pétion saw a section of the southern peninsula secede from the republic under the separatist government of André Rigaud, known as the Scission du Sud.[24]

The few examples of early southern newspapers that we do have evince a continuity in the project of republicanism and republican symbolism that Pétion established at the start of his republic in 1806. The republic's first paper, *La Sentinelle d'Haïti, Gazette du Port-au-Prince*, appeared in the first days of January 1808, and was printed "chez Fourcand, imprim. de la Répub." in Port-au-Prince.[25] Juste Chanlatte's brother, François Desrivières Chanlatte, whom Pétion had named general secretary of the Senate earlier, is listed as editor of *La Sentinelle*. The younger Chanlatte likely worked on the rest of the republic's official papers alongside Pétion's other secretaries, Inginac, Colombel, Milscent, Frenel, Delaunay, Modé, and Pelage, among others (see chapter 3).[26] The layout of *La Sentinelle* was similar to the earlier iterations of the northern *Gazette*, with one important change: the addition of the words "liberté" and "égalité" in the top left and right corner, respectively, of the masthead reaffirming the paper as an organ of Pétion's liberal republican state and staking out its status in opposition to Christophe's military authoritarian "Etat d'Hayti," which eschewed individual rights and equality in favor of a single, strong leader in the interest of stability and control. It bears noting that Christophe's royal motto was "Liberté, Indépendance"—a clear continuation of the Dessalinean notion of *liberté* and in contrast to the southern republic's emphasis on *égalité*.

La Sentinelle was replaced in 1809 by *Le Bulletin officiel, Gazette du Port-au-Prince*. The new paper offered a redesigned masthead which further touted the liberal republican symbolism that *La Sentinelle* had introduced. The front page added what is likely one of the first printed images of the Haitian republican coat of arms (and which adorns the Haitian flag today): spears, bayonets, cannons, and flags fanned out in all directions. In the very middle is a Phrygian cap hanging atop a spear, which sits between two shields topped with laurel, with the words "Rep. d'Hayti" and "Union, Force, Constitution" on each. The words "liberté" and "égalité" are printed to the left and right of this image. Philippe Girard's recent work has noted the similarity between the Haitian coat of arms and the late-French republican coat of arms under Napoléon.[27] Though where Girard sees an "odd" origin story to the symbol of Haitian (republican) independence in the adaptation of Napoleon-era letterhead, I see a quite logical continuity in the symbolism of French republicanism. Pétion's southern republic considered itself the radical instantiation of the republican values of liberty, equality, and democracy that had sprung forth after 1789—symbols that had faltered in France under Napoléon just a few short months after his failed expedition to retake the island. We can read Pétion's adoption of the late-republican symbolism of Napoléon's consular republic as a

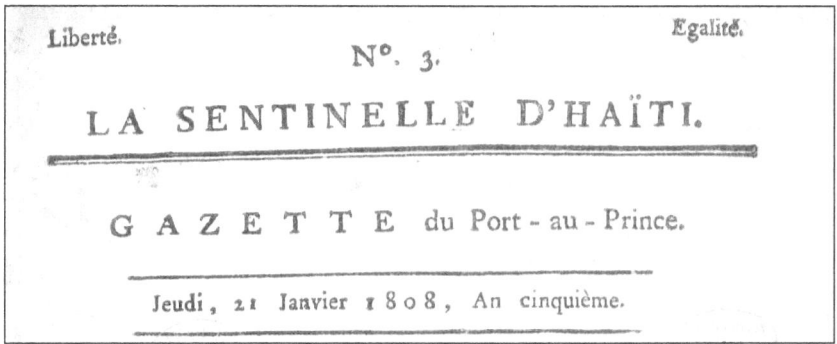

Figure 2.3. Masthead of Pétion's first official newspaper, *La Sentinelle d'Haïti* (Port-au-Prince), January 21, 1808. Courtesy of the Bibliothèque nationale de France.

Figure 2.4. Masthead of Pétion's second official newspaper, *Le Bulletin officiel* (Port-au-Prince), November 18, 1809. Courtesy of the Bibliothèque nationale de France.

reminder, perhaps even subversive provocation, that Haiti was now the sole remaining site of the ideals that republicans in Saint-Domingue/Haiti *and* in France had defended since 1791. This was not about imitation or borrowing, but about projecting and performing the republicanism that France no longer embodied.[28] As we shall see in chapter 3, Pétion's republicanism took on new meaning during the civil war with Christophe; it deployed the symbols of republicanism and preached the virtues of liberalism and progress (talent, reason, intellectual free will) as a weapon to challenge and discredit Christophe's northern military authoritarian state-turned-monarchy.

It is unclear how long *Le Bulletin officiel* lasted. The next republican government paper did not appear until January 1814, with the founding of *Le Télégraphe*. This time, the republic's official government newspaper would enjoy greater stability and regularity.[29] When *Le Télégraphe* debuted, it boasted a new eight-page pamphlet-style layout without columns and without the coat of arms. The paper eventually switched back to the standard four-page, two-column format and reintroduced the same republican coat of arms that had first appeared in *La Sentinelle*. In terms of quality, all three of the first southern newspapers are inferior to their northern counterparts: they were printed on thinner paper of lesser quality, which often bled through or was pressed too hard. By contrast, northern *Gazettes* appear printed on better paper and with better materials and presses. This suggests that the southern republic lacked both the technical expertise and the financial means to launch a sustained government print operation in the early years of the civil war.

Aside from the material-formal and political-ideological differences, northern and southern papers differed in their approach to content. The content of early southern republican papers (from 1807 to 1817) was less prolific and less developed than those under Christophe. The newspapers existed primarily for the purposes of reprinting and circulating information, mostly foreign news articles (as was common practice in New World newspapers of the early nineteenth century) and government laws, decrees, and proclamations. Southern papers included little editorializing or news commentary; the locally produced content that did make it into these early southern papers took the form of short satirical poems, most often written in response to written salvos lobbed at them from the northern state.[30] In the North, on the other hand, we see a quite different picture: in addition to foreign news, mostly excerpts from the London paper *L'Ambigu*, whose editor, Jean-Gabriel Peltier,[31] also served as Christophe's paid agent in London, northern *Gazettes* included extensive local content.

The prominence of local intellectual and cultural production in northern print culture attests to the robust printing operation under Christophe and the emphasis that he and his secretaries placed on the printed word, very much in the spirit of Dessalinean print culture.[32] The sheer volume of pages they produced evinces the importance that Christophe, too, placed on printing as a weapon of anticolonial independence.

Christophe's *Gazettes* printed editorial articles, news commentary, accounts of public ceremonies and celebrations, and government decrees, as well as creative production. This included couplets, usually reproduced from public ceremonies and commemorations, but also provocations and *répliques* that were part of a continuous *guerre de plume* with the South: *acrostiche* poems, epigrams, and essays, such as Chanlatte's *Réflexions sur le prétendu Sénat de Port-au-Prince*. Indeed, I would argue that Christophean secretaries enacted what was essentially a continuation and development of the politics and poetics of Dessalinean writing. They engaged in a collective and collaborative textual production that subordinated individual authorial or creative intent to the collective, secretarial duty that performed the monarchy internally in Haiti, and for the Atlantic world. I differ here from Deborah Jenson's assertion that Dessalinean writing was "very different from the two centuries of literature that would follow it in Haiti."[33] Indeed, I am arguing in this book that Dessalinean writing (both in the writers themselves, and also in their rhetorical strategies, styles, forms, and tropes) shaped a kind of writing that gets evoked and deployed throughout Haitian literary history by different actors seeking to reactivate its heritage. Dessalinean writing is the discursive foundation for a long heritage of writing (and, as we shall see in chapter 5, image production) in Haiti.

In this early phase of the civil war, and certainly in light of the South's meager print operation, the paper war appears relatively one-sided, at least as far as the archive goes. Most of the texts that we have from this period are those that come out of Christophe's northern state, such as Chanlatte's 1807 pamphlet, and though they undoubtedly elicited a written response from the South, we find few examples of them in the archive.[34]

* * *

In order to understand the paper war between North and South, we must note the real, on-the-ground battles that also took place during the civil war and shaped the contours of each rival state and their political futures. Immediately following Christophe's failed siege of Port-au-Prince, Pétion dispatched troops into Christophe's territory. Republican forces occupied Gonaïves between May and June 1807, a short-lived but major symbolic victory for the southern forces at the start of the civil war.[35] Pétion sent out another expedition under General Lamarre, which became a three-year battle in the North (1807–1810). Lamarre seized control of areas of the Northwest, specifically in Port-de-Paix and Môle Saint-Nicolas—zones that had been faithful to Dessalines but which had sparred with Christophe in the early post-independence period. Historians of the period refer to the military skirmish as the Guerre du Môle because it was there that the great republican hero General Lamarre became a martyr to his cause. As Christophe's forces closed in on Fort Georges, the republican army's last stronghold in the North, Lamarre sacrificed himself to spare the lives of many of his republican compatriots.[36] For these actions, Lamarre was immortalized by Antoine Dupré in the play *La mort du Général Lamarre*.

While the failure of Lamarre's expedition in 1810 marked the end of Pétion's military action in the North, the republican president still faced considerable unrest in the southern peninsula, which undoubtedly contributed to the irregularity of his print operation and its meager quality. There was Goman's separatist peasant government in the mountains surrounding Jérémie and the radical republican opposition in the South, headquartered in the liberal republican center of Les Cayes.[37] Things became even more complicated with André Rigaud's Scission du Sud, which established a fourth separate government on the western side of the island, which now included la République d'Haiti (Pétion, Port-au-Prince); l'Etat d'Haïti (Christophe, Cap-Haïtien); l'Etat du Sud (Rigaud, Les Cayes); and Goman's peasant state (Grand'Anse). Not to mention the Spanish side of the island, which in late 1810 was Spanish Santo Domingo (the French having finally left the eastern part of the island in 1809). Christophe took advantage of Pétion's trouble in the South to transition his government to a monarchy in 1811, a plan that had likely been in the works since the start of his separatist northern state, but which became possible with the end of the Guerre du Môle. Christophe tried once more to retake the South after he had established his monarchy, but failed again.[38] Thus while the North and South had sparred since the beginning of the civil war, the conflict became primarily textual after the end of the Guerre du Môle.

Christophe would try once more to retake the South in 1815, though this time he would not use force; instead, he tried a print campaign. To understand the shift in Christophe's tactics, we must first contextualize the world historical events that catalyzed them—namely, the French Restoration government's effort to retake the colony in 1814. As I argue below, the events surrounding this failed attempt, known as the Malouet affair, mark a turning point in Christophe's reign in foreign and domestic matters.[39] After facing down the real possibility of yet another French military expedition to recolonize the island, Christophe emerged resolute to reassert the northern kingdom's military might and its radical anticolonial stance in the international public sphere. Domestically, Christophe devised a plan in the new year 1815 to unify the independent nation under his rule. Pétion had suffered a blow to his public image after the Malouet affair revealed his favorability toward an indemnity payment to the French government in exchange for official diplomatic recognition, something Christophe had heavily publicized. In these efforts, a new secretary emerged on the scene, replacing Chanlatte as the primary wordsmith of Christophe's regime: Jean Louis Vastey,[40] or Baron de Vastey. As discussed above, Chanlatte dominated northern print culture in the early stages of the civil war up until Vastey's appearance in text in October 1814. Indeed, it was during the 1814–1815 period that Vastey became central to Christophean writing, while Chanlatte dropped out of sight for a number of years. My interest in Vastey, here, is to shed more light on the evolution of Christophean writing under Vastey's stewardship.

The Malouet Affair

Napoléon abdicated power in April 1814, ushering in a period of cautious optimism for leaders in the North and South of Haiti. A regime change offered the possibility of thawed relations, trade, and, most desirable of all, official recognition. It quickly became apparent, however, that the new Bourbon Restoration government planned to restore the wayward colony to its former status, having decided to name Pierre Victor Malouet, a former colonist and plantation owner in Saint-Domingue, as minister of the navy and of the colonies.[41] Recall from the previous chapter that Malouet was a well-known pro-colonial French adversary. The Restoration government's choice to name Malouet colonial minister was a symbolic and highly antagonistic one—a sure signal to independent Haitians, monarchist and republican, that the French intended to attempt once more to retake the territory and return it to a regime based in chattel slavery and racial hierarchy. As early as May 1814, Malouet had begun preparing an expedition to Haiti. Upon urging from the new administration, however, Malouet agreed to send out French diplomatic agents who would attempt to secure an agreement with one of Haiti's leaders in advance of the military expedition. A certain Draverneau, from Bordeaux, would go south to Les Cayes to treat with General Borgella,[42] Jean-Joseph Dauxion Lavaysse would treat with Pétion in Port-au-Prince, and Agoustine Franco de Médina would go north to Christophe's kingdom. Each agent was armed with a set of secret instructions from Malouet that stressed among other things King Louis XVIII's resolve to retake the colony, but to make it as bloodless as possible: "His majesty has resolved to deploy his powers to return the insurgents of Saint-Domingue to their obligations only after having exhausted all measures that his clemency commands."[43]

Malouet's plan, specifically his choice of agents, speaks to his deep knowledge of colonial Saint-Domingue as well as the post-independence regional and political divides. First, by sending an agent to Les Cayes, Malouet treated the southern peninsula as a separate sphere of influence from Pétion in Port-au-Prince. He thus acknowledged, or attempted to provoke, the South's separatist position that it had held since the start of the Haitian Revolution. Surely Malouet was also aware of Rigaud's short-lived Scission du Sud and the possibility that this separatist spirit could be reactivated. Malouet's choice of Médina as the agent to the North was even more provocative. Médina was known to Haitians since Dessalines's failed expedition to the East in 1805. He was a planter and a former president of the Conseil des notables of the town of Santiago (Saint-Yague) who had fled south to Santo Domingo when Christophe's army, charged by Dessalines with taking the northern band, invaded the Cibao region. Médina marched north back to the Cibao and successfully rooted out Christophe's positions, pushing the Haitian forces back to the West. For his efforts, Médina was named commander of the Cibao department by the French general Ferrand, then occupying the eastern side of the island for Napoléon. Médina continued to make excursions into Haitian territory even after the end of Dessalines's expedition, antagonizing Dessalines, then Christophe.[44] Médina likely returned to France when Dominican rebels expelled the French from the island in 1809. Malouet's choice to send Médina, a pro-colonial planter whose antagonistic relationship with the North stretched back to the first years of independence, was part of a larger strategy to provoke and destabilize the already fractious regional relationships in post-independence Haiti.

The actual events of the Malouet affair—Lavaysse's rogue actions specifically—are worth summarizing briefly here. Draverneau apparently fell ill and went back to France, leaving Lavaysse to his own devices. He made a series of risky and unsanctioned plays, identifying himself as a diplomatic agent of France, which was untrue, and going against his explicit orders from Malouet and the Restoration government.[45] He sent Christophe a threatening (and unsanctioned) letter in advance of Médina's slated arrival in the North, in which Lavaysse provokingly suggested that the weight of France and England's armies was ready to come down upon the northern state: "the sovereigns of Europe, though they have made peace, they have not yet returned the sword to its scabbard."[46] When Médina finally arrived in Cap Henry (he had stopped to check on his plantation lands in the Northeast), he was promptly arrested and interrogated by Christophe's agents, who "discovered" on Médina's person the incriminating secret instructions from Malouet.[47] Lavaysse's tactics were discovered, but not before he had created a diplomatic embarrassment for the new Restoration government, which distanced itself in the months that followed the debacle in Haiti and officially reprimanded him for his behavior. Malouet, for his part, would not have to face any consequences for his selection of agents and the bungling of his mission: he died on September 7, 1814, just a day after Lavaysse landed in the Caribbean, though Haitians would not find out about his passing until months later.

It is important here to consider the Malouet affair in the context of civil war: how each government, the republic and the monarchy, chose to engage with the colonial agents sent to them. Their approaches evince the opposing views their governments took on French diplomatic recognition, anticolonial independence, and, most importantly, the question of indemnity payments. Pétion agreed to treat with his assigned agent, Lavaysse, but refused outright to recognize the sovereignty of the French monarch. The republican president did, however, propose the possibility of an indemnity payment in exchange for official recognition of Haitian independence.⁴⁸ Lavaysse refused anything short of full recognition of French rule on the island, and the negotiations stalled there. Nevertheless, Pétion's official, public offer to pay an indemnity for colonial property losses would become a symbol of the combat between North and South: between an outward-looking, French-affiliated southern republic that was willing to grant some concessions in order to achieve recognition, and a northern monarchy that placed independence (economic, political, intellectual) above all else, and was willing to sacrifice personal liberties and life itself in order to protect it. To be sure, the idea of an indemnity payment was not an outlandish southern republican invention; it seems to have been the standard way of thinking about Haitian recognition among European abolitionists. Thomas Clarkson himself in his correspondence with Christophe indicated that an indemnity would likely be necessary for any successful trade or recognition treaty with France.⁴⁹ What is exceptional, then, is the Haitian monarch's refusal to consider even the possibility of paying an indemnity in the first place.

But an indemnity was anathema to the monarchy's stance on *liberté* as anticolonial, antislavery independence at all costs. Christophe wanted to achieve international recognition based on his power as a sovereign monarch, the strength of his military, and the civilization that reigned throughout his kingdom: "We will only treat with the French government as equals, power to power, sovereign to sovereign."⁵⁰ Again, this is a far more radical position on sovereignty and independence than Pétion's indemnity concession, but one that is consistent with Christophean policy. In fact, Christophe wasn't just critical of the indemnity question; he refused to treat with Malouet's agents altogether. Upon receipt of Lavaysse's incendiary letter and learning of the provocative choice of Médina as negotiator, Christophe convened his General Council, a governing body in the kingdom that included over 150 men: members of the nobility as well as officers of the army, administrators, counselors, and judges, many of them veterans of Napoléon's previous expedition to retake the colony a decade earlier.⁵¹

More important for our purposes, Christophe convened his General Council on October 21, 1814, for the express purpose of working together to analyze and produce text: first, to process Lavaysse's hostile letters and other documentation related to the affair, and then to draft a written resolution in response to the French government's aggression.⁵² In so doing, he brought together lettered secretaries and unlettered soldiers (many of them former slaves who had survived the violence of the colonial regime and the genocidal tactics of Leclerc and Rochambeau) in order to produce a text that could adequately express the northern monarchy's anticolonial, antislavery stance.⁵³ The council minutes are a key resource on the procedural practices of the northern monarchy because they include transcriptions of Christophe's directives to council members regarding practices of documentation and dissemination of information via the printing press. More important still, they reveal much about the collective, oral, and collaborative nature of northern political theater and textual production—especially the granting of voice and representation in print to illiterate and multilingual corps of generals in Christophe's army. Christophean writers sat together in large audiences and listened while one of their colleagues read a text aloud, and then collectively discussed their reactions, which became the basis for various written pamphlets produced and disseminated by the government presses. This indicates a continuity in the method and rhetoric of Dessalinean textual production from the early post-independence period: theirs was a writing entirely bound up in performing state power and in which a corps of writers produced iterations of the same arguments, using the same metaphors, imagery, and even turns of phrase—much as it functioned for Dessalines's secretarial corps. While individual writers signed their names to pamphlets, they were inscribing these texts into the collective textual endeavor of the northern kingdom.

The council minutes reveal that Christophe addressed the members directly: "Haytians! contemplate these documents with composure and wisdom, as is befitting of free men who have won their independence after much bloodshed. Contemplate them as befits agents who represent the nation, and who . . . must come to a decision about their fate and the most precious interests of their fellow citizens!"⁵⁴ The council's written resolution to "live free and independent or die" as well as the council minutes (*Procès verbal des séances du Conseil général de la Nation*) and all documentation related to the affair (copies of correspondence, reproductions of excerpts from French colonial publications, government proclamations, minutes of council meetings, and refutation pamphlets written by northern lettered men in defense of the kingdom) were sent to press, published en masse, and then distributed widely—domestically and internationally.

A close reading of the council minutes includes a curious detail from the meeting: Toussaint Daut, Prince de Saint-Marc, had requested that the council extend its session for another day in order to listen and to analyze another colonial text, the published memoirs of the colonial minister Malouet. His request called upon one of the council members to read aloud selections from Malouet's 1802 introduction to volume 4 of the *Collection de mémoires sur les colonies, et particulièrement sur Saint-Domingue*, a text well known in Saint-Domingue/Haiti since its publication.[55] The minutes reveal that Daut suspected the colonial minister of scheming to implement the colonial system that he had proposed a decade earlier in his memoirs. As the passages were read aloud, they were met with "bursts of indignation" in the room.[56] The minutes do not provide a transcript of the selected passages Daut had requested, nor what specifically was shouted in protest against them. I would suggest, however, that they are preserved in the written record via another text—a text that marks the first published text of Christophe's most prolific secretary and political writer, Jean Louis (Baron de) Vastey, entitled *Notes à M. le baron V.P. Malouet . . . en réfutation du 4e Volume de son Ouvrage*.[57] Vastey's first published work, which appeared alongside the *Procès verbal* in the mass of pamphlets and broadsides published by the northern regime in October 1814, consists of a series of quotes from the 1802 introduction to Malouet's *Mémoires*, each followed by a lengthy rebuttal from Vastey. Vastey thus reproduces in print form the collective, oral process of citation and rebuttal that took place in the General Council meeting.

Postcolonial Refutation

Vastey is far from unique: his is but one pen, and one voice, in the profusion of refutation texts churned out by Christophe's presses in the September–December 1814 period: pamphlets by Vastey, Chevalier de Prézeau (Sylvain Prézeau), Baron de Dupuy (Alexis Dupuy), Comte de Limonade (Julien Prévost), and many others.[58] These Christophean refutation pamphlets all shared a core concern: language. Each pamphlet followed a similar structure: in the title, the pamphlet announced the piece of writing that it would be refuting in the pages that followed: a letter, an article, or a published work. What is most fascinating—and I think most convincing—is the way Haitian pamphlets perform this adaptation-reiteration-displacement of authority on the space of the page.[59] Central to each refutation pamphlet was the presentation of excerpts from the original text, through citation of blocks of text that the pamphlet set out to refute—much in the way that Toussaint Daut requested that a series of excerpts from Malouet's text be presented to the General Council for analysis. The Christophean writer then responded to each citation with his own text, providing real-time evidentiary rebuttals in which he demonstrated the false premises of the arguments for the maintenance of the colonial system and racial hierarchy put forth in the French colonial text. Visually, this has the effect of disassembling, or breaking apart the erstwhile coherence, legitimacy, and sovereignty of the text he is refuting. The claiming of space by inserting a formerly silenced voice into conversation with—and ultimate refusal of—the colonial text is highly effective visually and rhetorically. The refutation text overwhelms the original with textual proof. Christophean writers thus put into pamphlet form the same practices of the Dessalinean sphere: displacing and destabilizing the (heretofore univocal) authority of French colonial discourse.

Vastey's first text, written "en réfutation" of Malouet's *Mémoires*, exemplifies a form that I am calling the "postcolonial refutation pamphlet," which dominated northern print production during the Malouet affair. Indeed, I would argue that the core of Christophean writing is this act of disassembling, unweaving, or piercing through of the original colonial text. Different Haitian writers did this in different ways, though all are performing the rebuttal and critique on the space of the page. Despite the recent profusion of scholarly work on Christophean writing, scholars have yet to take up the refutation pamphlet as a form.[60] Here I seek to push that further, interrogating the form of refutation pamphlets, which were common in eighteenth-century Atlantic print, and which Christophean writers used as models for their own textual refutation projects.[61]

What do I mean by "refutation"? I insist here on the term *réfutation* instead of *réplique* or *réponse*, first, because the Haitian pamphlets choose the term *réfutation* in their titles, self-consciously engaging a tradition of refutation pamphlets in eighteenth-century Atlantic print culture. The word "refutation" is drawn from the Latin *refutatio*, a classical rhetorical concept that is used in argumentation as one of the five parts of discourse necessary for persuasion. During the Enlightenment and the Age of Revolution, however, refutation took on a new form: the pamphlet. We see refutation pamphlets addressing Rousseau and Voltaire's most recent works, for example, among a host of other publications: *libelles* (pasquinades or lampoons), religious texts, and historical memoirs, among others. What unites the classic rhetorical idea of *refutatio* and the later Enlightenment-era refutation pamphlets is their common goal: a writer sets out to disprove and ultimately negate an opposing argument *made in a written, published text* by providing evidence.

Yet Christophean writers were not simply borrowing from existing forms. There is something far more significant at work in their use of the refutation pamphlet. Recall Chris Bongie's observation that Vastey's writing "adopts and adapts, revises and resists, generic conventions that were available to it at that time."[62] Refutation pamphlets were central to abolitionist debates and more often than not were written by pro-slavery advocates to refute abolitionist tracts. Take, for example, Paul-Edme Crublier de Saint-Cyran's 1790 *Réfutation du projet des amis des noirs,* which aimed to disprove the arguments put forth by Jacques Pierre Brissot and the members of his abolitionist society in support of suppressing the slave trade and abolishing slavery in the French colonies. Or take the 1810 text by François Richard de Tussac entitled *Le cri des colons contre un ouvrage de M. l'évêque et sénateur Grégoire,* written in refutation of Abbé Grégoire's 1808 *De la literature des Nègres.*[63] The titles of their own pamphlets—Juste Chanlatte's 1810 *Le cri de la nature* (subtitled *Hommage haytien, Au très-vénérable abbé H. Grégoire, auteur d'un Ouvrage nouveau, intitulé: De la littérature des nègres*) and Vastey's 1815 *Le cri de la patrie* and *Le cri de la conscience*—refer directly to de Tussac's 1810 pro-colonial, anti-abolitionist pamphlet. In using the refutation pamphlet, Vastey, Prézeau, Prévost, and others were adopting a form that was associated with colonial argumentation and then repurposing it for their own anticolonial arguments. They are thus enacting the same strategy that Dessalinean writing used to approach French pro-colonial discourse: by appropriating the pro-colonial form of the refutation pamphlet, and even adapting the same titles, Christophean anticolonial pamphlets disarmed and defused the textual weaponry that France used in an attempt to retake the island.

Let us consider Vastey's 1814 refutation pamphlet in more detail here to see precisely how this process of refutation—of neutralizing pro-colonial discourse through rebuttal and critique—is enacted on the page. Though I focus on Vastey's pamphlet specifically here, it bears repeating that the pamphlet was the product of a collective, public oral argument in the General Council meeting, and that this pamphlet was one of many penned by different Christophean secretaries in response to the affair. From the introduction of the pamphlet, Vastey makes clear his preoccupation with language, and colonial discourse more specifically, proclaiming his intention to break down the textual fabric of Malouet's *Mémoires*. He promises that he will do his very best to "thwart [breach] the treacherous machinations [thread, weft] devised by the bad faith and subtlety [artifice, finesse, chicanery] of men who think themselves inscrutable [impenetrable, unreadable, enigmatic]" (*déjouer les trames perfides inventées par la mauvaise foi et la subtilité des hommes qui se croient impénétrables*).[64] He takes on a refutation of Malouet's pro-colonial text, but takes aim at all pro-colonial advocates who believed their language and their logic to be impenetrable, inscrutable—a belief that Vastey intends to breach with his pen (if not his sword).

It is worth spending some time here on Vastey's phrasing, starting with his use of the term *trame*. It is not new: it was prevalent in eighteenth-century pamphlet writing more generally, especially during the revolutionary era. It can be translated literally as "threads," or even "weft"—the series of threads that are woven across the warp threads on a loom. Vastey's use of it in his text is paramount, as it refers us directly to the world of the text and the fabricated or textile nature of discourse (*text* from the Latin *texere*, "to weave, to construct"). The verb *déjouer* adds further dimension to Vastey's textile metaphor: it is usually taken to mean "to foil" or "to thwart" (as in a plot or a ruse). And certainly this is what Vastey is trying to do to Malouet's text, and to pro-colonial discourse more generally: to foil it, to cause it to fail. But how does he achieve that? I would suggest another translation of the word *déjouer* in the context of the metaphor Vastey uses that brings us closer to the image that Vastey is trying to paint with the weaver's loom and the threads of discourse: "to break" or "to breach," to cause something to fail by breaking through or breaching the structure. Vastey wants to breach pro-colonial discourse to create a space, expose the gaps, and cause it to fail.

Vastey enacts this breach on the pages of his refutation pamphlet, situating his own textual production in between—in the breach of—Malouet's once-dominant, "impenetrable" text. Visually, this use of citation and rebuttal creates a powerful effect: he is breaking apart Malouet's text, performing visually the claims of structural weakness that he doubles in his written analysis of Malouet's discourse. Indeed, within his rebuttals of each selected passage from Malouet, Vastey focuses almost exclusively on Malouet's words. He rails against Malouet for his use of "absurd language" and his blasphemous characterizations of black Haitians.[65] He also claims that Toussaint himself would roll over in his grave if he heard the "language of these loathsome colonizers."[66] As an example, he cites Malouet's recommendation that the term *non libre* be used in place of *esclave* in the new colonial system. He points to the grotesque absurdity of Malouet's plan: that he would ask free men (*hommes libres*) who enjoyed civil and political rights that they had won in battle to voluntarily reenslave themselves under a different, worthless word: to "trade in these eternal, inalienable rights for substitute words, badges, trinkets suitable at best for distracting children."[67] If Vastey's emphasis on the treachery of French pro-colonial language seems familiar, it should: this line of argumentation is inherited directly from the Dessalinean writing we studied in chapter 1.

Vastey also renders moot the pro-colonial arguments put forth in Malouet's 1802 text because of the radical political and existential transformation of 1804. The slaves that Malouet knew during the colonial period no longer exist, and Vastey implores the minister to disabuse himself of the "false opinion" of the Haitian people that he has espoused in his 1802 text: "this people is not the same one that you once knew long ago; we are now called *Sir*, we have a great King whom we love; Princes, Duke, Counts, etc."[68] Vastey offers this capacity for self-rule and the maintenance of order as the proof that northern Haitians cannot be duped into accepting Malouet's new colonial system: "You will still find this people impervious [*inaccessible*] to seduction."[69] Vastey's choice of the word *inaccessible* here relates directly back to his statement in his introduction to the pamphlet. Vastey aimed to breach or permeate

Malouet's pro-colonial discourse, exposing its gaps and structural flaws. And in so doing, he aims to render such discourse powerless to penetrate Haitians' own susceptibilities.

Emboldened by the performance of refutation throughout the pamphlet and the accretion of written evidence, Vastey switches from the mode of rebuttal to a bellicose and straightforward list of Haitians' demands in the final paragraph of his pamphlet. In this, he echoes the colonial agent Lavaysse's list of demands to Christophe's government in his threatening letter, adapting it and turning it back on the colonial minister to claim precisely what it is that Haitians want of the French Restoration government:

> Ô Malouet! souffrez que je vous donne une fois et pour toujours notre sine qua non, car nous sommes en garde contre tous les pièges que vous pourriez nous tendre, vous et vos pareils. C'est la reconnaissance de notre indépendance qu'il nous faut. . . . Sans cette base préalable, point de traité, point de composition; nous voulons être libres et indépendans; et nous le serons en dépit des infâmes colons; car la garantie de notre indépendance est à la pointe de nos bayonnettes!

> (O Malouet! Allow me to give you once and for all our *sine qua non*, for we are on guard against all of the traps that you might set for us, you and your *ilk*. The recognition of our independence is what *we* need. . . . Without this basic precondition, no treaties, no arrangements; we wish to be free and independent and so we will be, in spite of the loathsome colonists; because the guarantee of our independence is at the tip of our bayonets!)[70]

Vastey's last sentence is particularly noteworthy for our purposes. In essence, he neutralizes Malouet's writing—and colonial discourse more broadly—by arguing that power does not reside on the tips of men's pens (*pointe* in French) but at the point (*pointe*) of their swords. His repetition of the negative adverb "point" (*point de traité, point de composition*) further contributes to this imagery, emphasizing the futility of written, contractual engagements that do not first recognize Haiti's legitimacy, while also creating a cumulative effect that further emphasizes the noun "pointe" in the final phrase. Here again, the imagery he uses links back to his initial statement of his aims in the introduction: Haitians wield weapons capable of piercing not only through the fabric of colonial discourse, but through the bodies of French soldiers who would seek to reoccupy their lands. It also echoes back to Dessalines's pen/sword language in the 1805 constitution (see chapter 1). These words also find their echo in the Haitian proverb cited in the epigraph at the start of this chapter: "Konstitisyon se papye, bayonet se fè" (Constitutions are made of paper, but swords are made of steel). It also echoes the crossed pen/sword imagery that adorned Vastey's coat of arms and many others in Christophe's nobility.[71] Vastey's refutation does not merely breach or break through Malouet's pro-colonial discourse with his own; ultimately, he argues that pro-colonial writing is powerless in the face of the sword, especially when wielded by men who are willing to live free or die.

The refutation pamphlet's approach to discourse analysis—to breach the perfidious web of duplicity, nuance, and opacity—revealed the arbitrariness of the arguments, language, and logic upon which France justified the maintenance (or in this case, reestablishment) of the colonial system.[72] Or, in other words, Vastey deconstructs Malouet's French colonial text—a strategy in Vastey's writing that Marlene Daut identifies as "*avant la lettre* deconstruction of colonialist print culture."[73] We must recognize the degree to which Christophean refutation writing was indebted to the Dessalinean sphere and the strategies of unmasking, undermining of authority, and rescripting of language that Boisrond Tonnerre and Chanlatte had previously deployed to disarm and delegitimize French pro-colonial discourse. But Dessalinean and Christophean writers themselves were indebted to the practices of pamphlet writers before them, who relied heavily on the metaphors of fabric, text, and the breach in order to challenge, slander, unmask, or refute the texts of their rivals. Here, I would reiterate the need to approach these postcolonial refutation pamphlets beyond a hermeneutic based in the bourgeois public sphere.[74] As evidenced in the process by which Vastey constructed his pamphlet—from the public reading of Malouet's colonial text, to the collective call-and-response in the council meeting, to his visual deconstruction of the text on the page itself—there is a collective, oral, performative dimension to this text that goes far beyond questions of authorship and "literature." There is a sense of collective responsibility, of speaking for and giving voice to a larger public than could access the narrow confines of the print sphere.

Textual War on the South

In early 1815 Christophe sent an olive branch to Pétion—or perhaps, what he hoped was a Trojan horse. After the Malouet fiasco, he was resolute to try once more to unify the independent nation under his rule.[75] He used Pétion's willingness to treat with the colonial agents and the southern president's favorability toward an indemnity payment to justify the need to retake the South. In aiming the power of his printing presses southward, Christophe hoped to have influential men of power in the republican government to support a takeover from the inside, making it possible for Christophe's army to finally enter the city of Port-au-Prince.[76] Pétion had indeed suffered a blow to his public image in the North and in the South (especially among economic nationalists) in the fallout of the Malouet affair, something Christophe heavily publicized. He seized upon the patriotic sentiment that had been generated by the General Council's resolution, and began to roll out his new tactic: a print campaign against Pétion's southern republic. If southern lettered men of mixed race were the implied audience for the series of pamphlets written in refutation of French colonial discourse published in late 1814, these same lettered men were the explicit addressees of the series of pamphlets that followed in 1815.

Under a cover letter entitled "L'olivier de la paix," Christophe sent Pétion a packet of pamphlets penned by Christophean secretaries appealing to the good reason and fraternity of their southern "frères" (addressed "à mes concitoyens)" along with a portfolio of northern press articles from the Malouet affair. Prézeau's January 1815 *Lettre à ses concitoyens de Partie de l'Ouest et du Sud* and Vastey's January 1815 *A mes concitoyens* urged southern republicans to consider the northern monarch's offer of peace and protection in the face of France's overtly treacherous actions. To do so they emphasized the unity and the connections that northern writers shared with their southern counterparts. For instance, Prézeau appealed to his southern origins and his close ties with notable men of color who still resided in Pétion's republic in order to establish his credibility and the shared national interest that motivated his pamphlet. Vastey affirmed the same in his January 1815 pamphlet *A mes concitoyens*. But the "olive branch" packet was hardly a peace offering. For, while the cover letter and individual pamphlets heralded Christophe's magnanimity and his paternal benevolence, it also came with the demand that the southern republicans submit to his regime. Writing as the secretary of state and minister of foreign affairs, Prévost penned a letter to Pétion (copied in the olive branch packet) stressing that, given the discovery of Malouet's plans ("Les projets des implacables ennemis d'Hayti découverts"), Haitians needed to come together ("se réunir") and mount a joint force capable of repelling what he determined was an inevitable invasion by pro-colonial French forces.[77] The terms and details of such a reunification were made clear in a numbered list for Pétion's consideration. Once again, Prévost's letter mirrors the menacing letter that Lavaysse sent Christophe: it appeals first to Pétion's reason and his duty to protect the interests of his country, then it threatens him with invasion and proposes a list of offers they are making in exchange for recognition of Christophe as the sovereign leader of Haiti (the accordance of titles, conservation of rank, property, and so on).[78] Having disarmed French colonial discourse in its attempt to retake the colony in their refutation pamphlets, Christophean writers were free to repurpose these same discursive strategies in their campaign to retake Pétion's southern republic.

These early "olive branch" pamphlets were highly rhetorical, employing various strategies to "reveal" the error of southern republicans' political choices and loyalties, and convince Haitians in the West and the South to "gather under the banner of Royal authority."[79] They also focused heavily on language. One of Vastey's main critiques is of the comportment of men of color since the start of the revolution—himself included—for changing loyalties between *les blancs* (the French) and *les noirs* (insurgent and former slaves): "A permanent feature since the start of the revolution is that Haitians of color have always wavered [*tergiversés*], sometimes for the *noirs*, sometimes for the *blancs*, and they have always been victims of their fickleness. O you, to whom I now speak! come back to the true point of stability, to your own cause, to the *noirs*' cause, the Haytians' cause."[80] His use of the term *tergiverser* (to waver, to equivocate, to prevaricate) is noteworthy: Malouet's secret instructions introduced it in a swipe at Christophe, and Vastey repurposes it here against Pétion. Vastey's use of the term encompasses both the embodied experience of changing sides in the revolutionary battle *and* the discursive practice of equivocation—of using inconsistent or ambiguous language to mislead others or conceal the truth. Vastey critiques free men of color as especially deficient because of their inconsistency or flip-flopping, a quality that he argued was plaguing Haiti's political class and could be resolved in a more hierarchical and orderly political practice that foregrounded the interests of all Haitians ("les noirs . . . les haytiens") and, crucially for our purposes, a more frank and straightforward kind of writing.

According to Madiou's account, Christophe sent a group of emissaries (Toussaint Dupont, Comte du Trou; Baron de Dessalines; Baron de Ferrier; and Edouard Michaux) south to deliver the olive branch texts to Pétion in February 1815. Upon their arrival, they were met with general ridicule by members of Pétion's government, who mocked the absurdity of their northern brothers' royal costumes and seigniorial titles. Pétion declined to address Christophe's representatives by their official titles and thus refused to legitimate the northern monarchy, which he dismissed as founded on bizarre and unseemly (*inconvenantes*) ideas.[81] In response, Christophe ordered another round of texts to be sent south—this time more aggressive in their approach. Here, we see Christophean writers sharpening their critiques of southern inconsistency and equivocation, effectively repurposing their earlier refutations of French colonial discourse into attacks on Pétion and his surrogates. On the specific question of language, Vastey depicts Pétion as a perfidious double-speaking traitor, guilty of using the same language of false *liberté* that the French had espoused: "With the words *république, égalité, liberté*, Pétion and the French *blancs* would like to see us in chains [*nous enchaîner*]."[82] He also deploys a critique of Pétion's deceptive use of language that is near-identical to the Dessalinean critiques of French colonialism we studied in chapter 1. Vastey calls out Pétion's "deceitful phrases, with double meaning" (*phrases artificieuses, à double sens*), "obscure plots" (*complots ténébreux*), and "secretive language" (*langage mystérieux*) that were revealed in the documents and correspondence between Pétion and Malouet's colonial agent, Lavaysse.[83] He marshals a similar Dessalinean critique when he calls Pétion a "Proteus in the extreme" (*archi-protée*), resurrecting (and amplifying) the specifically negative depiction of the shapeshifting figure of Proteus, used earlier by Chanlatte to describe members of Pétion's Senate.[84] Vastey presents Pétion as the embodiment of this tergiversating man of color who is innately hypocritical: "Nothing paints Pétion's diabolical character better than this amalgamation of heterogeneous principles that repel each other.... He is truly an extraordinary spendthrift of hypocrisy."[85]

Vastey's repurposing of the anti-French tropes of deceptive language, hypocrisy, and inconsistency in his attacks against Pétion is worth unpacking briefly here. Marlene Daut has pointed to Vastey's use of the language of "monstrous hybridity" in his descriptions of Pétion as evidence of his "internalization . . . of the implicit 'racial' grammar undergirding discussions of Haiti."[86] Vastey is undoubtedly deploying the language of "monstrous hybridity," though I read his activation of the trope as a strategic deployment rather than a passive internalization. That is, Vastey seized upon a potent, recognizable trope in early nineteenth-century Atlantic discourse about Haiti to denigrate Pétion, assigning him all of the characteristics of a monstrous hybrid *and* offering a solution to this problem: Christophe's monarchy. Vastey did not present the problem of "monstrous hybridity" as an inherently racial one, but rather one linked to government form and *choice*. Vastey adapted the language of monstrous hybridity to the Haitian civil war context, both to refute Pétion's characterizations of the northern monarchy as despotic in the context of the Haitian civil war, and to valorize a Christophean, monarchical practice of order and hierarchy that solved all of the problems of flip-flopping, shape-shifting, and hypocrisy that he identified in Pétion's southern republic.

Vastey demonstrates the "solution" to the problem of monstrous hybridity by offering his own experience as proof. He describes his experience during the War of Independence as a free man of color as being beset by this same inconsistency, this hypocritical flip-flopping between opposing camps. He pinged between Toussaint's army and Leclerc's expeditionary forces before finally seeking shelter in Ennery among the former slaves of his family plantation. He describes Christophe's regime as providing salvation in the stability, consistency, and order it created. In particular, he points to the motto bestowed upon him by the king when he received his seigniorial title: "truth, sincerity, candor" (*vérité, sincérité, franchise*)—words that stand in stark opposition to the inconsistency and equivocation of his previous "tergiversation." His motto undoubtedly gestures to the emphasis Christophean writers placed on unveiling the dangerous, deceptive eloquence of French colonial writing first evinced by Dessalinean writers. In opposition to Pétion's use of language as inherently treacherous, designed to trick and mislead (*égarer*) Haitians, Vastey proposes Christophean writing as an alternative. He casts his own writing, and Christophean discourse more broadly, as clear, sincere prose that is dedicated solely to unveiling and exposing the hypocrisy and false *liberté* of the southern republic. His own textual production performs this motto: first, through acts of discursive illumination, casting the light of his discourse analysis onto the shadowy corners of prevarication and doublespeak in order to unveil "truth" to his readership; and second, through its style and syntax. Vastey utilizes a simple, clear language that is comprehensible first and foremost to a Haitian readership *and* listening audience. He deploys this frank, Haitian form of writing (what he calls a "tournure haytienne") as a direct challenge to southern republican "literary" writing that we will study in chapter 3.

* * *

Christophe placed a great deal of political importance on print: for example, he demanded that all correspondence related to the Malouet affair be printed in mass quantities and sent throughout the kingdom, the southern republic, Europe and its colonies, and the United States. As we saw above, Christophe used the power of discourse through the printed word in order to neutralize the medium through which colonists justified the colonial system. It was also self-consciously performative of state power. Christophean writing was a weapon of the state, evinced in Vastey's imagery of piercing through the fabric of colonial discourse, and in the dual quill and sword imagery that adorned the armorial symbols for Christophean writers. As we shall see in the next chapter, southern republican writers conceived of a different defense against foreign invasion: through the promotion of an image of Haiti as a place of civilization, of progress, and of the realization of the revolutionary ideals of 1789. Their approach was to achieve recognition from world powers through negotiation, persuasion, and contact rather than military might. Southern republicans were elaborating decidedly European, modern "literary" sensibilities, concerned for their image and reputation on the world's stage, and attempting—not always successfully—to stay above the fray of the northern monarchy's bellicose paper war.

Northern and southern writers would continue to spar until the end of the civil war, as southern writers began to elaborate their own republican state project of writing in opposition to, and in dialogue with, Christophean writing. Where Vastey's, Prévost's, and others' writing eschewed figural language and finely wrought ("châtié") style—in a word, literariness—as we shall see in the next chapter, southern writers embraced these qualities as foundational to their duty as patriots and citizens of the liberal republic.

3

Southern Republic of Letters

The years 1815–1820 marked a turning point for the southern republic. Against the backdrop of Christophe's northern paper war to retake the southern half of the island, France's conservative Bourbon Restoration, and Simón Bolívar's Spanish American War of Independence, the republican Senate reelected Alexandre Pétion and set about reworking the republic. Southern republicans wanted to highlight their government as the purest remaining instantiation of the liberal Enlightenment ideals of 1789. As such, ideas of civilization, progress, reason, *liberté*, and *égalité* became central to the republic's messaging: in the new constitution, but also in state newspapers, journals, and speeches, and in the creation of the Lycée national.[1] As we will see in this chapter, partisans of the southern republic turned specifically to literary writing and literary criticism as the central medium through which they established themselves as liberal subjects and performed the ideals of liberal enlightenment in the bourgeois public sphere. Via a new form, the literary and political journal (or *revue*), southern republicans heralded individual reason and literary writing as a direct expression of the autonomous author and the liberal mind. Criticism served a similar role, providing intellectuals with the forum to exercise the important qualities of taste, sensibility, and discrimination. Southern republican writers' turn to the *revue* served a dual purpose. First, it allowed them to distinguish their literary writing from the North's militarized, performative court writing, establishing an important distance between their republican state and the northern monarchy to outside observers. Second, it gave them a platform from which to publicize the southern republic's role as one of the few remaining sites of Enlightenment liberalism. To be sure, southern republican writers were engaged in an equally performative and political act: deploying their artistic and creative sensibilities as a form of resistance to and differentiation from the northern monarchy.

Crucially, the literature and criticism based in *l'esprit* and *l'imagination* that southern republicans embraced were recent formulations of the eighteenth-century bourgeois liberal order and the literary public sphere—still very much developing into the modern forms that we recognize them as today. What we see emerge in this phase of southern republican writing is precisely the embrace of the "essentially associated" concepts of *littérature* and *critique* in their early nineteenth-century iterations that Raymond Williams historicizes in *Marxism and Literature*.[2] This is particularly important for our purposes because, while southern men of letters embraced these concepts in a broader Atlantic Enlightenment context, I argue that they also deployed them specifically (and in a no less political way) in opposition to the writing practices of the northern kingdom. As we recall from the previous chapter, northern writers conceptualized a different approach to print and the "public sphere" that was closely linked to the Dessalinean sphere of symbolism, performance, and collective textual production. Indeed, northern writing stood in opposition to the worldly concepts of literature and criticism that the southern republic embraced.

In this precise moment in the civil-war-as-paper-war, then, we see a highly political tension between the northern and southern regimes in Haiti with regard to the use and meaning of writing. Southern republican writers responded to northerners' textual warfare in newly created publications such as *L'Abeille haytienne* (1817) and *L'Observateur* (1819). Though scholars have noted the importance of these early publications for Haitian literature, few have analyzed them as politically engaged periodicals with a specific, republican agenda.[3] This is because the *revue* itself is the privileged medium of the bourgeois public sphere: a medium for the exchange and expression of individual reason, critical analysis, and rational debate outside the state.[4] And yet, by reconsidering these early Haitian publications in the context of their production, both in the civil war *guerre de plume* with the northern monarchy and in the context of the historical transformations of the southern republic, I show that the *revue* is no less complicit or enmeshed in government power, no less "scribal," to use Chris Bongie's term.[5] Or rather, the concerns for the literary, the critical, and the political are not mutually exclusive, but rather part of a politicized performance of southern republican writers' use of literature. This is not how southern republicans present their own writing, of course. They self-fashion their intellectual production as existing outside any motivation beyond the free and *liberal* expression of the mind and the heart. It is this southern tradition of literary writing associated with republicanism that historians have most often identified as the beginning of independent Haitian literature. Instead, as I argue here, the emergence of a southern republican literary tradition was conditioned by the continued civil war and *guerre de plume* with the North and its militarized, performative court writing. Indeed, this is precisely what Haitian historian Hénock Trouillot is pointing to with his provocation that Haitian literature is essentially always a "partisan, combat literature."[6] Southern literary writing was the end result of a period of textual warfare in which both sides contested the meaning of writing and its uses in post-independence Haiti.

This chapter therefore analyzes the emergence of a decidedly modern "literary" sensibility in southern writing during the latter half of the civil war period (1814–1820) that reflects the transformations of the republican state in Haiti under Pétion. I show that the southern republic created new literary publications in order to perform the successes of the liberal republican model by heralding literary writing as a direct expression of the liberal mind, and the creative and intellectual abilities of the individual, autonomous author—characteristics that they formulated in direct opposition to Christophe's collective, militarized, and performative approach to textual production.Nevertheless, for all of its emphasis on intellectual autonomy and authorial genius, and its critiques of Christophean writing as complicit with state power, a publication like *L'Abeille* was very much a government publication. In what follows, I establish the contours of Pétion's "new" republicanism, which he elaborated within the Atlantic world transformations of the mid-1810s. Next, I analyze the new republican publications that resulted from the North-South paper war, paying specific attention to southern writers' efforts to define their intellectual production according to the emergent bourgeois concepts of literature and criticism. Finally, I trace how this nascent notion of literary writing, forged in the crucible of civil war, gained hegemony under Jean-Pierre Boyer's reunified republican state after the fall of Henry Christophe in 1820. Here, I perform a close analysis of the southern republican writer Hérard Dumesle's *Voyage dans le Nord d'Hayti, ou Révélations des lieux et des monuments historiques* (1824).

I argue that his piece of early domestic Haitian travel writing fixes the terms of the paper war between North and South from the position of southern republican hegemony.

Saint-Dominguan "Refugees," Haitian Returnees, and Pétion's New Republicanism

Between 1815 and 1816, hundreds of Saint-Dominguan "refugees" returned to the island after decades away.[7] During the revolutionary tumult and subsequent post-independence civil war, tens of thousands of men and women fled the island, creating new lives for themselves in the United States, France, and the Caribbean. Crucially, the 1815–1816 returnees whom we will study in this chapter represent a different trajectory than those earlier returnees we studied in previous chapters, such as Etienne Mentor and Juste Chanlatte, who returned to the island from exile in 1803 committed to Dessalines's military regime. The returnees of 1815–1816 were part of a different group: the republican diaspora in the Atlantic world.[8]

We can count among these returnees names like Delille Laprée, Jules Solime Milscent, Noël Colombel, Joseph Courtois, and Jonathas Granville, as well as well-known French Jacobins and abolitionists such as Jean-Nicolas Billaud-Varenne, Civique de Gastine, Horace Camille Desmoulins, and Barincou fils.[9] But who were these republican "refugees," and what kinds of ideas did they bring back with them when they returned to Pétion's republic in 1815–1816? The stories of Jules Solime Milscent and Joseph and Sévère Courtois present illustrative case studies of this Atlantic republicanism among men born in the colony of Saint-Domingue and exiled during the revolutionary tumult. Milscent had a strong connection to journalism and the world of print: he was the son of the former colonist-turned-abolitionist and Jacobin journalist Claude Michel Louis Milscent de Mussé (also known as Milscent-Créole), who was guillotined in Paris in 1794. A free man of color, Jules Solime Milscent had departed the colony in 1790 and remained in France during the Napoleonic period, even publishing an ode celebrating Napoléon's coronation as emperor in 1805.[10] He returned to Pétion's republic in 1816. The twin trajectories of Joseph and Sévère Courtois, whom Vanessa Mongey has studied extensively, reveal a similar transit through Napoleonic France and commitment to the world of the press and republican ideals. Joseph Courtois traveled to France in 1799 as a French republican to study at the Institut nationale des colonies. He served in Napoléon's army in the first decades of the nineteenth century, finally returning to Haiti after the Bourbon Restoration. He returned to Pétion's republic committed to the principles of liberalism, equality, and civilization, founding—alongside his wife, Juliette—a newspaper, the *Feuille du commerce*, and a coed school.[11] He was also central in the effort to encourage other Atlantic republicans to settle in Haiti's southern republic, a "repatriation of the St. Domingue diaspora" that included free men of color as well as white French republicans—likely also seeking refuge from the Restoration.[12] The younger Courtois brother, Sévère, represents a different though no less republican trajectory. Mongey calls him a "traveling republican," one of the many men in the post-1791 Atlantic world who believed that his duty was to "fight for the republican cause wherever he could" against royalist forces of all nations in the Caribbean: in Louisiana, the First Republic of Cartagena, Les Cayes, Haiti, Galveston Island, Texas, the Republic of the Floridas, Providencia, Venezuela, and beyond.[13]

It was not just Saint-Dominguan exiles who sought refuge in Haiti, but "traveling" republican revolutionaries of all nations, as many as two thousand by early 1816, according to Sibylle Fischer's estimates.[14] Most notable among these "refugees" was Simón Bolívar, who landed in Les Cayes on December 24, 1815, after the fall of Cartagena. Bolívar's letter to Pétion requesting asylum highlights the language of republicanism that was currency during this period: he depicted Les Cayes as the privileged zone of republican refuge in the New World: "the asylum of all republicans of this part of the world," and appealed to his shared sentiments with Pétion "regarding the defense of the rights of our common *patria*"—that is, the singular, universal *republic* that was struggling to find a foothold in the Caribbean.[15] In the Courtois brothers' trajectory, in Bolívar's story and many others', there is an unmistakably universal conception of the republic and of republicanism: the republic was not a place but an idea, one that could exist anywhere so long as it was formed through virtue, talent, equality, and rights. It was a republicanism formed in exile in the Atlantic world, committed to the values and ideology that they had seen falter in Europe. And yet, for all of its Enlightenment ideals, Atlantic republicanism remained ambivalent on the question of the plantation system, slavery, and the rights of men *other* than propertied, free men of color. Famously, Bolívar was slow to enforce the abolition of slavery in Gran Colombia, and many of the "traveling" Atlantic republicans themselves engaged in the slave trade, profiting from smuggling slaves in the Caribbean region.[16] Moreover, Bolívar ultimately devised a republican constitution in 1826 that installed a presidency for life and created a two-tiered system of citizenship (similar, as we shall see to Pétion's nomination of president for life in 1816 and to Jean-Pierre Boyer's restrictive approach to Haitian citizenship).[17] The Dessalinean wariness of what Enlightenment universalism would do for black, unlettered, and unpropertied men resonates here.

The universal, as-yet-unrealized ideal of republicanism that shaped the republican diaspora in the Atlantic world differed in important, sometimes paradoxical ways from Pétion's embattled—but very real—republican state in southern Haiti. The latter was an antislavery republic, and in that way, it was the most radical instantiation of Enlightenment liberalism in the Atlantic world. But in other ways, Pétion's southern state was less ideal, and less *free*, in practice, than the diaspora's republican ideals. Indeed, the republican state he presided over from 1806 to 1815 was antidemocratic, with few legitimate checks on the president's power. Recall from the previous chapter that after the republican revolution's 1806 assassination of Dessalines and proclamation of a new democratic constitution in December 1806, Pétion suspended the republican Senate and assumed full power of the government for nearly a year. Even after he reinstated the Senate, he found that the 1806 republican constitution excessively curtailed his power, and so he largely disregarded it, alienating and dismissing most of the more liberal members of the Senate.[18] Many of these disenfranchised senators left Port-au-Prince during this early phase of Pétion's consolidation and relocated to Les Cayes, a liberal republican stronghold since before the revolution. From a safe distance, they criticized Pétion for having violated the constitution and installing a dictatorship.[19] Pétion's increasingly undemocratic rule drew such criticism from the southern peninsula that the region briefly declared the Scission du Sud, naming Rigaud commander in chief of their independent state, the "Gouvernement départemental du Sud," headquartered in Les Cayes.[20] By proclaiming a separatist government, they hoped to encourage Pétion further toward their liberal economic and individual liberties–based goals.²¹ Had it lasted, the Scission du Sud might have pushed Pétion to reform the institutions of his republican state, but Rigaud's death in 1811 allowed Pétion to once again consolidate power in the southern peninsula. The 1816 republican constitution finally codified his authoritarian governance structure by naming him president for life with the right to choose his successor.²²

At the same time, the 1816 constitution proved itself to be more radically liberal in other ways, most notably in its free soil policy, which further radicalized the free soil guarantees decreed by the National Assembly in 1791. In this sense, Pétion's republicanism sought to further codify Haiti as the purest remaining instantiation of liberal Enlightenment ideals, further radicalizing and realizing the guarantee of freedom and rights that were no longer possible for men of color in the Atlantic world. Pétion remained entirely committed to assuring the legacy of the antislavery, human rights–based project of the Haitian Revolution in Atlantic world republicanism. When Pétion provided Bolívar with arms, munitions, soldiers, even a printing press, for his republican revolution, it was on the condition that Bolívar agree to abolish slavery in his South American republic, and pledge to turn over any African slaves captured in the Caribbean to Haiti rather than selling them back into slavery.²³ The Haitian Republic thus promoted itself as a *terre d'asile* for the enslaved *and* for republicanism itself in the Atlantic world during this period. The guarantees of rights and freedoms that came out of the 1815–1816 period were central to the Haitian Republic's self-fashioning as a sovereign, antislavery state in the Caribbean. The differences between stateless Atlantic republicanism and the realities of Pétion's southern state speak to the limits, possibilities, and contradictions of nineteenth-century republicanism in the Caribbean. On the one hand, we see clearly the distance between the rhetoric of liberal republicanism and the reality of statehood: the idea of Haiti that the southern republic and its lettered men had a vested interest in promoting, largely to the lettered outside world, and the realities of their state practices.²⁴

* * *

The influx of Saint-Dominguan-turned-Haitian returnees to the southern republic in 1815 and 1816 were crucial to enacting Pétion's new republicanism. The transformations of the republican state during the period and the new republicanism it brought—a new constitution, the creation of the Constituent Assembly, new schools, new publications—were the efforts of a group of lettered republican men who sought to (re)make in Haiti what had been cut short elsewhere in the Atlantic world: a republic that embodied the universalist principles of the French Revolution. As we shall see, for as much as the southern republic cast itself within the Atlantic, universal debates about freedom and rights, their discursive self-fashioning was still constructed in dialogue—paper war—with Christophe's northern kingdom. Which is to say, the southern republic demonstrated its universal republicanism by negating the legitimacy of the northern kingdom as a state form, and negating its writing as literary.

L'Abeille and *L'Observateur*

Nous n'écrivons pas pour complaire à la puissance et par telles et telles considérations, mais bien pour rendre hommage à la vérité et sous l'inspiration seule de notre conscience.

(We are not writing to try to please power and for such and such an issue, but to pay tribute to the truth, prompted by our conscience alone.)
—Noël Colombel, *Examen d'un pamphlet* (1819)

When Delille Laprée, Jules Solime Milscent, Noël Colombel, Joseph Courtois, Jonathas Granville, and others returned to Haiti from their various corners of the republican diaspora, Pétion made good use of them. Recall that in the earlier stage of the civil war, Pétion did not have the same print capacity as the northern monarchy, nor did he have as many talented writers as Christophe. Once back on Haitian soil, republican returnees became integral to Pétion's efforts to reassert, and perform, republicanism in Haiti and in the Atlantic world. For example, Pétion immediately named Colombel to serve as his personal secretary, and set about to the formation of new republican institutions: schools, the new Chamber of Representatives, and especially for our purposes here, the press, founding a number of newspapers and magazines, including independent Haiti's first *revue*.²⁵ Laprée helped found the Lycée Pétion in 1816, and in 1817, joined Milscent and Colombel to found *L'Abeille haytienne: Journal politique et littéraire*, the government's first programmatic literary writing project. Where literature and discussions about it occupied a marginal position, if at all, in the dry, informational government paper, *Le Télégraphe* (and had been even more marginal in the official government papers that preceded it), such concerns finally found their place in *L'Abeille*. Importantly, new literary and political journals such as *L'Abeille* defined southern republican intellectual production as the *free* expression of the liberal mind, which they contrasted to what they argued was politically compromised, utilitarian court writing coming out of the northern monarchy.

The title and front matter of the journal draw heavily upon French republican symbolism: the skep, or woven straw beehive, that adorns the front cover is one of the main revolutionary icons and represented work, equality, and community.²⁶ In addition to the apian imagery that was synonymous with 1789 republicanism, the journal's subtitle, *Journal politique et littéraire*, indicates the political uses of the literary writing that Milscent and others define in its pages. The epigraph presents as a subtle but significant shift from the pen-sword interchangeability in northern militant writing: in *L'Abeille*, military glory (*l'épée*) was separate from literary glory (*talents*). Talent was, of course, a revolutionary republican idea that took aim at the old system of order and privilege and allowed for social distinction based on merit, aptitude, and individual genius. Indeed, for Milscent and other southern writers, literature was possible only when writing turned away from political and military action (utilitarianism) and toward the domain of the imaginative and the aesthetic—a position that put them in stark contrast with the Christophean pamphlets coming out of the North.

Milscent makes clear the connection between the politics of his print endeavor and Pétion's liberal republican state in the journal's prospectus, which was the sole article to appear in the first issue: "At the budding sight of Haiti's prime, some friends of the arts wished to assist the liberal intentions of the government."²⁷ Here, a reference to Christophean pamphlet writing seems implicit in Milscent's formulation. Where northern writers linked their print projects intimately to their beloved, august majesty the king, Milscent makes it clear that "friends" of the arts *chose*

Figure 3.1. Front cover of *L'Abeille haytienne: Journal politique et littéraire* (Port-au-Prince), 1819. Courtesy of the Bibliothèque nationale de France.

to support the liberal intentions of the government with their own intellectual labor. To this end, Milscent's prospectus called on his fellow lettered republican compatriots to submit their articles to the paper in support of this liberal project. According to the guidelines Milscent set forth for these submissions, they could be on any subject—politics, science, literature, commerce, the rural economy—and in any form (prose or verse), so long as they were written "in the common interest," reminding prospective authors that "the elegance of discourse must add to the luster of your literary productions."[28] In the end, however, the journal served mostly as the organ for Milscent's literary production and his own musings on politics and the craft of writing.

Milscent further expounded upon the position he believed writing should occupy in a liberal republic in his manifesto "Des devoirs du journaliste." Here again, Christophean writing and its political role in the northern government loom large in Milscent's formulation. The manifesto establishes a value system in which utilitarian writing produced by "workers" (*ouvriers*) is deemed inferior to creative or literary writing ("œuvres de l'esprit") produced by "those who profess literary talent."[29] In the former category, "talent" is defined by the writer's ability to follow commands and fulfill orders ("exécuter avec goût la pièce qui lui est demandée"), while in literary production, talent is measured by the creative capacity of the writer and his sense of taste and discrimination ("du discernement, de l'intelligence, du génie même").[30] Milscent's hierarchy of literary value distinguishes between writing that is commissioned or ordered and writing that is the direct expression of the mind, the creative and intellectual abilities of the individual author that he sees as central to the task of illustrating and performing the successes of the liberal republican model.

Milscent makes his case that the journalist must be held to—and aspire to—the same rigorous standards as the literary writer of talent: he mustn't merely echo the news of the world, nor serve as a "simple copyist" (*simple copiste*) of government decrees. Milscent's republican journalist is called to a higher service: assisting the liberal republican state by embodying its principles of individual freedom of expression and erudition. To illustrate his meditations on the duty of the journalist, Milscent offers two pieces of writing from the North as examples of the kind of writing he deems antithetical to the liberal model, and against which he juxtaposes the southern republic's journalistic project: two proclamations "that were incited ... by the theatrical King of the northern part of our country."[31] Milscent's use of the passive voice to describe the unfree conditions of production (ordered, as opposed to, say, created through the inspiration and free will of the writer-artist) establishes his view of Christophean writing as lacking the agency or creative expression of the autonomous author. His sarcastic denunciation of the "theatrical king" is designed to denigrate Christophe's power as only performative and thus illegitimate, and to imply that his pamphleteers were simply performing a role that had been created for them in the elaborate spectacle of the northern monarchy. Indeed, Milscent derides the writers of these proclamations (lesser-known Christophean writers Chevalier de Jean Louis and Louis Lubin) as Greek chorus singers ("les Coryphées"), in contrast to his own definition of literary production that valorized individual textual production. Milscent appeals to the liberal Enlightenment narrative of reason and progress: northerners were unenlightened and in a state of subjugation, but if they were exposed to liberal ideas (or if they are simply allowed to follow their hearts—and Milscent sees no distinction between the former and the latter), then they would inevitably join Pétion's republic. According to this logic, the North is deficient, premodern, unenlightened, but also capable of being transformed or put back on some path toward progress and ultimately, liberty. Milscent reasons that if northern writers were exposed to the liberal concepts of Pétion's republic, they would recognize the king's tyranny and abjure all of the titles of nobility: "If all of our fellow countrymen of the north were educated in the liberality of the Republican Government; or rather, if they were permitted to follow their hearts, they would come savor with us the sweet pleasures of liberty."[32] Milscent's statement is the very quintessence of republican publicity: if only they were allowed to follow their individual desires (something the monarchy does not allow), they would be able to experience true freedom.

Hérard Dumesle founded his own literary journal, *L'Observateur: Journal périodique,* in 1819 in Les Cayes. It was styled in the same vein as Milscent's *Abeille*, particularly in its elaboration of the concepts of literature and criticism as central components of liberal republicanism. Born in Les Cayes in 1784, Dumesle was a contemporary of writers like Milscent, Chanlatte, and Vastey, and had also come of age during the civil war between North and South. His role within this intellectual field was to the liberal left of Milscent, Colombel, and others. In this way, Dumesle embraces the liberal, southern, Cayenne tradition that stretched back to the colonial era and had manifested itself in the Guerre du Sud and the Scission du Sud. For Dumesle and his fellow Cayennes, Les Cayes was the center of the southern liberal tradition—the birthplace of liberal republican ideas and the final resting place of its greatest champions: "where republican ideas formed the network of opinion."[33] That he founded his literary journal in 1819 is significant: it would serve as the liberal opposition paper in the new regime of Jean-Pierre Boyer, who had succeeded Pétion as president in 1818. Dumesle had been a strong supporter of Pétion, and gave one of the eulogies at his funeral (as reprinted in *L'Observateur*). He would take an important role as a liberal opposition member of the Chamber of Deputies: he was elected as a deputy from Les Cayes in 1822 and then president of the house in 1824. His position as a liberal voice of

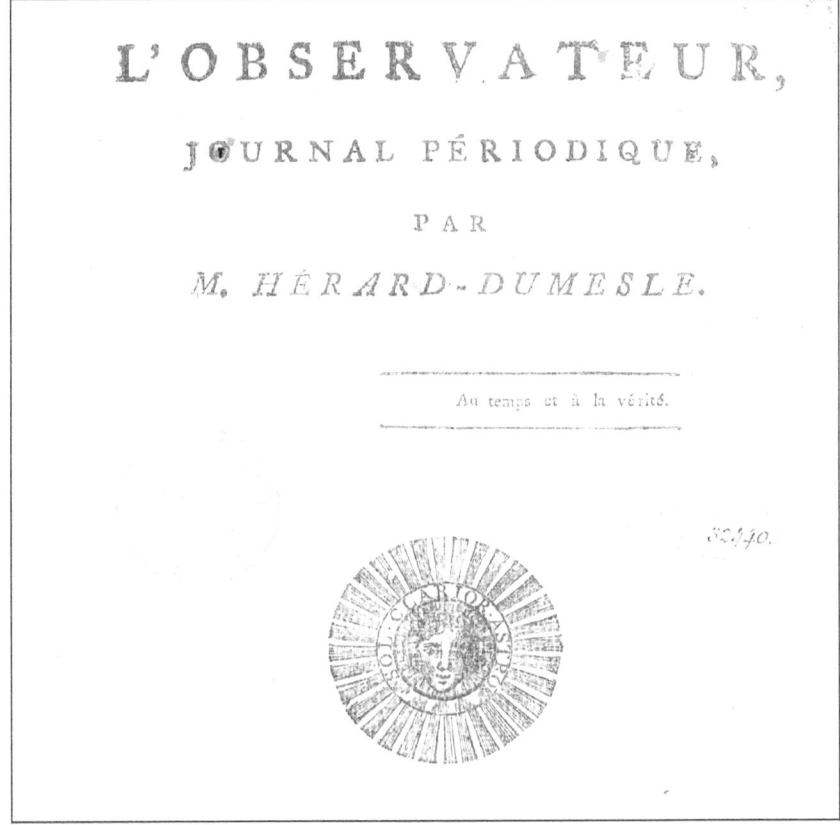

Figure 3.2. Front cover of *L'Observateur: Journal périodique* (Les Cayes), 1819. Courtesy of the Bibliothèque nationale de France.

parliamentary opposition turned more critical in the 1830s, as he took on an increasingly public and oppositional stance in politics. He was instrumental in the 1843–1844 Liberal Revolution to overthrow Boyer, and install his cousin, Charles Rivière Hérard, as president (some even accuse Dumesle of running the government for him). Rivière Hérard lasted only a short time in power—the liberal government could not hold against continued *piquet* rebellions in the South, Dominican independence in the East, and secessionist state unrest in the North. Dumesle and Rivière Hérard (along with their supporters) went into exile in Jamaica, where they spent the remainder of their lives.[34]

As far as *L'Observateur* was concerned, with very few exceptions Dumesle was the sole producer of content for the journal. In the paper's prospectus from April 1819, he laid out the main subjects he intended to cover: literature, agriculture, trade, and politics. However, he made it clear in the "Prospectus" that literature (which Dumesle defines alternately as "l'art de penser," "belle littérature," and "belles lettres") and literary criticism ("l'analyse de quelques ouvrages d'esprit") would receive pride of place. Like Milscent, then, Dumesle is working with the emergent concepts of literature and criticism in their restrictive, modern sense of anti-utilitarian creative works of the autonomous liberal mind. From this perspective, Dumesle speaks from a rather narrow subject position: southern lettered men of mixed race who had initially fought for equal rights in the colonial context during the early phase of the French Revolution—a social group from which Dumesle descended. He situates his journal and its literary endeavor as an example of the evolution of independent southern republican literary writing, from its persecution and *oppression* during the colonial period, to its flourishing in the independent republic: "During the long oppression under which our heads were bowed . . . those individuals of our class who showed a glimmer of talent [*étincelles du génie*] were harassed the most, and so to enjoy some peace they ceased to make a show of their erudition, content to worship the arts in secret [*rendre un culte secret aux beaux-arts*]."[35] Dumesle thus relies on an antislavery language and rhetoric—not to denounce chattel slavery, but to describe the metaphoric slavery of social and legal inequality and arbitrary government. What suffered in this context, says Dumesle, was the development and progress of literary production among free men of color in the colony. He attempts to rectify this with *L'Observateur*.

Dumesle makes a fascinating and quite early cultural nationalist argument regarding Haitian national literature in his journal. He makes the case that a new biography of great men must be written, one that places the nation's first men of letters side by side with its military heroes (echoing Milscent's epigraph in *L'Abeille*). Great nations have progressed toward enlightenment, he says, by conserving and venerating the works of their first writers, just as they venerate the great acts of their military heroes.[36] Dumesle proposes that writers such as Pierre Pinchinat, F. Braquehais, Louis Boisrond Tonnerre, and "a host of other writers, such as J. Chanlatte," be included in a new history of the origins of Haitian literature.[37] This literary pantheon, Dumesle argues, will have an important function in shaping the public mind: "To develop the public mind it is equally useful to take an interest in the history of the progress of literature and humanities, and to diligently gather the works of our first writers. It is an asset that belongs to the nation."[38] Even in 1819, before the fall of Christophe and the unification of the country under Boyer's republic, Dumesle had begun to define a national Haitian literature: its progenitors, its function in shaping national sentiment, and its role in projecting an image of civilization and progress to the Atlantic lettered sphere. That Dumesle limited his literary pantheon to one sole writer from the North, Juste Chanlatte, did not go unnoticed by Christophean writers, who took issue with the southerners' narrow and exclusionary notion of what constituted Haitian national literature.

It would be useful to look specifically at Dumesle's uses of a narrowly defined notion of literature and the literary public sphere to oppose what he sees as the illiberal, monarchical—even feudal—writing from Christophe's northern regime. Here, Dumesle builds upon Milscent's tactics in *L'Abeille* but also radicalizes them. Where Milscent's *Abeille* approached its condemnation of Christophe's monarchy with some restraint (no direct address, allusion and metaphor instead of naming), Dumesle's journal calls out Christophe directly and passionately, injecting a personal fervor that goes beyond Milscent's measured indignation. Throughout the journal, he criticizes the servitude and inequality inherent to a monarchy, and makes evident his anger and desire for vengeance against the North. In the various articles that touch on the subject of Christophe and the northern monarchy, most written in the first person, Dumesle describes in real time to his readers the visceral, emotional reaction that the king provokes in him: "When I think of this ferocious usurper who is oppressing a large swath of my cherished land, my soul is afflicted with a cruel unrest: I must take a breath before continuing."[39]

His articles convey a palpable urgency to save the North from what he deems its slow, painful demise. In a subsequent article, he sounds the bell: the North is on the brink of collapse and must be liberated. Citing a letter published in the French paper *Le Constitutionnel*, Dumesle warns grimly of a state of "wasting and desolation to which Christophe's ferocity has reduced the beautiful region he usurped, and which is soon likely to become nothing but a vast desert, for *His Majesty* has long proven that his paternal heart only wishes to rule over the dead."[40] In 1819, then, Dumesle is asserting the position that the North is an illegitimate secessionist monarchy ruled by a cruel usurper who had turned the country to dust. His use of the first-person possessive adjective "my" communicates the sentimental, subjective view of the North as a lost province that he longs to liberate from its oppressor and bring back into the republican "nation."

Dumesle pursues this idea of the oppressed, suffering North in an improbable fictional story: "Portfolio of a Pick-Pocketed Spy" (*Porte-feuille d'un espion dévalisé*). As the story reports, a British spy had traveled throughout the country noting his "observations" (a nod, undoubtedly, to the title of Dumesle's journal) in a small portfolio. On his last night in town, he wandered into a bad part of the city and ended up having his briefcase stolen, including the portfolio, which conveniently ended up in the hands of a literature enthusiast (*amateur des lettres*), who delivered it directly to Dumesle. The journal "reproduces"—inexplicably in French—a letter written to a certain "Mylord S" that recounts the British spy's observations. If we consider the piece as a fabricated premise for Dumesle to celebrate the unity of the republic and dismiss the North, we see an early sketch of Dumesle's own travels and observations in his 1824 *Voyage dans le Nord d'Hayti*. The short fictional story includes descriptions of the topography, flora, and fauna of the two regions, as well as a brief political history of the post-independence civil war told favorably from the southern perspective (among other themes upon which Dumesle elaborates in *Voyage*: women, religion, youth, civilization, and humanity). Such similar themes abound in discourses about the republic and representations of the North in the immediate post-unification period, when writers like Dumesle and Milscent could control the narrative of the civil war uncontested. In this particular moment in 1819, however, Christophean writers could still respond and refute such depictions, as they did in the pages of the French paper *Le Constitutionnel*, and in their own paper, *La Gazette royale*.

Bad Books

Il n'est pas étonnant si mes écrits fourmillent de fautes de littérature; mon but en écrivant, n'est pas d'aspirer à la gloire d'être homme de lettres, mais bien d'être utile à mes compatriotes, de les éclairer et de dévoiler la vérité aux européens.

(It should come as no surprise if these writings of mine abound with literary infelicities. Aspiring to the glory that comes from being a man of letters is not the reason I write; my goal is to be of use to my compatriots, to enlighten them, and to unveil the truth to Europeans.)[41]
—Baron de Vastey, *Le système colonial dévoilé* (1814)

Southern writers engaged protocols that were part of an emergent literary critical hermeneutic based on the narrow, Habermasian bourgeois liberal paradigm. It is precisely for the failures of northern writing to embrace "liberty" of creative expression and autonomous authorship that southern republican writers criticized and ultimately dismissed northern writing as unliterary and bad. It is this value judgment that I am aiming at, somewhat playfully, with the section title "Bad Books." In the seventeenth and eighteenth centuries, the label of *mauvais livres* was assigned to anti-absolutist pamphlets that challenged the authority of the state and church.[42] And yet in this new post-Enlightenment and postrevolutionary paradigm, the value system of good/bad had changed. Writing was "good" when it reflected the new liberal values, and it was "bad" when it did not. Southern writers brought such judgment to bear on northern writing, as we saw above, but it is important to note that this valuation was not yet hegemonic. Northern writers had their own ideas about what made "good" writing (namely, a frank, accessible style and the ability to pierce through colonial rhetoric like a sword), which they deployed in response to southern literary criticism of their work.

We see the tension between northern and southern valuations of writing at work in Christophean refutations of the negative press the northern monarchy received in the emergent southern literary tradition of Pétion's new republic. In his 1819 *Essai sur les causes de la révolution et des guerres civiles d'Hayti*, Vastey responded to southern republicans' recasting of writing in a narrow, specifically *literary* sense. For example, Vastey assailed Milscent's emphasis on literariness—erudition, style, taste—as evidence of his perfidious attempt to veil the truth that Pétion intended to sell the Haitian people back to the French with an indemnity payment. Vastey links this to Milscent's use of language specifically, based on superiority and erudition rather than clarity or candor. He finds Milscent's use of irony particularly suspect, a rhetorical device based on sarcasm and incongruity that stands in stark opposition to sincerity and frankness. Milscent "flattens other writers with the weight of his knowledge and his erudition; with his impish, naughty pen he makes his ex-colonist friends smile with satisfaction, and spreads the most bitter irony about Haytian writing."[43] For Vastey, southern republican writing obscures and veils instead of revealing, clarifying, or enlightening.

Vastey connects his attacks on republicans' writing and style to larger concerns about their indigeneity (nativeness) and their commitment to Haiti's independence from colonial rule. Elaborating and embellishing his critique of Pétion during the *guerre de plume*, which was adapted from his earlier critiques of French colonial discourse, Vastey denounces southern republicans such as Milscent as Haitian in name only: they did not fight alongside their black compatriots in the War of Independence and spent most of the revolutionary and civil war period in exile. Indeed, for Vastey, Milscent challenged the very idea of Haitianness as it was defined by Dessalineans in 1804. He embodied a kind of Atlantic, universal republicanism that threatened to bring the island into the orbit of some other power, and some other identity. I insist on Vastey's characterization of Milscent's non-Haitianness, his non-nativeness, because it rehearses a core tension that will replay throughout the nineteenth and especially early twentieth centuries between "indigène" and French, between authentic and Francophile, between a nationalist, *repli sur soi* focus and an outward, cosmopolitan world republic of letters that was centered in France. Such tensions are at work in the early post-independence paper wars between North and South and, as we shall see in subsequent chapters, condition the rearticulation of these original tensions in subsequent Haitian writing.

It is against the artifice and subtlety of Milscent's style and his questionable "Haitianness" that Vastey proposes his own idea for a specifically Haitian, *native* style of writing, or what he calls a "tournure haytienne." He favors a conversational, straightforward prose that performs and reiterates his seigniorial motto of truth, sincerity, and candor. There is also an unmistakably oral quality to the text: he makes ample use of repetition, direct addresses to his audience, and explicit, descriptive transitions, such as "Let us stop here for a moment and contemplate," "I am picking back up here," and so on.[44] These strategies allow Vastey to summarize points and remind the audience where he is in the larger arc of the story, and suggest that he wrote his piece knowing that it would be read aloud at length. Such techniques are part of Vastey's particular mode of expression, which consists of repetition, spoken, oral style, and grammatical constructions that are accessible to a larger listening public:

> Je me suis conformé à la connaissance que j'ai du génie, du caractère, des lumières de ma nation, d'un peuple encore nouveau, qui n'a pas assez vécu dans la civilisation pour posséder la connaissance des lettres; je suis donc dans la nécessité, dans des écrits politiques faits pour éclairer le peuple, de me mettre à la portée de la masse de mes compatriotes, de me répéter, de me rendre clair et intelligible à leur entendement, et de donner, si je puis m'exprimer ainsi, à ma construction grammaticale, une *tournure haytienne*. (Emphasis added)

> (I have reconciled myself to the knowledge that I have talent, character, insight from my nation, of a still-young people, who have not yet lived enough in civilization to possess the knowledge of literature [*posséder la connaissance des lettres*]; thus I have no choice, in these political works designed to enlighten the people, to come down to the level of the majority of my countrymen: to repeat myself, make myself clear and intelligible for the purposes of their comprehension, and, if I may so put it, to give to my grammatical construction a *haytian form* [*une tournure haytienne*].[45]

Vastey's description of his "tournure haytienne" gestures to the oral-based reality of the communication and dissemination of information in the northern kingdom. He aims to create a style of writing that is more accessible—in writing and in speech—to a wider audience of Haitians, those who do not yet possess "la connaissance des lettres." Though Vastey does not define the term any further in his text, here we can imagine that he is referring to the specific northern iteration of Saint-Domingue Creole that relied on various dialects and regional languages of French, African languages, Amerindian languages, and elements of Spanish, Dutch, and English.[46] Here again, however, we must also recognize the multiple audiences for whom Vastey is writing this work. His focus is on orality and the clear and intelligible language in which he targets, as he states, the vast majority of his fellow countrymen, the newly independent, illiterate members of Christophe's kingdom. And yet, as we saw in the previous chapter, he is aiming his work primarily at and in opposition to southern lettered men in the republic and their writing. His populist message and his accessible, "native" form of expression (the "tournure haytienne") is designed to cast Milscent's French-focused erudite and eloquent literary style as inauthentic or non-Haitian.

Vastey evokes similar arguments in his refutation of Dumesle's attacks on the northern kingdom in *L'Observateur*, which he says he wrote to correct the various inaccuracies and omissions in Dumesle's presentation of the North, including his "hideous portrayal of the situation in Cap-Henry."[47] Vastey refutes the binary that Dumesle establishes: that the republic is the site of abundance and vibrancy, while the monarchy is the site of "sinister calm" and desolation. He argues that freedom and abundance exist in the North, the product of the order and good administration that reigns there: "Sirs, the writers of the Southwest, do they think that there are free men only in their Republic? . . . in well-organized monarchies, do we not enjoy real liberty, the guarantee of people and of property that are the goal of all well-administrated communities?"[48] Vastey sarcastically wonders what languishing commerce, empty port, and fearful countryside Dumesle could have witnessed "from his armchair in Les Cayes," and counters these observations with evidence of the "wealth," "abundance," and "flourishing state" of commerce and educational institutions in the northern kingdom.[49] The reality of life in the kingdom lies somewhere between Dumesle's republican critiques and Vastey's Christophean propaganda. There *were* vibrant schools, hospitals, educators, painters, and culture in the northern kingdom, certainly more than there were in the South, but this was made possible because of a forced labor regime that limited the rights and liberty of the majority of the northern masses. Vastey's emphasis on the wealth and plentitude of the northern kingdom was an attempt to actively counter the republican narrative that linked Christophe's North to desolation and destitution—a narrative that would become hegemonic in Dumesle's post–paper war writing, as we shall see below.

In the context of the paper war, and in response to Dumesle's specific critiques of northern writing and expression, Vastey takes issue with the restrictive definition of literary writing that Dumesle puts forth in *L'Observateur*. He accuses Dumesle of excluding northern writers (Vastey, Prézeau, Prévost, and others) from his proposed literary pantheon because they did not adhere to Dumesle's narrow, emergent sense of writing as *literary*: "because they don't write in the same way as M. Hérard Dumesle, and because these patriotic writers have endeavored to defend Haytians' common cause, which is, clearly, very far from his own."[50] For Vastey, Dumesle is concerned only with a limited, elite conception of literature, whereas Christophean writing aims to be accessible to a wider audience in order to address the "general cause" of all Haitians. According to Vastey's metrics, northern writing is valuable—*good*—because of its militant, militarized, *anticolonial* stance. He measures its value according to the very real, political gains it made in defending Haitian independence. He reminds his readers that northern writers were the only ones to pen refutation pieces of pro-colonial French texts, an act that rendered northern writers as important as the generals of independence: "they rival our great military heroes who fought off our oppressors: they destroyed the framework [*échafaudage*] of the colonial system and felled the Hydra of slavery."[51] Here, then, Vastey's refutation in the *Gazette* counters Dumesle's argument that civilized nations must recognize literary glory as *separate* from military glory. Indeed, for Dumesle and other southern writers, literature was possible only when writing turned away from political and military action and toward the domain of the imaginative and the aesthetic. For Christopheans they are not separate; they never were—something we saw clearly in Vastey's refutation pamphlet from chapter 2. The point of the pen and the point of the bayonet were the same.

Vastey defends the Dessalinean-Christophean conception of writing-as-weapon in his work. In response to the accusation that Christophean writers were merely mercenary pens for hire, subject to the "tyranny" of their king, he proclaims: "I followed the spontaneous urging of my heart, it is the Cry of my Conscience! I write to you as a free man, revealing [*dévoilant*] to you the depravity, the hypocrisy, and the treason of a traitor.... If it were any other way, if I were not able to freely express my feelings [*exprimer librement mes sentiments*] in my personal writing, I would put down my pen and stay silent."[52] The title of his response pamphlet, *Le cri de la conscience*, emphasizes Vastey's insistence that his own conscience, not Christophe or any other power, drove his response. He assures his critics that he can indeed *freely* express his feelings in his personal writing, refuting the notion that his southern detractors put forth: that freedom existed only in Pétion's republic.

* * *

Pétion's personal secretary, Noël Colombel, got the last word in the paper war between North and South, and thus set the terms of the valuation of writing and literature that had been contested by each side. In his refutation of Vastey's *Essai*, Colombel rejects the possibility that a monarch's secretary could be anything other than a "hotheaded lampoonist" (*fougueux libelliste*), performing his wretched duties as scribe of the king: "Let this mercenary pen for hire on the payroll of the most bloody and savage of despots, shout abuses at us, slander us, hurl the bile and the venom that is infecting his heart at us, heap lie upon lie to plant the seed of unfavorable ideas of us in the mind of our countrymen, he is only doing his job; using his favorite weapons; he is earning his loathsome salary."[53] Colombel casts his response to Vastey's massive *Essai* explicitly as a literary criticism of the work: "We will speak on Vastey and on his literary production" and will give "our opinion on the literary merits of his production with the same frankness that we spoke about his moral qualities."[54] Colombel's insistence on his literary critique of Vastey seems to challenge Vastey's continued insistence that his work was not to be evaluated as a purely literary endeavor (such as in the epigraph cited above).

Colombel argues that Vastey has some literary talent, but that it is tainted by the hatred, vengeance, and bitter character that pervade his texts. Further, Colombel concludes that such qualities negatively influence Vastey's *style*, which the southern writer laments is not "châtié": "He has neither elegance nor fluidity, but rather quite a bit of stiffness; his diction is incorrect, often diffuse, always verbose and monotonous."[55] Colombel is most critical of Vastey's use of repetition and recycling: "he drags on endlessly with commonplaces; keeps on repeating himself with childish self-satisfaction, and in a flood of words, failed ideas that he has spun out twenty different ways in twenty different pamphlets."[56] Colombel's criticisms of Vastey (the unpolished, repetitive style) compared to Vastey's criticism of Colombel and other southern writers (the overly erudite, opaque style) highlight the different conceptions of writing and print publics in each regime.

But Colombel's writing was no less enmeshed in the cultural politics of Pétion's southern republic, despite his insistence on his own authorial autonomy and freedom of expression. Colombel's writing performed the liberal republican idea of writing, legitimating its own claims to authorial autonomy and free will. We see this clearly in Colombel's response to Vastey's claim in his *Essai* that southern writers were equally complicit in the politics of Pétion's regime as northern writers were in Christophe's.[57] Colombel takes great care to distance himself and other southern writers from republican governmental power, arguing: "We are not writing to try to please power and for such and such an issue, but to pay tribute to the truth, prompted by our conscience alone."[58] Here, Colombel echoes Vastey's phrasing in *Le cri de la conscience* on freedom of expression, and sharpens it for the purposes of the southern republic. Colombel's response to Vastey affirms in no uncertain terms the contours of southern republican writing: putative separation between politics and literature; individual artistic authority; critical reason; and free will. He constructed this emergent concept of southern republican writing in opposition to the complicit, compromised, "mercenary" writing from the North, and performed it for those who were watching, and reading, in the Atlantic world. It is here, with Milscent, Dumesle, and Colombel's late–civil war corpus, that we can trace the emergence of a particular tradition of literary writing that is associated with the southern republic: one that values the singular, autonomous author whose work is a pure expression of the liberal mind, which they formulated in direct opposition to what they depicted as Christophean writing's treachery against liberalism. It is this southern republican tradition that becomes fixed as Haitian "national" literature under Boyer's "reunified" republican state, something we see first with Hérard Dumesle's *Voyage dans le Nord d'Hayti*, to which we will now turn.

Writing after the Fall of Christophe

On August 15, 1820, Henry Christophe fell ill while attending mass in Limonade. He suffered a stroke in front of the parish and was rushed to his residence at Bellevue-le-Roi. He survived, but suffered from paralysis and was mostly bedridden in the weeks that followed. Soon after, opposition leaders within his kingdom seized upon his weakening power. In the southern port town of Saint-Marc, soldiers rose up in revolt against the monarchy, rallying to Boyer's republic. In the Cap, meanwhile, some of Christophe's generals (most notably Richard, Duc de Marmelade, and the chevalier de St Henry, Nord Alexis) began plotting to form their own provisional government. By early October, the tide had turned definitively against Christophe. His troops refused to march south to quell the Saint-Marc rebels, and his own guards joined the revolt against him. Recognizing that his reign had ended, Christophe committed suicide on the night of October 9, 1820, in the Sans Souci palace.[59] Northern separatists initially proclaimed a rebel state in the North. Boyer, however, was eventually able to force most of the insurgent generals and the magistrates to submit to the republic, signing an act on October 21, 1820, that declared, "Today, there is in Haiti only one government and only one Constitution."[60] With that, Boyer officially integrated the former kingdom into the republic. He and his army entered the city on October 26, 1820, promptly renaming it Cap-Haïtien.

Hénock Trouillot remarked that after Dessalines's death, a writer with ideas like Boisrond Tonnerre's "could only live in the North."[61] After the death of Christophe, a writer like Vastey couldn't live at all, or if he wanted to, he had to change his tone dramatically. This is precisely what Christophean writers did in the weeks and months that followed Christophe's suicide. In order to consolidate power, the northern separatists killed Christophe's heirs as well as his most loyal aides and generals, bayonetting them in the yard of the prison on October 18 and 19, 1820.[62] Vastey was killed alongside other prominent members of Christophe's nobility. Those Christophean writers who did survive emerged under Boyer's unified republic as entirely new versions of their former selves. The former Comte de Rosiers now presented himself under the republican title General Juste Chanlatte when he welcomed Boyer and his republican troops into Cap-Haïtien with a special address, and penned a pamphlet that condemned Christophe as "the scourge of Hayti, a disgrace to human kind," corrupted by "nocturnal orgies" and "obscene depravities."[63] Other prominent northern writers also avoided Vastey's fate by putting their pens in the service of the republic. Julien Prévost, formerly Comte and then Duc de Limonade, served as director of *La Concorde*, the first republican state-funded newspaper to be published in post-Christophe Cap-Haïtien. As the title suggests, the paper cultivated the "internal harmony or Concordia" that Boyer sought in his newly unified republic.[64] The northern *Concorde* lasted two years, until Boyer, fearing opposition in the North, stopped funding for the paper in 1822. The newspaper would be the last periodical printed in the North for nearly four decades.[65] It is in the context of a silenced North—and the rescripting and republicanization of the reunified Haitian state— that Hérard Dumesle penned his early domestic travel piece entitled *Voyage dans le Nord d'Hayti, ou Révélations des lieux et des monuments historiques*.

* * *

On December 2, 1820,[66] less than two months after the tumultuous events surrounding Christophe's suicide, Hérard Dumesle boarded a boat in the port of Les Cayes and began his trip to the North of Haiti.[67] He landed in Le Môle, the former kingdom's northwesternmost point, and moved eastward to Port-de-Paix, Cap-Haïtien, and Milot, then turned south to make his return trip by land: from Gonaïves, through the Artibonite, to Port-au-Prince (where he paused to pay respects at the tomb of the great republican leader Pétion), and then back to Les Cayes. Dumesle's northern itinerary is of symbolic significance: he begins and ends in Les Cayes, the birthplace of republican ideas in revolutionary Haiti, and made his first stop in Le Môle, the last bastion of republican opposition in the North during the early years of the civil war between Pétion and Christophe.[68] Over the course of his trajectory, he recorded numerous observations that revealed themselves to him from the monuments and spaces of the former kingdom, many of which take the form of poetry.

I read Dumesle's text as a highly political effort to reestablish republican dominance over the North.[69] He sought little less than the complete remapping of the Haitian North and its great sites of revolutionary history to reintegrate and "nationalize" them into a southern liberal republican narrative of Haiti's past. He revisits key national historic sites, rediscovering for his readers the geography and inhabitants of a region that had been closed off to the republic for nearly a decade. Dumesle's text symbolizes republican unification and, in so doing, strategically silences the Christophean tradition of northern print culture and the meaning of *liberté* it espoused. Dumesle's *Voyage* is thus one of Haiti's first foundational fictions: a text of national consolidation that attempted to narrate—and perform—a unified republic.[70]

The text itself takes the form of an epistolary travel narrative: a series of impressions and reflections on the former kingdom, "this region [*contrée*] that still echoes with Christophe's name," that Dumesle addresses to his wife, "ma Rose-Estelle," whom he identifies as his muse.[71] Dumesle's use of the *récit de voyage* genre is key to understanding his remapping of Haitian history from a position of liberal republican hegemony. It allows Dumesle to present a personal account of events, of "truth" that was unmediated by power. The truth about the northern monarchy and the facts surrounding the history of the revolution and civil war revealed themselves directly to the writer via the ruins of the great monuments of the North. There are additional generic intertexts at work in Dumesle's text that we must note here. As Carl Hermann Middelanis has pointed out, Dumesle drew from Constantin-François Volney's 1791 account of his voyage to Egypt and the "Near East" entitled *Les ruines, ou Méditations sur les révolutions des Empires*.[72] Dumesle's use of the orientalist travel narrative genre is significant, as it lends an exoticist, exploratory tone to his "discovery" of the secessionist northern state. I would argue that the more significant element of Volney's work, however, is the poetics of ruins. In the romantic tradition of the late eighteenth and early nineteenth centuries, ruin poetry emphasized the poet's imagination, his emotional, personal response to the experience of looking upon and contemplating ruins. Dumesle is thus engaging with the tradition of "ruins" work from Joachim Du Bellay, Denis Diderot, Jacques Delille, and François-René de Chateaubriand, among many others.[73] However, as I will argue in the conclusion to this section, Dumesle did not engage this tradition of ruin poetry via Volney or any other European romantic ruin poets. Rather, I suggest that Dumesle arrived at the poetics of ruins via his northern nemesis, Vastey—an intertext that Dumesle purposefully obscures. Dumesle's text is thus at the origin of the invention of Haiti's republican literary heritage—a heritage based in the co-optation and silencing of the Christophean writing that preceded it.

Dumesle's subtitle, *Révélations des lieux et des monuments historiques*, and the epigraph (pulled from his own text) place him squarely within this romantic context of ruin poetry and the intimate, personal emotion it communicates. Indeed, ruins dominate Dumesle's *Voyage* (and echo his earlier writing in *L'Observateur*). The North that Dumesle "discovers" is dusty, desolate, and in ruins. An emptiness and eerie silence pervade his description of the countryside: the peasantry are entirely absent from the landscape, hidden away in their homes. He describes his first impression upon disembarking in Le Môle: what had been a grand, beautiful port city fourteen years ago "now offers to the dismayed traveler nothing but ruins, rubble [*des ruines, des décombres*], . . . everything has disappeared."[74] The grand symbols of Christophe's monarchy, the Sans Souci palace and the Citadelle, are both in ruins. Furnishings and artifacts, once finely ornamented, are now tarnished and covered in soot; the once orderly palace grounds are strewn with debris in the wake of looting and bloodshed.[75] His poems surge forth at various points throughout the text, inspired by the "révélations" brought about by his observation and "interrogation" of the ruins of the North. Take, for example, his account of the visit to the Sans Souci palace, undoubtedly the most poignant symbol of the ruined monarchy. Dumesle is overcome with grief while visiting the site and reflecting on the horrors of Christophe's despotism. To escape the "oppressive ideas of despotism" (*accablantes idées du despotisme*) evoked by the destruction and disarray of the palace ruins, he goes into a garden to seek refuge among the rows of trees and plants that had fared somewhat better. Inspired by the harmony of nature, he inserts into his prose reflections a four-syllable verse poem that summarizes his observations, ending with these lines: "This harmony / That tyranny / Never had / In spite of its evidence" (*Cette harmonie / Que n'eut jamais / La tyrannie / Malgré ses faits*).[76] In spite of the pages and pages of "faits" produced by Christophean writers in defense of the monarchy, Dumesle bears witness to its inevitable demise. A monarchy based in order and discipline failed to create lasting harmony or unity.

The hybrid nature of Dumesle's text—epistolary, travel narrative, romantic ruin poetry, oral history, documentary revolutionary history—is worth considering in more detail as it relates to Christophean writing and the heritage of the civil war *guerre de plume*.[77] Recall from the previous chapter that in Christophe's kingdom, creative, poetic writing was composed primarily for oral, commemorative, *collective* purposes: sung poems or operas were performed aloud in the kingdom and then later printed and circulated in newspapers and pamphlets. The quintessential example of this kind of Christophean approach to creative, poetic production can be found in Julien Prévost's 1811 *Relation des glorieux événements*, which chronicled Christophe's royal coronation.[78] Prévost's text is a multi-genre assemblage of texts: it includes a historical précis on the Haitian Revolution and civil war written by the author as well as reproductions of official historical documents, edicts, and proclamations related to the creation of the monarchy. Interspersed throughout Prévost's "relation" of the coronation are reproductions of the various speeches, poems, and performances that fêted the occasion.

Dumesle's poetic production stands in stark contrast to the ceremonial pomp of commemorative verse produced in the northern monarchy. In his work, poetry epitomizes the liberal values of self-expression and personal inspiration, in opposition to the militant pamphlet-writing from the North during the *guerre de plume*. More specifically, the way he integrates poetry into the personal, epistolary narrative of his travel account serves to illustrate the praxis of individual, autonomous writing made possible by a liberal republican government. Indeed, I would argue that Dumesle's interspersing of personal, sentimental ruin poetry, peasant testimonials, and Haitian history throughout his first-person, epistolary travel narrative imitates the multi-genre or hybrid assemblage of previous northern texts (from Vastey, Prévost, and others) but recasts them within the realm of the individual, autonomous writer and his personal poetic intimacies. Where order, hierarchy, and royal decorum conditioned the production of ceremonial poetry that honored the king and legitimized his power, in Dumesle's *Voyage* it was the contemplation of nature, personal experience, and emotion that conditioned the production of poetry in the liberal, republican state. The romantic idea of individual inspiration from nature that Dumesle showcases in his poetic production—poetry surging forth from nature and captured on the spot by the autonomous author—is a definitive refusal of the Dessalinean sphere and its political, weaponized combat literature.

Dumesle's text develops many of the arguments he and other southern republican writers deployed during the civil war. We see this in Dumesle's treatment of the tropes of veiling/unveiling, dark/light, and oppression/liberty that had been so contested during the civil war and *guerre de plume*. He rehearses the metaphors and polemical language claimed by each side of the *guerre de plume* and fixes them in the service of liberalism and the republican government (and against the memory of Christophe's regime). In his text, he bears the torch of truth and enlightenment: light with "the benefits of civilization" is on the side of the liberal republic, while Christophe's monarchy is the shadowy zone of "illiberal" oppressive rule, a "monstrous assemblage of despotism."[79] Dumesle's pen unveils and sheds light on the shadowy, treacherous dealings of the monarch and his secretaries in the text, describing "Christophe's shadowy government" as "this dreadful power that covered the North under a gloomy veil," while it is Christophe who is revealed as the Machiavellian monster, "always walking in the shadows" and hiding truths and facts from his subjects "under the veil of secrecy."[80] Fittingly, the sun, which adorns the frontispiece of Dumesle's journal *L'Observateur* with the Latin motto "Sol clarior astro" (The sun is brighter than the star), returns to play a key role in *Voyage* in Dumesle's depiction of the North. Dumesle happens upon a sculpture of the sun that decorated a pediment on Christophe's palace. It is darkened by the soot of too many ceremonial lanterns (an obvious gibe at the ritual pomp of the monarchy) and lends a gloomy tinge (*teinte lugubre*) to the scene—a metaphor for tyranny and the failure of the northern monarchy.[81]

In Dumesle's *Voyage*, liberal ideas of rights and freedoms could penetrate the shadows of Christophe's government and inspire oppressed subjects to think for themselves. Dumesle affirms that this process had already begun to bear fruit: "Everywhere liberal ideas have been able to enter [*pénétré*], the Republic has found supporters."[82] The fall of the monarchy proved to Dumesle that liberal values would ultimately prevail over the shadowy, treacherous reign of despotism. Having witnessed the consequences of despotism on the North and the achievements of liberalism in the South, Dumesle concludes: "I am more and more convinced [*Je me pénétrai de plus en plus*] . . . of this immortal truth: Liberty is the beacon of science, it is the soul of agriculture, commerce, and the arts; while despotism addles [*abrutit*] man, its oppressive grip strangles thought."[83] The capacity of liberalism to penetrate abounds in Dumesle's text. Dumesle himself plays the role of liberal beacon, of penetrating light in the *Voyage*: his writing penetrates the darkness surrounding Christophe's reign, revealing the monarchy as an aberration that is no match for the lasting, progressive achievements of liberalism. To challenge this fact, Dumesle argues, would be to go against the physics of space and time: "To question it would be to want to travel back in time, and even the partisans of despotism are obliged to admit that liberal principles never go backward."[84]

Dumesle's take on northern writing in *Voyage* is particularly important for our purposes here, as he returns to his idea for a literary pantheon of Haitian writers that he had proposed in *L'Observateur*. In many ways, he treats northern writing in the same way he treated the great sites and northern monuments: he summarizes and confronts the major writers from Christophe's kingdom one by one and engages in a literary critique of their work. By engaging with northern writing as he would a revolutionary site or a monument, he is acknowledging the heritage of Christophean writing as a necessary part of his symbolic remapping: it is essential for him to explain, categorize, and ultimately claim dominance over the northern writing from the kingdom in order to neutralize its political power and subversive potential. This is what he had done with the monuments and ruins he visited in the North: reclaiming them for the republic and rescripting them into a national heritage by emptying them or cleansing them of their monarchical associations. Such a task was easier with symbolic monuments and historic sites, which do not speak, and whose symbolism lends to easy rescripting. The task proved slightly more difficult with northern writing, not only because many northern writers left a prolific oeuvre to contend with, but also because it forced Dumesle to confront the fundamentally political nature of the work he himself was doing. He explains, "I thus decided to attend to the different works that appeared in the North, both because I am inclined to [*par goût*] and because I desire to know all of the literary production of my compatriots."[85] It is interesting to observe how Dumesle walks the tightrope of liberal, free-thinking author and ardent supporter of the republic, a stance that was politically compromised from the start. In order to avoid the charges of scribal complicity with Boyer's government—the very grounds upon which he criticizes Christophean writing—Dumesle must present himself as an independent actor who has chosen, of his own volition, to engage in a critique of northern writing.

Dumesle's assessment of northern writers is particularly useful for its broader statements about the value of literature and its purpose within a republic: we get to see how he evaluates literature, whose writing he praises and on what grounds, and whose he dismisses as *not* literature or literary. Dumesle's text thus performs and concretizes the specific arguments about literature and literariness that had emerged as part of the southern republic's new literary program during the *guerre de plume*.[86] Dumesle's primary metric for measuring northern writing for fitness within the national literary pantheon was the independence and autonomy of the author; he believed resolutely that genius could not express itself under conditions of surveillance, limits, and proscriptions. Predictably, he dismissed most of it as unliterary, mercenary, and thus unworthy of inclusion in Haiti's "national" republican literary pantheon. For Dumesle, the biggest problem with northern writing was that it was written under the yoke [*férule*] of the northern monarch, rather than being the product of a free mind and an expression of "la liberté." He criticizes Prévost's Christophean writing as afflicted by this fundamental illiberalism. Though Dumesle sees some literary merits, it is essentially "commandé" and thus not guided by his personal expression: "his heart did not guide his pen."[87] He is similarly critical of Prézeau and Dupuy, who served alongside Prévost, Vastey, and others during the *guerre de plume*.

Dumesle had greater difficulty disarming and assimilating Juste Chanlatte into "national" Haitian writing because of the massive role Chanlatte had played in Dessalines's and Christophe's governments, his substantial list of anti-republican publications (including scores of *Gazette* articles and pamphlets aimed directly at delegitimizing Pétion's republican government), and his supreme talent. Recall that in 1820, Chanlatte had once again managed to get out in front of the changing political tide, avoiding the fate of the bayonet by aligning himself with Boyer's new government. Dumesle's account of Chanlatte's earlier non-republican writing needed to convincingly explain it away without entirely discrediting its producer, who was now writing in support of the republic. In general, Dumesle is quite complimentary of Chanlatte and his work, but concludes that the problem with the latter's writing under Christophe was that it had been constrained by the monarch's despotism: "writing under the yoke of a tyrant to whom the arts and the sciences paid tribute, his work shows the effects of this influence that, by setting limits to thought, deprives talent [*génie*] of the independence necessary for it to bloom."[88] Rather humorously, Dumesle describes a number of Chanlatte's works in the service of Christophe's regime as having "escaped, as it were, from his pen."[89] Such a depiction has the dual effect of removing all agency from the creation of the work, absolving Chanlatte of his role in their creation, and also reinforcing the notion that individual creation and even thought itself were impossible under the king's despotic rule. Dumesle concludes that these works by Chanlatte and their subject matter are best forgotten altogether.

On the other hand, Chanlatte's theatrical works are much easier for Dumesle to assimilate into the national literary pantheon because of their literary qualities, which are precisely what Dumesle emphasizes in his assessment of them. Chanlatte's *Néhri*, for example, deserved "high standing in our literature" because Chanlatte respected the three classical unities of drama, and because of his harmonious, energetic (*mâle*) versification.[90] Crucially, Dumesle does not engage the collective, performative, and courtly nature of Chanlatte's *opéras comiques*—all of the elements that would place him in a Christophean tradition of writing. Dumesle ends his assessment of Chanlatte's writing with a liberal, forward-looking gesture: Chanlatte's forthcoming work. The former Christophean publicist was putting his Christophean past behind him, hard at work preparing a didactic poem entitled "La Haïciade," a particularly republican formulation that Dumesle assures his reader will be the embodiment of liberal poetic creation: "inspired by the spirit of liberty [*génie de la liberté*]," which is to say a perfect emanation of the poet's free will and inspiration, "his muse will celebrate ... the dawn of the arts in Haitian climes"—after the fall of Christophe, of course.[91]

Naturally, Dumesle reserves the strongest criticism for Vastey, the writer who for him represents the most odious mercenary writing. Dumesle is particularly critical of the negative idea of Haiti that he believes Vastey's work projects to an international public sphere: "how many of the works written by a despot's favorite pen are unworthy to appear among the creations by which the intellect [*l'esprit*] of a fledgling people and their advances in knowledge will be judged."[92] He is equally negative in his reading of the stylistic characteristics of Vastey's work, "flat and lifeless" (*plat et sans nerf*), which is understood to be a symptom of his sycophancy (*basse adulation*) and lack of freedom to think or follow his own personal inspiration.[93]

Buried in a footnote, however, Dumesle does acknowledge one moment in which he observes Vastey transcend his scribal complicity as a "despot monger" (*fauteur du despotisme*) and produce writing worthy of being called literary. In this footnote, Dumesle quotes a long passage from the first section of *Le système colonial dévoilé* and concludes, "And it is next to such disgusting sycophantic platitudes that we find beauties like this!!!"[94] It is worth reproducing in full the passage from Vastey that Dumesle found worthy, not least of all because I believe that Dumesle closely models his own text on it, and because it contradicts the very premise upon which Dumesle bases his exclusion of Vastey's writing from the Haitian literary pantheon. The long passage is indeed one of the more striking from Vastey's oeuvre. In it, he laments the Spanish massacre of the Amerindians, "the first Haitians," and the origins of the slave trade, linking his own writing to the poetics and rhetoric of Haitian anticolonialism through Dessalines's radical act of "avenging America":

> O terre de mon pays! en est-il une sur le globe qui ait été plus imbibée de sang humain? En est-il une où les malheureux habitans aient éprouvés plus d'infortunes? Partout où je porte mes pas, où je fixe mes regards, je vois des débris, des vases, des ustensiles, des figures qui portent dans leurs formes l'empreinte et les traces de l'enfance de l'art; plus loin dans les lieux écartés et solitaires, dans les cavernes des montagnes inaccessibles, je découvre en frémissant, des squelettes encore tout entier, des ossemens humains épars et blanchis par le temps; en arrêtant mes pensées sur ces tristes restes, sur ces débris qui attestent l'existence d'un peuple qui n'est plus, mon cœur s'émeut, je répands des larmes de compassion et d'attendrissement sur le malheureux sort des premiers habitans de cette île! Mille souvenirs déchirans viennent assiéger mon cœur; une foule de réflexions absorbent mes pensées et se succèdent rapidement; il existait donc ici avant nous des hommes! ils ne sont plus; voilà leurs déplorables restes! ils ont été détruits! Qu'avaient-ils fait pour éprouver un aussi funeste sort? Il a donc passé une race d'hommes exterminateurs? Ces malheureux n'avaient donc point d'armes? Ils ne pouvaient donc point

se défendre? A cette pensée, je saisis mes armes, et je rends grâces au ciel d'avoir mis dans nos mains l'instrument de notre délivrance et de notre conservation. O armes précieuses! sans vous que serait devenu mon pays, mes compatriotes, mes parens, mes amis; dès ce moment, je considérai mes armes comme le plus grand de tous les biens.[95]

(O land of mine, is there any other on this planet whose soil has been more soaked in human blood? Is there a land whose ill-fated inhabitants have experienced greater misfortunes? Everywhere I step, everywhere I look, I see shards, vases, utensils, figurines, the forms of which bear the imprint and the traces of art's infancy. In more remote and solitary locations, in the caves of inaccessible mountains, I come across skeletons still intact, human bones scattered about and blanched over time, and I tremble. As my thoughts pause over these sad remains, these shards bearing witness to the life of a people who no longer exist, my heart is moved, I shed tears of pity and compassion for the wretched fate of those first inhabitants of the island! A thousand rending memories lay siege to my heart; a multitude of reflections crowd upon me, one after another in quick succession. So, there were men here before us! They no longer exist, here are their pitiable remains! They were destroyed! What had they done to suffer such a calamitous fate? Did some race of exterminating men happen upon them? Had they no weapons, those unhappy souls? Could they not defend themselves? At this thought, I seize hold of my own weapons and thank the heavens for having placed in our hands the instrument of our deliverance and our preservation. O precious force of arms! Without you what would have become of my country, my compatriots, my kinsfolk, my friends? From that moment on, I looked upon those weapons of mine as the greatest of all possessions.)[96]

No wonder Dumesle had to bury the passage in a footnote; it entirely contradicts his dismissal of Vastey's style. What is more, it reveals the extent to which Dumesle simultaneously *relied upon* and *silenced* the poetic practice of individual, artistic inspiration from ruins that Vastey inaugurated in this passage from *Le système colonial*. We can see how Dumesle enacted this dual appropriation/silencing if we further probe this curious footnote. First, we note that Dumesle does not cite from Vastey's original 1814 text, nor does he even correctly name it (he lists the incorrect—and indeed nonexistent—title "Réfutation de Leborgne de Boigne"). Rather—or, so he says—he came across the Vastey passage in an article written in *La Revue encyclopédique.* Dumesle seems purposefully murky on the details of these texts in his footnote: he incorrectly identifies the title of Vastey's original work, he doesn't identify the title of the *Revue encyclopédique* article or its author, and he fails to indicate the date or number of the issue in question. To clarify things here: Dumesle's footnote is referring, albeit obliquely, to Antoine Métral's 1819 article in *La Revue encyclopédique* entitled "De la littérature haïtienne," in which the French author correctly cites the page numbers of Vastey's *Le système colonial dévoilé* and only somewhat mistakes the title as "Système de colonization." Métral heaps praise upon the Christophean writer for his eloquence in the above passage, comparing him to Rousseau and none other than Volney: "Here is a magical, moving eloquence, like what we find in Volney."[97] It bears noting that Métral praises Vastey's writing *as literary* and for its *literary* qualities specifically—an assessment that clashes with Dumesle's invention of Haiti's republican literary tradition. In a sense, it is as if Dumesle simply removes Vastey from the equation and fashions his own writing, and southern republican literary writing more broadly, in the style that Métral so vigorously praises.

Recovered from Dumesle's purposeful obfuscation and placed within its original context, we see that Métral praised Vastey's text for exactly what it was: an exemplary romantic ruin text. Vastey walks among the debris, the ruins of Haiti's first Amerindian inhabitants. Upon reflecting on these ruins, he describes his emotional response, making ample use of the romantic, plaintive "O" to lament the massacre of these unfortunate, first inhabitants of Haiti. It is not just raw emotion that Vastey feels. His experience among the ruins inspires him to write—just as Dumesle is inspired to write down the poems that come to him as he walked among the ruins of the North. The fundamental difference was that Vastey considered his pen to be among those weapons he clutched dear to his heart. Writing—*publishing*—was among the weapons Vastey considered central to Haiti's arsenal of independence, an instrument of Haitian deliverance and preservation. For Dumesle (and Milscent and Colombel before him), the key to liberal republican textual production was keeping the pen and the sword separate. By relying on the narrow terms of the emergent concepts of literature and literariness, Dumesle is authorized to simultaneously adopt Vastey's romantic ruin text and disavow its author as complicit with power. In so doing, he strategically silences the Christophean tradition of northern print culture in his origin story of Haiti's national literature. These are the fraught foundations upon which Haiti's "national" literature is based.

From his literary analysis of northern writers, Dumesle concludes that the government form has an impact on "the nature and the progress of the mind."[98] He determines that "republican eloquence" (*l'éloquence républicaine*) developed quickly and primarily in the South because of "the impetus provided to it by the freedom of thought [*libre faculté de penser*]."[99] As we shall see in the next chapter, these kinds of conclusions about the impact of government on the mind of its citizens will take on nationalist and *imperialist* significance under Boyer. His desire for unification and *concorde*—and to protect against foreign invasion—would call upon such justifications for his occupation of the eastern side of the island in 1824, to create the unified Republic of Island Haiti.

* * *

Hénock Trouillot has argued that if scholars would do the work to contextualize Dumesle's *Voyage*, they would be unable to deny that the work "is essentially a combat book."[100] Indeed, by considering Dumesle's project in the longer heritage of the paper war between North and South, and the uses and meaning of literature, this chapter has revealed some of the key political and literary ideologies at work in his text. What Dumesle puts forth as national "Haitian" history is not a geographically integrated approach to the newly unified Haitian Republic, but rather an example of southern republicanism from its position of hegemony. In this context, Dumesle's text seeks to establish Pétion as the historical Père de la Patrie and *the* father of Haitian independence, disavowing Christophe's past claims to glory in the Haitian Revolution and his role as "paternal" protector of the nation and its people as king of the North after Dessalines.

Beyond political and historical rewritings, however, Dumesle's work also engages in a textual recasting of national literature, effacing and disavowing the sixteen-year heritage of Dessalinean and Christophean writing by claiming southern liberal republican writing as *the* origin and foundation of Haitian literature. In other words, Dumesle asserts one notion of "national" Haitian writing while simultaneously delegitimizing its former rival tradition from the northern kingdom. We can see the work Dumesle has done to set the terms of the debate and subsume any other kinds of writing under the banner of "national" writing. When he is done, Christophean writers and their critiques of Pétion's regime and his publicists are delegitimized. The rhetorical figures of light and dark, torches of enlightenment and shadowy perfidiousness, frank sincerity and treacherous doublespeak that had been claimed by each rival state and its publicists during the civil war become fixed in Dumesle's symbolic text that remaps a unified nation under the banner of liberal republicanism. What is more, the tradition of literary writing and criticism gained hegemony under the label of an emergent Haitian "national" literature under Boyer's "reunified" republican state after Christophe's fall in 1820. In this sense, we can read post-unification texts such as Hérard Dumesle's *Voyage dans le Nord d'Hayti* as one final, definitive "réplique" in the *guerre de plume* between the North and South that fixes the terms of the debate about writing and its uses in Haiti.

4

The Myth of the Universal Haitian Republic, or *Deux Nations dans la Nation*

After the Treaty of Ryswick (1697) officially divided the island colony between Saint-Domingue (French) and Santo Domingo (Spanish), the border between East and West became a defining feature of the political tensions on the island. The border, and more specifically its porosity and its contingency, played a particularly important role during the revolution and the early years of post-independence in the nineteenth century. Toussaint briefly unified the island under his rule in Saint-Domingue, abolishing slavery in 1801. The victory was short-lived: Leclerc's expedition retook the eastern side of the island, from which Napoléon's forces launched their attacks to retake the colony. Dessalines invaded the East once more in 1805 in an unsuccessful attempt to root out the French *colons* who fled when he began his program of expulsions and mass executions after independence.[1] The French remained in the East until landowners and their army of plantation slaves finally pushed them out in 1808, restoring Spanish colonial rule. From 1809 to 1821, a period known as España Boba (Stupid Spain), the Spanish flag hung over the port cities and interior towns of the eastern part of the island.[2] Throughout the Boba period, various factions emerged in the East, each proposing a different possible future for achieving independence from Spanish colonial rule.[3] The most prominent factions divided fairly cleanly along geographic lines: those in favor of unification with Haiti resided in the north-central border towns. Those in favor of an alliance with Bolívar's Spanish American revolution in Gran Colombia were centered in the southern coastal capital city of Santo Domingo.[4]

On November 15, 1821, the north-central border towns of Dajabón (Laxavon in Haitian texts) and Monte Cristi (Monte-Christ) hoisted the Haitian flag to declare independence from Spain and establish unity with Jean-Pierre Boyer's republic. In response, a rival faction of "creole elite,"[5] led by José Núñez de Cáceres in Santo Domingo, declared the creation of an independent state, el Estado independiente de la parte española de Haití on December 1, 1821, that would seek integration with Bolívar's Gran Colombia. Núñez de Cáceres sent members of his *junta* to proclaim the independent state to residents of the Northeast, who promptly refused. According to Madiou, the Northeast rallied to the pro-Haitian group in the north-central borderlands area. By December 30, 1821, all of the major towns in the northern band (Cotuy, la Vega, Puerto Plata, Macoris, and—most important—Santiago) had hoisted the Haitian flag, proclaiming their alliance with the republic. Nevertheless, the pro-Bolívar/Gran Colombia alliance faction in the Southeast refused to yield, and Boyer concluded that it was necessary to march on Santo Domingo to quell the opposition and officially unite the island under his rule. According to Madiou, Boyer went to the Senate to consult them on how to approach the opposition in the East, and was counseled that the constitution mandated that there be only one, unified republic on the island: "a State separate from the Republic cannot exist in our territory."[6] His choices were to rally the opposition to the Haitian Republic or to take them by force. The pro-Bolívar faction in Santo Domingo surrendered when Boyer's troops arrived on February 9, 1822, thus marking the start of twenty-two years of Haitian rule in the territory.

Boyer's invasion was motivated at least in part by concerns about security: instability or regime change in the East could have marked the end of Haiti's independence. Indeed, in 1820 rumors began circulating in Haitian journals that there might be yet another attempted French invasion of the former colony, via the eastern side of the island.[7] Yet the rhetoric of Boyer's invasion was also to spread Haiti's universal republicanism: he would extend the Haitian system of (putatively) democratic government to those residents of the East who had toiled under the yoke of Spanish despotism, abolishing slavery for good. But was this republican abolitionism also a form of imperialism? Are the two mutually exclusive? Certainly not. In fact, Boyer's universalist republican empire predates the same reasoning that undergirded France's Third Republican imperial expansion.[8] David Geggus has suggested that Boyer's decision to invade the East was both imperial and abolitionist: "Like the imperial powers in the scramble for Africa, the Haitian state in 1821 used its abolitionist credentials to justify annexing the Dominican Republic."⁹ Anne Eller refers to Boyer's system of governance as "autocratic, but defiant, republicanism."¹⁰ Boyer's desire to create a unified republic on the entire island of Haiti—largely to protect against foreign invasion, but also to further establish Haiti's liberal republican credentials in the international sphere—relied upon the virtues of republicanism to justify his occupation of the eastern side of the island in 1822.

I emphasize the historical details here surrounding the unification¹¹ of l'Ile d'Haïti (the official term for the unified territory during the Boyer presidency) not only because they are so little known in early post-independence studies of Haiti, but because they tell us a lot about Boyer's presidency and the meaning of his republican state. Specifically, they tell us about the way that unity, or *la concorde*—a crucial republican concept linked to *fraternité*—functioned in Boyer's unified republican island state (over which he served as president for life from 1822 to 1843) and the realities of disunity and division within it, which is the subject of this chapter.¹² I begin by unearthing the tension between territorial *concorde* and internal strife to reveal the limits and possibilities of Boyer's unified island state, which I argue are based in the myth of the universal Haitian Republic. Central to Boyer's attempts to create territorial *concorde* is Beaubrun Ardouin's little-studied *Géographie de l'Ile d'Haïti* (1832), analyzed in the next section. While Ardouin's *Géographie* performatively narrated the unified republic by symbolically and spatially integrating the eastern side through the social scientific genre of the geography, it nevertheless did little to address the internal tensions that fueled opposition to Boyer's regime.¹³ Instead, it stoked the smoldering coals of civil war by vilifying Dessalines and Christophe and excluding them from the pantheon of national heroes. The final section contrasts Ardouin's social scientific, imperial island strategy with the attempt to represent and create internal *concorde* among the island's diverse populations in the liberal newspapers *Le Républicain* and *L'Union*. These newspapers focused on addressing and even ameliorating internal divisions within Haiti by attempting to narrate a more capacious and inclusive Haitian Republic through an early example of the cultural nationalist movement known as *indigénisme*. The editorials, essays, historical studies, poems, and short stories published in these newspapers highlighted the shared culture and patrimony of the island's inhabitants:

from East to West, from rural dweller to urban elite. In particular, they rehabilitated the memory of the revolutionary hero Dessalines by paying homage to the rich repository of oral and Africanist traditions among Haiti's peasant and former slave populations, in an attempt to create a more profound sense of internal unity among all of Haiti's inhabitants—something Boyer's republicanism had failed to do.

Boyer's *Concorde*, or The Myth of the Universal Haitian Republic

Boyer's presidency, which he assumed in 1818 after Pétion's death, was focused on portraying an image of civilization, progress, and perfectibility to the Atlantic world that often contradicted the internal divisions and imperial practices at home.[14] What resulted in Boyer's presidency was a paradoxical republicanism: his focus on the ideal of regeneration, the spread of universal rights through emancipation, and the pursuit of economic liberalism is contradicted by his suppression of the press, his rule as president for life, and his general undemocratic *élitisme* that created a two-tiered citizenship regime that excluded the mass of the population from accessing any of these liberal ideals.[15] This was the instantiation of Pétion's new republicanism designed to strengthen the power of the executive and create stability—and unity—at home, while promoting the image of universal republicanism to the Atlantic world. Boyer sought to counter the libelous image of post-independence Haiti in US newspapers and recruited enslaved black Americans to work in Haiti as free men.[16] In many ways, Boyer realized what Pétion's 1816 republican renewal sought to create: he unified the western side of the island under a single, republican rule for the first time in Haitian history.[17]

Boyer's performance of—perhaps even obsession with—the idea of unity points to an important reality: Haiti in the 1820s was far from unified, nor was the republic universal, or necessarily liberal. There was near-constant opposition from the North, which stoked Boyer's legitimate fears that the region would rise up and found a secessionist state or monarchy. Indeed, mere weeks after Boyer reunified the nation under a single republican state in November 1820, there was a new uprising among former Christophean generals that sought to create an independent state of the North and Artibonite.[18] Though it failed, it would be followed by countless attempts and even successful foundations of independent, separatist regimes in the North and South of Haiti throughout the nineteenth century. Moreover, Faustin Soulouque abolished the republic entirely, ruling as Emperor Faustin I from 1849 to 1859 (see chapter 5). Dessalines, Christophe, and Soulouque (not to mention other failed attempts to reestablish monarchies and empires) point to the existence of a tradition of governing and an idea of statehood that remained different from—often oppositional to—the idea of the Haitian Republic that Boyer had succeeded in making hegemonic in 1820. There was also great opposition from various factions from within the republic: from nationalists who criticized Boyer for favoring foreign merchants, and from liberals who sought greater individual freedoms.

Boyer's response was to pursue the legal codification of unity and *concorde* through a commission for the consolidation of Haiti's legal codes for the entire island republic during the period 1825–1835. This included Boyer's infamous Code Rural, but also many other legal codes that Kate Ramsey has argued were central to Boyer's performance of civility and civilization in an Atlantic world context.[19] Crucially, however, Boyer's strategy of legal unification across geographic space also codified a system of deep *inequality* within Haitian society. The 1826 Code Rural was a strict labor code that rendered rural inhabitants (*cultivateurs*) second-class citizens, tying them to the land as forced agricultural laborers and refusing them the rights accorded to full-fledged city dwellers (*citadins*).[20] As such, it worked against the idea of *concorde* by codifying two classes of Haitians, or as Louis Joseph Janvier argued, creating "in a country that claimed to be egalitarian, two nations in the nation."[21] As Claire Payton's research reveals, the vast majority of Haiti's inhabitants had few rights and no representation in the political sphere: they could not build homes, for example, enter the city limits, or travel outside their commune without the written permission of their plantation employer. Schooling laws were irregular and poorly enforced, and *cultivateurs* certainly could not vote. In this new "postcolonial geography of power," as Payton terms it, "rurality replaced blackness as the fundamental category of exclusion and cities became the legal category of privilege."[22] The Code Rural fractured the unity of the republic from the inside, sharpening the urban-rural divide and stoking peasant resentment, and laying bare the paradoxes of Boyer's universal Haitian Republic.

Like Pétion before him, Boyer was focused on official recognition from "civilized nations," and followed the path that Pétion had forged, agreeing in 1825 to pay an astronomical indemnity (150 million francs) to compensate French *colons* for their lost revenue in exchange for official recognition.[23] The indemnity was a key piece of Boyer's economic liberalism: he believed that the only path forward for independent Haiti lay in attracting foreign trade. In an article Boyer penned for his official paper, *Le Télégraphe*, the Haitian president derided Dessalines for chasing away trading partners with his violence and rhetoric, arguing that in order to attract foreign business to the country, it was necessary to inspire confidence "by giving them freedom" (*en lui laissant la latitude*).[24] Boyer's negotiation of the 1825 indemnity payment to France was closely linked to the Code Rural (Boyer looked to agriculture and peasant labor to raise much-needed funds), and was equally disastrous for internal *concorde*. The indemnity agreement stoked internal tensions and unrest from opposition groups: southern liberals, northern Christophists,[25] the peasantry, and pro-independence groups in the East. Indigenous traders and businessmen saw their livelihoods threatened, while Christophists saw the move as treason. They reactivated the earlier critiques of Pétion during the *guerre de plume* and accused Boyer of having "handed the country over to the French/whites/foreigners" (*livré le pays aux blancs,* which had now become an opposition refrain), casting the indemnity as tantamount to a loss of sovereignty and the end of Haitian independence.[26] Even residents of the East were troubled by the decision, and questioned whether Haiti was "truly, fully independent" (*réellement pleine et entière*) in a letter from Santo Domingo published in *Le Télégraphe*.[27]

Boyer also relied upon the law to silence internal opposition and impose unity by setting clear limits to a free press and opposition dissent—for example, jailing the liberal journalist Joseph Courtois and, in a more extreme case, executing Félix Darfour. The case of Darfour, which unfolded precisely during the early phase of Boyer's presidency between 1818 and 1822, is a particularly complex one that is worth exploring here. Darfour's challenge of the putative color-blind ideals of the government illustrates the practical limits of Boyer's color-blind republicanism, and more broadly illustrates the narrow and often paradoxical practice of republicanism in Boyer's island Haiti. As his name suggests, Félix Darfour was Sudanese but had lived for nearly two decades in France, having emigrated as a young child during Napoléon's campaign to Egypt. He was thus among the many African and "Indian" immigrants to Haiti who sought to take advantage of the free soil protections in article 44 of the 1816 constitution. Upon his arrival in Port-au-Princ in 1818, he joined the growing republican press, founding a political, commercial, and literary newspaper, *L'Eclaireur haytien, ou Le Parfait patriote,* which first appeared in August 1818.[28] Darfour embraced the liberal guarantees of the 1816 constitution, which promised liberty of expression and freedom from censorship, and engaged in a spirited critique of the republican government. He sparred first with Milscent in *L'Abeille* and then set out to engage in larger government reforms, changing the name of his paper to *L'Avertisseur haytien* (the "Haitian Alarm")—which announced an increasingly critical, reformist tone in his journalism.

Darfour was critical primarily of the government's overly liberal stance on commerce (liberal in the sense of favoring free commerce largely controlled by foreign merchants) and for not doing enough to promote and protect the interests of indigenous merchants.[29] Specifically, he pressed Boyer's government on its failure to promote the interests of black businessmen and traders, which he argued was a failure to uphold the constitution and its guarantee of equality of opportunity and of rights. In an 1819 article in *L'Avertisseur* entitled "De l'abus du pouvoir," he criticized the government for not consulting or deferring to its citizens, and—most damning—for excluding black men from the governing class: "To be able to govern men and decide their fate, it is generally enough to be born or to descend from one specific race [*d'une race particulière*]."[30] Indeed, it was precisely for Darfour's emphasis on color in his critique of the Haitian Republic that Boyer's republican government sentenced him to death a few years later.[31] On August 30, 1822, Darfour penned an address to the Chamber of Representatives and petitioned to have it read aloud on the floor. It consisted of a compendium of his earlier critiques of the republican government: that foreigners had a monopoly on commerce at the expense of Haitian merchants; that the government was codifying inequality between black men and men of mixed race; that in reality Boyer gave advantages to this latter group to the detriment of black men; that he did not do enough to educate black men; and that he put only men of mixed race in positions of authority.³² Délide Joseph notes that Darfour's address was not just a list of attacks, but also a reformist program, which included his proposals to combat the exclusion of blacks, to institute a system of social inclusivity and equitability, and to work to better integrate black Haitians into the government.³³ Still, Darfour had uttered a phrase that activated republicans' fears of a Christophist-style uprising: he accused the republican president of wanting to "hand over the country to the French/whites/foreigners" (*livrer le pays aux blancs*).³⁴ Darfour's accusations reportedly set off "horror and indignation" in the Chamber. He was arrested and immediately tried by a military commission, which condemned him to death for having "sown discord" among Haitians.³⁵ He was publicly executed just three days after his address to the Chamber, while his few allies in the government were also arrested, stripped of their duties, and imprisoned.³⁶

Boyer's execution of Darfour for "sowing discord" by raising the specter of race and inequality reveals the limits of Boyer's universal republicanism to address the problem of racial inequities in Haitian society.³⁷ In this sense, the Darfour affair quite resembles Simón Bolívar's political execution of Manuel Píar in 1817 for having fomented "race war" among the Spanish American republican revolutionaries.³⁸ Indeed, the color-blind republicanism of Haitian and Spanish American republican governments had much in common. The ideal of universal, color-blind republicanism in these early Caribbean republics is rooted in the founding myth of the French Republic: that it is unitary and universal, and excluded difference in the accordance and exercise of individual rights.³⁹ When it came to the practical instantiation of these universal principles, or the legitimate critiques that reformers like Darfour articulated, Boyer's government answered with violence and silence.⁴⁰

Color-blind republicanism is one of the many myths of the Haitian Republic that emerged under Boyer. By "myths" I mean specifically narrative constructions (the written "stories" that get told) and the beliefs that result from them. These texts narrated the inevitability of the republic by casting Dessalines's empire and Christophe's kingdom as perversions or aberrations of the inexorable march toward civilization and liberal republicanism. We can see clear examples of this republican myth at work in Beaubrun Ardouin's *Géographie de l'Ile d'Haïti* from

1832, written during the height of Boyer's rule in Haiti.⁴¹ If, as we saw in the previous chapter, Hérard Dumesle's personal travel narrative *Voyage dans le Nord d'Hayti* aimed to symbolically reintegrate Christophe's former kingdom into the republic by reclaiming—and rewriting—its story, Ardouin's 1832 *Géographie* aimed to achieve a similar end, but for the entire island of Haiti.

Alexis Beaubrun Ardouin (1796–1865) was a long-standing member of the republican establishment. He came of age under Pétion (for whom his father had briefly served as a personal secretary) and began working for the republican administration in his young teens, first as a typesetter in the national press under Pétion and later as secretary to General Borgella under Boyer during the successful campaign against Goman to unify the southern peninsula in 1819. He was a staunch Boyerist and worked closely in the service of the regime: as a judge, as a commissioner of the civil court, and in the Senate, first as an elected member and secretary, and eventually president. His *Géographie* is arguably the only major piece of "Haitian" history written from the perspective of the unified island and represents some of the earliest social scientific writing in republican Haiti.

The text begins with a short thirty-page historical "précis" of the dates and key events in Haitian history from 1492 to 1830. This is followed by a timeline of important events; a fifty-page descriptive "géographie" that names and explains the main features of the entire island's topography, government administration, territorial divisions, army, education system, and major industries; and finally, a seventy-page detailed description of all of the island's notable cities, market towns, and villages. Ardouin draws heavily from Moreau de Saint-Méry's *Description topographique, physique, civile, politique et historique*, announcing in the preface that he set out to create an abridged and updated version of this earlier colonial geography in order to map the current political geography of the unified republic under Boyer.⁴² Crucially, however, Ardouin is also asserting Haitian power *over* another space: the eastern side of the island. Ardouin's *Géographie* is not only a postcolonial, national project, but also an imperial project that sought to extend Boyer's republic over previously independent regions of the island. In this sense, he performed Boyer's ideal of *concorde*—territorial unity—by mapping the island republic as a coherent and contiguous space from Abricots to

Verettes, from Altamira to la Vega, assimilating and integrating the recently annexed territories in the East (but also the South and the North) into the official, geographic space of the republic.

Ardouin's historical summary narrates the inevitability and universalism of the island republic. He casts the key events surrounding Haitian independence as a process of liberal progress that culminated in the founding of the Haitian Republic. In Ardouin's historical narrative, the republic's greatest enemy were regressive forces—anything that would hinder the revolution's progressive goals. This enemy takes numerous forms in Ardouin's history: first, the counterrevolutionary French *colons*, and next, the authoritarian faction of Haiti's revolutionary leadership. Indeed, he reserves his strongest criticism for the Haitian revolutionary leaders who instituted governments that challenged republicanism: Toussaint, Dessalines, and, especially, Christophe. Ardouin argued that Toussaint's greatest mistake was the despotism ("le régime tyrannique") he extended across the eastern side of the island, a gesture to the unified island republic his text performs.[43] It was the general discontentment that came out of the "unjust rigors" of Toussaint's dictatorial regime that Ardouin blames for France's return to the island in 1802.[44] Ardouin heralded Dessalines's heroic actions in the creation of an independent nation, but chastised him for making slaves of his fellow citizens—slaves not to the master's whip but to the despot's whims: "General Dessalines soon came to see his fellow citizens as little more than slaves, made to blindly obey his whims."[45] Even more damning for Ardouin, however, was Dessalines's choice to reestablish Toussaint's despotic form of government. Perhaps most notable is Ardouin's description of Dessalines's assassination, which was, he argues, like Toussaint's demise, entirely self-inflicted—the natural, proportional result of the despot's unwise political choices. Yet it was Christophe's regressive antiliberalism that was the most problematic for Ardouin because it was of his own volition. He depicted Christophe's actions during the civil war as a direct attack on *fraternité* and *concorde*: Christophe spilled the blood of his own countrymen and brought desolation to the North (picking up here on the main tropes in Dumesle's *Voyage*): "He divided Haiti's children once again, and brought desolation to a country that had just barely risen from the ashes of war [*renaissait à peine de ses ruines*]."[46] It is interesting to note here how Ardouin reverses Christophe's own motto "From my own ashes, I rise" (*Je renais de mes cendres*) and uses it against him: the new nation was just emerging from the ashes of revolution and Christophe plunged them back into the horrors of civil war.

Against this portrait of the virulently antiliberal northern monarch, Ardouin presents Haiti's first republican leader, Pétion, as a *virtuous*, civilized patriot, extolling "his mild manner, his public and private virtues, his exemplary moderation, his courage and his military genius."[47] And while Ardouin notes that it was Boyer who ultimately "delivered our brothers" from Christophe's tyranny by promulgating the republican constitution in Cap-Haïtien, Ardouin paints it as the natural outcome of Pétion's liberal republican regime, proven by "the superiority of the legal system over despotism, of justice over tyranny."[48] Ardouin describes Pétion and Boyer as a different kind of leader than their despotic predecessors; they did not need violence and bloodshed to achieve dominance, but rather wisdom, faith in laws and justice, and above all the republic. Ardouin's presentation turns, of course, on a disavowal of Pétion's assassination of Dessalines. His description of the event in *Géographie* is entirely in the passive voice (the only agent is Dessalines and his capacity to menace and destroy) and it is evoked obliquely through a metaphor of natural disaster: "A government built upon principles so against those of social order was inevitably bound to crumble [*s'écrouler*] with the slightest blow: indeed, it only took an instant to knock down [*renverser*] the formidable Emperor who, just a minute before, was threatening to crush everything under the weight of his iron scepter."[49] There are no republican generals behind the ambush, but rather the logical order of things: liberty must always prevail over despotism.

It is fascinating to trace the lacunae, the euphemisms, and the metaphors of Dessalines's assassination throughout early republican writing. Republican writers cannot ascribe violent agency to Pétion in the assassination of Dessalines. The republic was founded on the idea of promoting an image of civilization, progress, and perfectibility—Haiti's radical instantiation of Enlightenment universalism—to a wider Atlantic public for whom those values indexed virtue and sovereignty. Nevertheless, as we shall in the next section, this republican stance on Dessalines was becoming increasingly untenable as popular opposition to Boyer grew in the late 1830s. Indeed, among Haitian peasants and former slaves, Dessalines and his memory—his heroic exploits during the revolution;

his massacre of the French; his own brutal assassination at the hands of southern conspirators—remained ever-present in their songs, Kreyòl proverbs, and Vodou practices during the first forty years of independence.[50] Haitian poets, artists, and historians finally grew wise to this fact, and began to probe the paradoxes of Boyer's universal republicanism and the peasantry's continued subjection even under putatively democratic regimes. These texts, which I analyze below, cannot be reduced to simple pandering to the peasantry. Rather, I argue that they attempted to wrest open the narrow story of the Haitian Republic by imbuing one of its disavowed heroes with the peasant, oral, and Vodou significations associated with his memory.

Island Haiti's Indigenous Literature

If Boyer's presidency can be summed up as the pursuit of territorial unity, it must also be understood as the continued confrontation and attempt to master forces of disunity and regional opposition within that territory. While Boyer successfully quelled opposition in the early years of his regime, pressure from opposition groups—namely, southern liberals (led by Hérard Dumesle and David Saint-Preux) and northern Christophists—reached a fever pitch in the 1838–1839 period. That southern liberals and northern military authoritarians would find common cause in their opposition to Boyer is somewhat surprising, given their opposing political ideologies, but it also speaks to the tangible, increasingly negative effects the 1825 indemnity payment had created in Island Haiti.[51] Madiou notes that Dumesle's liberal opposition grew stronger and more audacious—he and Saint-Preux were kicked out of the Senate in 1839 after accusing Boyer of despotism.[52] In the East, various anti-Boyerist political factions began vying for power during the same period.[53] Meanwhile, northern Christophists had been agitating since the mid-1830s to make the North and Artibonite independent of Boyer's government. They hatched a failed conspiracy to assassinate the president, then decided instead to try to take down Boyer's secrétaire général, Inginac, who had been a target of their ire since Dessalines's assassination. This northern conspiracy even included some southern liberals, whose commercial interests had been constrained under Boyer and who were eager for the chance to overthrow him.

Haiti's internal divisions and the growing opposition to Boyer's presidency became a central preoccupation for writers and intellectuals of the late 1830s. If Ardouin's earlier *Géographie* was able to perform Boyer's territorial unity largely by leaving internal opposition and tensions unaddressed, the increasing political and popular unrest led a new group of southern republican writers to try a new tactic to confront the sources of discord and create new unity from within: *indigénisme*.[54] The poets, historians, and statesmen involved with the newspapers *Le Républicain: Recueil scientifique et littéraire* (1836–1837) and *L'Union: Recueil commercial et littéraire* (1837–1839) attempted to theorize an inclusive, capacious national culture that resonated with the various societal factions across the "unified" island territory. These two papers brought together some of the most notable intellectuals of the period, such as Ignace, Laurore, Emile, and Eugène Nau; Céligny, Coriolan, and Beaubrun Ardouin; Dumai Lespinasse and Massillon Lespinasse, and even some of the earliest historical writing from Thomas Madiou, among other contributors. The literary writing and literary criticism published in *Le Républicain* and *L'Union* has led many to refer to the group of contributors to these papers as the Ecole (or Cénacle) de 1836, though I would note here that their apparent coherence as a literary school belies the heterogeneity of their political views—particularly in the degree of their liberal opposition to Boyer. The Ardouin brothers, for example, maintained a Boyerist stance in their political and poetic contributions to the papers, while the Nau brothers embraced the reforms of the liberal opposition and pushed for change beyond the status quo. Indeed, while the papers were not flagrant in their liberal opposition stance (Dumesle, for example, was far too liberal for these papers), the newspapers did refuse to follow a strict Boyerist line, and were both quickly shut down by the government.[55]

In their short-lived print runs, the publications attempted to distill a national culture from those aspects that rendered it singular, original, and island-wide: their Amerindian past that linked East and West, African cultural transmissions born of the slave trade, and local expression, local color, language—in a word, their *indigénisme*. In addition to their attempts to link East and West, contributors also aimed to bridge social divides by highlighting the African heritage of the peasantry and the original trauma of the slave trade, and honoring the role that Dessalines held in peasant and Vodou traditions as the great liberator of the nation. For these reasons, *Le Républicain* and *L'Union* constitute two of the first sustained cultural nationalist projects in Haiti, and the only ones that sought to encompass Haiti as it existed in the 1830s by exploring its ties to the eastern side of the island. The editorials, essays, historical studies, poems, and short stories published in these newspapers had the goal of illustrating—and creating—an island republican identity. Indeed, Hénock Trouillot has referred to the group's work as a form of "cultural nationalism in the extreme," which promoted the unique nature of Haitian national culture, history, language, and *génie* (talent, spirit, genius).[56]

These two newspapers endeavored to bear witness to a more capacious idea of Island Haiti's national culture, from East to West, from rural peasant to learned elite. Emile Nau published a series of articles that highlighted the island's Amerindian history, bringing the East and West together in their shared Amerindian heritage. This included an essay on the poetry of the Taino Indians and the "Histoire indienne" of the cacique leaders Caonabo, Mayobanex, and Anacaona—each of which served as early sketches for his later masterwork *Histoire des caciques d'Haïti*.[57] In addition to this shared Amerindian past, the newspapers included essays on important figures from the East such as Juan Sánchez Ramírez, who led the uprising that expelled the French from the East in 1808.[58] Interestingly, *Le Républicain* also highlights the story of José Núñez de Cáceres, whom they recognize as a key figure in the fight for independence from European colonial powers, despite the fact that he opposed unification with Haiti in 1821. In addition, the papers included excerpts, reproductions, and translations of documents from the East, such as the "Histoire de l'Université de Santo-Domingo," written by a former student and a manifesto from the "Society of the friends of the country" in Santiago.[59]

The African heritage of Haiti's peasant population and life in the countryside were represented in poetry and short narrative vignettes—what we might consider an early precursor to the *récit paysan*—such as "Une veillée de campagne," "Scène de mœurs: Un jour de l'an dans la campagne," and "Tradition africaine: Conte créole."[60] Each of these short stories was written as a serial, ending on a suspenseful note to be continued in the following issue. They included dialogue and Kreyòl phrases spoken by peasant characters, highlighting aspects of Haitian life and African traditions that, up to that point, had received little attention in the republican narrative of Haiti.[61] Ignace Nau penned a three-part "conte créole" that recounted episodes of the Haitian Revolution and included dialogue and numerous terms in Kreyòl that remained untranslated, and thus assumed to be understood by most readers.[62] There was even a series on Haitian national song and dance that described popular peasant practices in great detail.[63] *L'Union* also reproduced excerpts from a series of Coriolan Ardouin's earlier poems on Africa and the slave trade, including "La danse des Betjouanes" and "Chant de Minora."[64]

Lastly, Thomas Madiou published some of his first writing in *L'Union*, including the story of Macandal, the great maroon leader of the North whose memory was of critical importance to the insurgent slaves during the revolution, and to the peasant population thereafter. Importantly, Madiou's account of the story incorporates the northern legend, which held that Macandal broke free in a "superhuman effort," only to be killed by a French colonial soldier as he tried to escape the Cap.[65] He also published accounts of Toussaint Louverture's rise and fall at the hands of the French, as well as the story of the siege of Crête-à-Pierrot—one of the decisive battles of the Haitian War of Independence.[66] As a stylistic side note, it is fascinating to read these early texts from Madiou. In some of the essays, like that on Crête-à-Pierrot, he is the historian that we know from his eight-volume *Histoire d'Haïti*, more or less measured though given to some "melodramatic detail."[67] In some essays for *L'Union*, such as his account of Toussaint Louverture, however, he is positively lyric.[68] He describes Toussaint's final moments thus: "Before closing his eyes forever, he cursed France and asked God for an avenger [*un vengeur*]. We know that his prayer reached the heavens."[69] Madiou's use of the word "vengeur" here is powerful and cannot be overlooked. Not only did it reactivate the tone and lexicon of Haiti's early post-independence textual production, but it also created a new facet to Dessalines's role as avenger—not just of the New World, but of the revolutionary leader Toussaint.

Indeed, Madiou's reactivation of Dessalines's vengeance narrative was part of a new, more inclusive approach to Dessalines's memory from within the republic, one that celebrated multiple facets of his legacy—not just his role as the great liberator, but also his foundational act of vengeance. This was something that liberal writers took on in opposition to Boyer's republican regime in the 1830s. Writers like Madiou, Nau, and others in the 1830s turned to poetry to rehabilitate Dessalines's memory within a wider, more inclusive national Haitian identity. Here, I consider two different attempts to rethink Dessalines's place in Haitian national identity in poetry: an 1835 poem from Coriolan Ardouin that toed a Boyerist line, but introduced new elements of Dessalines's story into the national conversation; and second, a slightly later poem by Ignace Nau that offered a radically new representation of Dessalines, which appealed specifically to the place of the peasantry within the national narrative by gesturing to oral traditions, African heritage, and the role of Dessalines as both liberator, avenger, and emperor of Haiti.

Let us begin with Coriolan Ardouin's poem, "Le Pont rouge."[70] Similar to Beaubrun Ardouin's version of Dessalines in his historical preface to *Géographie*, Coriolan Ardouin presents Dessalines as the great liberator who sullied his own victory and that of his fellow revolutionaries by founding an empire. It is worth considering the first stanza in its entirety, which evokes Dessalines's assassination but does not name it, instead presenting the powerful liberator whose thirst for glory and power sullied the glory of the Haitian Revolution with his own blood:

> C'est là qu'il est tombé dans toute sa puissance
> Celui dont le bras fort conquit l'Indépendance!
> Que lui pesaient à lui [sic] sa gloire et son grand nom?
> Sous son pied d'Empereur il foula cette gloire,
> Et du sang fraternel il a tâché l'histoire
>   De notre révolution!
>
> (There he fell in all his glory
> He whose iron fist conquered Independence!
> Did his glory and his great name burden him?[71]
> As Emperor, he trampled that glory underfoot,
> And with fraternal blood he stained the history
>   Of our Revolution!)

Ardouin laments that Dessalines destroyed his own great reputation as liberator, and by extension the glory of *all* the Haitian people ("notre révolution"), by installing an empire. Here, we see an echo not only of other Boyerist writers, but also of Boyer himself and his remarks on economic liberalism in *Le Télégraphe*, in which he blames Dessalines's monstrous and violent massacre of the French after independence for chasing away all foreign commerce. In Ardouin's poetic depiction, it was Dessalines who had tarnished the *history* of the Haitian Revolution with "du sang fraternel." And yet, Ardouin's poem maintains some ambiguity in the violent act it references in the final lines. Recall from our discussion of Beaubrun Ardouin's *Géographie* above that the charge of spilling brotherly blood was most commonly used in reference to the civil war infighting between Toussaint and Rigaud or Christophe and Pétion. Certainly, Dessalines spilled the blood of the remaining Frenchmen and foreigners in the mass killings of April 1804, but this was hardly "fraternal" bloodshed. Here, I would argue that Coriolan Ardouin is doing something new with his reference to Dessalines and the spilling of brotherly blood, in keeping with the Indigenist revision of Dessalines's memory. Ardouin is referring, obliquely, to Pétion's assassination of Dessalines: Dessalines sullied Haiti's revolution *with his own blood* by forcing Pétion and his army of southern republicans to remove him from power. In this way, Ardouin's poem is one of the first pieces of post-1820 republican writing to index, albeit indirectly, the complicated and thorny issue at the heart of the republic's founding—the forced spilling of fraternal blood because of Dessalines's choice to establish an empire.

If not a rehabilitation of Dessalines's memory, the poem does go further than previous republican accounts of Dessalines's role in Haitian history. In contrast to the portrayal of Dessalines's demise (an emperor, felled by his thirst for power) in the first stanza, the second stanza begins with the conjunction "Pourtant, il était beau," announcing a series of stanzas that celebrate the glory that preceded Dessalines's despotic turn. The poem concludes with a slightly more nuanced appreciation of Dessalines's role in Haitian history than, say, Dumesle's depiction of the emperor in *Voyage* or Beaubrun Ardouin's depiction of him in *Géographie*.

> Oh! s'il voulut détruire après son propre ouvrage,
> Si contre des écueils sa barque fit naufrage
> Et qu'il s'ensevelit sous un triste linceul,

C'est qu'il faut que d'un ciel la clarté se ternisse,
Que le flot se mêlant au sable se brunisse,
C'est que la pure gloire appartient à Dieu seul.

(Oh! If he insisted on destroying his own work,
If his boat wrecked against the reef,
And he was buried beneath a somber shroud,
It is because a clear sky always sullies,
Because the tide darkens when it mixes with sand,
It is because pure glory belongs to God alone.)

To be sure, Coriolan Ardouin still makes mostly the same point here as the earlier, euphemistic republican representations of Dessalines's fall: Dessalines wrecked his own ship, destroyed his own good work, and died because he chose to found an empire. The line "s'ensevelit sous un triste linceul" is as close as we get to even the word *death* here, let alone *assassination* or *regicide*. And yet, Ardouin's account is devoid of the anger and frustration that we saw in earlier republican accounts. Instead, he seems to forgive Dessalines here by saying, in so many words, that men are fallible. Indeed, this last line might also be read as a tacit explanation and expiation for Pétion's (mis)deeds as much as for Dessalines's.

Ignace Nau offers an even more nuanced presentation of the liberator-emperor figure of Dessalines in his poem "31 décembre 1838," which marks an important departure from previous republican poetry on the Haitian leader. Unlike Ardouin's poem, and other representations of Dessalines before that, Nau's poem undertakes a radical shift by emphasizing the African and oral traditions of Dessalines's memory that were common among the former slaves who comprised almost all of the peasantry. This is not to say that other republican writers from the 1830s did not valorize African culture: both *L'Union* and *Le Républicain* were replete with African and peasant themes, which they saw as crucial to their *indigéniste* cultural nationalist project (Coriolan Ardouin's *Les Betjouanes* series, for example, celebrates the beauty of Africa and the horrors of the slave trade). Rather, I argue that Nau's poem tackled the complicated question of Dessalines's memory for cultural nationalist purposes in order to create unity in the republic, particularly by addressing the popular, peasant class. He did this by directly connecting Dessalines's role in Haitian history with Vodou and oral peasant traditions. What is more, he did so in a piece of writing that was not destined for the pages of a republican literary newspaper—or not solely—but rather a poem written expressly for the purposes of a public performance of a national holiday for *all* Haitians: the January 1, 1839, Independence Day celebrations. It is worth recalling here that the year 1838 had witnessed extraordinary pressure on Boyer's republic from opposition groups, including assassination attempts and conspiracies to secede from northern Christophists, and accusations of despotism and authoritarianism from liberals. The issue of *L'Union* in which Nau published the poem offers a short lead article and another poem, "A l'an 1838," both of which depict 1838 as a "cursed year" in which the republic seemed lost, paralyzed by its divides and without any forward direction.[72] Nau presents his poem as a reflection written from the waning hours of this cursed year, the darkest moment before the possibility of the new year presents itself to the republic.

This immediate context further attests to the political import of Nau's portrayal of Dessalines, and his attempt to reach a wider, popular audience. As I argue here, he sought to offer a reset: a new strategy to address the divides and disagreements that had paralyzed the republic in 1838. This involved thinking differently about Dessalines and how he was treated during the republican Independence Day celebrations. More specifically, Nau considered the independence celebrations on January 1 as an opportunity to start not only a new year, but a new approach to thinking about Haitian independence by encouraging his compatriots to show reverence for Dessalines instead of the disdain that was customary among Nau's intellectual and political class. His publicly performed poem evokes earlier, Dessalinean and Christophean traditions of pomp and political celebration. Moreover, his poem, like so many of the Dessalinean texts that preceded it, incorporated oral and Vodou traditions of Haitian independence—popular traditions that had been kept out of print for many years. Indeed, we cannot grasp the meaning of Nau's Independence Day poem if we do not understand the metaphors and Vodou referents in the Dessalinean writing that precedes it. Nor can we understand the full significance of Nau's return to these Dessalinean forms if we do not take into account the context of the post-independence civil war and the myths of republicanism that followed in its wake.

The first line of the poem contains a direct address to the republican revelers, proposing that for the first time, the official government celebration of independence make a gesture of honor and respect to Dessalines. The poet suggests, in the first-person plural imperative, "let's take off our hats" when we hear Dessalines's name:

> Dessaline! . . . à ce nom, amis, découvrons-nous
> Je me sens le cœur battre à fléchir les genoux
> Et jaillir à ce nom un sang chaud dans mes veines.
> Demain, quand le soleil reluira sur nos plaines,
> Quand son disque demain ira de ses rayons
> Réveiller l'harmonie et l'encens de nos monts,
> Qu'au bruit de la fanfare et de l'artillerie
> Le peuple salûera le jour de la Patrie,
> Suspendez vos plaisirs, recueillez votre cœur,
> Songez à nos héros, songez à l'Empereur!
>
> Quand cet aigle africain parut sur nos campagnes
> On dit avoir senti tressaillir les montagnes,
> Vu ployer leurs sommets comme un noble coursier
> Qui fléchit et reçoit son royal écuyer,
> Et tout à coup le sol osciller sous les maîtres,
> Les repoussant partout comme ennemis et traîtres.
> A voir l'aigle promis que long-tems il rêva,
> D'un seul cri, d'un seul bond l'esclave se leva,
> Et, surprenant l'impie au milieu de ses fêtes,
> Rompit son joug de fer contre ses mille têtes.
>
> Et ce peuple nouveau qui d'esclaves naquit,
> Fier des libertés que sa force conquit,
> Dédaigne de s'asseoir autour des mêmes tables
> Pleines encore de vins et de mets délectables.
> Cette orgie insultait à ses mille douleurs;
> Le vin était son sang et le pain ses sueurs.
> —"Purifions le sol des péchés de l'impie,"

Dit le peuple, et la torche alluma l'incendie,
Et Jean-Jacques, semblable à quelqu'esprit de Dieu,
Dicta l'indépendance à la lueur du feu! ...

Ecoutez ... le canon! La montagne en tressaille
Comme autrefois de joie aux sons de la bataille!
—Oh! demain le soleil se lèvera plus pur
Et plus majestueux dans sa courbe d'azur!
L'oiseau nous chantera des chants d'amour encore,
La voix de nos forêts redeviendra sonore,
Et nos fleuves taris jailliront en torrents,
Et nos lacs rouleront des flots plus transparents,
Et toi, peuple héroïque, et toi, mon beau Génie,
Demain vous salûerez une ère d'harmonie!

(Dessaline! Friends, when we hear his name, let's take off our hats
I feel my heart beat as my knees slack
And when I hear his name, hot blood flows through my veins.
Tomorrow, when the sun glistens across our plains,
When tomorrow the orb's gleaming rays
Awaken the sounds and the smells of our mounts,
When to the sound of the trumpet blares and the cannon blasts
The people greet our Independence Day,
Postpone your delights, collect your emotions,
Think of your heroes, think of the Emperor!

When the African eagle appeared over our fields
They say you could feel the hills tremble,
They say you could see their summits yield, like a noble steed
Who bends down to let his royal cavalier mount,
And suddenly the ground shook beneath the masters,
Everywhere repelling them as enemies and traitors.
Seeing this promised eagle that he had dreamed of for so long,
The slave sprung up in a single leap, with a single cry,
And, catching the impious unawares in the midst of his feast,
Broke his iron yoke against a thousand heads.

And this new people born of slavery,
Proud of the freedoms they conquered by force,
Refused to be seated around the same tables
That were still full of wine and delectable dishes.
Insulting these excesses were to the peoples' thousand wounds,
The wine was made of their blood, the bread of their sweat.
—"Let us cleanse the earth of the sins of the impious,"
Said the people, and their torch lit the fire,
And Jean-Jacques, like some spirit of God,
Dictated independence by the light of their flame.

Listen . . . the cannon! The mountain trembles with its sound
As it once did with joy from the sounds of battle!
—Oh! Tomorrow the sun will rise even purer
And more magnificent in its clear-blue skies!
The bird will sing us love songs once more,
The sounds of our forests will echo once more,
And our dried up rivers will flow in torrents,
And our lakes will roll with the most transparent waves,
And you, heroic people, and you, my beautiful Spirit,
Tomorrow you will greet an era of harmony!)[73]

The first stanza of the poem suggests to Nau's fellow republicans that they might think differently about Dessalines this year. In addition to showing reverence by removing their hats and bending a knee, he asks that they find a moment of calm in all of the fanfare to think about Haiti's national heroes *and* its former emperor: "Suspendez vos plaisirs, recueillez votre cœur / Songez à nos héros, songez à l'Empereur." The syntax here indicates that Dessalines is not considered a hero by most, but that Nau is asking that he be included among the other heroes in their reflections on independence. It is particularly notable that Nau replaces the proper noun "Dessaline" that he used in the first line of the stanza with his imperial title, "emperor," which ends the first stanza. Yet unlike Ardouin's poem, which casts Dessalines the emperor as sullying the glory of Dessalines the liberator, Nau presents Dessalines as both the hero and the emperor, carrying the theme of Dessalines's multifaceted legacy throughout the poem. At the sound of Dessalines's name, Nau describes an almost involuntary reaction in which he finds himself genuflecting: "Je me sens le cœur battre à fléchir les genoux / Et jaillir à ce nom un sang chaud dans mes veines." Read out of context, this line seems to suggest a reaction of fear. However, in the context of a historical revision that I have outlined above, I believe we can read it as Nau's connection with the oral, peasant tradition of Haitian independence and Dessalines's role therein. Indeed, the poem seems to play upon reversing the reader-listener's expectations and assumptions about Dessalines, and Nau's poetic representation of him. What at first reads as Nau's fear or anger could also be read as reaction awakened inside him: his knee bends without him realizing it, he feels hot blood coursing through his veins as if he's giving in to a part of himself that has been cut off, repressed, ignored.[74]

The poem's second stanza enacts an important but subtle temporal shift back in time: to the slave uprisings that initiated Haitian independence. Nau's use of the phrase "On dit" is key, here: he is tapping into the oral tradition and the lore that surrounds these historic moments of the revolution. Nau is recounting the myth, the heritage, the collective (oral) story of Dessalines. The second stanza introduces Dessalines under another name, "cet aigle africain," a symbol in Vodou and peasant lore of Dessalines. Nau's poem depicts Dessalines's legacy as both the great liberator and the great emperor. The connection between Dessalines as "l'Empereur" in the first stanza and "cet aigle africain" in the second is further borne out in the lexicon that Nau employs. Nau likens the mountains to a noble steed bowing down (*fléchit*—the same verb Nau used in the first stanza to describe his subconscious ancestral connection) to let the African eagle mount before the two ride together to victory. The significance of the mountain imagery cannot be overstated in the oral, peasant depictions of the Haitian Revolution: mountains are the symbol of resistance, marronnage, and the power of the insurgent slaves.[75] The northern mountains were the stronghold for insurgents and maroons and the location of the greatest battles of the Haitian Revolution. That the mountains serve as a noble horse for Dessalines's royal cavalier (un noble coursier / Qui fléchit et reçoit son royal écuyer) serves as a metonym for the thousands of insurgent slaves and free people of color who took to the mountains to seek refuge from the French, and to prepare for the final battles of independence. In Nau's poem it is Dessalines, the African eagle, who encouraged them to rise up and throw off the iron yoke of slavery. Further, the figural depiction of the mountains-as-horse and African eagle-as-rider gestures clearly to the Vodou tradition of spirit possession, in which spirits or *lwa* are said to "mount" a Vodou initiate, as one would ride a horse.[76] It is worth insisting here again on the paradigmatic shift that Nau was enacting in the presentation of Dessalines and his legitimation and oral performance of Vodou and peasant traditions in the public celebration of Haitian independence. It indicates his attempt to move toward a more inclusive remembering of the father of Haitian independence and a more capacious performance of Haiti's national, indigenous culture.

The third stanza of the poem recounts a scene from the drafting of the proclamation of independence, still in the mode of oral history. Here, Nau presents Dessalines under a third title, Jean-Jacques, the most intimate of his titles in the poem. The context in which Nau presents the drafting of the independence proclamation and the calls to rid the island of the remaining French is significant because it further humanizes Dessalines's foundational act of vengeance. It presents the call for violence against the French as the direct discourse of the new Haitian people ("Purifions le sol des péchés de l'impie"), thus legitimizing Dessalines as a leader precisely because he fulfilled his duty to enact the people's will. Recall from chapter 1 the debates that surrounded the violent, fiery tone that Dessalines and Boisrond Tonnerre used in the Haitian Declaration of Independence. Nau's emphasis on the words and the will of the insurgent slaves, rather than a secretary's pen, emphasizes that Dessalines was a man of the masses, and that their will colored the language and the content of the Acte de l'indépendance.

The final stanza of the poem brings the reader back to the present day, returning from the oral portion of the poem to the ceremonial and commemorative mode of the first stanza. In the original newspaper version of the poem, this final stanza is set apart by a dotted line to indicate this temporal shift. And yet, the line is entirely artificial: Nau's lexical and syntactical structures in the last stanza encourage the reader (and the listener, for whom this connection would be more powerful) to link all of Dessalines's glorious historical acts that Nau recounted in the middle stanzas into the final, future-looking stanza. Nau begins the final stanza as he began the first, with an imperative, though this time it is a command rather than an invitation: he tells his republican compatriots to listen to the celebratory cannon fire echoing against the mountains: "Ecoutez . . . le canon! La montagne en tressaille." The cannon fire that shakes the mountains of Port-au-Prince during the Independence Day celebrations directly evokes for the reader-listener the image of Dessalines from the previous stanzas: the African eagle who made the mountains tremble as he flew overhead, activating the desire for liberty among the insurgent slaves and maroons who inhabited them. Further, we can read the command "Ecoutez" followed by a suggestive ellipsis in the first line of the final stanza as referring not only to the sound of the cannon, but back to Dessalines and the words of the Acte de l'indépendance he dictated by the light of the insurgents' torches. That is, the imperative "Ecoutez," though semantically linked to the sound of the cannon, is also symbolically linked to the previous stanza in which Dessalines proclaimed Haitian independence. What is more, it serves to bridge the temporal moments in the poem, connecting the past memory of Dessalines's heroic acts with the present moment of the eve of independence celebrations thirty-four years later.

Nau's rehabilitation of Dessalines's memory and his activation of Vodou and oral peasant traditions are exemplary of this more capacious, wide-ranging approach to achieve a unified national identity that unblocks, unveils, and brings into the light Dessalines's role as the liberator of Haiti *and* its first leader. Indeed, he seems to be suggesting that only by recognizing Dessalines as both the liberator and the emperor, by acknowledging Dessalines's wider importance to African traditions and peasant culture, will Haiti achieve *concorde*—the ideal that Boyer had been touting for so many years. Nau ends the poem with his hope for harmony and unity, not only in the new year but for a new era. Here again, we can see a connection to Coriolan Ardouin's earlier poem. Where Ardouin had presented a fatalistic, negative presentation of Dessalines's emperor as a fact of nature in dictums like "a clear sky always sullies," "the tide darkens when it mixes with sand," and "pure glory belongs to God alone" (similar, again, to earlier nature-based republican depictions of the emperor's "fall"), Nau presents a more positive possible future for the Emperor's memory. Indeed, Nau seems to be responding to, even correcting Ardouin's vision, when he presents future time with an "even purer" sun, "magnificent in its clear-blue skies" and lakes with the "most transparent waves." This future time is the Independence Day celebrations of January 1, 1939, which he addresses in the final lines of this forward-looking stanza to le peuple: "Et toi, peuple héroïque, et toi, mon beau génie, / Demain vous saluerez une ère d'harmonie!"[77] The "toi, peuple héroïque" he addresses here, in the context of the previous stanzas, now reads as a purposeful, inclusive reference to *all* Haitians—those who venerate Dessalines as their great liberator, the African eagle, and the fallen emperor. Furthermore, "mon génie" here should be read as a reference to the "génie de la patrie"—the spirit of the nation, which is in line with the eighteenth-century use of the term *génie* to mean "an allegorical being personifying a principle [or] an abstract idea."[78] Dessalines—his memory, his mythic existence in African-based peasant culture, his complex set of titles and identities—is vital to the spirit of the nation. Only once his full existence is recognized might the Haitian nation move toward welcoming an era of harmony ("saluerez une ère d'harmonie"), rather than recognizing a day of independence ("saluera le jour de la Patrie"). Yet Nau's emphasis on the possibility of an era of harmony to come suggests, necessarily, that *concorde* does not exist in the present day. Nau's rehabilitation of Dessalines simultaneously highlights the failure of republicanism to come to terms with Dessalines's complicated, problematic memory. As we shall see in the next chapter, the question of what to do with Dessalines and his memory would only become more politically charged.

The Liberal Revolution of 1843 the World of 1848, and the Return to Empire

The 1838–1839 period was the flash point that forced Boyer to put down the liberal opposition to his regime; Haitian intellectuals and politicians had put their finger on the paradoxes of his putative universal island republic and had begun proposing their own way forward. He responded by shutting down the newspapers *Le Républicain* and *L'Union*, but new opposition papers soon cropped up: *Le Manifeste* (1841) and *Le Patriote* (1841).[79] These liberal opposition papers took an even bolder stance than their predecessors, embracing new socialist ideas by French philosophers Henri de Saint-Simon and Charles Fourier that focused on the working class, such as promoting education, public libraries, and savings banks for workers.[80] Boyer responded by creating a new government-sponsored paper, *Le Temps* (1842) (with the epigraph "Public order. Peace, Prosperity. Change is the work of Time") and tapping his moderate, faithful republican supporters Beaubrun Ardouin and Charles Séguy Villevaleix to run it.[81] In spite of his suppressive efforts, the liberal opposition continued to gain ground, winning seats in the 1842 parliamentary elections (mostly in the southern peninsula, around the capital, and in the East in Santo Domingo). Boyer tightened his grip by refusing to let them take their seats in the Chamber.[82] It was not just the liberal opposition that was putting pressure on Boyer, either, as he began to feel increased pressure from the northern, Christophist opposition, who continued to plot against Boyer's nominal republic.

A natural disaster ultimately brought Boyer's regime to an end and ushered in the Liberal Revolution of 1843. On May 7, 1842, a massive earthquake hit the northern band of the Island of Haiti, causing damage from Port-de-Paix to Puerto Plata and killing more than half the population of Cap-Haïtien—as many as six thousand people in a city of less than ten thousand.[83] The aftermath was chaotic, with pillaging, looting, and sickness crippling the northern cities. For a few days, Boyer remained silent. He did not send military reinforcements to maintain order or bring aid to the devastated regions surrounding Cap-Haïtien, Fort Liberté, and the rest of the northern band; rather, he dispatched a mission "to assess the extent of the destruction and pillaging."[84] When he finally issued a statement in the official government paper, *Le Télégraphe*, he implored residents to cease the looting and pillaging. Even then, he could not help making a political point, drawing parallels between the violence of Christophe's monarchy and the devastation of the earthquake: "The city of Cap-Haïtien, which was just beginning to prosper after having suffered so much under the regime of tyranny, has been completely destroyed."[85] Boyer's inaction in the face of the earthquake and his denigration of the northern region, coupled with a financial crisis triggered by the depreciation of paper money, revealed his weakening power base. A regime change was soon to come.

I am interested specifically here in the importance of geography and regional identity in the revolutionary tumult of the 1840s. For, if Boyer's presidency had performed, mythologized, and militarized Haitian unity for his quarter century of rule, Haitian regionalism remained a powerful force that surged to the fore in his absence. In late 1842, the South rose up in a social revolution, drawing on a powerful liberal heritage that was autochthonous to this region of Haiti. In Les Cayes, Hérard Dumesle created the Société des droits de l'homme et du citoyen, directly referencing earlier republican revolutionary movements and undoubtedly drawing upon revolutionary social agitation in France. Dumesle nominated his cousin, Charles Rivière Hérard, to lead the insurrection in Les Cayes, while the southern town of Jérémie proclaimed a provisional popular government headed not by military leaders but a committee of civilians.[86] The southern military troops, led by Rivière Hérard, easily defeated Boyer's—largely owing to the mass defections among the government troops to the opposition side. On March 15, 1843, Port-au-Prince rose up in arms and adhered to the revolution, welcoming Rivière Hérard on March 21 into the capital city, which they had renamed Port-Républicain—another direct link to the radical Jacobin revolutionary era in 1793.[87] The southern liberals also drew upon a concept that was synonymous with 1789 liberalism: *régénération*.[88] They were seeking not just reform, but rebirth as a nation, and dated their government proclamations "An 40e de l'Indépendance et le 1er de la Régénération."[89] In evoking regeneration, the liberal revolutionaries were staking their project as part of a longer heritage of Enlightenment revolutionary ideology that had emerged in Haiti's southern peninsula in 1791 and again in 1810 with the brief Scission du Sud. The constitution of 1843 that they penned was Haiti's most democratic yet: it instituted a four-year term instead of a presidency for life and insisted on a robust parliamentary system based in civilian leadership that checked executive power.[90] The goal of the 1843 revolutionaries was to finally realize what had been started in 1791, and partially enacted under Pétion: a liberal republican state according to the Enlightenment principles of inalienable individual rights, equality, and democracy.

This was the goal, at least. As soon as Rivière Hérard's government assumed power in April 1843, the cracks began to show, as the liberal revolutionaries vigorously debated exactly what kind of government should replace Boyer's nominal republic.[91] Factions of the Liberal Revolution sparred over the terms of the constitution, the form of their government, and the role of the army within it, and civil war again broke out across the island. Opposition groups in the North, South, and East—

each with its own opposition ideas—began to agitate against the Liberal Revolution. The East moved first, officially declaring its independence from Haiti on February 28, 1844, and proclaiming itself the República Dominicana.[92] Rivière Hérard responded by immediately calling up his troops to march on the East. He recognized the need to contain the uprising and bring the territory back into Haitian control in order for his fledgling government to survive. Meanwhile in the South, armed bands of small landholders and cultivators who had initially supported the liberal revolutionary movement—and indeed, were instrumental to its success in late 1842 and early 1843—had begun to question the priorities of the liberal government and its commitment to the peasantry and the socialist promise of equality for all. He further angered them by ordering the arrest of Lysius Salomon, an elite landowner from Les Cayes who had long championed the cause of the southern peasantry and opposition to the government's status quo. Led by Jean-Jacques Acaau, a band of armed southerners (known as the *piquets* for the wooden sticks that they armed themselves with) rebelled against the liberal government, demanding Salomon's return from exile and chastising the liberal government for failing to address the peasants' demands.[93]

While Acaau and his *piquet* army rebelled in the South, the North was planning its own scission from Rivière Hérard's liberal government. Jean-Louis Pierrot (or Pierrault, as it is sometimes spelled) was a former nobleman in Christophe's kingdom who was named military commander of the North under Rivière Hérard. When Pierrot refused to march east to quell the uprising there, Rivière Hérard demanded his arrest. In response, Pierrot proclaimed a separatist government in the North. It is worth quoting the preamble to Pierrot's April 26, 1844, manifesto in full, to glean the degree to which the northern secessionists were drawing upon the long history of northern silencing and alienation following the fall of Christophe's monarchy in 1820: "The people of the Northern Department, tired of being the plaything of an unprincipled Government, has freed itself from the Government of Rivière Hérard on the following grounds: Ex-President Boyer, called upon in 1820 to join us, stole our treasury, our arsenal, and in return, bequeathed us with division in Society and corruption in our politics after having, during his presidency, exiled the Capois elite and thrust them into humiliation."[94] And so, after years of simmering unrest and many failed attempts, the

North finally reinserted itself back into the national sphere of power. Pierrot's plan was to maintain the scission of the North until he could install Philippe Guerrier, a venerated northern general (and himself a former member of Christophe's kingdom), to replace Rivière Hérard as president.[95] The secessionists even produced their own separatist flag, adding a white star—*l'étoile du Nord*—to the blue of the flag, that would remain there until their demands were met.[96] It was actually Beaubrun Ardouin, still hoping to restore a Boyerist republic after the Liberal Revolution, who helped pen the Manifesto of May 3, 1844, which named Guerrier president of Haiti and brought the secessionist North back into the republic.[97] Soon Jean-Jacques Acaau rallied the South and they too recognized Guerrier as president. While marching on the East, Rivière Hérard learned that he and his liberal opposition government had been overturned by the northern secessionists.

Rivière Hérard's radical social revolution had ended, yet unrest continued: the elderly general Guerrier died on April 15, 1845, after just a year in office. The Conseil d'Etat promptly named Pierrot to replace him. In his first address to the nation, Pierrot echoed Christophe's earlier rhetoric when he called for order and discipline to maintain independence.[98] He also set out to reform the government in the spirit that Guerrier had begun (but failed to enact): he returned the capital city to its prior name, Port-au-Prince, and enacted a series of exiles (*bannissements*) of southern liberal opposition members, or *riviéristes*, who he claimed had sought to provoke civil war ("exciter la guerre civile").[99] Pierrot's attachment to his Christophist roots and his devotion to the northern region, however, led him to make another significant and highly questionable change to the structure of the republic: moving its capital. In a proclamation published in the official government paper, *Le Moniteur*, Pierrot explained that he had decided to move the seat of the national government back to the North.[100] Why did he make this risky decision? Madiou posits that Pierrot had always felt uneasy in Port-au-Prince and did not trust the men of the capital, and that he relied on questionable advice from his northern advisors.[101] This may be true, but what Madiou doesn't note is that the South and West were still a tinderbox of revolution. The liberal opposition (*riviéristes*), at this point exiled in Jamaica just off the southwest coast of Haiti, continually threatened to invade the southern peninsula. Pierrot undoubtedly felt safer in the

North. He might have been able to rule effectively from Haiti's second city, had it not been for his second questionable decision: to send a military expedition to retake the East.[102]

The army in Saint-Marc rose up against Pierrot on February 27, 1846, leveling charges of "la dictature" against the northern leader and demanding that the Boyerist general Jean-Baptiste Riché replace him.[103] The North was defiant: Pierrot's generals raised an armed resistance against the republican delegation sent North to depose him (as Madiou described, "all of the old traditions of Pétion versus Christophe awakened in them").[104] The northern resistance lasted only a month: on March 29, Cap-Haïtien adhered to the revolution and submitted to Riché's presidency.[105] Riché's brief presidency was an attempt to return to the status quo of Boyerism. Many of the main players in Boyer's government who had been exiled by Rivière Hérard's liberal opposition government, or sidelined by Guerrier and Pierrot's Christophist military regimes, returned to prominent roles in Riché's government: Céligny Ardouin, for example, was assigned to the interior and agriculture, while Beaubrun Ardouin was named vice president of the Senate.[106]

Riché died abruptly after a year in office. It was a Saturday. The Senate reconvened on Monday, March 1, and proclaimed Faustin Soulouque the new president of Haiti.[107] In his first address to the people of Haiti, Soulouque cited his Christian faith and his promise "never to deviate from the path forged by the illustrious President Riché."[108] Just two years later he would be proclaimed emperor of Haiti.

* * *

Soulouque's proclamation of empire in 1849—a date, attentive readers will note, that well precedes Louis Napoléon's proclamation of empire in France—must be considered within this wider Atlantic context of liberal, social revolution and return to empire. This is an especially important context to reconsider, given that the historical details surrounding the 1848 southern liberal uprising against Soulouque are surprisingly slim—there is no consensus on the actors and events, and even less on Soulouque's repression of the uprising. The "standard account" of Soulouque's actions during the 1848 uprising in written histories of the period is based on character traits and racialist tropes rather than documentation, often sliding into sensationalism and hyperbole.[109] These explanations, which rely on personal vendetta and racial animus, mask the actual political motivations behind Soulouque's actions. Marlene Daut has argued powerfully against the use of race as a "key" or indicator to explain why Haitian historical actors, writers, and historians did, said, and wrote what they did.[110] We would do well to apply this critique to accounts of Soulouque and his empire. Soulouque undoubtedly targeted wealthy southerners from the towns of Jérémie and Les Cayes who were generally, but not always, of lighter mixed race. Still, to conclude that Soulouque targeted them *because* they were of lighter skin is a radical simplification and more important still, precludes us from seeking a more nuanced analysis of the period. Soulouque's violent repression of the 1848 liberal uprising and eventual proclamation of empire is less an absurd or violent example of black despotism (as Spenser St. John would have it) than a calculated political choice based in populism and made in response to the global dimensions of the 1848 revolutions—of which Soulouque was undoubtedly well aware.

Indeed, the "world" of the 1848 revolutions (which began in France and Italy, then spread eastward and westward, throughout Europe and the Americas) is a critical but overlooked piece to understanding the eventual proclamation of empire in Haiti.[111] In February 1848, protesters seized government power and declared the Second French Republic. The revolutionary government's first acts were to strip the nobility of their titles and privileges and definitively abolish slavery in all of France's colonies—reinstalling the radical gains of the First Republic. News of the Paris events quickly spread eastward throughout Europe as a moment of democratic revolutionary fervor toppled princes and kings from power, albeit only briefly in most cases. While these events were received throughout the Caribbean, they held particular significance for Haitian republicans who had, since the Haitian Revolution, believed that Saint-Domingue/Haiti was the site of the most radical instantiations of liberal Enlightenment ideals. *Their* island was the place where slavery was abolished for the first time, *their* ancestors had fought for racial equality in the National Assembly and given their lives to the cause on the ground in Saint-Domingue. Haitian republicans witnessed France finally returning to a republican abolitionist government—one that aligned with their own political goals, and with whom they likely sought to manifest their solidarity and alliance. The prospect of a Haitian-French republican alliance was indeed quite real: the French republican government signed a commerce treaty with the newly independent Dominican Republic in October 1848.[112]

Haiti's own 1848 took place in April of that year. According to Soulouque's government's account of the uprising published in the official newspaper *Le Moniteur*, a liberal opposition group tried to raise its flag in the capital city on April 16, 1848.[113] The rest of the southern peninsula rose up simultaneously, in coordination with the revolutionaries in Port-au-Prince. On May 16, Soulouque's troops put down the insurrection in the southern towns of Aquin and Miragoâne and ordered that the revolutionary leaders be put to death. Meanwhile, hundreds of wealthy southern men, women, and children fled, mainly from the towns of Jérémie and Les Cayes (both strongholds of liberal opposition), to take refuge in the neighboring islands of Jamaica and Saint Thomas, among others. More than seven hundred southern Haitians fled as Soulouque meted out his reprisal against the southern insurgents.[114] In response, Soulouque issued a decree barring these wealthy southern families ("who never ceased to ignite civil war in the country") from reentering, revoking their citizenship and seizing their property for having "abandoned" the country.[115] Finally, in July, *Le Moniteur* reported that a special government council had found a number of these residents guilty of threatening national security and fomenting civil war, and had sentenced them to death.[116] Most were found guilty in absentia, though the paper includes a list of others who had been arrested (*saisis*) and would be put to death in Aquin. Sufficiently cowed and purged of their most liberal residents, the remaining citizens of Jérémie came together and wrote a petition denouncing—and naming—the "traitors" who had worked to "overturn the established order and replace it with anarchy and civil war," professing their support of Soulouque's government for good measure.[117]

Having stamped out the threat of liberal revolution in the South, Soulouque turned to the problem in the East, and its troubling republican alliance with France. Soulouque pointed out in *Le Moniteur* that by recognizing Dominican independence, France was tying Haiti's hands as far as their 1825 indemnity agreement was concerned, which had been drawn up according to the borders of the unified island republic: by signing a commercial treaty with the East, "does France not paralyze us in our legitimate efforts to bring this part of the republic back under our legal government, and does she not also make it impossible for us to pay the indemnity to which we only consented in the first place because we were counting on the resources afforded to us by the entire island, and notably the eastern side?"[118] He rallied his troops for an eastern campaign, which took place during March and April 1849. He was able to bring some key central and southwestern towns under the Haitian flag (notably San José de Las Matas and Azua), but quickly realized that he would not be able to take Santo Domingo. He retreated to Port-au-Prince, but not before issuing a public oath to return to take the East at some future date: "I swore to maintain the indivisibility of my jurisdiction. I will remain faithful to this oath."[119] Soulouque would remain faithful to this pledge, refusing to recognize Dominican independence for the entirety of his regime, treating the East as a wayward territory that was necessary to retake for the territorial integrity and independence of the island nation.[120] Soulouque's decision to turn back rather than risking more bloodshed in Santo Domingo—whether it was because he saw defeat as imminent, or to save face with his critics— earned him the respect and support of his army. When he returned to Port-au-Prince in May 1849, the idea of proclaiming an empire was already beginning to circulate among Soulouque's army and civilians in his government.

On August 26, 1849, the Haitian congress proclaimed Faustin Soulouque emperor of Haiti. Though it would be another three years before Soulouque's official coronation ceremony (*sacre*), the August 1849 celebration did include some celebratory pomp and even a crown, which had apparently been hastily constructed out of pasteboard.[121] One hundred and one cannon blasts marked the occasion: the senators entered the imperial palace, followed by Soulouque and his empress, then by members of the army. The president of the Senate, Laroche, crowned Soulouque and placed a gold cross upon his chest, to the cries of "Vive l'Empereur!" The procession then headed to the church for a ceremony, after which Soulouque mounted a horse and made a tour of the city, flanked by his army officers.

In his first address as Emperor Faustin I, he announced to his subjects: "Haitians! May the new era that opens before us [*la nouvelle ère qui s'ouvre pour nous*] be marked by the fullest uniting of hearts; may it calm passions, if there still exist any between us, and let us all join hands in reconciliation upon the sacred altar of the country [*l'autel sacré de la patrie*]."[122] The language of this proclamation is worth exploring here in some detail. He undoubtedly evokes earlier republican calls to Haitian *concorde*, and especially Ignace Nau's hopeful call for a new "ère d'harmonie," which Soulouque proclaims to inaugurate.[123] Indeed, the spirit of Nau's *indigéniste* poem—the populism, the veneration of peasant practices, and the valorization of Dessalines's memory—undergirds Soulouque's imperial project. But there is also a gesture back to Dessalines's original proclamation of Haitian independence and the threat of the "tepid heart" (*cœur tiède*) to the oath of national unity. Soulouque sought to impose the unity that Dessalines had maintained as leader of the Armée Indigène, and later through his empire as the paternal leader of his Haitian progeny, but with one difference. As we shall see in the next chapter, Soulouque had learned from Dessalines's mistakes. Where the first Haitian emperor had failed to contain his republican opponents, who ultimately orchestrated his downfall, Soulouque would make no such mistake: under his empire, the republic would live in exile.

5

The Second Empire of Haiti and the Exiled Republic

No one would have expected to find in this "illiterate" emperor a patron of the arts.
—Michel Philippe Lerebours, *Haïti et ses peintres* (1989)

Rereading events in France through the quizzing glass of Haiti is to clarify the reciprocal dependencies, the uncanny resemblances that no ideology of difference can remove. Who are the *true* cannibals? Who is "aping" whom?
—Colin Dayan, *Haiti, History, and the Gods* (1995)

In his masterful two-hundred-year study of Haitian painting, Michel Lerebours argues that the misconception of Emperor Faustin Soulouque's regime has led many historians and scholars—foreign and Haitian alike—to neglect the major role that art served in the empire: "Faustin Soulouque went down in history as a symbol of 'ignorance and cruelty.'"[1] Lerebours maintains that no other Haitian leader was as engaged and interested in artistic production. Soulouque accorded noble titles to his official painters—for example, Colbert Lochard and Bernadotte Ulysse—and also sought to democratize the fine arts through a new law on public education that vastly expanded the national education curriculum.[2] The law called for the creation of new educational institutions, including an *école normale* for teacher training, farm schools, rural schools, a school of *arts et métiers*, an Académie impériale de peinture, an Ecole impériale de médecine, a Maison centrale, and Collèges impériaux, among others.[3] Forty-three new primary schools were built during Soulouque's regime and the government imposed strict punishments on families that did not send their children to school.[4]

The assumptions about Soulouque that Lerebours works against—that an illiterate general could be a protector of the arts—is an important starting point for this chapter, as it captures the problem of "civilization" when it comes to Soulouque's regime. If, as we saw in previous chapters, the concept of literature became actively ideological through a "powerful and foreboding system of abstraction" in the eighteenth century, so too did the concept of "civilization." Indeed, the two are closely linked. As Raymond Williams argues, the earlier concept of "civilization" as "an achieved state, which would be contrasted with 'barbarism,'" transformed in the eighteenth century into "an achieved state of *development*, which applied historical process and progress. This was the new historical rationality of the Enlightenment, in fact combined with a self-referring celebration of an achieved condition of refinement and order."[5] This emergent concept of "civilization" was at work in Jean-Pierre Boyer's consolidation of legal codes, which his republic used "as both an index and a force of civilization."[6] Indeed, Boyer sought to apply this emergent notion of "civilization" in all aspects of his regime: the creation of an elaborate system of legal codification that excised the rural peasantry from participation in the "civil" state; the tight control over dissidents and critics that threatened *concorde*; and the sponsorship of mythologizing works of Haiti's republican history like Ardouin's *Géographie*.

Soulouque's return to empire not only represented a challenge to the emergent notion of "civilization" that Boyer had so ardently cultivated for the Atlantic world—he actively sought to critique it, to create space for alternative possibilities. That is, Soulouque's empire was itself a response to Boyerism and the exclusionary and elitist notion of citizenship, civility, and "civilization" in accordance with the dominant Western norms that the republican president had imposed in Haiti. Soulouque shaped a populist, more capacious sense of Haitian identity that transcended the narrow manifestations of nationhood and citizenship that had preceded his empire, thereby challenging the dominant notion of "civilization" that was operational in the Atlantic world. As we shall see in this chapter, Soulouque's return to empire posed a problem for his political opponents—republicans in exile—who still sought to perform Haiti's "civilization" according to the ever-evolving terms of the concept in the white, Western world. It also poses a challenge for our own scholarly (mis)understandings of Haiti and the arc of Haitian history, wedded as it is to the myth of the Haitian Republic. Soulouque's empire troubles the narrative of liberal republicanism and the progress of "civilization," and so it is treated as an aberrant event, a regression or regrettable blip in the march of progress.

In this chapter, I analyze two concepts of "civilization"—the Western, dominant notion and its critique—at work and in tension between imperial Haiti and the republic-in-exile. Among exiled republicans, we see a refined, nonviolent notion of "civilization" and "culture" that sought to cultivate and rehabilitate Haiti's image in France. In imperial Haiti, on the other hand, we see Soulouque mounting a challenge to the exclusionary, racialized notion of "civilization" itself through an active cultivation of popular religion and culture. Soulouque's patronage of artistic production, coupled with an emphasis on the visual symbolism of power, attests to the central role that visual culture played in his regime. First, I explore the role of visual and popular culture in Soulouque's empire as part of the Dessalinean heritage of citation, iteration, and critique of the concept of Western civilization or "modernity." Next, I consider the parallel—but opposite—effort among exiled republicans to allegorize and tell the story of the founding of the Haitian Republic precisely according to the dominant norm of Western civilization, establishing Haiti's parentage with the French Revolution and the liberal Enlightenment values of 1789. As we shall see, the form of the Haitian state and the heritage of 1804 were still highly contested well into the nineteenth century.

Trolling Napoléon

It is absolutely mistakenly said that he was nothing but a servile and useless copy of the empire of Napoléon I.
—Louis Joseph Janvier, *Les constitutions d'Haïti* (1886)

The assumption that Soulouque's regime was a medieval dark age is a pervasive one: studies of Haiti's nineteenth century give Soulouque's empire remarkably short shrift, often dedicating only a few pages to a crucial decade in Haiti's political and social history.[7] To date there is no historical monograph dedicated to studying Haiti's second empire; indeed, we might even say that there is a "black legend" that surrounds the history and legacy of Soulouque's rule, one that is not too dissimilar from the memory (or forgetting) of Napoléon III in France. I argue that this oversight is traceable, at least in part, to the potent myth of Haitian republicanism, discussed at length in the previous chapter. Soulouque was not a bloodthirsty tyrant, no more so than any nineteenth-century Haitian leader (or Atlantic world leader, for that matter), and the ten years of his rule were not akin to a regressive dark age. The Soulouque years were, however, an embrace of a less outwardly focused, more populist notion of Haitian culture that embraced oral tradition, visual culture, and popular religious practices. That is, if Boyerism was interested in portraying an image of "civilized" Haiti to the outside Atlantic world, at the expense of peasant rights, Soulouque was most interested in engaging Haiti's popular classes and addressing at least some of their demands—despite what it might look like to the outside world. This is particularly true of Vodou, which was practiced publicly and widely during the empire.[8] As Kate Ramsey's research has shown, Haitian oral tradition has a positive memory of Soulouque's empire "for its open association with popular religious practice and organization."[9] Indeed, Soulouque's regime embraced the public practice of cultural elements associated with Vodou and officially sanctioned the public expressions of dance, music, and drumming, by "observing and honoring a distinction" in the actual, popular practice of Vodou that the previous laws did not allow for.[10] Soulouque's treatment of Vodou is just one example of the empire's complex and nuanced understanding of popular Haitian cultural practices. We see in Soulouque's empire, then, a reactivation and a continuation of previous efforts to create space for a more capacious, popular conception of identity and cultural expression that spoke to the diverse class, race, and religious lived experience of all of Haiti's inhabitants.

Beyond popular religion, Soulouque also privileged other popular, collective practices: artistic production and the public performance of song, poetry, and speeches to commemorate events and celebrations. Lerebours has noted a robust practice of landscape, portraiture, political-historical themes, and especially, religious painting. He describes the ceremonial inauguration and benediction of numerous ex-voto paintings patronized by the Impératrice Adélina and other notable women and men in the court.[11] In order to connect with the widest swath of

Haitian society, Soulouque travelled frequently around the country, inaugurating statues, presiding over ceremonies, commemorations, and holidays, and giving speeches throughout the northern departments and the southern peninsula addressed to a diverse cross-section of Haitian society. A speech that Soulouque made in Gonaïves, for example, addressed soldiers and rural peasants, while in Jacmel he addressed an assembly of local schoolchildren. Indeed, Soulouque's performance of power and nationhood was constructed around the rhythm of celebrations and commemorations and key historical events: from the Independence Day and Jean-Jacques Dessalines celebrations on January 1 and 2, to the agricultural festival in May, the fête Dieu in June, the fête de l'institution de l'Empire in September, and the funeral ceremonies to honor Dessalines in October. It is via these collective, oral, public performances that written texts came to serve a purpose in Soulouque's regime, mostly reproduced for print in the empire's official newspaper, *Le Moniteur haïtien*.

Indeed, *Le Moniteur* thrived under Soulouque. Though the famously illiterate general emphasized painting and visual culture as the privileged form of Haitian cultural production more than any other Haitian head of state—a choice that he thought befitting of a primarily oral, Kreyòl-speaking, peasant-based nation—it was not as if writing stopped altogether in the empire. *Le Moniteur* as well as the commercial trade journal the *Feuille du commerce* appeared regularly during Soulouque's regime. The eminent historian Thomas Madiou served as the managing director and editor of *Le Moniteur* during the empire, and was named "chevalier de l'ordre imperial de la legion d'honneur" and later "Rédacteur des Actes Officiels du Gouvernement," and "Notaire du Gouvernement."[12] *Le Moniteur* is a key resource for understanding Soulouque's empire: it published all parliamentary debates and legal proclamations, but also included accounts of public ceremonies and celebrations, and reproductions of commemorative speeches and sung poems, hearkening back to the uses of poetry under Dessalines and Christophe and away from the liberal republican notion of the autonomous author.

The official paper also reproduced speeches, songs, and poems from residents—both men and women—throughout the empire from various social groups. We see poems from well-known, high-ranking figures in his government, such as Dalgé Philippe, Brisson Ainé,

Jean-Baptiste Romane, and even a baroness, a certain Almonor de Gorgues, composed a sung poem, "Hymne à la famille impériale," for the patronal fête of the emperor.[13] *Le Moniteur* also included a more popular component, incorporating a wider swath of historical figures and events, as well a more diverse, representative cross-section of Haitian social sectors and geographic groups than any previous publication to date. There were, for example, poems from teachers and school directors from cities throughout Haiti, highlighting the respect for public education and educators in the empire. *Le Moniteur* also published other texts in serial, many of which had been published in other newspapers in France, such as excerpts of Alexandre Dumas *père*'s *Mes mémoires* (1852), undoubtedly for the information it provided on the life of his father, the great black general Thomas-Alexandre Davy de la Pailleterie, native of colonial Saint-Domingue, and a translation of Harriet Beecher Stowe's antislavery novel, *Uncle Tom's Cabin* (1852).[14]

As many scholars have noted, the publication of *Uncle Tom's Cabin* was a literary event in the mid-nineteenth-century Atlantic world.[15] In the case of Haiti, it captivated both sides of the imperial-republican divide: it was lauded by Soulouque (who is said to have greatly appreciated it when it was read to him) and by Haitian republicans in exile, many of whom dedicated their works to "Madame, Mistress Harriet Beecher Stowe, auteur du roman philosophique."[16] Mary Grace Albanese's recent research on the Atlantic life of Stowe's novel suggests that these transatlantic uses of the novel reveal "a number of antinomies in Haitian nationalist appropriations of Stowe."[17] Indeed, it is precisely the contested notions of Haitian "civilization" and Haiti's role in the mid-century Atlantic world that are at play in the imperial and republican uses of Stowe. Haiti's diverse political and ideological landscape shared a common commitment to the antislavery cause—from the earliest moments of the revolution, through the civil war, and beyond. That is, both a supporter of the imperial regime and a liberal republican exile could celebrate Stowe's abolitionist work, and celebrate Haiti as the radical, successful antislavery state in the Americas. And both sides could also still vehemently disagree about what political shape that post-independence antislavery state should take, well into the mid-nineteenth century.

Figure 5.1. Quillenbois and Théo-Edo, *Fauxteint 1er, empereur d'Haïti, et son auguste famille*, in *Le Caricaturiste*, October 21, 1849. Courtesy of the Bibliothèque nationale de France.

In sum, Soulouque's empire, though its popular cultural practices challenged the dominant Western notion of "civilization," was not a dark age devoid of artistic or cultural production. Such a revision puts into even starker relief the silence surrounding his empire within Haitian historiography. Indeed, Haitian history's silencing of Soulouque becomes all the more remarkable when we consider that he is one of the better-known—or at least the most ridiculed—nineteenth-century Haitian leaders *outside* Haiti. His simian, cartoon likeness was printed and reprinted in the French and Atlantic press,[18] such as the one reproduced in figure 5.1, by the French caricaturist and *légitimiste* Quillenbois (Charles-Marie de Sarcus) and the engraver Théo-Edo.

While most scholars have interpreted these 1850s caricatures of Soulouque as a convenient way for European satirists to criticize Napoléon III and the Second Empire, there is something rather more complicated going on here, at least in the example of the Quillenbois caricature. First, the date should give us pause: Louis Napoléon Bonaparte had been elected president of France's Second Republic on December 20, 1848—a bitterly ironic end to the wave of democratic transformations ushered in by the revolution in France, and especially to France's first democratic presidential election. Bonaparte would not stage his coup d'état until December 1851 and did not officially become Emperor Napoléon III until a year later, on December 2, 1852.[19] In addition to a *légitimiste* critique of Bonaparte, we must also read Quillenbois's caricature as a direct response to news of Soulouque's elevation to emperor on April 26, 1849 (see chapter 4). In this sense, it is also a *légitimiste* critique of republicanism, especially the Haitian republicanism that Boyer had so vigilantly promoted to the Atlantic world, which Quillenbois saw come to a fitting end in what he depicted as Soulouque's ridiculous empire.[20] Quillenbois's satire turns on Soulouque's choice of Napoleonic finery: he makes him ridiculous by draping him in the robes of France's first emperor—replete with the imperial hand of justice, starkly colored black in the focal point of Quillenbois's caricature. The emperor's bare leg, prominently uncovered above the knee, mimics Napoléon's famous pose and renders it savage and ridiculous. The Empress Adélina is grotesque, almost unrecognizable as a female figure, save for her ill-fitting, too-short empire-waist dress that reveals her bare feet, the square, low neck and puffed sleeve—an exact replica of the Empress Joséphine's coronation gown. Indeed, the caricature's title, *Fauxteint* (*faux teint*, or fake complexion—a play on the emperor's forename, Faustin), further conveys this racist charge of mimicry: Soulouque is draping himself in Western culture's finery, playing white and adopting a political form that was not made for black Africans.

The timing of Quillenbois's caricatural depiction of Soulouque-as-black-Bonaparte indicates that, despite the historiographic silences around his regime, news of Soulouque's elevation to emperor on April 26, 1849, was widely publicized in the Atlantic world. But Quillenbois's 1849 caricature also seems to anticipate, with supernatural prescience, Soulouque's April 11, 1852, imperial coronation ceremony in which he and his wife, Empress Adélina, adorned themselves in exact replicas of Bonaparte and Josephine's coronation robes. The timing of Quillenbois's caricature is all the more surprising when we consider that there is no evidence suggesting that Soulouque was already planning to stage a rep-

Figure 5.2. Dridier, *(Cristoforo) Enrico I. Re de Hayti* (1811). In *Prints, Drawings and Watercolors from the Anne S. K. Brown Military Collection*, Brown Digital Repository, Brown University Library, https://repository.library.brown.edu/.

lication of Napoléon I's coronation ceremony in 1849. Was Quillenbois an oracle capable of precognition? Of course not. Rather, I suggest that we situate Soulouque's elaborate performance of Napoleonic imperial statehood in 1852 precisely in dialogue with and in *refutation of* Quillenbois's caricature and those like it. Touched off by Louis Napoléon's election as president of the Second Republic in 1848, scores of caricatures of Soulouque-as-black-Bonaparte circulated in France and the Atlantic world.[21] It was the circulation of denigrating, Western images of Haitian figures, dating back to the earliest days of Haitian independence, that prompted Soulouque's decision to stage, photograph, and disseminate an elaborate re-creation of Napoléon I's imperial imagery in 1852.

Quillenbois's depiction of a black Bonaparte begins to look less prescient if we consider the 1811 portrait engraving of Henry Christophe reproduced in figure 5.2. The portrait, by the Italian engraver (*incisore*) Torchiana after a sketch by the designer (*disegnatore*) Dridier, is a little-studied depiction of Christophe.[22] It is curious for many reasons: first, and most important, it depicts Christophe bedecked in Napoléon I's coronation regalia: the saber on his left side, the neck kerchief, gold embroidered robe, white slip, boots, golden laurel leaf crown, even the pose, with one foot forward, are virtually synonymous. And yet, this is entirely erroneous: Christophe hated the French, and Napoléon even more, and would never have dressed in Napoleonic regalia. He is known to have dressed deliberately in the British royal style, a Haitian version of King George III, and had purchased British-style (and English-made) regalia for his ceremonial attire.[23] The 1811 date is telling: news of Christophe's coronation circulated throughout Europe with various degrees of exaggeration and misinformation. He was denigrated as a black emperor in some accounts, and a model coin of his likeness crowned with a laurel wreath was produced in England.[24] Still, the engraving does not strike me as a particularly negative representation of Christophe: his features are not caricatural or disproportionate, and the composition of the portrait itself resembles very closely one that the designer Bosio created of George III, also produced by Torchiana. Both engravings appear in different volumes of the work *Serie di vite e ritratti de famosi personaggi, degli ultimi tempi* (Series of lives and portraits of famous characters of recent times), which included portraits of Abbé Raynal, George Washington, Tippoo Saib (Tipu Sultan), Louis Philippe d'Orléans, Charlotte

Corday, and Voltaire, among many others, each accompanied by two-page narratives of their life and accomplishments.[25]

The engraving thus participates in what Tabitha McIntosh and Grégory Pierrot describe as the "imagined faces of Henry Christophe . . . extensively circulating and circulated throughout the Atlantic world."[26] The engraving did not draw upon Christophe's actual likeness, nor did it even seek necessarily to achieve it. Rather, in the spirit of neoclassical portraiture, it activated a diverse iconography in order to evoke the subject by marrying the background, dress, and paraphernalia (books, instruments, nature, or in the case of Christophe, his subjects) with the written biography that accompanied it. Dridier clearly designed his portrait using the ubiquitous image of Napoléon I in his imperial regalia painted by Robert Lefevre. Yet there is another curious intertext that we might consider: the engraving of Dessalines's coronation, published in Louis Dubroca's 1806 biography of Dessalines, *Vida de J. J. Dessalines* (figure 5.3).[27] A notoriously racist, negative account of Dessalines's life and rule as emperor of Haiti, the biography depicts Dessalines as naturally ferocious and barbarous, owing to his African blood. The crowd of faces gathered at the balcony in the Dridier 1811 engraving of Christophe resembles the crowd of black subjects gathered at the emperor Dessalines's feet in this 1806 engraving. As Deborah Jenson notes, it is hard to say whether the Dubroca text and images influenced other contemporaneous depictions of Dessalines, though the text was "parroted in media sources in multiple locations in the Euro-American world."[28] While there may or may not be a direct connection between these two portraits of Haiti's monarchs, it is clear that they each activate the same pictorial trope of despotism: the crowd of subjects gathered in the foreground. It is worth noting that of the roughly three hundred portraits of famous figures from throughout the world that appear in *Serie di vite e ritratti*, the only other portrait that employs a similar crowd of human subjects is that of Hyder Ali, sultan and reputed "despot" of Mysore.

Quillenbois draws upon this pictorial trope of despotism in his caricature of Soulouque. Where Dessalines and Christophe were despots, they were effective despots: the human subjects who crowd around them are uniform and seemingly under the strict control of the monarch. Quillenbois's caricature, on the other hand, presents the monarch on the same visual plane as his ridiculous court, who surround him

Figure 5.3. Manuel López López, *Coronación de Juan Santiago Desalines primer emperador de Hayti* (1806). Courtesy of the John Carter Brown Library.

in a chaotic, undisciplined jumble. Meanwhile, Soulouque's subjects appear to have abandoned the ceremony altogether. They do not bear witness to the pomp of Soulouque's coronation, reverently posed in the foreground looking up at their sovereign. Instead, they are off in the background, participating in an entirely different ceremony: Vodou. They are clearly in movement, gesticulating wildly and dancing in a circle around what is unmistakably a *poto mitan*: the central pillar (literally and figuratively) of a Vodou temple around which ceremonies take place. The two figures depicted on the pole are Haitian spirits, or *lwa*, who enter via the *poto mitan*, by descending it into the temple. Quillenbois's depiction of this intimate detail of the Vodou ceremony evinces a deep knowledge of Haitian popular religion. It is worth noting that Quillenbois's caricatural depiction precedes the series of salacious articles depicting Vodou under Soulouque that Gustave d'Alaux (Maxime Raybaud) penned in 1850–1851 for the *Revue des deux mondes*. Whatever his source, Quillenbois's caricature of Soulouque leaves little ambiguity to his meaning and motive: he invokes a racist trope of mimicry that denies Haitians' capacity for self-rule, no matter what their government form.

Soulouque responded to the satirical, racialist representations of his regime in true Dessalinean fashion: he refuted them. But instead of the written, published texts that denigrated Haiti, Soulouque focused on the images: the Quillenbois caricature and the scores of others like it. He utilized the Dessalinean strategy of performance, iteration, and ultimately, delegitimization of Western representations of Haiti that circulated in the Atlantic world. More specifically, he adopted and adapted the caricatural presentations of his rule by deliberately, spectacularly fashioning his imperial power in relation to Napoléon I. As Louis Joseph Janvier and Colin Dayan maintain (cited in the epigraphs above), the charges of ignorance and mimicry against Soulouque's creation of the second Haitian empire are simplistic at best. Indeed, we must look to the conditions that produced Soulouque's empire, "the reciprocal dependencies, the uncanny resemblances" that are implicated in France and Haiti's shared colonial *and* postcolonial history of royalism, republicanism, and imperial rule—on both sides of the Atlantic.[29] We see these resemblances clearly at work in Soulouque's April 11, 1852, coronation ceremony. The program for the ceremony, published in *Le Moniteur*, reveals the magnitude of the

Figure 5.4. *Faustin 1er, Emperor of Haiti*, in *Album impérial d'Haïti* (1852). Library of Congress Prints and Photographs Division.

affair. A huge tent was erected in the Champ de Mars to house the ceremony, which was planned out to the minute and according to the smallest detail, beginning at three o'clock in the morning.³⁰ Soulouque had also negotiated, unsuccessfully, with Pope Pius IX to sign a concordat with the Haitian empire and provide an archbishop for an official *sacre*.³¹ What do we make of the three-year delay between Soulouque's elevation to emperor and his official coronation ceremony? Certainly, some of it can be attributed to the elaborate planning: it was a massive spectacle of power and pomp. But it is equally likely that it was designed to coincide with Louis Napoléon's elevation to "prince-président" in order to preempt the proclamation of the second Bonapartist empire.

The lithograph in figure 5.4 depicts Soulouque posing in an exact replica of Napoléon I's imperial regalia—the scepter, hand of justice, and other symbolic ornaments, gilded bees and all, which he had ordered from Paris (and one for the Impératrice Adélina as well).³² This portrait comes from Soulouque's *Album impérial*, a lavish collection of lithographs that he commissioned as his official coronation book.³³ What is most striking is the new photographic technology that Soulouque harnessed in the visual representation of his imperial power: daguerreotype. He commissioned the New York–based photographer Hartmann to produce daguerreotypes of the ceremony, which various artists used as the basis for the lithographs that were then reproduced, bound, and mass-distributed. The effect is remarkable: the lithographs present the most lifelike, realistic portrait of a Haitian leader, his family, and his advisors that had ever been created. Most important, Soulouque controlled the mechanisms of its (re)production. It must have been an extremely powerful image to behold and disseminate, and one that Soulouque and his advisors had taken great pains to make possible.

To return to Colin Dayan's incisive question: who is "aping" whom? There is indeed something much more complicated than mimicry at play here: a complex internal and external performance of power in the visual culture of Soulouque's regime. It was not just the 1840s and 1850s caricatures of the Haitian emperor to which this daguerreotype-lithograph responded: it was an entire Western tradition of caricature and denigrating portraits of Haiti's revolutionary leaders that had been circulating in the Atlantic world since the earliest days of the Haitian Revolution. Carlo Célius sums up the stakes of nineteenth-century Haitian portraiture: "It was imperative for the new Dominguan and Haitian elite to achieve perfect mastery and absolute control over their own likeness."[34] Soulouque was finally able to respond resoundingly to this need with his cutting-edge *Album impérial*: a perfect mastery of and a perfect control over his own image—and his empire—that he could circulate throughout the Atlantic world.[35] There are clear connections between the rhetorical and representational strategies Soulouque employed to the earlier traditions of the Dessalinean sphere. What Dessalinean and Christophean writers did with Western discourses, adopting the colonial form to neutralize its power, Soulouque did with images—borrowing, adapting, and ultimately deconstructing their power. Here, technological mastery was key: much in the way that Dessalines and Christophe used print technology to perform self-mastery, order, and power in the Atlantic world, Soulouque used image technology.

In the specific context of the racist, denigrating caricatures of Soulouque that permeated the 1850s Atlantic press, Soulouque was claiming legitimacy in the medium of the image while at the same time besting the simplistic, mass-produced satirical press with a precise, high-tech daguerreotype. Soulouque was taking control of his own image and responding directly to Quillenbois's denigrating, caricatural depiction of his imperial power and, by association, the broader practice of racist characterizations of his regime. We might extend this analysis to the fraught concept of "civilization" itself that shaped the West's denigrating views of Haiti, and which Boyer had sought to cultivate through a repressive, elitist, color-blind republicanism. Soulouque's daguerreotype-lithograph presented a realistic portrait of a black emperor using the most recent technology in image production to challenge the notion that Haiti was "uncivilized" while refusing to accede to the ever-narrowing notion of the concept of Western civilization or "modernity."

What is more, we can read Soulouque's visual presentation of imperial power as a direct challenge to Louis Napoléon's rule in France. Indeed, for as much attention as scholars have given to France's caricaturing of the black Haitian emperor, little thought has been given to the possibility that Soulouque was preempting or even deliberately antagonizing Louis Napoléon, not yet Napoléon III, by evoking the heritage of Napoléon I. First, by framing his empire in a Napoleonic context, Soulouque is evoking the memory of Napoléon I's abject failure to retake the

Figure 5.5. Kehinde Wiley, *Ice T* (2005). Private collection, courtesy of the Rhona Hoffman Gallery.

colony in Saint-Domingue and thus, independent Haiti's superiority over the supposed military prowess of France's first emperor.[36] Second, we must remember that Soulouque was operating within a system of Haitian critique, established by Dessalinean precedent, in which citation and adaptation within the Atlantic sphere were shown to neutralize the power of colonial texts. Within the tradition of anticolonial textual production that preceded him, Souloque and his advisors were adept users of the print public sphere: they used spectacular visual performance and provocation to preempt and undermine France's would-be emperor. If Deborah Jenson has called Toussaint a "spin doctor," we might call Soulouque a "troll."[37] The elaborate coronation ceremony, the sumptuous collection of lithographs in the *Album impérial*, and the technological mastery communicated through the daguerreotypes, all placed within the frame of Napoléon I, amount to a complex act of Atlantic trolling. Soulouque framed his own power within the symbolism of Napoléon I in order to draw attention to Napoléon I's failure to retake Haiti, in an effort to antagonize and ultimately neutralize Louis Napoléon's power by preempting his claims to that heritage.

Understanding Soulouque's strategy of adapting and iterating Napoleonic symbolism to contest and delegitimize dominant notions of Western power and civilization sheds important light on the "black legend" that surrounds Soulouque's rule. It also adds crucial contextualization and precedent to a contemporary example of this practice in Kehinde Wiley's work. Wiley is renowned for his portrait work of black subjects and is best known for his official portrait of the former president Barack Obama that now hangs in the National Portrait Gallery. Wiley's 2005 portrait of the rapper Ice-T (figure 5.5), commissioned by the television network VH1 for its hip-hop hall-of-fame awards show, is near exact in its composition, light, and style to the 1806 portrait of Napoléon on his imperial throne, painted by the French neoclassicist Jean-Auguste-Dominique Ingres.[38] What differs, starkly, is the sitter himself and his contemporary dress, painted with an exactitude and a verisimilitude that create a tension between the neoclassical "original" and the familiar, contemporary sitter. The tension is a key piece of Wiley's style, and also of his message, which is more involved than a simple "remix" of Old World styles and contemporary black popular cultural figures, as his work is usually described. As André Carrington has recently argued, Wiley's work calls into question "the norms of racial, gendered, and class representation inherited from modernity."[39] This is most certainly true of Wiley's early work from the 2000–2005 period, which, in the context of my reading of Soulouque's complex use of citation and adaptation above, has its roots in the radical Haitian critique of "civilization" and Western modernity. That is, Wiley is not simply countering the absence of black subjects or sitters from the archive of Western portraiture. Through a practice of citation, iteration, and ultimately critique, his work challenges the dominant, white Western notion of "civilization" and "modernity" by calling into question the putative dominance of the terms of the debate—white, Europe, empire—in what we might call a profoundly Dessalinean critique.

(Re)Writing the Revolution in Exile, or Dessalines Disavowed

If Soulouque's focus on visual culture, popular religion, and public ceremony drew on the Dessalinean sphere, the liberal bourgeois sphere of Pétion and Boyer's republicanism continued in exile. Recall from the previous chapter that the uprisings in the 1840s had atomized Boyer's ideal of republican *concorde*. After Boyer's fall in 1843, southern republicans (and staunch Boyerists) such as Pierre Faubert, Emeric Bergeaud, and Beaubrun and Céligny Ardouin spent much of the 1840s shuttling back and forth from exile in Jamaica and Saint Thomas.[40] Ardouin returned briefly to politics in opposition to Rivière Hérard's liberal government: he supported Guerrier and Pierrot's regimes in the mid-1840s, and even served briefly as minister to France under Soulouque. This service ended abruptly when Soulouque clashed with Beaubrun's brother Céligny Ardouin (then serving as his interior minister) and had the younger Ardouin executed by firing squad.[41] All had their citizenship revoked after the April 1848 uprising in the South and spent the remainder of Soulouque's regime in exile: some in Saint Thomas, like Bergeaud, and others in Paris.

These exiled republicans engaged in a prolific production of texts during Soulouque's imperial reign. Importantly, this literature-in-exile was dedicated almost entirely to revisiting Haiti's revolutionary moment: the biographies and memoirs of its revolutionary heroes and the story of the Haitian Revolution aimed to situate it firmly within a liberal Enlightenment heritage. Joseph Saint-Rémy published *La vie de Toussaint-L'Ouverture* (1850) and *Pétion et Haïti* (1854) and wrote critical prefaces to Louis-Félix Boisrond Tonnerre's 1804 *Mémoires pour servir à l'histoire d'Haïti* (1851) and Toussaint's *Mémoires du général Toussaint-L'Ouverture écrits par lui-même* (1853); Pierre Faubert revisited the early moments of the Haitian Revolution by reprinting his 1841 play, *Ogé, ou Le préjugé de couleur* with an expanded historical introduction (1856); Beaubrun Ardouin published his eleven-volume *Etudes sur l'histoire d'Haïti* (1853–1860) and also edited and posthumously published Emeric Bergeaud's *Stella* (1859), an allegorical retelling of Haiti's revolution, to name only a few of the reworkings of the Haitian Revolution that flooded the Parisian scene in the 1850s.

Recent scholarly engagement with these 1850s writers has emphasized the importance of the "civilization" that they were performing within a European sphere.[42] Nevertheless, this scholarship only scratches the surface of the question of the *internal* strife, civil war, and political exile in the production of these various (re)writings of Haiti's revolution. I argue here for a reading of the exiled histories of the Haitian Revolution in the 1850s that considers the longer heritage of political-ideological divides that characterized the near-entirety of Haiti's post-independence statehood, and which contested the very meaning of liberty, independence, and civilization. The context of civil war, the global context of liberal revolutions of 1848 and their failures on both sides of the Atlantic, and the advent of Soulouque and Napoléon's empires seems crucial here to further probing exiled republicans' depictions of Haiti's revolutionary history. What was their goal, their politics? Who was their audience? What did it mean to rewrite the Haitian Revolution in exile, while an emperor reigned in Haiti?

Bergeaud, Ardouin, and the other exiled republicans allegorized and retold the story of the founding of the Haitian Republic in order to establish its fundamental parentage with the French Revolution and the liberal Enlightenment values of 1789. In fact, as I argue below, these exiled republican writers made the case that Haiti represented the purest instantiation of the ideals that had sparked the French Revolution—more so than France itself. This is not an outlandish claim: those Haitian republicans living in exile had seen many more years of republican government (even if nominal) than the French, who had seen their revolutionary First Republic cut short by Napoléon I, the Bourbon Restoration, and then another return to empire under Napoléon III. Nevertheless, Haitian republicans' claim of liberal revolutionary parentage required coming to terms with Dessalines's violent act of anticolonial vengeance: the 1804 massacre of the remaining French on the island.

The "Dessalines problem," as I'll call it, had become increasingly complicated for the Boyerist faction during the uprisings of the 1840s. Recall from the previous chapter that 1830s *indigéniste* writers had upended the long-standing Boyerist stance of disavowing Dessalines by calling for a more positive memory of Haiti's liberator and for a more capacious idea of Haiti's revolutionary history. Rivière Hérard acceded to the demands of a mobilized peasantry, signing a petition to accord a pension to Dessalines's widow. In January 1844, he honored Dessalines publicly during the official Independence Day celebrations—the first time ever under a republican leader.[43] Subsequent regimes each recognized the importance of paying homage to Dessalines's memory among the peasant and popular classes. In response to "unanimous public opinion," one of Pierrot's first acts as president was to proclaim that a national funeral service be celebrated in every commune to commemorate Dessalines, empereur d'Haïti.[44] Though his Boyerist successor, Riché, remained silent on the question of Dessalinean commemoration during his short term in office, Soulouque further formalized Dessalines's official state recognition by signing a law that declared January 2 the Fête de Jean-Jacques Dessalines, Empereur. The law required that the January 2 day be fêted with the same amount of pomp and celebration as the January 1 independence celebrations. It also required that five portraits of Dessalines holding the Acte de l'indépendance be commissioned and placed throughout the national palace.[45]

Recall that Dessalines's foundational act of Haitian independence was based in vengeance: the massacre of the remaining French *colons* on the island. His April 28, 1804, proclamation to the newly independent inhabitants of Haiti (the famous "I have avenged America" speech) called for unity among brothers, the creation of a singular whole, through a foundational act of vengeance. Dessalines proclaimed:

> Oui, nous avons rendu à ces vrais cannibales, guerre pour guerre, crimes pour crimes, outrages pour outrages. Oui j'ai sauvé mon pays, j'ai vengé l'Amérique. Mon orgueil et ma gloire sont dans l'aveu que j'en fais, à la face des mortels et des dieux. Qu'importe le jugement que prononceront sur moi les races contemporaines et futures? J'ai fait mon devoir, ma propre estime me reste; il me suffit.

> (Yes, we have retaliated against these true cannibals: war for war, crime for crime, indignity for indignity. Yes, I have saved my country, I have avenged America. My pride and my glory are in my confession of it, in the face of men and gods. What does the verdict that present and future

races [*races*] might deliver matter to me? I did my duty, my self-respect [*estime*] remains; that is enough for me.)[46]

As we saw in chapter 1, Dessalines revealed the violence of the French colonial system and enslavement by an act of retributive, justified violence: barbarians against colonial barbarity.[47] The French colonizers were "uncivilized" in their colonialism and their practice of chattel slavery, and in their violent attempts to regain control of the colony during the insurrection. Dessalines thus refused the eighteenth-century Enlightenment conception of "civilization," rooted as it was in the barbaric, inhumane institutions of colonialism and slavery. Yet in the post-1804 Atlantic world, it was precisely for Dessalines's critique of Enlightenment "civilization" in his act of anticolonial vengeance that he—and the Haitian state, and the Haitian people—were deemed uncivilized. This was a pressing problem for republicans, whose politics and statecraft were based in performing Haiti's accordance with, perhaps even radical perfection of, Enlightenment ideals. If, within Haiti, Dessalines finally received statues and celebrations as Haiti's liberator and emperor, outside Haiti it was a much more difficult balance to strike. How could exiled republicans celebrate Haiti's antiliberal emperor, the architect of Haiti's foundational act of anticolonial violence? The simple answer is: they didn't. Instead, they attempted to retell Haiti's revolutionary story. As Marlene Daut has argued, this group of 1850s writers sought to create "a non-violent (non-vengeful) 'civilization'" through histories and allegorical retellings of the Haitian Revolution.[48] Taken together, the Haitian republicans writing in exile—Faubert, Saint-Rémy, Bergeaud, and Ardouin—engaged in a project of rescripting the heritage of the Haitian Revolution within a paradigm of Enlightenment republicanism and "civilization." In many ways, we might consider it a coordinated campaign in which the terms, the ideas, the symbols, and the heritage of Haiti's revolution were rescripted, reappropriated, and disavowed. They defined their ideas of republican virtue against Dessalinean violence, their commitment to "civilization" against Dessalinean vengeance.

The question of Dessalines's violence and vengeance in the Haitian Revolution is central to Pierre Faubert's didactic play, *Ogé, ou Le préjugé de couleur* (1841, 1856), which restages the failed 1790 uprising against colonial administrators in Saint-Domingue led by Vincent Ogé and

Jean-Baptiste Chavannes.[49] Faubert had originally conceived of the work in 1841 as a performance—based, no doubt, in the Aristotelian tragic principle of catharsis—for the students at Port-au-Prince's Lycée national, where Faubert was director. Faubert's choice to republish a previous work with an expanded historical preface while in exile in Paris is fairly standard among his fellow Haitian writers in exile; many of the works they published were reprints or publications of other writers' memoirs. Daut offers a compelling reading of the play as Faubert's response to US and European accusations of Haitian color prejudice, and as a call for Haiti to fulfill its duty as a "beacon" in the abolitionist Atlantic.[50] When placed within the longer heritage of 1804/1806 and Haiti's civil war, however, the play also reads as a stark repudiation of Dessalines's legacy: his foundational act of vengeance and creation of the Empire of Haiti.

In Ogé and Chavanne's 1790 uprising, Faubert finds a powerful allegory for rewriting 1804 and Dessalines's decision to "venger l'Amérique" by ordering the massacre of the remaining French soldiers and planters in Haiti. Via the main character, Alfred (a fictional character who joins the insurrection led by Ogé), Faubert offers a passionate speech in the didactic spirit of his play. The scene takes place as Ogé, Chavannes, and other army officers are discussing the fate of the French prisoners they have captured. While Chavannes and other officers suggest killing them by firing squad, building into a cacophony of voices chanting "Bravo! la Mort! la Mort!," Alfred passionately, convincingly, dissents:

> Qu'une généreuse pitié envers un ennemi vaincu ne peut que profiter à une noble cause. Oui, prouvons notre énergie dans les combats, mais soyons humains après la victoire: c'est ce qui caractérise, en général, les peuples civilisés, à moins qu'ils ne soient dans des époques de crise où ils ne méritent pas toujours d'être pris pour modèles. Or, nos amis d'Europe pensent que notre race est aussi susceptible de civilisation qu'aucune autre: montrons-leur, dès notre début, qu'ils ne se trompent pas. . . . Messieurs, ce sont les fondements d'une société nouvelle que nous jetons en ce moment: eh bien, tâchons de lui donner pour base la plus sociale de toutes les vertus, l'humanité. . . . Et pour la misérable satisfaction de punir quelques hommes cruels, nous priverions nos frères et nos enfants l'héritage d'une telle vertu! Non, mes amis; nous avons autre chose à faire

qu'à exercer des vengeances: il faut réhabiliter toute une race d'hommes injustement déchue de l'estime du monde.

(Gracious mercy for a defeated enemy can but benefit a noble cause. Yes, we shall prove our vigor in battle, but let us be humane after we have won: this is what, in general, distinguishes civilized peoples, unless they are in a time of crisis, in which case they are not always worthy models. For our friends in Europe believe that our race is as capable of civilization as any other: let's show them, from our beginning, that they are not mistaken. . . . Gentlemen, we are at present laying the foundations for a new society: well, let us endeavor to make its base the most social of all virtues, humanity. . . . And for the paltry satisfaction of punishing a few cruel men, we would deprive our brothers and our children of the legacy of such a virtue! No, my friends; we have more important things to do than mete out vengeance: we must rehabilitate an entire race [race] of men unjustly fallen from the world's respect [estime].)[51]

How can we read Alfred's didactic speech and not hear a rescripting of Dessalines's April 1804 proclamation? Dessalines's proclamation states forthrightly, performatively, that he is unconcerned with how the outside world will judge his act of vengeance. Conversely, Alfred's speech is concerned precisely with the world's judgment of Haiti: in the historical moment of the revolutionary uprising, and in the contemporary Atlantic world. Placing these two passages next to one another reveals a fundamental distinction between the legacies of Dessalinean and republican thought in Haiti: one, concerned chiefly with its internal dynamics and a refusal to accede to the Western notion of "civilization," the other, preoccupied with the face Haiti showed to the outside world and its standing therein. Indeed, in its hypothetical return to the moment of possibility before 1804, Alfred's speech reminds the future leaders of Haiti's revolution that their choices will have consequences for post-independence society and the new nation's standing in the world.[52] Their revolutionary acts will serve as the metaphorical foundation upon which the free, independent society is built ("ce sont les fondements d'une société nouvelle que nous jetons en ce moment"). Alfred warns the revolutionary leaders that by choosing vengeance for short-term satisfaction or petty score-settling, they will rob future society of a solid foundation. The metaphor of the national foundation that Faubert evokes here is an important one that gets continually conjured and repurposed in Haitian thought. Faubert was not the first to make it; it goes all the way back to Dessalinean independence writing, which cast the 1805 constitution as securing Haitian rights on "solid ground" (*assied vos droits sur des bases invariables*).⁵³ In evoking this language, Faubert points to its failure: violence was not expiatory, as Dessalines said it was, or at least, it did not make for a solid foundation upon which to build a nation and a people.

Moreover, I read the final statement, "il faut réhabiliter toute une race d'hommes injustement déchue de l'estime du monde," as again referring us back to Dessalines's April 28 proclamation of vengeance. To be sure, with Alfred's speech Faubert was activating the protocols of abolitionist discourse and Haiti's Enlightenment universalism, as Daut argues: it was Haiti's duty to rehabilitate an entire race of men who had been stripped of their humanity in slavery. But Faubert was also engaging Dessalines's legacy in contemporary (1840s and later 1850s) Haitian society. This makes sense in the 1841 context in which Faubert first produced the play: as we saw in the previous chapter, the 1830s had seen a transformation in intellectual opinion on Dessalines and the rehabilitation of his memory among the *indigénistes*, especially Ignace Nau. Faubert appeared to be putting down a definitive, if oblique, assessment of what he thought of Dessalines's legacy. Dessalines was not humane after Haitian victory, and thus an entire race was deemed uncivilized in the wider Atlantic world. Dessalines's act of anticolonial vengeance was the cause of Haiti's "fall" from "civilization." Faubert thus casts it as the duty of Haiti's postcolonial republicans to rehabilitate an entire people—Haitians—who had been unjustly deprived of the world's respect (or, translated somewhat more liberally: who had fallen from the world's esteem) because of the violent acts committed by Haiti's revolutionary forefathers. Faubert's comment on Haiti's fall from the world's "esteem" in its 1856 reprint in Paris surely doubled as a commentary on Soulouque's empire: an unfortunate but foreseeable outcome of the politics of vengeance that Albert warns against in the play.

If Faubert allegorized his critique of Dessalines's legacy and the heritage of Dessalinean vengeance, Joseph Saint-Rémy was much more forthright in his preface to Boisrond Tonnerre's *Mémoires pour servir à l'histoire d'Haïti*, which he published in Paris in 1851.⁵⁴ In order to recast—and disavow—Haiti's violent anticolonialism and especially Dessalines's foundational act of vengeance, Saint-Rémy's preface discredits the handful of political actors who perpetrated these violent, vengeful acts, Boisrond Tonnerre chief among them. According to Saint-Rémy, Dessalines was struck by the ingenuity and violence of Boisrond Tonnerre's style, which aligned with Dessalines's own violent tendencies: his "horrible words corresponded perfectly to the feelings of savage vengeance that filled his heart."[55] Saint-Rémy depicts Boisrond Tonnerre as bloodthirsty, vicious, and one of the main architects of the 1804 massacres of the French: "he loved blood and gave his master a taste for this infernal brew [*breuvage infernal*]."[56] Saint-Rémy's spectacular language places the responsibility for the revolution's violent anticolonialism in the hands of a few deranged actors. By disavowing the 1804 massacres and delegitimizing Dessalines's political strategy, Saint-Rémy made way for more "enlightened," "civilized" narratives of Haiti's revolutionary act and its post-independence future.

Civilizing the Haitian Revolution in Emeric Bergeaud's *Stella*

Republicans in exile attempted to come to terms with the problem of violence and vengeance for Haiti's "civilization" by rewriting the revolution through allegory.[57] Emeric Bergeaud recasts the story of the Haitian Revolution through allegory in Haiti's first novel, *Stella*.[58] Much in the way that the other 1850s writers-in-exile sought to disavow the violence of the foundational acts of Haitian independence, Bergeaud sought to replace the Dessalinean act of anticolonial vengeance with the republican virtues of unity, fraternity, and above all, *liberté*. By assigning allegorical characters and their mythical and supernatural experiences to the historical factions in Haiti's civil war, Bergeaud is able to transcend the realities of Dessalinean vengeance in order to showcase the main tenets of liberal republicanism upon which the Haitian Republic was founded. He does so by retelling the main events of the Haitian Revolution—the first slave uprisings, the war against the French, and civil war between Toussaint and Rigaud and later Dessalines-Christophe and Pétion—as the extended, allegorized fight between the novel's fictional brothers, Romulus and Rémus, which I will summarize briefly below.

The story is set in colonial Saint-Domingue, in the humble slave quarters (*ajoupa*) of the brothers and their mother, Marie l'Africaine, built in the shadow of the master's house (the Colon). We learn in the story that Marie's father was the chief of a powerful tribe and that her mother was descended from an African king.[59] She was captured and sold into slavery by a rival tribe who had declared war on her father. Romulus, the elder brother, is described as the color of ebony; he was conceived in Africa and born during the tragic placelessness of the Middle Passage, an origin that makes him the idealized, collective stand-in for the great generals of the Haitian Revolution: Louverture, Dessalines, and Christophe. Romulus's younger brother, Rémus, is the color of mahogany and was born on the island as a result of the Colon's rape of Marie, and serves as a stand-in for André Rigaud and later Alexandre Pétion. At the start of the novel, Marie is beaten to death by the Colon, orphaning the brothers and setting into motion their eventual uprising against their master. The brothers burn down the Colon's house and escape to the mountains as maroons, setting up a camp from which they launch successful attacks against the Colon and his ilk (these events stand in for the historical events of the Bois Caïman ceremony and the burning of plantations in the North). The brothers are aided in their fight by the titular character of the novel, the allegorical Stella, or "star," a guiding light that is the near-universal symbol of liberty in the nineteenth-century Atlantic world.[60] The character Stella is liberty incarnate: an angel, a messenger from God, a celestial spirit who takes the form of a young woman. Her apparition in the novel is indeed otherworldly: she emerges out of the flames of the Colon's home after Romulus and Rémus set fire to it to exact revenge for their mother's death. Though she keeps her true identity a secret from the brothers—the story culminates with her triumphant revelation as the corporeal incarnation of *liberté*—Bergeaud makes it clear to the reader that this young woman belongs in the realm of the supernatural, the marvelous.

I am most interested here in the historical events that Bergeaud's novel allegorizes in his story of the revolution that allows him to transform vengeance and violence into unity and *fraternité*. First, Bergeaud references the mythic founding of Rome by naming his main characters after the twin brothers Romulus and Rémus. Bergeaud is not the first to connect Haiti to this Roman mythology. In his 1848 *Histoire d'Haïti*,

Thomas Madiou likened Dessalines to Romulus as the founder whom the Haitian people eventually overthrew: "the Romans freed themselves of Romulus because he became a tyrant, but they still put him in the heavens [*le placèrent au ciel*]."[61] Here, Madiou seemingly acknowledges Dessalines's status as a *lwa* in the Vodou pantheon.[62] Bergeaud's allegory took a different tack than Madiou, using it to emphasize—and perform—the foundation of the Haitian Republic.[63] Through its narration of the two brothers' infighting, the novel thus allegorizes the revolutionary factions who competed to define liberty in post-independence statehood, coming down resolutely on the side of the republicans. Bergeaud changes the ending of the Roman myth: instead of Romulus killing Rémus, the two brothers come together in peace to found the republic together. This is a particularly interesting reversal of the foundation of the Haitian Republic, given that it was founded in Pétion's assassination of Dessalines in 1806—that is, of Rémus killing Romulus.

We see a similar departure from the history in Bergeaud's allegory of the civil war between Dessalineans and republicans. In Bergeaud's allegory, Romulus (standing in for Dessalineans) is duped by the Colon into carrying out terrible acts and initiating a civil war against his brother Rémus (standing in for republicans). Rather than fighting back, however, Rémus allows himself to be vanquished for the future good of the nation. Bergeaud acknowledges to his reader that Rémus's actions seem to defy reason and reveals to the reader a hidden truth of Haiti's "history": the mystical and spiritual source of Rémus's "loss" in the civil war against Romulus. Squarely in the domain of the fictive and the marvelous, then, Bergeaud depicts a chance meeting between Rémus and an old man in the forest. The man asks Rémus to cease all activity in the civil war, to allow himself to be vanquished and accept humiliation (here, echoing Faubert's warning against the desire for vengeance in *Ogé*). He acknowledges Rémus's quest for glory in battle and commends his courage, but tells him that there is a more important, noble role for Rémus to play in the war ("young man, . . . you are necessary to the completion of my plan").[64] Though the identity of this mysterious giant remains unknown to Rémus, Bergeaud reveals his identity to the reader as the "spirit of the nation" (*génie de la patrie*), another mythic force at work in the foundation of the Haitian Republic.

Meanwhile, without the "light" of Stella's liberty or the counsel of his brother, Romulus is "doubly blind" and decides to establish an authoritarian government. Bergeaud attributes this choice to Romulus's "mauvais génie"—a sure contrast to the mystical "génie de la patrie" who had counseled Rémus to allow himself to be vanquished for the greater good of the nation. When the French come to retake the island, Romulus realizes his error and pleads with Rémus to help him protect against the reestablishment of colonial rule. Rémus accepts the penitent Romulus and they kneel together on the tomb of their mother and pledge an oath of reconciliation—an oath that precedes the final battles in the war for independence: "unity is strength!" (*l'union, c'est la force!*).[65] Together with Stella, the brothers vanquish the French and proclaim Haitian independence, each taking turns reading from the Acte de l'indépendance. This is, of course, not what actually happened: the southern faction joined Dessalines's Armée Indigène with the oath "Liberté ou la mort," and it was Dessalines alone who proclaimed independence. Bergeaud's allegorical telling of these foundational fractures allows him to rewrite a unity between "brothers" that did not exist in Haiti's historical record.

As for the allegorical treatment of Dessalinean vengeance, the novel addresses it twice: once in the narrative and again in Ardouin's historical coda.[66] Ardouin's coda explains the massacre as a result of the fear of French reinvasion and some psychological release brought about by the liberation of a class of men, long oppressed in chains. He likens the furor of the former slaves to indiscriminate, impetuous, forces of nature, in a language that draws upon the republican revolutionaries' defense of their act of parricide in 1806 (see chapter 1):

> L'incendie détruit, sans conscience de ses ravages, les métaux les plus vils et les plus précieux. . . . Ainsi s'assouvit cette colère populaire, impétueuse comme l'ouragan, terrible comme l'incendie. . . . Les villes, les campagnes furent inondées de sang. Il semblait que ce sang eût la vertu de purifier le sol des souillures de l'esclavage, tant on mettait d'ardeur à le répandre.

> (Fire destroys the most lowly and most precious of metals indiscriminately. . . . So this popular rage satisfied itself, furious like a hurricane, terrible like a fire. . . . Town and countryside were inundated with blood.

It seemed as if this blood had the power to cleanse the earth of the stains of slavery, so much blood did they spill and with such fervor.)⁶⁷

In Ardouin's description, there are no leaders behind the order, no political reason behind Dessalines's command of island-wide massacres. It is the result of indiscriminate, illogical popular anger, presented in the passive voice and via the metaphor of a natural disaster. In this presentation of the events, Ardouin disavows the popular spiritual belief in the power of blood, as we saw in previous chapters. Indeed, Ardouin's use of the subjunctive mood in "il semblait que" creates a measure of distance and doubt in the popular justification of the massacres: it *seemed* as though blood had the ability to heal the wounds of slavery.⁶⁸

Within the narrative, Bergeaud addresses Dessalinean vengeance through the character Romulus, whom he casts as the architect of the misguided plan to send eight hundred sick and wounded French soldiers out to sea to be drowned. The narrative thus alters the scope and method of the historical massacre of men, women, and children that Dessalineans meted out across the island from February to April 1804.⁶⁹ It was actually the French who had used their ships in the harbor as a staging ground in 1803 for their mass drownings of insurgents during the final phase of the War of Independence. By replacing the actual act of Dessalinean vengeance with another, marginally less violent act, Bergeaud moves away from the sensational and bloody depictions of Haiti's anticolonial violence. Moreover, by replacing Haitian anticolonial violence with a known act of French colonial violence, Bergeaud's narrative insists on the violence of Western civilization, albeit in a circuitous way. It is not just the violence of the French expeditionary forces that Bergeaud evokes in his discussion of revolutionary violence. He also points directly to the bloodshed of the French Revolution: "The spirit of humanity was sincerely at work; and, despite the immense support of intelligence and virtue [*d'intelligences et de vertus*], the cornerstone was set in blood."⁷⁰ The narrator reasons that, despite this fact, the revolution in France was not "cursed" and so neither should it be in Saint-Domingue/Haiti. Bergeaud's insistence that Haiti's violence not be considered uncivilized or cursed by pointing to France's own bloody revolutionary history is a recognition that there is some double standard in the way the French and Haitian Revolutions are treated differently when it comes to violence.

Bergeaud's references to the French Revolution are instructive: as much as he attempted to recast Haiti's foundational fractures through an allegorical story of *fraternité*, he was also recasting its connection to the French Revolution through the allegory of *liberté*: Stella. Stella *is* French Enlightenment liberty. Her story is, in effect, the story of how the Enlightenment ideas of liberty and equality saturated the public sphere in the years leading up to the French Revolution. But as quickly as they took hold, they also transformed: into the radical Jacobin era of the National Convention. The events of the Terror that consumed the French Revolution went against the Enlightenment principles that inspired the events of 1789, and so, Bergeaud says, liberty *fled* France and came to Saint-Domingue. She describes her "upbringing" in France in terms of the Enlightenment and emergent public opinion of the eighteenth century: she grew up in public squares and on street corners in Paris.[71] She explains that the popular masses honored her like a divinity, but that their passion soon turned to delirium: "They fought each other, they killed each other, they slit each other's throats, all in my name."[72] Stella grew frightened; the men who had once glorified her now killed violently and indiscriminately in her name. She fled, throwing herself onto the first boat out of France, which, by chance, brought her to Saint-Domingue. When she landed in the colony, the Colon captured her and imprisoned her, but the brothers saved her by burning down his plantation. The brothers' act, burning down the Colon's home and "rescuing" the ideal of liberty that was born out of Enlightenment ideals and the heroic actions of 1789 in France, thus stands in for the insurgent slaves and free people of color's decision to revolt against the planter class in colonial Saint-Domingue.

Bergeaud's allegory of the brothers "rescuing" liberty from the clutches of the Colon's prison is another way of telling the same story about the Haitian Revolution that liberal republicans long believed: that the actions of the slaves and free people of color in revolutionary Saint-Domingue had rescued *liberté* from the theoretical prison of French colonialism, and thus, that Haiti was the most radical, revolutionary example of liberal republicanism.[73] Bergeaud maintains that the Haitian revolutionaries represented the staunchest French republican patriots: "The elders of the revolution made a name for themselves in 1790 and 1791; their military warrants [*brevets*] date back to the era of the French republic. They were also enthusiastic republicans, fanatic patriots, and had been for a long time. They did not even consider independence until they learned they could no longer trust the metropole."[74] By forcing the revolutionary government to abolish slavery in Saint-Domingue in 1793, revolutionaries there succeeded in realizing the Enlightenment principles of human rights that had so far existed only in theory in France. Stella, *liberté*, was the legitimate child of 1789 who chose to reside in Haiti, the place that remained the most faithful to the liberal Enlightenment ideals of the revolution and the First Republic.

Emile Nau's *Histoire des Caciques* and the Problem of Western Civilization

Back on the other side of the Atlantic, in imperial Haiti, Emile Nau engaged in his own allegorizing of Haiti's revolutionary past. It was part a different project, one that reinvested in Dessalines's foundational act of vengeance as part of Haiti's indigenous heritage, reinscribing 1804 into a longer history of anticolonialism and antislavery activism on the island. Nau's *Histoire des caciques* was one of the few texts published in Haiti during the 1850s, and the first Haitian study of the island's Amerindian history and the conflict between tribal leaders (*caciques*) and Christopher Columbus's conquest of the island (1492–1528).[75] Recall from the previous chapter that Emile Nau and his brother Ignace were among 1830s indigenist writers in *Le Républicain* and *L'Union* who highlighted the island's Amerindian history. Though Ignace had died in 1845, Emile was a signatory of the 1849 constitution and was named baron and then chevalier in Soulouque's empire. He also played an important role alongside Thomas Madiou in the written culture of imperial Haiti, and his *Histoire* further developed the valorization of Dessalines's memory as the liberator, avenger, and emperor of Haiti.

Exiled republicans' rescripting and allegorizing of the Haitian Revolution sought to move the idea, and the image, of Haitians away from vengeance and bloodshed and toward some new image of civility and of civilization. But Nau sought to further flesh out the connections between the massacre of Ayti's Amerindians and the enslaved Africans in Saint-Domingue, and Dessalines's foundational act of anticolonial violence.[76] His work offers an important contrast, and a different political and ideological approach, to the Haitian writing published in exile in France. Whereas writers like Ardouin, Faubert, Saint-Rémy, and Bergeaud retold a republican origin story that excised, epiphenomenalized, or allegorized Dessalinean violence, Nau embraced an indigenist approach that filled in the historical backstory to Dessalines's 1804 act of American vengeance.[77] By way of conclusion to this chapter, then, I propose analyzing Nau's *Histoire des caciques d'Haïti* in counterpoise to the allegorical rewriting of the Haitian Revolution on the other side of the Atlantic.

Though Nau's work was a historical text, it nevertheless sought to write its own origin story of Haiti by linking—through an extended historical study—the enslavement and extermination of the island's Amerindian tribes and Dessalines's radical act of anticolonial vengeance. Nau is more fully fleshing out, giving written word and historical significance to Dessalines's naming of the Armée Indigène and Haiti's original symbolic connection to the Taino Indians. That is, he is not recasting or rescripting the Haitian Revolution, but rather putting an already-extant idea—that of the link between the Taino Indians and the African slaves of Saint-Domingue—in the form of a written history.[78] Recall that the island's Amerindian predecessors were key to Dessalineans' radical form of independence, the naming of Haiti, and the black, anticolonial, antislavery state's path forward. In the Acte de l'indépendance, Dessalines announced that Haitians needed to reject the French example and follow another path, that of their Taino predecessors, their brothers in chains who preferred to die rather than lose their freedom: "Let's follow in other footsteps; let's imitate those people whose concern for the future and fear of leaving an example of cowardice to their descendants, chose to be exterminated rather than stricken from the ranks of free people."[79] By returning to this original Amerindian "path" in Haiti's radical anticolonial independence and fleshing out its documentary history, Nau is writing a profoundly Dessalinean, indigenous story in several respects: first, because it continued the approach to popular cultural belief that he and his brothers had elaborated in the 1830s; second, because he sought to complete a cycle of Haitian history written by indigenous, Haitian historians; and third because, as he expressed in his preface, he sought to write the history of the Columbian conquest from the point of view of the island's native inhabitants: "It is by standing among them, and from this point of view, that I tell of the discovery and conquest of the island."⁸⁰ Nau is thus continuing a form of Haitian indigenism that Dessalines inaugurated, and which writers like Baron de Vastey and Ignace Nau further elaborated in their work.

In the preface to his historical study, Nau declares that collective suffering and continued heroic martyrdom define the island's identity: "From the discovery until now, so much suffering, so many murders, so much heroism, so many martyrs!"⁸¹ He admits that Amerindians and enslaved Africans were not linked by any blood relation ("par aucune sympathie de consanguinité") but rather by their communal suffering under enslavement: "The African and the Indian were two of a kind in chains. It is by such a brotherhood of misfortune, such a shared suffering that their fates became intertwined."⁸² Sibylle Fischer has identified Nau's as an allegory of the Haitian Revolution in its presentation of vengeance and radical liberty.⁸³ Indeed, the key allegorical link between Amerindian history and Haiti's revolutionary story is the act of vengeance itself. In his description of the African slaves' self-liberation—breaking their chains and exterminating the French troops—Nau concludes, "To free a country this way, it meant avenging all who had been oppressed, it meant avenging themselves and at the same time avenging the unfortunate Indians" (*Rendre un pays ainsi libre, c'était venger tout ce qui y avait été opprimé, c'était se venger soi-même et venger en même temps les malheureux Indiens*).⁸⁴ Nau's repetition of the very word itself "venger" creates an enumerative effect, one that stands in contrast to the act of metaphoric and allegorical treatment of the word—and the act—among Haitian writers in exile. Nau *emphasized* vengeance as foundational to Haiti's national identity, linking it to the anticolonial struggles of Ayti/Saint-Domingue's first inhabitants. That is, where the 1850s republican works in exile seek to move away from violence and vengeance, through dramatic catharsis, didactic dramatization, or allegorical, magical realist retellings of Haiti's revolution, Nau returns to violence and vengeance as the source of Haiti's indigenous, and thus national, identity.

Nau's insistence on linking the long history of the island and its many inhabitants *with* bloodshed, instead of the metaphoric and allegoric elision of that violence, is striking: "It is the most beautiful island to be born of the seas and under radiant skies, but it is also the ground that has perhaps imbibed the most human blood on the planet. Posterity must know this, must feel pity with all of its mercy. Posterity will admire this island too, I hope, for perhaps glory will be the end and the crowning achievement of its misfortunes." (*C'est la plus belle île qui soit éclose au sein des mers et sous des cieux splendides, mais c'est aussi la terre du globe qui a peut-être bu le plus de sang humain. Il faut que la postérité le sache, il faut qu'elle plaigne de toute sa pitié. Elle l'admirera aussi, je l'espère, car la gloire peut-être sera la fin et le couronnement de ses infortunes.*)[85] Here, Nau borrows directly from Vastey's romantic ruin passage in *Le système coloniale dévoilé*: his use of superlatives, the image of earth imbibed with blood, and the misfortunes of its many inhabitants ("O land of mine, is there any other on this planet whose soil has been more soaked in human blood? Is there a land whose ill-fated inhabitants have experienced greater misfortunes?").[86] Nau's choice of text and of author is itself a provocation: as we saw in previous chapters, Dessalinean and Christophean writing was systematically silenced and disavowed by republican critics in the post-1820 period. Yet where Vastey's text presents the image of Haiti's past bloodshed in somewhat less anthropophagic terms with the passive construction of the verb "imbiber" (the earth has been penetrated, soaked, saturated with human blood), Nau transforms it into the active construction of the verb "boire" in what is an equally purposeful provocation. The island—Ayti, Saint-Domingue, Haiti—has drunk perhaps the most human blood of any on the globe.

I see Nau's description here in clear contrast to Joseph Saint-Rémy's depiction of a bloodthirsty Boisrond Tonnerre, discussed above. Where Saint-Rémy tries to explain away Haiti's foundational violence by assigning the genesis of Dessalinean vengeance to a few bad actors who had a taste for blood ("cet infernal breuvage"—a more negative connotation than, say, a "boisson"), Nau portrays violence as endemic, rooted in the violence of the Columbian conquest and French colonial rule—the bloodshed of centuries of conquest and colonialism in Ayti/Saint-Domingue. Nau wants to insist on the historical realities of the island's bloody colonial history as both the unifying source of Haiti's indigenous, national history and the legitimate cause for Haiti's vengeful anticolonialism. In Nau's history, it is not a deranged leader or his secretary who have a taste for human blood, but the earth that has absorbed the blood of entire civilizations—the chained, tortured, and martyred enslaved. Here, we are far from Ardouin's depiction of psychological break and natural disaster, and much closer to Ignace Nau's 1839 poem in which the liberated slaves refused to sit alongside their former colonizers and their wine of the slaves' blood, and their bread of the slaves' sweat ("Le vin était son sang et le pain ses sueurs"), and who proclaimed that they must purify the newly independent Haitian land with the colonizers' blood ("Purifions le sol des péchés de l'impie")—drawing upon the original texts of Haitian independence.

Emile Nau's history of Haiti's first inhabitants is thus a history of European colonialism from its origins, and the violence and oppression that were part of it. Bloodshed, violence, and vengeance are foundational to its story, and its history. Remarking upon the crime and glory of Columbus's conquest-exploration, Nau exclaims: "What a crime indeed to have slaughtered an entire people! But on the other hand, what glory to have discovered a new world for civilization, science, and religion! What is unfortunate is that this glory is stained with murder, torture and blood."[87] It is worth sitting with Nau's apostrophe for a moment here, and not just for its Vastey-ean style which revived the legacy of the disavowed Christophean writer. Nau's indigenous historian sheds tears over the fate of Haiti's Amerindian brothers and curses their executioners. Yet at the same time, he finds himself compelled to admire the spirit of these Christian explorers. The historian's apostrophe reveals his internal conflict—two voices in dialogue—that Nau performs for the reader in his preface and upon which he concludes, with no real resolution. Here, Nau is articulating what David Scott has identified among twentieth-century postcolonial Caribbean writers: "the paradox of colonial enlightenment."[88] Nau points to the frame in which he finds himself: the dominant Western tradition of the Columbian conquest and the creation of the modern, Christian West, the invention of *civilization* itself. Yet he feels deep anger and sadness at the bloodshed it created, and which conditioned his very existence. Nau is pointing to the paradox at the heart of Western liberalism, progress, and science: that it is profoundly marked, indeed compromised, by violence and bloodshed. He is also pointing to the central role that the New World had in the creation of that West—the soaked soil of Ayti/Saint-Domingue/Haiti that made the West possible.

Nau concludes his criticism of Western systems in a somewhat cryptic proclamation at the end of his preface: "All glory that sullies itself is atoned for" (*Toute gloire qui se souille s'expie*).[89] He clarifies what he means by giving two historical examples of what he calls *expiation historique*, what we might translate as "poetic justice" or "historical reparation," or even both. These two examples are Christopher Columbus and Napoléon Bonaparte. Columbus's glory was having discovered the New World for Western civilization, a glory that was sullied by Columbus's role in enslaving and exterminating an entire race. This sullied glory was atoned for when Columbus himself was put in chains some time later. Bonaparte's glory as emperor was sullied when he had Louverture arrested ("fait arrêter déloyalement Toussaint Louverture") and sent to the Jura mountains in France to die.[90] That sullied glory was atoned for when Bonaparte himself was imprisoned on Saint Helena and left to die. Nau's elaboration of an idea of historical justice or reparation places him within the Dessalinean sphere of Enlightenment critique and a clear understanding of Ayti/Saint-Domingue/Haiti in the invention of the West.

But what about the civil war context in Haiti? Nau remains entirely silent on this question, yet his declarative proclamation "Toute gloire qui se souille s'expie" would seem like an invitation to consider it within Haiti's own internal glories and their sullying, especially 1804 and 1806. Can we apply Nau's ethics of "expiation historique" to Dessalines's foundational act of Haitian vengeance? If so, is European colonialism the glory, the horrors of the slavery its sullying, and Dessalines's vengeance the atonement—the poetic justice and the historical reparation—for the horrors of the colonial system? This would suggest that for Nau, Dessalines's radical act of violent anticolonialism was cosmically justified or legitimate. Or, is Dessalines's proclamation of independence the glory, his decision to pursue anticolonial vengeance the act that sullies it, and his assassination the atonement? Or, is the creation of Haiti's republic in 1806 the glory, its sullying the assassination of Dessalines, and the atonement the tumultuous, fractured politics of Haiti's fifty years of postcolonial existence? Nau's text does not say. Yet if we look forward to future arguments that will be made about 1804/1806 at the turn of the twentieth century—that the republic's origin in parricide was a foundational fracture in Haitian history for which Haitians are still atoning—Nau's text leaves open the possibility of this interpretation and offers a language and ethics for expressing it.

Nau's presentation of Haiti's foundational anticolonial act in his *Histoire des caciques* stands in contrast with the radical argument about liberal republicanism that exiled republicans were engaging in. Their rescripting of Haitian independence—either through Bergeaud's allegorical rewriting or Saint-Rémy's efforts to delegitimize the architects of the violent anticolonial acts of 1804—sought to recast Haiti as the soil where the Enlightenment ideal of *liberté* truly took root. Nau's internal conflict, the opacity of his narration, reveals the fundamental paradox at the heart of these virtuous, republican narratives: the impossibility of separating the Enlightenment ideals of liberalism, progress, or humanism from the fundamental dehumanizing basis of colonialism and chattel slavery. What is more, he presents Ayti/Saint-Domingue/Haiti as born out of both traditions, born out of both the violence and the glory of Western civilization. Nau's work offers a new role for Haiti, one that differs from the idea of Haiti as the radical instantiation of 1789 that we see in the works of Haiti's exiled republicans. Instead, Nau argues that Haiti has something universal to say about *humanity*. For Nau, Haiti has as much to teach the world about humanity as any European country—indeed, more: "Haiti's history, despite what little space it takes up in the annals of world history, abounds with useful lessons for the study and instruction of humanity."[91] Nau's work on the early colonial history of Haiti heralds the fundamental humanity of Haitians' self-liberation, of their radical act of claiming personhood and humanity from within a system that was built upon the very rejection of that humanity. The Western system of science, progress, and "civilization" has something to learn from Haiti about what true humanity looks like.

6

Nationals and Liberals, 1904/1906

Faustin Soulouque temporarily defeated his liberal opponents by effectively exiling the republic, driving hundreds of southern liberal families out of the country after 1848. In late 1858 the town of Gonaïves rebelled against Soulouque's rule, proclaiming a republic on December 22, 1858. Soon other regions adhered: they deposed the emperor and named Fabre Geffrard, a southern republican who had served as the Duc of Tabara under Soulouque's empire, as the new president of the republic. Soulouque abdicated and departed for exile in Jamaica, while Geffrard proclaimed Haiti a republic once more and welcomed back its exiled citizens.[1] Geffrard also returned the country to the Boyerist stance on "civilization": an outward-facing performance of Haiti's status as a civilized nation and an internal repression of all that challenged it. In many ways, this was the reverse of Soulouque's political and diplomatic strategy, at least insofar as it related to government form and popular peasant practices. Geffrard signed a concordat with the Holy See in March 1860, reinstating Catholicism as the privileged and protected religion in the republic.[2] The concordat went hand in hand with government enforcement of the Code Pénal against Vodou ("superstition") intended to address the increasingly public practice of the popular religion under Soulouque and, as Geffrard proclaimed, "to remove from our land these last vestiges of barbarism and slavery, superstition and its scandalous practices."[3] Indeed, Geffrard's 1864 response to the Bizoton affair—publicly executing eight *cultivateurs* for "*sortilèges*, premeditated murder, and torture"—was a spectacular performance of Geffrard's stance on "civilization."[4]

While Geffrard was successful in reversing much of Soulouque's imperial populism, the republic was far from secured: civil war, uprisings, and attempted coups continued unabated under his presidency (1859–1867). Less than a year after he took office, northern Christophist generals hatched a plot to unseat Geffrard's republic and return the country to a monarchy. As Matthew Smith notes, seventeen conspirators were publicly executed, a number "larger than any under Soulouque."[5] A subsequent uprising by the southern general Lysius Salomon and his supporters in Les Cayes met similar repression: twenty-six conspirators sentenced to death, fourteen executed in one day alone.[6] Geffrard proved that a republican leader could be just as brutal as emperors and monarchs in putting down opposition movements.

The republic would finally take hold, durably, in 1869. It did not, however, achieve this status because of an intellectual or political movement, or because of an inevitable arc toward liberal republicanism. The republic took hold because Haiti's internal factionalism used up its remaining (metaphoric) fuel in a civil war that (literally) leveled the presidential palace—a spectacular event that finally shifted the paradigm from regionally based civil war to party-based national divisions.[7] But before the pyrotechnics, let us set the stage: Geffrard's early grip on his republican presidency gave way to nearly four years of insurrections and secessionist rebellions between 1864 and 1869, particularly around Sylvain Salnave, a northern general.[8] In 1865 a group of northerners, led by Salnave and his secretary and ally Demesvar Delorme, invaded and captured the North and seceded from Geffrard's republic for nearly seven months.[9] After a brief exile, Salnave returned in February 1867 to retake the country; Geffrard capitulated, resigning immediately and leaving for exile. Salnave was officially voted president of Haiti in June 1867 on a wave of support from the peasantry and the urban proletariat. His platform was indeed populist: he reignited the language of populist leaders Acaau and Salomon and was particularly popular among market women and urban workers for his financial and trade policies.[10]

Despite his popularity, he was never able to establish unity among Haiti's various factions. By mid-1868 the republic had fractured into a civil war between four separatist states, and Salnave considered imposing unity by proclaiming an empire (though he ultimately rejected the idea).[11] There was his military state in Port-au-Prince, which maintained a sliver of support from the North in and around Cap-Haïtien in the coastal band, as well as strong support among urban inhabitants throughout the country and the *piquets* in the South; there was also Nissage Saget's separatist republic in the North, headquartered in Saint-Marc and with strong support from the Artibonite, local elites, rival generals to Salnave, and armed *cacos* from throughout the northern region; there was Normil Dubois's liberal republican Constitutional Army of the South; and there was the Etat Méridional of the South led by Michel Domingue in Les Cayes—though, notably, neither of these southern governments had the support of the southern *piquets*, who remained loyal supporters of Salnave even after his capture and execution.[12]

Salnave's defeat was almost certain by mid-1869. As opposition troops closed in on Port-au-Prince, Salnave planned his escape: he rigged the presidential palace with explosives to blow up as he fled to the Dominican border. Had he been in the North he might have survived, drawing his support from the northern band (*banda norte*) on the Dominican side that was sympathetic to his separatist cause.[13] Instead, he was promptly captured by southern Dominican border guards, under the command of José María Cabral—a known supporter of Nissage Saget. Salnave was seized and brought back to Port-au-Prince, where he was executed on January 15, 1870. The remaining supporters of Salnave's regime were executed or exiled. Delorme, having already been unceremoniously cut loose from Salnave's government, remained in Europe while his family in Haiti was escorted to a US embassy and then into exile.[14]

* * *

As Louis Joseph Janvier remarked on the fracturing of the country during the Salnave revolution and civil war: "everything needed to be restructured after the crisis of 1868–1869."[15] Salnave's spectacular leveling of the presidential palace marked a symbolic end to a cycle of regime change and upheaval rooted in fundamentally opposed government forms: republic versus military-imperial state. Out of the violence and upheavals of the post-Soulouque decade, the political landscape in Haiti emerged transformed: political and social actors reoriented their ideological differences around a single government form: the republic. From the smoldering ruins of Sylvain Salnave's revolution, a new paradigm of internal factionalism and civil war conflicts emerged. Whereas earlier postrevolutionary conflicts were marked by a primarily regional, factional divide based in oppositional government forms (monarchism versus republicanism), post-1869 divisions were contained to the ideological, partisan, and parliamentary divides within the republic. These divides cut across regional zones and were determined by newly formed party lines: Nationals and Liberals. The crisis of the 1868–1869 period thus marks a transition toward a modern party-based model that would convert and co-opt the previous regional and ideological divisions in Haiti into two different groups. The significance of this moment cannot be understated. As Michel-Rolph Trouillot has argued, in the post-1860s reaction and the creation of a party system, "Haiti came as close as it ever has to an effective parliamentary experience."[16] And yet it was indeed only a moment: civil wars, insurrections, exiles, and coups continued unabated in the post-Salnave era, but under the newly formed—and constantly evolving—political categories, parties, and regional affiliations.

This chapter traces the continued civil war in Haiti that manifested itself along these newly formed post-1869 divides: between Liberals and Nationals in politics, in divergent approaches to education and cultural policy, and in new approaches to commemorating Haiti's foundational 1804/1806 division at the turn of the new century. Yet these new divides were not invented out of whole cloth: they drew heavily upon Haitian history while responding to ever-changing Atlantic currents of thought. That is, the post-1869 divides were marked by both the divisions that shaped Haiti's first fifty years of civil war and the ideological debates that marked the nineteenth-century Atlantic world: specifically, France's Third Republican debates on nationhood and imperial republicanism and the rise of a new US hemispheric imperialism at the turn of the century. Thus, the divides between government forms that had driven the first fifty years of Haitian civil war gave way to a new set of factions that reactivated and adapted these earlier divisions.

Nationals and Liberals

What exactly did it mean to be a "National" or a "Liberal" in late nineteenth-century Haiti? As their names perhaps suggest, Nationals were agriculturalists and populists, drawing their power from rural elites and from the support of the peasant majority. Liberals were economic progressives but anti-populists: they hoped to put an end to the reign of political divisions in Haiti by installing a regime of skilled elites.[17] Crucially, however, Nationals and Liberals were both republicans; in the post-1869 reorganization both parties were committed to republican governments and republican constitutions. Jean-Pierre Boyer Bazelais and Edmond Paul founded the Liberal Party in February 1870 in response to the crisis of the 1865–1869 civil war and the seemingly interminable back-and-forth between republic and military state. Shortly after the Liberal Party appeared, the Cayenne deputy Septimus Rameau founded the National Party in the heritage of the peasant-focused populist politics that Lysius Salomon and other residents of Les Cayes had promoted since the 1840s.[18] After early parliamentary gains for the Liberal Party, the National Party seized power in 1874 by boycotting parliamentary sessions in order to stop the Liberal candidate, Sénèque Momplaisir Pierre, from getting elected. When the sitting republican president, Nissage Saget, finished his term, he was thus without a successor, and handed over power to the head of the military, the National Party leader Michel Domingue. In 1876, Liberals in exile organized an invasion and uprising in Jacmel that killed many, including the founder of the National Party, Rameau. The Liberal uprising successfully overturned Domingue and installed Pierre Théoma Boisrond-Canal as president of the provisional government.[19] Boisrond-Canal and the Liberals briefly held power, until a surge of populist support brought Lysius Salomon back after decades in exile and the Nationals to power in 1879. With Salomon's election as president, the Nationals would control government for nearly a decade, though not without numerous, often violent attempts to unseat them, including the failed 1883 Liberal uprising in Miragoâne, led by the former parliamentarian and founder of the Liberal Party, Boyer Bazelais.[20]

While the creation of parties was itself new, we must not overlook the half century of civil war factionalism and oppositional political ideology that preceded the post-Salnave political reorganization—something to which historians of the 1870s and 1880s period have tended to give short shrift. What was different about the new party organization was that it allowed for political expression and filiation to cohere across geographic space in ways that had not been previously articulated, breaking down the southern peninsula's stronghold on liberal republicanism and the northern band's military authoritarian identification. For example, Claude Auguste's research has shown that after the 1883 failure at Miragoâne, the Liberal Party actually transformed into a party that aligned more closely with northern planters than with southern elites. In this sense, we have to distinguish between the pre-1883 Liberal Party, concentrated mostly in the South, and the post-1883 Liberal Party, which sought inroads in the North among planters and represents a transversal breaking down of a geographic division that had originally structured the party.[21]

Readers may have noted that I have chosen not to cite David Nicholl's color-legend argument in my discussion of the post-1869 redrawing of party lines. I find Nicholls's analysis of the Liberal/National divide problematic because he asserts the primacy of color difference in these political divisions: between "ultranational *noiristes*" and mulatto Liberals.[22] He argues that intellectuals and politicians of the 1870s and 1880s organized their interpretation of Haitian history according to skin color, creating black and mulatto "legends" of the past. Indeed, while Nicholls applies his color thesis to the whole of Haitian history, I would argue that the genesis of the theory itself came out of Nicholls's misreading of Louis Joseph Janvier's Nationalist political project.[23] Nicholls's anachronistic use of the term *noiriste* to characterize both Janvier and the National Party should give us pause. The term itself appears nowhere in Janvier's work. Instead, it reveals the presentism that shapes Nicholls's assessment of the post-1869 moment, more specifically the *noiriste* color politics of the Duvalier dictatorship and its violent *makoutisme* in the 1970s. Indeed, I would argue that by anachronistically attributing *noirisme* or *noiriste* ideology to nineteenth-century Haitian thought, Nicholls creates a teleology of Haitian color politics and political ideology that obscures the social and political realities of the late nineteenth century.

If the crux of Nicholls's color-legend turns on his reading of Janvier, it would be useful here to briefly summarize Janvier's biography and the main elements of his Nationalist program.[24] Janvier was born in Port-au-Prince in 1855 to a well-off and well-connected family. Raised in the Protestant faith, he attended a primary school run by English missionaries and later studied at the Lycée national and then the Ecole de médecine in Port-au-Prince. Like most well-off and well-educated men of his standing, Janvier received a government scholarship to continue his studies in Paris when he was twenty-one years old. He left in 1876, in the midst of the Liberal Party's uprising and the death of the National Party leader Rameau. Janvier spent the next decade and a half in Paris, completing studies in medicine and political science, and establishing himself as an important Haitian intellectual in France. His work appeared frequently in French newspapers and in collected editions with noteworthy Parisian publishing houses. The publishing house Rougier et Cie even helped Janvier and his young colleague Jean-Joseph Chancy establish a series with their press, the Bibliothèque démocratique haïtienne, under which Janvier published many of his works, including his short story "Le vieux piquet" and his essays *L'égalité des races* and *Les antinationaux*.[25] Janvier associated himself with a number of notable intellectual circles in Paris, most notably an emerging gathering of French nationalists in the Jeune France group (including Maurice Barrès and François Coppée) who engaged in their own critique of liberal republicanism in post-1870 France.[26]

Janvier's Nationalist program is best summed up in a phrase he proffered in his 1884 work, *L'égalité des races*, "To take action for the good of the greatest number, for the honor of all" (*Agir pour le bien du plus grand nombre, pour l'honneur de tous*), or in his dedication to "Le vieux piquet": "For the welfare of all" (*Nous voulons le bien de tous*).[27] Importantly, these phrases are as close as we get to the "power to the greatest number" (*le pouvoir au plus grand nombre*) slogan that is erroneously attributed to Janvier (and to the National Party more broadly), which does not appear anywhere in his oeuvre and miscasts their populist approach.[28] In opposition to an outward-facing, Atlantic-oriented Liberal Party, Janvier's Nationalist Party encourages his fellow compatriots to "withdraw to ourselves, to commune with one another," "be ourselves first and foremost," and "live autonomously."[29] Janvier espoused an economic nationalism: he was against laissez-faire market liberalism and opposed foreign ownership of property and land, trade monopolies, foreign banks, and debt. He was a vehement critic of Boyerist legal codes, especially the Code Rural, and championed Lysius Salomon's February 1883 law, which proclaimed that any *citoyen* engaged in the cultivation of important export commodities (coffee, sugar, cotton, and so forth) "will have the right to possession of three to five carreaux [9.5 to 16 acres] of public land."[30]

Janvier's Protestant faith informed his attempts to advocate for the Haitian peasantry, especially in support of what he believed were their legitimate claims to landownership. Land reform was the central tenet of Janvier's Nationalist program: "the grand reform, ... land to the peasant, it's the keystone of the edifice of our reconstruction, the cement of the system, the foundation of granite [*assise de granite*] upon which we can build everything."[31] Janvier was a self-proclaimed "progressiste": he proposed a social reform project that was built around the goal of raising the peasantry out of misery by getting land into the hands of peasants, and pursuing an ambitious literacy and educational program that would democratize access to skills and knowledge. For Janvier, education was liberatory and democratic, and essential for peasants so that they might participate more fully in the political process. As we shall see in the next section, Janvier elaborated this political and ideological program through various different modes, including the short story or *lodyans*.

With a better grasp of Janvier's Nationalist program and oeuvre, let us return to Nicholls's color-legend argument here: that "the division between the Liberal and the National parties ... was fundamentally a question of color," and moreover that Janvier was the leader of a group of "*noiriste* ideologists" who "wished to establish a 'black' view of the past which ascribed the evils of Haiti to the selfishness of mulatto politicians and the weakness of those black heads of state" who agreed to serve them.[32] A close reading of Janvier's oeuvre reveals a more complex approach to color, politics, and the nineteenth-century Atlantic world than Nicholls's dismissive assessment would suggest. While Janvier decries color prejudice in Haiti—the disproportionate hegemony of a light-skinned elite over the black, peasant masses and the virtual caste system that separated them in the Code Rural—he is hardly the only Haitian to do so. In fact, Janvier is reactivating the long heritage of critiques of color prejudice in Haiti, such as Félix Darfour's critique of Boyer's putatively color-blind republicanism (see chapter 4). What Janvier is pointing out on color prejudice in Haiti is in line with his larger critique of Haitian republicanism in the post-1806 moment: it failed to live up to its promises and its guarantees of freedom, equality, and rights. Janvier thus advocated for a republicanism that would embrace these fundamental tenets and called out the Liberal Party for failing to critique its republican forebears for their own failures on the question of rights, equality, and democracy. Very much in the spirit of Darfour, Janvier attempted to reveal the inconsistencies and hypocrisy of Haiti's putatively liberal, democratic, republican regimes that systematically refused rights and full citizenship to Haiti's former slaves, the peasant masses. To reduce Janvier's critique to a simple question of color is to miss the more complex, historically rooted critique of republicanism that resonated throughout Haiti's nineteenth century.

I would make a second and final point about Nicholls's accusation that on the subject of color prejudice and "some other" matters (such as Janvier's claim that all Haitians spoke and understood French), Janvier was "patently dishonest and unreliable."[33] I advocate a more nuanced reading of Janvier's published texts that analyzes them in the context of their enunciation and the longer heritage of Haitian writing that he engages: one that takes into account addressee, genre, and performativity. Just like Haitian polemicists before him, Janvier was aware that he was addressing—performing for—multiple print publics, both local and foreign, ally and adversary. Janvier thus deployed different subject positions throughout his oeuvre depending on the audience he was addressing, and also on the political point he was trying to make. The fact of Haiti's unequal power relationship to the "civilized nations" of the world meant that writers were hyperaware that they were never just writing for a specific addressee, but also for a larger North Atlantic print public that was measuring their "progress." Janvier's oeuvre is indeed wide-ranging in terms of audience and form: his first published works in France were journalistic refutation pieces aimed to refute libelous articles and specious claims made about Haiti and Haitians in the French press.[34] In representing Haiti in these early polemical articles, Janvier played to his audience and specifically, to the linguistic politics of the French Third Republic and its nascent *mission civilisatrice*—the spread of the French language (and thus, of "reason" and "civilization") through colonization. His later works, inspired in large part by the 1883 Liberal uprising and subsequent civil war, are highly critical of Haiti and focus on internal Liberal/National divisions. Is it so outlandish to speculate that Janvier might have misleadingly portrayed Haitians' linguistic capabilities in order to shield them from France's colonizing "civilizing mission," all while calling for the need to expand and democratize education and literacy internally within Haiti? I think an equally significant problem here is Nicholls's search for a "reliable" narrator of Haiti's social and cultural realities in the 1880s. There is a difference—indeed, a chasm—between the fact that Janvier took conflicting positions on color prejudice for different audiences (that it did not exist when he wanted to defend Haiti against its racist detractors, and that it did exist when he wanted to score points against Haitian political opponents) and the notion that race or color was a motor or source of Janvier's decision making.

Instead, I consider the inconsistencies in Janvier's style and the evolution of his treatment of Haiti's internal divisions as central to understanding the Liberal/National divides of the late nineteenth century, especially as they related to representing Haiti to the outside world. As Catts Pressoir and Hénock and Ernst Trouillot have noted, Janvier's style, especially in these post-1883 texts, departed from that of many of his Haitian contemporaries in the degree to which he was unafraid to criticize Haiti's way of life or its institutions. His writing went "straight to the point" and offered "the most penetrating critique" of Haiti's politics, its institutions, and its traditions.[35] Indeed, his work seems to have evolved such that, by the time he was writing his reflections on the 1883 civil war, he had dispensed with any illusions that he needed to represent Haiti according to some aspirational ideal, or perform a kind of "civilization" to protect against foreign criticism and mask the reality of the internal political situation. Indeed, he called into question the idea—dear to Anténor Firmin—that Haiti should aspire to some kind of civilizational ideal. Instead, he critiqued the idea itself, in Dessalinean fashion: "What is civilization, anyway? All pastiche or copy."[36] In the postface to his revisionist *Les constitutions d'Haïti* (1886), Janvier reflects on his choice to write in a frank, clear style: "Man reflects himself in his style. . . . With these lines, I am protecting myself against the prejudices of those who can never put their feelings out in the open, I am taking precautions against the secret machinations [*manœuvres occultes*] of those who would never dare clearly speak their views [*ouvrir des avis en langage clair*]."[37] Here, the reference to the earlier, Dessalinean sphere of frank discourse versus occult eloquence is unmistakable: it most resembles that of Baron de Vastey, who wrote of the wounds caused during Haiti's first civil war between Pétion and Christophe. While Pétion wanted to paper over the recent history of the civil war, and especially Dessalines's empire and assassination, as he presented the republic to the Atlantic world, Christophe wanted to plumb its depths: "Why expose our wounds out in the open? Must we lift the veil that covers them? Well! How can we heal them if we don't have the nerve to plumb their depths?"[38] Janvier's focus on Haiti's contemporary National/Liberal civil war divides embraced the Vastey-ean impulse to expose and reveal Haiti's weaknesses and propose new ideas for moving forward.[39]

Janvier's engagement with earlier Haitian intellectuals of the Dessalinean sphere offers important insight into the intellectual stance that he was adopting in the post-1869 cultural field. He was positioning himself as a different kind of Haitian Atlantic intellectual than had traditionally represented Haiti to the outside world (such as the earlier generation of 1850s republicans-in-exile that we saw in the previous chapter). Janvier self-consciously deployed a different set of cultural references, a different style, and a different approach to the "cosmopolitan" lettered sphere. He positioned himself as a Nationalist representing Haiti abroad after a long line of Haitian "cosmopolitan" liberals, a position he proclaimed clearly in his published work: "So often I see the task of representing the country abroad entrusted either to people who have been gone since 1848, when it was considered good form to disown it, or to those who pride themselves on never reading what Haitians publish."[40] He saw himself as operating according to a different set of codes than the liberal republicans exiled in Paris before him, who, as I have argued in previous chapters, sought to perform a kind of Haitian identity (liberal, perfectible, civilized) within the Francophone cosmopolitan lettered sphere. While an earlier generation of Haitian republican writers believed that Haiti's defense lay in presenting its cultural production to the lettered sphere, Janvier asserted that it lay in defending, indeed *refuting*, Haiti's detractors in writing, reactivating the long heritage of that practice in Haiti's early post-independence writers.

"Le Vieux Piquet," or Nineteenth-Century Haitian History from Below

Janvier emphasized the Haitian peasants and their rights throughout his 1880 writings, though perhaps none more so than in his little-studied story (or "simple récit," as he titles it), "Le vieux piquet: Scène de la vie haïtienne" (1884). Janvier's text is a brief historical narrative that recounts some of the major events in Haitian history as they were experienced by the rural peasants of the extreme Southwest, from below, as it were, and their continual fight to obtain their source of true freedom: *la terre*. The story's main character Bon Dos is essentially the mouthpiece for Janvier's Nationalist program, and thus the story serves as another format through which Janvier made the same points and argued for the same action: a Nationalist rallying cry that was highly critical of the Liberal Party and its failure to address the lives and welfare of the peasantry. As I argue in this section, it is a kind of revisionist history from below, telling the story of the peasants' fight for their right to land since Dessalines's empire, the 1844 *piquet* uprisings, and Salomon's 1883 land rights law, from the perspective of the peasants themselves, through their privileged medium, the *lodyans*.[41]

The short story takes place in the Macaya mountains in the southern peninsula, located to the southeast of Jérémie, in the village of Grand Doco. We are taken by a narrator through the virgin forests of the Macaya to a valley where, next to a stream, sits a cluster of houses (*cases*) built around a yard on land belonging to the family of a *cultivateur*, Jean-Louis Bon Dos. That Janvier uses the juridical term *cultivateur* instead of *paysan* is significant, situating his reflection within the terms of the labor regimes of the early post-independence period and Boyer's Code Rural: Bon Dos is a rural dweller without the full rights of a *citadin* under the Code Rural. The title and the setting also carry obvious significance: the village of Grand Doco had served as the capital of Goman's separatist peasant republic during the early post-independence period, and then again as the stronghold of peasant resistance during Acaau's *piquet* rebellion of 1844–1845, which attacked Rivière Hérard's revolutionary liberal government for failing to enact the reforms it had promised that would improve the peasants' lives and livelihood.[42] The main character's name is also straightforward in its symbolism: the peasants—their bodies, their labor, their families—are the backs upon which the nation is built. Though the third-person omniscient narrator never indicates the year in which the story takes place, we learn that Bon Dos was thirty-seven years old during the final battles of the *piquet* uprising in 1846, and that he is seventy-five when the story takes place. The old *piquet* Bon Dos was thus born in 1809 and is dying in 1883, two dates that bookend the question of land reform and peasant rights, and Janvier's larger Nationalist argument. Elsewhere in his oeuvre, Janvier argued that Pétion's 1809 decision to distribute national lands to military officers in recompense for their service marked the beginning of the peasants' quest for equality and rights: "Beginning in 1809, personal independence secured by landownership, which is true liberty [*la vraie liberté*], has been the peasant's constant wish; *cultivateurs* want only one thing: to escape from their dependence on landowners or farmers and enjoy their natural freedom [*liberté naturelle*]."⁴³ The year 1883 marked Salomon's law according peasants rights to own land they were actively cultivating.

The story begins as the family returns home from a day in the fields: one by one, the children and grandchildren of the patriarch return to the yard and congregate inside the main house belonging to Bon Dos. The family gathers close around Bon Dos, who prepares to tell them an important story, imparting lessons and knowledge through the didactic, oral genre of the *lodyans* (or "audience"): "Listen, my little one, and remember this well. All of you."⁴⁴ Janvier's use of the genre is part of his larger Nationalist project to promote a peasant-focused argument for land rights. The *lodyans* follows a generic structure based on a traditional oral form that Jean Jonassaint defines as "the popular Haitian mode (or code) of telling or relating (orally) social or political anecdotes [*petite histoire*] of the country, the village, or the locality."⁴⁵ While the *lodyans* would become more widely used in later turn-of-the-century novels and short stories by Nationalist writers Fernand Hibbert, Frédéric Marcelin, and Justin Lhérisson, Janvier's early example straddles the divide between fiction and politics, between indigenous narrative and didactic essay.⁴⁶ Indeed, though Georges Anglade has identified Lhérisson as the first "lodyanseur à l'écrit" for his short stories published in *Le Soir*, I would argue that Janvier's 1884 "Le vieux piquet" served as a model, if not an inspiration, for the later texts. In fact, Janvier's fictional prose production must be considered as part of the boom in social realist novels at the turn of the twentieth century.⁴⁷

With his audience assembled, Bon Dos commences his *lodyans*. He reveals that he is dying, but he is dying happy because he will see his children receive what he and his ancestors had fought for since before independence: land. Sitting at the threshold of the very home where he was born, surrounded by his progeny, Bon Dos recalls the night they brought his father across that same threshold, mortally wounded. It was 1846, and his father had been gravely injured saving the life of one of his comrades during a battle. One of his grandchildren asks what they were fighting for, setting up the narrative structure for the remainder of the story: a revisionist history of Haiti's nineteenth century from below, told from a single location—the far southwest—from the perspective of an old peasant who had lived it. Bon Dos begins by recalling how his own father had suffered under the yoke of slavery and had fought along with his fellow island-born slaves (*noirs créoles*) to break their chains and become their own masters. According to Bon Dos, Pétion and Gérin assassinated Dessalines because he promised to distribute land to the former slaves like his father. In response, Bon Dos's father joined Goman's secessionist state and fought in the campaign against Pétion, aided from time to time by Christophe, who provided them with arms and ammunition. After Borgella's successful campaign against Goman and his insurgents in Grand Doco, Bon Dos's father surrendered, and was put to work on a plantation owned by a "city dweller from Jérémie" (*citadin de Jérémie*)—here again, insisting on the juridical term that distinguished urban dwellers (*citadins*) as citizens with full rights.[48] He recounted to his son his experience of traveling as a rural inhabitant into the cities—on the specified days that the Rural Code allowed—to sell his agricultural products. The *citadins* sneered at him, calling him "negro from the hinterland, Goman's negro" (*nègre des mornes, nègre de Goman*).[49] Bon Dos's father and brothers all died in 1846 in the last phases of Acaau's *piquet* rebellion; his father's last words were to implore his son to continue fighting for his birthright, his right as a citizen of Dessalines's Haiti: his right to land. Bon Dos sharpened his own *piquet* and took up his father's fight, first alongside Salnave, whom Bon Dos describes as more of a friend to the peasantry than any of the "so-called liberals" (*soi-disant libéraux*), and then Salomon, whom Bon Dos reveres as a great father figure who will assure the safety and livelihood of peasant families.[50]

Bon Dos's praise of leaders like Goman, Salnave, and Salomon is put in further relief by his negative presentation of Haiti's putatively democratic, constitutional republican regimes, which he argues did little for the peasantry (an echo of Janvier's denouncements of the Liberal Party as the "pseudo-libéraux," the "antinationaux" and "constitutionalists" elsewhere in his writing). Bon Dos expresses the disappointment that his father and his fellow men-in-arms felt when the 1843 revolutionaries' radical liberalism found its end point in the creation of a new constitution but not in the accordance of rights to the peasantry: "a paper Constitution. The whole Revolution stops there for them."[51] This is a clear evocation of the Haitian proverb "Konstitisyon se papye, bayonet se fè." For Bon Dos, legal regimes on paper were particularly insidious because they entrenched the divisions between those who had access to the levers of power—full citizens of the urban or landholding status—and those who were second-class. Legal documentation became a system according to which the rural residents could be arrested, punished, and deprived of what little livelihood they had, while conversely those in power or who sought it could simply write new paper regimes to suit their needs.[52] Bon Dos gives the example of Salnave: when his opponents captured and killed him, they used the constitution to justify their actions and faced no legal consequences. Bon Dos warns his children: "constitutions, they make them to restrain us, but they themselves never obey them: they think themselves too noble [*trop nobles*] for that."[53] Bon Dos's use of the term "noble" here links up with his denunciation of the liberal residents of the southern city of Jérémie as "aristocrats" created by Boyer's land reforms ("une véritable aristocratie terrienne").[54] Bon Dos's critiques thus reproduce Janvier's critique of Haitian Liberals: their name suggested that they were against tyranny, monarchs, and hierarchical forms of government, but in reality they reproduced that very system for the Haitian peasantry. Liberals' approach to the peasantry and rural labor regimes created a tiered class system that effectively rendered democracy or universal *liberté* impossible.

Here again, we see that the notion of *liberté* remained fraught and contested among various factions of the nation well into the late nineteenth century. In an extended play on the meaning of *liberté*, Bon Dos describes the hypocrisy of liberty and liberalism he saw in the post-1859 civil wars. He described the military members of the Liberal Party ("all of these so-called friends of liberty") who captured and killed Salnave and who put down Bon Dos and his fellow *piquet* agitators as acting according to the principle of individual liberty: "friends of their own freedom, arch enemies of ours. . . . Our leaders were executed. It was in the order. The liberalism of our enemies wanted it so."[55] He described the Liberal Party's opposition to Salomon's 1883 law in similar terms: those who proclaimed themselves Liberals were against the "loi libératrice" that freed the peasantry from their second-class existence and provided them with the path to full political participation in the nation. Bon Dos concludes that the notion of *liberté* enshrined in the paper constitutions so prized by the Liberal Party only reproduced inequality and systems of servitude for the rural peasantry.

The *lodyans* ends with Bon Dos's own dying words to his children. It is a didactic string of imperative phrases, commands, and directives according to which the new peasant generation must live, and a transparent reification of Janvier's Nationalist agenda—one we can easily imagine being read aloud to a group of peasants or translated into Kreyòl. The patriarch tells his children what to plant, how to rotate crops, when to harvest. Now that they have land after Salomon's 1883 law, he wants them to work to become "citoyens complets"—literate members of political and social life, invested in the future of the nation. He wants them to see their true value ("it's our welfare that makes the welfare of all"), to believe that they are more than just the backs upon which the country is built, but essential members of Haitian society.[56] Via this fictive *lodyans*, Janvier once again elaborates the keystone of his political program: *la terre au paysan*.

Janvier's *lodyans* enacts a revisionist critique of Haiti's history from below, a critique of the previous putatively republican, democratic regimes' failure to address the needs and the *rights* of the peasantry. It is a critique that he repeats throughout his work, in various genres and forms: "the complaint of the nation that has been betrayed too many times since 1806 by those she pinned all of her hopes upon."[57] His work is one of revisionism, or of *resurrection*, to bring forth the stories of those who had been obscured and to give voice to those who have not been included in the annals of Haitian history—*cultivateurs* like Bon Dos, but also artisans, soldiers, and peasants. In this, he is not fashioning his work according to the dominant, normative codes of the world republic of letters, but rather as a social literature or "littérature d'action" to complement his Nationalist platform. Via Bon Dos's story, he seeks to reveal the myths, misconceptions, and deliberate elisions of nineteenth-century Haitian historiography, insofar as it failed to address the government's continued "betrayal" (*trahison*) of Haiti's peasant masses. As he wrote in *Les constitutions*, "In history, truth always has a way of breaking through, no matter what precaution is taken to hide it, whatever care was taken to disguise it."[58] His use of the metaphor of truth, veiling, and piercing through recalls the earlier Vastey passage, but updated to the context of the armed peasants and their *piquets*. The armed peasant will always pierce through the regime or historical narrative that seeks to disavow him: "they alone are the font of our glorification [*apothéoses*]."[59]

Firministes/Nordistes, 1904/1906

The turn of the century saw an intellectual and social renaissance in Haiti during the 1890–1915 period, especially in the North, though it was not without considerable political turmoil.[60] The Nationalist, peasant-focused, populist Salomon had been able to hold on to power after the civil war of 1883, but not without constant pressure from Liberal opposition groups and rival Nationalist would-be leaders. In 1888 there was an uprising in the North and South; the North proclaimed a separatist republic, the République Septentrionale, under Séïde Thélémaque in 1888, while the southern Nationalist François Légitime briefly replaced Salomon as president of the republic in 1888. The northern general Florvil Hyppolite (who had replaced Thélémaque when he died) led a successful uprising against Légitime. Hyppolite was named president of the unified republic in October 1889 and ushered in an era of relative calm. Hyppolite exiled many in the National opposition, brought back Liberal leaders Edmond Paul and Anténor Firmin, and gave them positions in his government (Firmin especially pursued financial reform, schools, and public works). The North benefitted especially from the Hyppolite government, which initiated modernization projects throughout the country and was able to broker a peace, albeit ephemeral, between Liberal and National political factions. Tirésias Simon Sam, another northerner, came to power after Hyppolite's death in 1896, and served out his six-year presidency until the end of his term in 1902. The transition of power proved less obvious. The North and the South split along National/Liberal lines: the South was divided in its support between two candidates, the wealthy Liberal Calisthène Fouchard and the former secretary of war Sénèque Momplaisir Pierre. The North supported the Nationalist military general Pierre Nord Alexis (and were known as "Nordistes"). However, Anténor Firmin's entry into the field as a progressive (and his supporters, the "Firministes") added a new angle to the divisions in the North: in cities throughout the North (Cap-Haïtien, Limbé, Plaisance) and throughout the Artibonite, Nord-Ouest, and Port-au-Prince, Firmin drew new supporters for his intellectual, civilian political candidacy.[61] From June to December 1902, the country was at civil war, primarily between Nordistes and Firministes. The 1902 civil war is notable for the possibility of a third way: a political and ideological program beyond the Liberal/National divide that Firminisme offered. It was an ephemeral political possibility, and yet one that generated a committed intellectual following of Firministes who ultimately died for their politics.

Anténor Firmin is arguably Haiti's most well-known intellectual of the period for his essay *De l'égalité des races humaines* (1885), which he wrote in refutation of Arthur de Gobineau's multi-volume biological racist tract, *Essai sur l'inégalité des races humaines* (1853–1855). But who was Firmin, and what was Firminisme? A native of Cap-Haïtien and a Liberal from his earliest days, Firmin completed his education in Haiti and worked as a teacher, a speculator, a lawyer, and a journalist. He sparred early with his fellow Capois Demesvar Delorme, a Nationalist, in the 1870s before founding his own liberal newspaper, *Le Messager du Nord*. Despite his Liberal politics, Firmin did not immediately go into exile when the Nationalist Salomon came to power in 1879. Indeed, he even served as a representative of Salomon's government to Venezuela for the celebration of Simón Bolívar's centennial in 1883—as a staunch progressive, liberal republican, Firmin was a logical choice.[62] After the 1883 civil war in the South, however, Firmin went into exile in Paris, where he served as a Haitian emissary (a post that was undoubtedly assigned to him by Salomon in an effort to keep Liberal Party ideologues out of the political fray). There, he met up with Louis Joseph Janvier, who had already established himself on the intellectual scene; Janvier likely introduced Firmin to the Société d'anthropologie de Paris, where both men were members.[63] But the two still differed in important ways. Janvier was a staunch economic nationalist, while Firmin's economic liberalism supported further relaxing foreign ownership prohibitions in order to develop the Haitian economy. The two also operated in different intellectual and ideological spheres of influence in Paris: Janvier associated with the Jeune France nationalists (as discussed above), while Firmin was pursuing an "engaged cosmopolitanism" of an "increasingly global and interconnected world."[64] Hyppolite called Firmin back to Haiti in 1889 to serve as his minister of finance, commerce, and foreign relations. He stayed for only two years; though he successfully navigated negotiations with the United States and blocked its attempts to obtain Môle Saint-Nicolas as a military base, his politics and public pronouncements in favor of economic liberalism led Nationalists to attack him for trying to sell Haiti to the United States.[65] He went in and out of exile throughout the 1890s, which Marc Péan argues only served to increase his popularity and raise his profile as someone whose rigorous political and economic beliefs challenged the corrupt politicians in office.[66]

He returned to Cap-Haïtien in 1902 to attend his daughter Anna's funeral. The timing was fortuitous: the country had fallen into a political crisis in preparations to elect a successor to Tirésias Simon Sam, who had resigned from his presidency a year early. Out of this political crisis, Firminisme emerged. It was the product of the Liberal/National party divide that had shaped the country's politics since 1869. In many ways, Firminisme was a third way out of the parliamentary divisions that drew on aspects of each party to form a new, progressive party of the turn of the century. Overall it was much more Liberal than it was Nationalist, though it challenged the technocratic, elitist position of the Liberals (which accorded political power to a capable few) and embraced a populism that was more in line with the 1843 revolutionaries as well as Louis Joseph Janvier's peasant-based progressivism.[67] Firministes saw in the civilian, intellectual leader an opportunity to replace the military authority with a constitutional republic that relied on laws and human dignity—a language that evoked the liberal revolutionaries of 1843. Firministes called to "replace the blind regime of the sword with a regime based in respect for the laws and for the human person."[68] In concrete terms, they wanted a leader like Firmin who was a specialist in financial matters to take control of Haiti's economic situation, to reduce the influence of the army on political action, and to enfranchise citizens in the political process. Firminisme spread throughout Haiti in mid-1902, cutting through geographic, class, race, and generational divisions that had been, up to that point, hegemonic. Nevertheless, Firmin's strongest support was among the professional and artisan classes, while he had the least support among the elite establishment. The youth were his greatest champions (men like Seymour Pradel, Pauléus Sanon, and Massillon Coicou), spreading the doctrine of Firminisme "in their circles, their associations or their communities."[69]

Despite its commitment to an innovative third way and a path out of factional civil war, Anténor Firmin's 1902 Firministe revolution failed. If a political party based in the idea of transforming the military regime and replacing the "saber" with laws and human rights was a worthy ideal, it lacked precisely the military strength to overcome Nord Alexis's troops (aided by German ships, no less). Firmin did, however, have a few Haitian military sympathizers: Jean Jumeau and Hammerton Killick, the latter controlling a Haitian naval ship poignantly named the *Crête-à-Pierrot* after the important revolutionary battle. When a German ship fired on the *Crête-à-Pierrot* and demanded its surrender (at Nord Alexis's request), Killick scuttled it—himself aboard—in a massive explosion and a spectacular act of Firministe resistance.[70] Firmin went into exile in Saint Thomas, and Nord Alexis held on as president until 1908.[71]

The experience of civil war from 1883 to 1902, especially the increasing role that foreign powers played in it, shaped intellectuals' approach to the centennial of Haiti's independence. If, as we saw in previous chapters, Dessalines's assassination had been silenced or obliquely referenced by various writers and political factions, by the turn of the century writers were much more direct, confronting head-on the heritage of 1804/1806, the original civil war fracture of Haiti's founding, and its consequences for an entire people. Though there were still disagreements on Dessalines's characteristics as a leader and what his legacy should be, everyone argued for a more straightforward, honest accounting of his life and his death in order to move the country forward. Rather than celebrations of Haiti's victories and future promise, then, the public commemorations and publications that surrounded the centennial read like an attempt to reset the board and find common cause after near-constant civil war. Intellectuals were eager to identify the root cause of Haiti's civil war and offer a solution. They did so by going back to Haiti's original fracture: 1804 and 1806. More specifically, they endeavored to come to terms with Dessalines and his legacy at the centennial of independence: his role in the founding and in the future of Haiti. It is fitting, then, that Haiti celebrated the two centennials: 1904 and 1906.[72]

Dessalines was the focal point of Haiti's centennial celebrations, though it is important to note that many of the ideas the centennial enacted to honor the liberator-emperor had been proffered as early as 1845, and likely even before: a mausoleum to the emperor, a column to the heroes of national independence in Gonaïves, a national holiday commemorating his assassination and his inclusion in the national pantheon of heroes.[73] We might consider one such proposal taken to the floor of the Chamber of Representatives in 1847 by representative Pradine Linstant as an example of the deep roots and continuity of the centennial celebrations with earlier efforts to remember Dessalines. Linstant argued that other representatives' proposals to build a mausoleum to Pétion and Riché were incomplete because they did not include Dessalines, whose remains still sat under a humble monument that went unnoticed by passersby. Linstant argued that posterity had judged Dessalines worthy of more: "Of all the heroes of independence, J. J. Dessalines distinguished himself by his courage and the noble leadership he gave to the immortal revolution, which ushered in a new era. The misdeeds of the great man are erased by the immensity of his service to the country."[74] Linstant's arguments about posterity and the relative measure of Dessalines's faults versus his achievements—a hero who broke the chains of slavery and liberated a people—served as the basis upon which the centennial celebrations presented Dessalines as a hero and a member of the Haitian pantheon. In 1893, President Hyppolite contracted and paid for a mausoleum for "L'Empereur Dessalines."[75] On February 7, 1903, a statue of Dessalines was inaugurated on the Champ de Mars and financed, in part, by President Nord Alexis.[76] On November 29, 1903, "La Dessalinienne" was sung for the first time to honor the first Declaration of Independence when Dessalines's Armée Indigène rode victorious into the city of Cap-Haïtien.[77] The North waited until 1906 to inaugurate its own statue of Dessalines, spearheaded and financed by the prominent northerner Charles Leconte. Jean Price-Mars gave the inaugural speech to his fellow "son of this Department, citizen of Grande Rivière-du-Nord."[78] President Nord Alexis proclaimed October 17 a national holiday in 1906 and ordered commemoration services throughout the country.

It is the 1906 centennial celebrations that are of most interest to us here; they are, I would argue, more significant than those of 1904 to the national narrative of healing and "expiation." Writers and intellectuals positioned 1906 as a symbolic end point to the century of fractious civil war that they argued Dessalines's assassination had set off. By moving beyond partisan passions and embracing the "historical truth" of Dessalines's life, rule, and assassination, they hoped to finally move past partisan divides and toward a stable democracy. It would turn out to be a vain hope. Let us consider two of these 1906 commemoration texts more closely: Massillon Coicou's two-act drama in verse, *L'empereur Dessalines*, and L. C. Lhérisson's pamphlet *Pour Dessalines: 17 octobre 1806, 17 octobre 1906*. I argue that authors and intellectuals like Coicou,

Lhérisson, and others operated within a closed system of Haitian imagery, reactivating the Dessalinean discourse of independence and, especially, the language of previous writers like Chanlatte, Vastey, and Nau who challenged the republican disavowal of Dessalines's assassination and the foundational fracture of 1804/1806. Both Coicou and Lhérisson structure their argument about the Haitian centennial and the heritage of Dessalines's assassination around an already extant language of posterity, sullied glory, and "expiation" (reparation or compensation for a crime, atonement). Indeed, I would argue that they developed the line of reasoning that Emile Nau established in his preface to *Histoire des caciques* (see chapter 5) and brought it to what they believed was its logical conclusion: that the republic's origin in parricide was a stain on Haitian history that demanded atonement or reparation, but also an honest accounting. They argued that 1806 was a crime for which Haiti was still atoning—which is to say, they saw in it the source of Haiti's continued civil war. Or, as Coicou put it in the preface to his play: "this crime that did incalculable harm to the country, a truly prolific harm, for we are still atoning for it today [*nous l'expions encore*]."[79]

Massillon Coicou is a fascinating Haitian figure about whom relatively little is written. Coicou was undoubtedly a product of the late nineteenth-century cycle of civil war; it was a near-constant theme in his poetry and led him to adhere closely to the Firministe "third way" as a possible solution to Haiti's national crisis. Coicou was an early member of the Association du centenaire de l'indépendance nationale, a literary and artistic organization that began in 1891 on the centennial of the first uprisings in Saint-Domingue.[80] Coicou dedicated his first poetry collection, *Poésies nationales* (1892), to the centennial association, and it is an example of the nationalist-patriotic poetry that sought to unify the country and lay the groundwork for the centennial. He organized the collection into three books that represent three periods of Haitian history: slavery, revolution, and independence in book 1; Haiti's nineteenth century in book 2; and a long series of reflections and lamentations on civil war and the current state of Haiti at the end of the century in book 3. In his poetry, Coicou is as comprehensive as he is tenacious in his critique of civil war in Haiti's history: he honors each of Haiti's founding fathers equally, and together: Toussaint, Pétion, Christophe, and Dessalines, but offers a scathing critique of Geffrard during the civil war with Salnave. Coicou was elected president of the centennial association in 1896, replacing the founder and president, Joseph Jérémie.[81] A staunch Firministe, Coicou was removed from his post and the centennial association disbanded in the wake of the 1902 civil war between Nordistes and Firministes. Nord Alexis allowed the committee to reconvene after the civil war, but Coicou and the other original members were not permitted to rejoin. Still, it was not as if Coicou was cut out of Haitian cultural life under Nord Alexis: he remained active on the intellectual scene, publishing in various magazines, giving speeches, and working in public theater. He founded the literary and theatrical society L'Œuvre, geared specifically toward Port-au-Prince's younger generation and the role of public theater in educating the broader Haitian public. He took over the position of director at the Théâtre Haïtien in 1905, where *L'empereur Dessalines* was first performed.[82]

Coicou's was the first Haitian play to dramatize Dessalines's assassination at Pont Rouge when it was performed on October 7, 1906 (or October 17, more likely), at the Théâtre Haïtien.[83] Though the events reached the stage, they did not make it into print: Coicou never published the second act of the play—likely because it was deemed too provocative or inflammatory.[84] As with his poetry, Haiti's civil war shaped Coicou's dramatic depiction of Dessalines's assassination in 1806. I am interested here particularly in the heritage of earlier narratives of Dessalines's assassination that Coicou draws upon, particularly the notions of "expiation," sullied glory, and historical posterity. In the preface to his play, Coicou argues that it is not a man's reputation or acclaim that constitutes his glory, but his deeds. He reminds his readers that whatever his reputation, Dessalines's emancipation of an entire race from slavery constituted his glory. Furthermore, while Coicou acknowledges that the republican faction's honorable actions in the War of Independence contributed to their glory, their crime of parricide also needed to be counted among their "deeds." Indeed, Coicou states plainly in his preface that Dessalines's assassination was a crime, and one that was grossly disproportionate to the offense Dessalines committed by installing an imperial regime. Coicou's plain, straightforward accusations of parricide are a marked contrast to the metaphoric, euphemistic presentations of Dessalines's death that prevailed in earlier republican narratives of the revolution (see chapter 4). Indeed, Coicou's bold assertions are much closer to the stark accusation of parricide that Chanlatte levied against Pétion and his republican senators in his 1807 pamphlet *Réflexions sur le prétendu Sénat de Port-au-Prince* (see chapter 2). Coicou argues that he is taking stock of the event one hundred years later; past the passions that animated partisans and toward an honest accounting of the motivations of the event. He follows the logic of posterity, which delivers the final word in his preface: "the time has come for posterity to carry out its task of revision, its work of elimination, its duty to provide justice."[85] Coicou presents his play—the public spectacle of Dessalines's assassination—as evidence of what Haitian history should revise, eliminate, and conserve of the events of 1806: Dessalines's glory as the nation's liberator, and the crime of parricide. He concludes his preface with this judgment: "history refuses to approve [*sanction*] the crime of Pont-Rouge" (*la postérité refuse sa sanction au crime du Pont-Rouge*).[86]

L. C. Lhérisson goes further still with the question of parricide in his pamphlet *Pour Dessalines*.[87] He denounces 1806 as a "monstrous act" (*une action monstrueuse*), challenging Dessalines's reputation as a savage and turning it back on his executioners: "The Revolution of 1806 . . . was an ambitious, fruitless, unjust, and barbaric deed."[88] Under a subheading entitled "Atonement" (*L'expiation*), Lhérisson outlines the consequences of Haiti's foundational parricide (which he follows with the subheadings "Forgiveness" and "Toward the Future"). Lhérisson stresses that though Pétion and his conspirators were not themselves punished for their crime, the nation suffered for their sins. Here, Lhérisson activates Emile Nau's cryptic declaration about poetic justice and historical reparation that we saw in the previous chapter ("Toute gloire qui se souille s'expie"). Lhérisson applies Nau's ethics of "expiation historique" to Haiti's internal civil war: the glory is the creation of Haiti's republic in 1806, and its sullying with the assassination of Dessalines. The punishment for this deed, Lhérisson maintains, is continued civil war. Lhérisson argues that a nation cannot kill its founding father and its liberator with impunity; logically, there must be a consequence: "You do not kill a head of state with impunity, let alone a breaker of chains! It is an unpardonable [*irrémissible*] crime, one that weighs heavily on the future of a nation."[89]

Both Lhérisson and Coicou looked to the past but also to the future in order to offer a way out of partisan divisions and continued civil war: the heroine Défilée.[90] Défilée-la-folle, or Dédée Bazile, is said to have brought Dessalines's dismembered body to its final resting place after his assassination on October 17, 1806.[91] Prior to the centennial celebrations, there had been only brief mentions of her in Thomas Madiou and Beaubrun Ardouin's mid-nineteenth-century histories of Haiti. Coicou's play dramatizes for the first time on stage and in print (in his preface, at least) the heroine Défilée. Coicou, Lhérisson, Joseph Jérémie, and many of the other members of the centennial and theatrical societies of the period saw Défilée as the emblem of the national conscience.[92] Coicou asks his reader in the preface about Défilée and her actions: "Isn't it true that when Défilé passed through Port-au-Prince, making a funeral shroud [*linceul*] for the emperor out of a muddy sack [*sac fangeux*] . . . that the most perfect embodiment of the national conscience is her, this madwoman in the midst of these madmen who thought themselves wise?"[93] There is much to unpack here: first, that Coicou is picking up on the imagery that earlier poets used to metaphorically index Dessalines's assassination. Coriolan Ardouin's "Le Pont rouge," for example, blamed Dessalines for having stained Haitian history with "fraternal blood." Ardouin portrayed Dessalines's fall as of his own doing: the emperor's choice to destroy his own work, to shipwreck *and bury himself*, "s'ensevelit sous un triste linceul" because of his ambition and his imperial designs (see chapter 4). Coicou reworks this by depicting Dessalines's assassination as a stain ("énorme tache de sang") that the national conscience cannot erase, and insisting on the republican conspirators' agency in the act: they stained Haiti's history with the blood of their liberator. Similarly, Coicou pushes back against the idea that Dessalines somehow buried himself under a sad funeral shroud. If not for Défilée, Dessalines would have had no burial at all: she alone assures a proper burial for Dessalines by creating a makeshift funeral shroud out of a dirty bag ("sac fangeux").[94] Finally, Coicou presents the "madwoman" Défilée as the sole defender of Haiti's national future; she alone performed this sacred act of national devotion amid the jeers and taunts of these crazed executioners who believed themselves to be the enlightened ones. It is a powerful image and an even more powerful rebuke of the republican narrative of 1806 that had dominated the nineteenth century.

We do not know how Coicou's Défilée appeared on the stage, though we do know that she was played by a prominent member of the intellectual elite, Sylvia Innocent. As we shall see in the next chapter, Défilée will become an even more prominent figure in nationalist poetry under the US occupation of Haiti, as will Coicou's argument about the crime of Dessalines's assassination and the ethics of historical expiation. Where Coicou, Lhérisson, Jérémie, and other writers of the centennial were concerned with Haitian civil war and the path forward toward a unified, functioning government, the next generation would contend with the loss of Haitian independence itself when the United States invaded in 1915. The ideas of sullied glory and atonement in the context of Haiti's civil war were one thing, but when mobilized against the loss of sovereignty and the US occupation of Haiti, they turned even more potent. A generation of nationalist writers would identify in 1806 the seeds of the US occupation and rally around a fascistic idea of national revolution to found the nation anew.

* * *

In January 1908, civil war again gripped Haiti when Firministes in exile attempted once more to overthrow Nord Alexis's government by secretly distributing letters and pamphlets written by Firmin, Rosalvo Bobo, and other exiles.[95] Firmin landed in Gonaïves on January 15 and rallied the Artibonite to rise up against Nord Alexis, whose repression was swift: he sent out his militia, known as "zinglins," to arrest and execute Firmin's supporters. On the night of March 14, 1908, Massillon Coicou, his brothers, and a group of their Firministe companions were seized and executed outside the walls of the cemetery in Port-au-Prince.[96] Ultimately the Firministe uprising failed, and the next six years descended into near-constant civil war. As Matthew Smith has noted on the defeat of Firminisme, Firmin's misstep was his failure to come to terms with Haiti's civil war and his belief that his movement could "erase a history of factionalism": "At the end of the first decade of the twentieth century, Haiti had to contend with the coalescence of the conflicts of the past century."[97] As we shall see in the final chapter, intellectuals and politicians focused not on erasing Haiti's factionalism, but probing its depths: focusing on Haiti's factional divides, its internal civil war, and its fractured foundations, in order to found the nation anew. Indeed, it is hard not to see in the public killing and dismembering of the sitting president Vilbrun Guillaume Sam in 1915 a haunting doubling of Dessalines's 1806 assassination. This was not lost upon some Haitians, who saw the events of the US occupation of Haiti through the lens of Haiti's original foundational fractures and civil war.

7

Haiti's National Revolution

Haiti's National Palace in Port-au-Prince collapsed in the 2010 earthquake. The heavy upper domes of the structure remained mostly intact after they had leveled the first floor, leaving ruins that resembled what can best be described as a fallen wedding cake. The palace that collapsed was Haiti's third on the Champ de Mars site in central Port-au-Prince. The first had been destroyed by Sylvain Salnave when the embattled president rigged the palace to explode as he attempted to flee across the border in 1869. A second palace was built in the 1880s and again destroyed in an explosion in 1912 that killed the sitting president, Cincinnatus Leconte. Haitian authorities had already selected plans from the Haitian architect Georges Baussan and started construction in earnest when the United States occupied Haiti in 1915. The United States took control of the construction and completed the structure in the 1920s.[1] It is fitting, then, that when the Haitian government decided to demolish the damaged structure, a foreign company completed the work: J/P HRO, Sean Penn's nonprofit organization, razed the crumpled edifice in 2012.[2]

As with any national symbol, the National Palace is fraught with competing interpretations about who is claiming it and who determines its meaning. While to many foreigners, the crumpled edifice, the stark white domes still intact above, represented a failure of the nation-state, to many Haitians, the fallen palace marked an end to the capital city's tyranny over Haiti's provinces, and to the centralization and corruption of the previous century. This is particularly true for northerners, who had viewed the National Palace with contempt from the moment of its inception in the mid-1910s. For them, the palace represented the unequal centralization around the capital city, the growing power of the elites in the capital, and an increasing ostracism of the North. Indeed, the palace construction plan was part of an unevenly enacted program of public works initiated by Port-au-Prince's elite bureaucracy that privileged the capital city over the northern province and its main center, Cap-Haïtien. One northern resident, describing the deplorable state of provincial infrastructure in the early twentieth century and the dire need for developments in schools, roads, and housing in regional town centers, noted wryly, "We're certainly not asking for palaces."[3] Another northerner, J. F. Magny, described the symbolism of the National Palace with a lexicon of decadence, depravity, and biblical corruption, bearing witness to the social and political views of the North in the 1930s:

> Divisions, hatred, ambitions, prejudices, slaughter, denunciations, treason ... this is the serpent that has bitten Mother Haiti! It is still alive and will continue its murderous work, until not a stone remains of the national edifice. Well! So be it! The house needs to be rebuilt on a stronger foundation—solid, eternal. We do not want it merely to be rebuilt, to be only the façade, a beautiful dome with a muddy substructure, a rotten, worm-eaten frame. ... O bleached tomb!!!–Continue your infernal work, cursed serpent. Finish your destruction and sweep the ground clean [*balayer*] so that we can erect [*édifier*] in the bedrock a new order of things [*un ordre de choses nouveau*] that your fangs will attack in vain.[4]

Magny's description here is nothing short of a call for national revolution, very much in the spirit of interwar European nationalist movements, as we shall see below. The title of his article, "1804-1915-1930," evokes the heritage of the Haitian Revolution by suggesting that 1930 serve as the end point of the US occupation and a new kind of 1804, a new Haitian independence. Though the occupation would not officially end until 1934, by 1930 the tide had turned against the United States. Nationwide protests had roiled the country in late 1929, catalyzed by a student protest at the US-run Service technique school in Damiens. After a violent confrontation between US Marines and protesters in Marchaterre on December 4, 1929, left as many as fifty dead, the end of the occupation was no longer a question of if, but when.[5] As the United States began preparations to withdraw its military forces, Haitians engaged more freely in the press in their own discussions on the future of the nation. With the election of the new Nationalist president, Sténio Vincent, the year 1930 represented a moment of national regeneration, returning to 1804 to create a new foundation for the nation. Importantly, Magny's focus on national regeneration does not blame the United States or cast his national critique as part of a reaction or response to the US occupation. Instead he focuses on Haiti's own house, the nation's internal decay that had been spreading since before the United States had arrived and, as Magny's compatriots would argue, was actually the cause of the occupation itself. Magny chooses the image of the biblical serpent to convey the idea that Haitian sin—hatred, ambition, greed—caused Haiti's current predicament. The US occupation was not the *cause* of this national failure; it was a result of this original sin, of the flawed foundation of the Haitian nation. The departure of US forces will simply "restore" Haitian sovereignty, but Magny is looking for more. Using the extended metaphor of nation-as-house, Magny does not want the Haitian nation restored: he wants it to be reconstructed, refounded entirely. Magny evokes the white domes of the National Palace when he argues that Haiti's national house must be rebuilt on a new foundation, one that is immune to these carnal sins. Its beautiful domes cannot mask what it is: a bleached, whitened tomb.

The metaphor of the nation-as-house, its rotten foundations, and the blame placed on the divisive, degenerate forces within participates in an extant Atlantic discourse of integral nationalism (or "Maurrassisme"[6]) in which northerners like Magny were well versed.[7] It is thus the Haitian heritage of 1804/1806 but *also* the powerful ideology of national revolution prevalent among far-right integral nationalists in Europe within which Magny frames his nationalist critique. This chapter considers the ideology of national revolution in 1920s and 1930s Haiti under the US occupation. In the first two section, I excavate the heritage of Haiti's occupation-era far-right nationalism by analyzing the little-studied literary magazine *Stella* (Cap-Haïtien, 1926–1930). I highlight the poetry and prose works published in the magazine, which the writers situated within the longer Haitian tradition of nationalist, Dessalinean intellectual production: that in order for the nation to heal and achieve unity, it was necessary to plumb the depths of Haiti's original fractures, its deepest wounds. Yet if the *Stella* writers placed themselves within an intellectual heritage, they also saw themselves forging a new, radical path for the post-occupation future. As I argue in a final section, *Stella*'s nationalist writers once again evoked the fracture of 1804/1806—not to mend Haiti's foundational fractures, but to definitively reject the liberalism of 1806.

Occupation-Era Cultural Nationalism

In many ways, the US occupation of Haiti was a *fait accompli*. In the decades that preceded the military intervention, Haiti can be best summed up as a nation challenged to maintain independence in the face of foreign penetration, against the backdrop of a larger, global struggle for hegemony, influence, and resources at the dawn of the new century. While the United States ultimately gained control, the early twentieth century saw France, Germany, and Great Britain each vying for a piece of the economy and a zone of influence in the region, relying on gunboat diplomacy to protect their citizens and capital on the ground. Haiti was an especially desirable base of operations for the world powers in the Caribbean, with its connection to transatlantic shipping routes and the potential for establishing a military base at Môle Saint-Nicolas, a deep-water harbor in the northwest. By the early 1910s the Haitian economy, tied almost entirely to coffee exports, was in a steep decline. This, in addition to continued political factionalism, further contributed to the nation's political instability and the inevitability of foreign intervention.

The events that played out over the years 1911–1915 rehearsed a familiar nineteenth-century story: regional opposition groups flexed their muscle, agitating uprisings and coups against the sitting leader in Port-au-Prince. It was a revolt against the sitting president Vilbrun Guillaume Sam, set into motion by northern opposition leader (and former Firministe insurrectionary) Rosalvo Bobo, that gave the United States the pretext it needed to enter Port-au-Prince on July 27, 1915. Sam's assassination only served to hasten the United States' intervention in Haiti, designed to secure its strategic economic and political interests in the region.[8] While some elite leaders and businessmen in Port-au-Prince welcomed the invasion to quell unrest and put an end to the regional power centers that fomented revolt and threatened their interests, the rest of Haiti resisted. Haitians of all political factions and regional affiliations opposed the US end to Haitian sovereignty in different ways: from the Latinisant poet Edmond Laforest, who drowned himself in protest, to the Firministe Rosalvo Bobo, who led a band of *caco* rebels in the North of Haiti, to the insurgent leader Charlemagne Péralte, whose effigy remains a symbol of Haitian resistance and independence. While many took up arms, still others looked to Haitian history and more specifically the heritage of

1804/1806 to find answers for their loss of sovereignty and independence under the US occupation. Their pursuit is the subject of this chapter.

One of the most significant publications to come out during the US occupation period was the northern literary magazine *Stella: Organe de la bibliophile* (1926–1930). Though it is largely forgotten today, eclipsed by its well-known southern counterpart, *La Revue indigène* (1927–28), *Stella* was the northern region's most notable and prolific literary magazine of the early twentieth century.[9] It served as a voice of the then-flourishing intellectual and literary community in Cap-Haïtien and an organ of the learned Capois society, Les Bibliophiles. The magazine's contributors were highly educated Capois from modest military or agricultural wealth. They were born and raised in the northern capital, educated at the Lycée Philippe Guerrier in Cap-Haïtien, and worked as teachers, lawyers, or members of local government. This included such prominent young Capois as Christian Werleigh, Jean-Baptiste Cinéas, Louis Mercier, and Cadet Dessources, as well as more prominent intellectuals like Luc Grimard and Jean Price-Mars.

It is *Stella*'s deep commitment to Haitian history, and Haitian revolutionary history specifically, that sets it apart from its better-known Port-au-Prince–based contemporary, *La Revue indigène*. To better grasp the wider intellectual field of the period in Haiti, it would be useful to present the two magazines in contrast here. The *Stella* group was slightly older on average and more heterogeneous in age than the *Revue indigène* group, although it is important to note that some of *Stella*'s main contributors, such as Cinéas and Werleigh, were born in 1895—only five or eight years older than the *Revue indigène* contributors. *Stella* was critical of the avant-garde innovation and *verslibrisme* practiced by the Young Turks in *La Revue indigène* (and in their earlier magazines, *La Nouvelle ronde* and *La Trouée*), though they never engaged in direct critique or refutation of *La Revue indigène*. Rather, *Stella*'s writers mostly ignored *La Revue indigène* and took aim instead at historians and intellectuals who challenged—in writing—their integral nationalist views.[10] Nevertheless, there is considerable ideological overlap in *Stella* and *La Revue indigène*. This was before the intellectual polarization of the 1930s, which impelled stricter ideological divides between the Haitian Communist Party, the nativist, ethno-nationalist movement that developed around the *Griots* magazine, and a far-right Catholic, integralist nationalism in magazines and newspapers like *La Phalange, La Lanterne, Maintenant,* and *Psyché*.[11] In the 1920s, most intellectuals engaged in the vogue for far-right nationalist thinkers, and expressed a nativism that was based in a particular Haitian idea of local cultural specificity. For example, in the 1920s Jacques Roumain praised Maurice Barrès for the idea expressed in "La terre et les morts" as the new foundation upon which Haiti's national fortress could be built: "These words from Barrès, here is the solid granite base [*le dur granit*] upon which we can erect [*édifier*] the nationalist fortress," echoing the nation-as house metaphor that the *Stella* magazine elaborated above, but also Louis Joseph Janvier's call for national reform that we saw in the previous chapter.[12]

The primary difference between *Stella* and *La Revue indigène* was audience—that is, their intended print public sphere. As I have argued elsewhere, the *Revue indigène* magazine privileged a cosmopolitan frame: the writers saw themselves as "citizens of the world," and considered the formal experimentation and free verse of early twentieth-century poetic modernism a central component of their cultural nationalist project.[13] Theirs was a cosmopolitan cultural nationalism, or "cosmopolitan patriotism" as Kwame Anthony Appiah terms it, an Atlantic-facing literary production that engaged in the world republic of letters.[14] Their poetry was anthologized and prefaced by Paul Morand, the French travel writer and literary critic, who gave them an audience on his trip through the Caribbean. Many of the young poets also networked with Valery Larbaud, the translator and *revuiste* of the 1920s who was arguably at the center of Paris's Atlantic literary and cultural exchange. In fact, a close read of the group's magazine reveals a curious detail: it did not provide any subscription information. This is a remarkable aberration: virtually all other Haitian specialized publications I have studied from the period include this information. I would argue that, simply put, the primary audience for the *Revue indigène* was not Haiti. The group, financed by the wealthy father of one of its contributors, created the *revue* as a calling card for entry into the 1920s world republic of letters.[15] As we shall see here, *Stella* writers were quite the opposite: anti-worldly, anti-*mondain*. They criticized worldly literary society and avant-garde literary innovation as decadent. They conceived of literature as an arm, a tool of their ideological mission: to regenerate and rehabilitate the Haitian nation through order, structure, tradition, and history.

If this sounds "bad," it is: *Stella* writers fully embraced the far-right nationalism that other Haitian intellectuals like Roumain merely flirted with, and built their cultural nationalist project around Maurrassisme and an idea of Haitian national revolution. But before we get there, it is worth asking why *Stella*'s far-right integral nationalism has not been the subject of more scholarly interest. This is not to say that scholars have ignored it; some have noted with considerable unease the preponderance of French far-right nationalist thought in early twentieth-century Haitian literary and cultural production.[16] Yet this connection has never been sufficiently explained. Certainly part of it is that the *Revue indigène* overshadows *Stella*: the modernist magazine is infinitely more interesting to scholars of French and Francophone studies than a "traditionalist," nationalist-integralist publication. Moreover, the *Revue indigène* is legible specifically within the cosmopolitan lettered sphere: it uses a language and set of references that were legible to—indeed, geared for—a modernist Atlantic audience. *Stella*'s anti-*mondain* writing, on the other hand, eschews the performance of the dominant norms of cosmopolitan, Francophone literariness. The magazine is focused inward and expressly on Haitian issues, Haitian history, and a Haitian readership.[17] While this focus may not be interesting to Francophone literary critics or literary historians—committed as we are to the construct that associates "goodness" with innovation—it is nevertheless a significant cultural and political position to take, especially in the context of this larger argument I am making about the history of writing in post-independence Haiti and the eventual rise to power of François Duvalier's nativist dictatorship.[18] That is, by focusing on a corpus of Haitian and Francophone writing that is shaped by the inclusion of "good literature" (that which innovates and accords with the hierarchies of aesthetic values set by the republic of letters) and the exclusion of "bad literature" (that which does not), literary critics have silenced an entire sphere of Haitian intellectual production. If we are to make sense of the Duvalier dictatorship and its link to Haiti's long nineteenth century of Enlightenment critique, we must dilate our focus beyond the capital-centric, cosmopolitan sphere of the world republic of letters.

Let us consider *Stella*'s anti-*mondain* intellectual production in action. In a speech entitled "L'étude de l'histoire," *Stella* contributor Guizot Mompoint explained why the group and its magazine put the study of history at the center of their poetic production. Mompoint argued that in a time of national crisis under the US occupation, it was history that would provide moral guidance for a people, showing them the follies of the past and offering them ideas for the future. For Mompoint, it was history that countered the dissolution of morals and values in society because it offered people guidance and a constant reminder of their civic duty, which he contrasted with the "moral and intellectual disorder" of worldly, literary society.[19] Mompoint's critique of the elite, worldly predilections of the "société mondaine et littéraire" is instructive here: he is criticizing the social and cultural politics of the elite, intellectual class (in Port-au-Prince) as much as he is criticizing their actual literary production. For, as we shall see here, *Stella* did engage with literature, a literature that subordinated the practice of creative writing to the moral imperative of history, and by privileging content over form. *Stella*'s cultural nationalism supported a literature that was didactic and commemorative, in the service of *Stella*'s national revolution, through two main forms: historico-patriotic poetry and the peasant *récit*.

Christian Werleigh, one of *Stella*'s main poets and a member of the magazine's central group of contributors, embodies the anti-*mondain* position of *Stella*'s sociohistorical poetry when he characterized the *verslibrisme* and avant-garde poetic innovation of the early twentieth century as a kind of literary "anarchy."[20] If order and hierarchy offered a solution to the crisis of decadence in Haitian society, order and structure in Haitian poetry was a response to the anarchy of *verslibrisme* that threatened Haitian national literature. In particular, writers like Werleigh pursued a kind of technical conservatism, using the alexandrine to maintain order and structure in poetry that would contribute to the political and ideological message within the magazine. *Stella*'s conservative approach to poetry is reflected in the magazine's appreciation of Dominique Hippolyte's 1927 poetry collection, *La route ensoleillée*. Not incidentally, Hippolyte chose a line from Charles Maurras's 1918 historical-patriotic poem *La bataille de la Marne: Ode historique*, "J'ai tout reçu du sol natal" (My native soil has given me everything), to serve as an epigraph for his poetry collection.[21] The historical thrust of the epigraph and the emphasis on nativism resonated with the *Stella* writers, as did Hippolyte's traditional versification: "The poet rightly ignores the free verse and symbolist revolutions, even more so the Dadaist and cubist revolutions."[22] Hippolyte's poetry embodied *Stella*'s approach to poetry: the simplicity and modesty of the alexandrine in the face of what the northern writers perceived to be pretentious and even anarchical experimentations in versification and form. For *Stella* poets, dodecasyllabic verse was an instrument of tradition, structure, and simplicity that allowed poets to more adequately express their historical-patriotic poetry.

Nearly all of the poems in *Stella* fulfilled this historical-patriotic poetic ideal, recasting Haiti's heritage squarely within an Amerindian-Dessalinean paradigm. Frédéric Burr-Reynaud contributed poems entitled "1804," "Défilée," "Dessalines, Christophe," and "Eloge funèbre d'Anacaona," while Louis-Henry Durand penned "Après le sacrilege," a poem denouncing the cowardly actions of Dessalines's assassins and redeeming the revolutionary hero's memory.[23] Of all *Stella*'s poets, however, Werleigh stands out for his Dessalinean production. His fellow contributor Louis Mercier celebrated his effort to rehabilitate the memory of Haiti's founding fathers and mothers: "to honor these nation builders whose memory has been sullied by historians full of hatred and prejudice."[24] Werleigh commemorated Dessalines's proclamation of Haitian independence in the poem "Dix-huit cent quatre," the liberator's hard-fought battle against the French in "La Crête-à-Pierrot," the patriotic act of Dédée Bazile in "Le miracle: Dessalines et Défilée," and his celebration of the native Indian queen who ruled the Xaragua kingdom of Hispanola until her death at the hands of the Spanish conquistadors in "Anacaona."

Werleigh's poem "Le miracle: Dessalines et Défilée" typifies the historical-patriotic nature of *Stella*'s cultural nationalist poetry.[25] It is a continuation of the nationalist politics of Massillon Coicou's play, further radicalized under the US occupation of Haiti (see chapter 6). Indeed, Mercier referred to Werleigh as Haiti's "barde national," a title used previously for Coicou, to inscribe Werleigh's poetics within this Dessalinean heritage. Werleigh's poem begins with the couplet announcing Dessalines's death: "He was dead . . . the horrible deed was done / And the great leaders and the masses celebrated," establishing from the first lines a tension between the loss of Haiti's liberator and the celebration that ensued.[26] It was a moment, according to Werleigh, of cruel irony: the people who celebrated the emperor's death believed they were celebrating the salvation of the nation, when they had in fact doomed it to failure. Werleigh presents Pétion as unwise and shortsighted, unable to foresee the disastrous effect of his plot to assassinate the emperor—the eventual loss of Haitian independence with the US occupation a century later. Here, Werleigh reactivates the debate over the meaning of *liberté* that characterized the early post-independence divide between Dessalineans and republicans:

> Et comment pourraient-ils s'empêcher d'exulter,
> Ceux qui disaient avoir sauvé la Liberté?
> Le croirait-il, ce peuple heureux qui chante et danse,
> Qu'il venait de tuer, déjà, l'Indépendance?
>
> (And why would they not be celebrating,
> Those who thought they had saved Liberty?
> Would they believe it, these happy, dancing folk,
> That he had just killed Independence, too?)

For Werleigh, 1806 was the moment that sealed the fate of the Haitian nation; republicans argued that they were saving *liberté* while Dessalineans argued that republicans had sacrificed *independence*. Werleigh thus identifies the root cause of Haiti's military occupation in 1915 with the unwise actions of Pétion and his republican supporters more than a century earlier.

Werleigh further makes this point by shifting to the future tense, from the position of having seen the effects of 1915 on Haitian independence. Here, the US occupation looms large—though unnamed—as Werleigh links Dessalines's assassination to the loss of effective independence under the United States' neocolonial intervention:

> Un jour, les Fils infortunés devront se battre:
> Ils verront tout à coup s'effondrer l'avenir
> Et repentants, ils sauront eux, se souvenir
>   Du Titan de Dix-Huit-Cent-Quatre.

> (One day, his unfortunate Sons will have to fight:
> They will see the future suddenly fall to pieces
> Repentant, they will know to remember
>   The Titan of 1804.)[27]

The "Fils" here are the descendants of the revolutionary leaders, Haitians like Werleigh. They will have to fight when the United States lands troops on Haiti's shores, the moment to which Werleigh refers when "ils verront tout à coup s'effondrer l'avenir." It is at this moment, a century later, that Haitians will realize that they should look to Dessalines for answers. Werleigh's use of the verb *s'effondrer* is important. It recasts the dominant nineteenth-century imagery of Dessalines's demise: that in one second, his rule crumbled (see chapter 4). Werleigh argues that it was not just Dessalines's empire that crumbled in 1806, but the nation's future. This vision of a crumbling national edifice caused by a faulty foundation implies that the US occupation was not the cause of Haiti's national crisis, but a symptom of it. In Werleigh's poem, Haiti's loss of national sovereignty—of *liberté* as independence—had been decided nearly a century before, by the sins of Haiti's revolutionary forefathers.

Werleigh's poem clearly echoes Magny's language describing the faulty foundations of the Haitian nation and the need to rebuild on new, solid ground analyzed in the introduction to this chapter. Werleigh develops this metaphor of razing the ground and starting anew with the story of Dédée Bazile, or Défilée-la-folle. Recall from the previous chapter that Massillon Coicou and other centennial writers cast Défilée as a symbol of national conscience in the centennial celebrations of 1904/1906, committing to print what had been, up to that point, an oral tradition. Werleigh draws heavily upon Coicou's work especially in order to cast Défilée as a redemptive force and a source of national hope in the context of the US occupation. He reminds the reader that she was the only person to act in the national interest when she gathered Dessalines's body for burial: "She alone chose to go to the cemetery, / Securing the future of the entire country."[28] The titular miracle of the poem was thus this "mad" woman's clarity of (national) purpose. Werleigh portrays it as a kind of momentary, divinely bestowed lucidity and patriotic presentiment for the future. Where Pétion, the wise, enlightened leader, had not been able to understand the omens that beseeched him to abandon his plan, Défilée alone saw the path forward to conserve the nation: "Hearing the name of this hero they were jeering / Suddenly lit up her vacant eyes."[29]

Werleigh ends his poem on the metaphor of Défilée as a maternal, life-giving force: she is the mother-womb of Haiti's national rebirth after the US occupation. Défilée's heroic act thus preserved Dessalines's memory and allowed for the eventual rebirth of the nation by sowing the seeds—with his bones—of Haiti's national regeneration. She protects the national idea, nourishes it, and conserves it so that one day it might be reborn again:

> O Défilée, épouse, mère, fille, sœur,
> Tu fus toute la Femme et tu fus la Patrie:
> ...
> Celle qui sur la terre a sauvé Sa mémoire.
> Ton nom obscur, de tous béni, sera plus beau
> Et l'on ira prier sur ta tombe fleurie,
> O toi qui n'avais rien et donnas un tombeau
> > Au Fondateur de la Patrie!
>
> (O Défilée, wife, mother, daughter, sister,
> You were all Women and you were the Fatherland;
> ...
> She who on earth saved His memory.
> Your humble name, blessed, will be finer
> And we will go to pray at your flowery tombstone,
> You who had nothing and gave a resting place,
> > To the Founding Father!)[30]

In contrast to the bloody, bellicose, masculine acts of parricide that destroyed national independence, Werleigh offers the feminine figure of Défilée, a protective, live-giving force.[31] Werleigh gestured to the recent but growing importance of female writers and intellectuals in the early twentieth century as part of his effort to rethink Haiti's national heroes: "Times have changed. That's why today we call Défilée the first Heroine of the Haitian nation."[32] Défilée's story offered the possibility of national regeneration for occupation-era Haiti, and was part of the magazine's larger focus on the memory of Dessalines's assassination. Like the 1904/1906 writers before them, *Stella* writers saw 1806 as an original fracture in the foundation of the Haitian nation—one that they sought to expose and ultimately, correct by refounding the nation on new ground.

The Peasant *Récit*

In addition to their focus on national history, the *Stella* magazine also explored short stories, scenes, and vignettes that highlighted peasant life in the northern region. Under the pseudonym "Campagnard," the Capois writer Jean-Baptiste Cinéas penned a series of *récits* in the pages of *Stella* that promoted agricultural reform, highlighted the long heritage of northern cultural traditions, and sought to restore dignity to the peasantry. In presenting himself as the "Campagnard," Cinéas assumes the role of intermediary, or even of native ethnographer. He uses an observation-based lexicon ("observe," "study," "witness") to present his methodology for the column: "we will see them at work, observe their unrequited love, witness the daily injustices to which they are subjected."[33] Cinéas's "Campagnard" thus navigates between the rural world of the peasant and the educated elite that constituted his readership. He describes his writing as a "picture of peasant life" (*tableau de la vie paysanne*) that would offer a studied, authentic representation of the peasant reality to the magazine's readers, including descriptions of peasant religion, marriage, and collective labor practices, or *konbit*.[34]

Cinéas was a true *homme du nord*;[35] he remained in the North for his education, completing a degree in law at the Ecole libre de droit du Cap. While writing for *Stella*, he also taught at the Collège Notre-Dame du perpétuel secours in Cap-Haïtien and served as the region's inspector of schools. Cinéas also served as George Eaton Simpson's translator and guide when the latter was doing his ethnographic field research in northern Haiti in 1937, and later coauthored a number of articles with Simpson on northern folklore. Cinéas shared a northern sensibility and a good relationship with the well-known Haitian ethnographer Jean Price-Mars (who hailed from Grande-Rivière-du-Nord). The two found common cause in their commitment to reforming Haitian society through their work: where Price-Mars sought to "restore the value of folklore in the eyes of the Haitian people" in *Ainsi parla l'oncle*, Cinéas sought to "restore the opinion" of the humble and indispensable peasant laborer in his peasant stories.³⁶ It is important to note here that the *Stella* writers enjoyed a much closer relationship with Price-Mars than the *Revue indigène* writers, who had little engagement with the northern ethnographer in the 1920s.³⁷ Price-Mars was a supporter of the *Stella* writers and contributed a number of excerpts and original articles to the northern magazine. He was a particular champion of the work of Cinéas, one of the main *Stella* contributors, whom some have called the father of the Haitian peasant novel. In 1933 Price-Mars wrote a glowing preface to Cinéas's first peasant novel, *Le drame de la terre*, praising the author for his ethnographic accuracy, telluric authenticity, and use of the *lodyans* style of storytelling: "The writer identified with his characters with such ease that we can no longer tell if he is a storyteller who has cut us off a slice of real life . . . or if his work is a transcription of the long chats that our elders of yore used to revel in."³⁸ Cinéas's dedication of his novel, *La vengeance de la terre,* to Price-Mars suggests a close, caring relationship that he describes in biblical terms: "To my knowledgeable, very dear friend, . . . the man who loves me and whom I love more than anyone."³⁹

Despite his prolific contributions and innovations to the peasant novel genre—the privileged form of "national" Haitian literary expression in the 1930s and 1940s—Cinéas's foundational role in the genre has been eclipsed by Jacques Roumain's *Gouverneurs de la rosée*, arguably Haiti's best-known novel.⁴⁰ I argue here that the peasant novel was the manifestation of the new, distinct cultural nationalist project that emerged out of a primarily regional context in the pages of *Stella*. Indeed, the peasant *récits* that appeared in *Stella* differed from the narrative short stories that were published in Port-au-Prince newspapers and magazines (*La Presse, La Revue indigène, Haïti-Journal*) during the same period. The *contes* and *nouvelles* published in Port-au-Prince typically recounted short intrigues that centered on one main (capital-dwelling) protagonist. On the other hand, the short narratives that appeared in *Stella* contained almost no dialogue, and privileged description and exposition over plot.⁴¹ Often the author introduced his subject, painted a detailed short vignette of the rural scene, and then provided trenchant social and political commentary on the scene for the reader. They shared much more with Louis Joseph Janvier's "Le vieux piquet" than with the contemporary short stories in Philippe Thoby-Marcelin's *Les héroïnes* or Jacques Roumain's *La proie et l'ombre*.

Cinéas's short *Stella* narratives served as the laboratory for his longer-format peasant novels published in the 1930s and 1940s and are key to understanding the regional foundation of the modern peasant novel genre. His full-length novels—*Le drame de la terre* (1933), *La vengeance de la terre* (1934), *L'héritage sacré* (1937), and *Le choc en retour* (1945)—feature the same characters and reproduce some word-for-word sections, while further developing the images, themes, and ideologies he had sketched out in the pages of *Stella*. His peasant contributions to the magazine reinforced and enhanced the cultural nationalist project of *Stella*, which sought to establish an alternative future for the Haitian nation based on decentralization, agriculture, and a reinvestment in the peasantry.

In fact, a close reading of Cinéas's first novel in the cycle, *Le drame de la terre*, reveals just how much Jacques Roumain's depiction of the peasantry and *la misère* in the rural hinterland borrowed from its little-studied predecessor. Cinéas's novel opens with a drought: he describes the dry, cracked surface of the earth and the repetitive, enumerative evocation of the rain, which still had not come. Roumain's *Gouverneurs* famously opens with Délira Délivrance's grave prognostication "We're all going to die," as the main character plunges her hand into the dust of the drought-wrought earth. Cinéas's depiction of the earth as a woman, a metaphorical womb that is forced to submit (undoubtedly in conversation with Werleigh's Défilée-as-womb-of-the-nation metaphor discussed above), also precedes Roumain's extended metaphor of fertility and the earth in *Gouverneurs*—of Manuel's phallic machete, the blade of the peasant's hoe, and the "lame" or blade of water that irrigates the land at the end of the novel that imitates its entry into the earth, and Annaïse's pregnancy that assures that life will continue.[42] Other similarities abound: Roumain's description of the *konbit*, one of the most cited aspects of his novel, includes all of the key aspects from Cinéas's earlier depiction. For example, where Cinéas depicted "the hoe and the machete [that] glistened in the sun, like flaming swords" in his 1933 text, Roumain depicted "hoes raised high, circling with flashes of light" in *Gouverneurs*.[43]

What did not translate into Roumain's peasant novel, however, is the clear influence of the northern, regional realities that structured Cinéas's approach to the peasantry, the earth, and agriculture, and which dictate the plot of the novel and the dramatic content. The main characters in Cinéas's novel represent the basic social structure of the northern countryside. First, "Cônel" Dubréus Macaya, or Frè Dubré: he is the leader or "chef" of this unnamed rural *section* of the North that Cinéas depicts and had called a *konbit* to clear his land. He knew how to read and write; he was a military man with experience, fortune, influence, and relationships. Next, Ti-Monsieur Servilius, also known as "Viejo" for his work as a migrant laborer in Cuba and the Dominican Republic, and occasionally as "Jouq-Boutt" (for his tendency to arrive first and leave last). He is a ludic, playful character, and it is the suspicious circumstances surrounding his death that set off the particular plot in *Le drame*. Mapou-Laloi, or Danilus Pierrecin, is the other strong man in the rural section (*lion de la section*) whose power rivals Dubré, though it comes from a different source: the spirits. Both Dubré and Mapou-Laloi exact their influence over Ti-Nonme, a lowly peasant who has little agency in the rural section, and who must rely alternatively on Frè Dubré and Mapou-Laloi. Each of these main, male characters have children, who represent the younger generation of this drama: Frè Dubré's son, Dubréard; Mapou-Laloi's son, Clermecin, and Ti-Nonme's daughter, Florida. Ti-Nonme and Florida are each instrumentalized by these more important actors, and it is Ti-Nonme's fate that is rendered the most tragic in the story.

As the drama unfolds between these main rural characters, Cinéas introduces a different social group: intellectuals and intermediaries or go-betweens with the state, who become increasingly important as the plot develops and Ti-Nonme is put on trial for Servilius's murder. There is Faustulus, the director of the rural grade school, who had tried to make a life for himself in the city, Cap-Haïtien, but failed and returned to the countryside. Though he is looked down upon as a lowly rural dweller by the *citadins* in the novel (his status is marked by an incorrect, creolized French: "Si j'été riche, je ne sais pas cé qué je sérai été dévini"), Faustulus is regarded as a man of intellectual authority in the countryside. He dazzles the peasants with his skills, his ability to read and write when they need it, such as the all-important marriage letter (*lettre de demande en mariage*).⁴⁴ We also meet Paul Desforges and André Flosel, characters who stand in for the contemporary political and intellectual schools of thought during the period as they related to the peasantry: those who wanted to eradicate superstitious practices, which they saw at the root of Haiti's backwardness, and those who believed that the peasants' religious and superstitious practices were legitimate cultural expressions, and that the source of their misery lay in the structural inequities codified by the state. Desforges, a lawyer from the city who is interested in facts, logic, and the law, is highly critical of superstitious practices and the role that he believes Vodou played in the murder. Against Desforges's strict anti-superstition stance, Cinéas portrays a more favorable intellectual, Flosel, who has studied psychology, religion, and sociology, and who refutes Desforges's argument that Vodou is responsible for the murders, and more broadly, peasant misery. In his defense of Ti-Nonme, Flosel argues that the state is to blame: "the indifference of the State, in the State-sponsored pillaging that helps itself to the workers' harvests and pays them nothing in return."⁴⁵ Flosel is at least partially modeled on Price-Mars and his peasant advocacy; certain passages of his speech to the jury are pulled from Price-Mars's *Ainsi parla l'oncle*. Desforges appears to be modeled on François Dalencour, who was highly critical of the North and of the superstitious practices that he believed were menacing Haitian society.⁴⁶

Yet there is one final character, the "grand planteur," Pierre Deslys, who troubles Flosel's position slightly, and adds further depth to Cinéas's presentation of the peasants' interests and the interests of the North more broadly. Deslys and Flosel are close friends, and the novel ends with them walking through the ruins of Frè Dubré's plantation, which was divided up and eventually fell into ruin in the years following his murder, as all of his heirs and relatives abandoned the countryside for the city. Deslys's advice to Flosel, his commentary on the entire *drame*, is thus the final commentary on the problems surrounding the countryside that concludes Cinéas's novel. For, while Cinéas applauds the Price-Mars–styled social scientist Flosel for his knowledge and his education, he also acknowledges that Flosel does not understand the earth and the practice of agricultural production like the northern planter Deslys does. In this summative, didactic conversation, Deslys tells Flosel, "It's all well and good to call for, to preach, a return to the land [*la retour à la terre*]," but adds that this initiative does not take on the real problems, the true *drame de la terre*. For the planter Deslys, all of the initiatives put forth to "save" Haitian agriculture—education, road construction, even hygiene—require "earning the confidence of the masses, recapturing their hearts. . . . But who is going to seriously study this problem? Who is going to take it on? Who is even thinking about it?"⁴⁷ Deslys the planter gets the last word in Cinéas's peasant novel, and the reader is left with a call to action: to find a way for the state, the intellectuals, and the local elites to regain the trust and confidence of the peasantry.⁴⁸

Cinéas's peasant novel cycle adds much more depth, texture, and regional difference to our understanding of the cultural nationalism that emerged during and after the US occupation of Haiti. Considered alongside the Dessalinean and Amerindian focus of Werleigh's poetry, the traditionalist, far-right orientation of *Stella*'s cultural nationalism emerges as a kind of right-wing *indigénisme*. Distinct from the cosmopolitan cultural nationalism of the *Revue indigène*, *Stella*'s cultural nationalism was rooted in the Haitian *sol* and in communion with *la terre et les morts*. In this sense, it is a more logical precursor to the subsequent cultural nationalist movements of the 1930s and especially the 1940s, characterized by the ethno-nationalist *Griots* magazine and the ethnological focus of the *mouvement folklorique*.

Stella's National Revolution

You are not Haitian if you are not Dessalinean.

(On n'est pas haïtien si on n'est pas Dessalinien.)
—Louis Mercier, qtd. in Laroche, "*La tragédie du roi Christophe*"

If Eugen Weber posited that Latin America was the logical place for Maurrassian thought to take hold outside Europe, it is only because he hadn't yet read anything from Haiti.⁴⁹ It should not come as a surprise that the ideas of Charles Maurras and the Action Française organization were not limited to the French hexagon. Maurras's integral nationalism is arguably the most important French ideology of the early twentieth century, one that scholars often ignore at the expense of fully appreciating the power and reach of this ideology during the period throughout the world.⁵⁰ Indeed, most scholarship on the early occupation era in Haiti has focused on Marxist radical thought to the exclusion of a substantive analysis of the countervailing presence of far-right ideologies. I argue that far-right, integral nationalism was hegemonic during this period; we cannot fully understand the emergence of the Duvalier dictatorship and its three decades of rule without understanding the integral nationalist ideologies that preceded it.

One *Stella* contributor clearly situated Haiti's January 1, 1927, Independence Day celebrations within a global current of integral nationalism: "Today, amid the irresistible surge of integral nationalism [*nationalisme intégral*] that is driving away the pestilent fumes of pacifism and cruel internationalism, all people are building up their heroic souls by cultivating the veneration and love of their greatest heroes."⁵¹ Haitians were in fact self-professed adherents of Action Française and its ideology *in the Haitian context*. The connections between Maurrassisme and *Stella*'s Haitian nationalism are unmistakable: a preoccupation with the decadence and decline of society, an emphasis on decentralization through a return to the earth, a valorization of the peasant as some mythic receptacle of national identity, and a new national paradigm based on work, order, productivity, and agriculture.⁵² The connection goes deeper still: as I argue, integral nationalism resonated strongly in Haiti because it activated the heritage of Haiti's radical Enlightenment critique that a faction of Haitian thinkers had engaged in since 1804. It is important here to note that Action Française was a royalist movement (though it drew from various legitimist, Bonapartist, and Bourbonist strands) and Maurras was a staunch antiliberal and counterrevolutionary. Maurrassisme was thus a counter-Enlightenment or even an anti-Enlightenment project.⁵³ Here, I see a logical—though no less troubling—fit between the Haitian desire to return to the country's foundational 1804/1806 fracture (inaugurated at the turn of the century with writers like Coicou and Lhérisson, as we saw in the previous chapter) and Maurrassian counterrevolution of the early twentieth century. Haitians' retrospective reflection on the problems of the Haitian Revolution's failure of liberal democracy, and Maurrassian nationalism's rejection of its own French Revolutionary heritage, coincided and interacted. Haitians' further radicalization of the 1904/1906 generation's arguments about Haiti's foundational fractures and the source of the nation's ills is a response to the loss of sovereignty under the US occupation: the failure of 1804 itself.

It is worth reiterating here what I have developed at length elsewhere: the degree to which the *Stella* contributors and northern elites more broadly were intimately familiar with Charles Maurras and the main thinkers of the Action Française group.[54] Sténio Vincent, Louis Mercier, and others subscribed to the organization's newspaper, and some even donated to its mission. In 1927 the future finance secretary, Abel Lacroix, donated eight hundred francs "to help spread integral nationalism [*pour la propagande du nationalisme intégral*]," to be hand-delivered to Charles Maurras.[55] The trajectory of Gérard de Catalogne evinces the clearest case for a global Maurrassian network in the early twentieth century; Catalogne was a veritable *passeur* (go-between) of Maurrassisme between France and Haiti. Catalogne is a fascinating though little-studied figure who played an important role in François Duvalier's dictatorship, which remained rooted in Maurrassian integral nationalism. Duvalier dedicated his collected works (speeches, essays, and articles) to the very concept of integral nationalism.[56] The title of Duvalier's collection, *Œuvres essentielles*, must be read as a direct gesture to the title of Maurras's collected works, *Œuvres capitales*. Naturally, it was Gérard de Catalogne who wrote the preface to Duvalier's collection. But long before he was known as the "white bear" of the Duvalier dictatorship, Catalogne had a long and storied history among far-right nationalist movements on both sides of the Atlantic.[57] Catalogne's life began, unsurprisingly, in Cap-Haïtien. He was born to a Martinican father and a Haitian mother in 1905 and, like most elites who lived in the Caribbean, left for France to complete his studies in 1916. He attended the prestigious Lycée Louis-le-Grand and later the Institut catholique and the Sorbonne. It was in the 1920s that he began to frequent the writers and intellectuals associated with Action Française—François Mauriac, René Groos, Jean-Pierre Maxence, and Charles Maurras. By 1928 he was publishing articles in the newspaper *L'Action française*—articles that were linked specifically to his Haitian heritage, such as "L'influence française en Haïti."[58]

When Catalogne returned home to Cap-Haïtien in 1927, he discovered an intellectual community that was committed to the ideas of Action Française. Catalogne proposed a public lecture at the Cercle

Printania social club on the editor of the *Action française* newspaper, Léon Daudet, an anti-Dreyfusard and increasingly anti-republican voice in interwar France. As Catalogne later described his trip in the *Action française* newspaper, the Capois elite were already well-studied in the topic at hand.⁵⁹ Catalogne would eventually take up with his fellow Capois Maurrassians in 1934, after the rise and fall of his star in France.⁶⁰ Once back in Haiti, Catalogne established himself as an important Maurrassian intermediary in Cap-Haïtien, giving conferences and selling books, and collaborating closely with the members of the *Stella* magazine.⁶¹ Thus, while *Stella*'s writers engaged in a profoundly inward-looking nationalist revolution—reactivating the foundational fractures, and factions, of Haitian intellectual and political thought—they organized and expressed these ideas through the dominant early twentieth-century far-right ideology of integral nationalism.

In an early issue of the magazine, the northern writer Luc Fouché clarified *Stella*'s stated purpose in a lead article entitled "Une revue est nécessaire."⁶² In it, he insisted on the magazine's role in reshaping Haiti's national future. The nation was at a crossroads, he argued, between rehabilitation and decadence. It was the duty of the magazine and its young contributors to work together for the regeneration of the Haitian nation:

> We are at a singular moment in our national history: following down the path we are on, it will either be a prelude to our rehabilitation or transport us directly to decadence. . . . Now is the moment, or never, to pull ourselves together [*nous ressaisir*] into a national soul [*âme nationale*], and by this I mean shared beliefs, emotions, and aspirations that bend . . . our collective energy toward the same goal: *the regeneration of our country*.⁶³

Fouché's article describes a turning point moment between decadence and its antidote, regeneration. To change the direction of the nation's future, *Stella* writers believed they must educate its future citizens and develop this national soul. Only then would they be able to provide the nation with the stability, the order, and the labor force that would secure its economic viability and national independence for years to come. The language of Fouché's "turning point" moment is intimately linked to the idea of national revolution: the national soul, the energy of Haiti's inhabitants, working toward the goal of national *régénération*. The idea of a national revolution—of regeneration, of revisiting Haiti's first revolutionary moment and founding the nation anew—abounds in the pages of *Stella*.

Stella's poetic project in response to the US occupation—the redemption of Haiti's forgotten or sullied heroes of the North through poetry as part of an attempt to regenerate, even re-found the Haitian nation that we studied above—is in line with the "repli sur soi" mentality of far-right nationalist movements. It is less an attack on the US occupier than a focused energy that looked inward and to the past, rethinking the revolution and the immediate post-independence period to re-found the independent nation. It is a desire to root out *internal* decadence and decay, to raze the dilapidated, decaying structures of the last century, in order to write the nation anew. One of the key elements of this national revolution was the definitive rehabilitation of Haiti's silenced or forgotten national heroes—Dessalines, Capois, Dédée Bazile, Christophe—which the magazine saw as critical to national regeneration ("le salut national"). Recall from previous chapters that Dessalines's memory had been a nineteenth-century battleground, and it was not until the turn of the twentieth century and the centennial of Haitian independence that Dessalines finally received recognition as the hero of the Haitian nation.

The young Capois historian Louis Mercier's proclamation, cited in the epigraph to this section, "On n'est pas haïtien si on n'est pas Dessalinien," further affirms the exclusionary definition of nationalist identity that he sets out. In response to the US occupation of Haiti, Mercier argued that one of the solutions was to probe the reasons why Dessalines had been so long silenced as the national hero of Haitian independence, despite the peasantry's veneration of him and his status as a spirit (*lwa*) among practitioners of Vodou. The US occupation effectively put an end to the debate and occasioned a definitive place for Dessalines in Haiti's national pantheon. As Cinéas reflected in an article, it was not until Haiti lost its sovereign status that it realized the true importance of Dessalines's memory and the need to keep it alive in every Haitian soul: "It took 1915 for us to understand Dessalines, to admire him even more and love him with the fervor of our souls."[64] Other articles communicate a similar sense of definitive change concerning Dessalines's memory under the US occupation. As Mercier declared in an aptly titled article,

"La vérité qui parle," Dessalines is no longer considered a barbarian: "No sensible historian would write today about how our founding father fell at Pont-Rouge, a victim of his own tyranny," nor would a Haitian head of state dare celebrate October 17 as a national holiday.[65]

Haiti's national revolution reached the level of doctrine in the writing of Louis Mercier. A historian, teacher, lawyer, and *New York Times*-renowned tour guide, Mercier was a prominent Capois intellectual of the early twentieth century, but very little has been written about him in subsequent years.[66] Born in 1893 in Cap-Haïtien, Mercier became one of the most passionate defenders of the North and is remembered by many as one of the nation's fiercest patriots. He was an active member of the Bibliophiles group and contributed a considerable number of articles to the *Stella* magazine. In his 1929 work *Une étape de l'évolution haïtienne*, Price-Mars described Mercier (with seemingly humorous hyperbole) as a "fierce defender of Christophe, defending the undying glory of the monarch like an unassailable citadel, repelling attacks from every which way."[67] Mercier counted among his closest friends his fellow contributors Christian Werleigh and Luc Grimard, and the three of them together became known as the "Trois Mousquetaires."[68] Mercier's writing is fervent and energetic, propelled forward by the idea of being on the threshold of some new order. He cites Mussolini as one of the century's "greatest men of action" and an inspirational source of his own revolutionary nationalism.[69] Mercier's forward-looking national project gestures toward a new order in which the decadence and decay of liberalism and individualism will be replaced by a fervent, unifying patriotism: "For each of the false dogmas, equality, liberalism, individuals, etc., you can substitute the concrete reality: Homeland! Homeland! Homeland!" (*A tous les faux dogmes, l'égalité, libéralisme, individualisme, etc. vous substituerez la réalité tangible: Patrie! Patrie! Patrie!*)[70]

Mercier's arguments, and the *Stella* magazine more generally, evince a deep knowledge of Haitian historical writing outside the liberal republican tradition, and thus build upon the heritage of paper wars, intellectual debates, and civil strife of the previous century of independent Haitian thought. Mercier drew a direct connection between the arrival of the occupation forces on Haiti's shores in 1915 and the historical memory of French efforts to retake the island during Christophe's reign (most famously with Malouet's secret mission in 1814) by reproducing texts from Christophe, Vastey, and Prévost. One contributor wrote of northern defiance to the occupying forces, evoking the bold promise of Christophe's coat of arms—that they, too, would rise from the ashes of the US occupation of Haiti. Another essay on Dessalines's memory compared Dessalines's death at Pont-Rouge to Caesar's assassination in the Roman Senate—evoking an intertextual link to Juste Chanlatte's *Réflexions sur le prétendu sénat de Port-au-Prince* pamphlet.[71] Mercier was a disciple of Vastey in particular, and cited his work at length in his contributions to *Stella* and many of his other works. As a fellow historian, Mercier was committed to rehabilitating the memory of Haiti's first historian (*du premier de nos historiens*): "this baron de Vastey, that historians thought they could dim because he was a high-ranking official under Christophe."[72] Mercier also took up Vastey's arguments about the importance of the press for northern writers, casting the *Stella* magazine as a continuation of this venerable practice. The magazine reproduced pages from Vastey's 1819 *Essai* in an essay entitled "Comment on défend un pays" about the role northern writers played in "enlightening" their internal enemies, and the role of the press in changing public opinion. The passage Mercier selected from Vastey's *Essai* provides a meta-commentary on *Stella*'s occupation-era cultural nationalist project: "Northern writers, distressed to see that the populations of the Southwest have been abused and driven to disgrace by their government, are pushing the presses to their capacity to shed light on public opinion in this region, and force Pétion to change the system."[73] Here, we can replace Pétion with Borno, or the liberal bourgeois establishment in Port-au-Prince, and Vastey's phrase becomes a potent commentary on *Stella*'s occupation-era cultural nationalism.

At the heart of Mercier's contributions to *Stella* is a profound questioning of the Haitian Revolution and its aftermath, of 1804/1806—which he places within the frame of Maurrassian antiliberalism. He describes the aftermath of the revolution as a fork in the road—between "power" and "liberalism." The first was a treacherous and rocky path, and the second was a flat, meandering route—the proverbial path of least resistance:

> A l'origine de notre vie politique, deux voies se sont offertes à nous, l'une dure, épineuse où l'on était obligé de marcher droit, tracée par Toussaint Louverture et Christophe, l'autre facile, attrayante, tracée par des pseudo-

libéraux, disciples de Danton, de Robespierre, des révolutionnaires français. Nous avons pris la dernière voie qui n'était pas faite pour nous et qui nous a conduites jusqu'à l'abîme.

(At the origin of our political life, two paths were offered to us: one difficult, thorny, where we had to walk straight, laid out by Toussaint Louverture and Christophe; the other, easy and appealing, was laid out by the so-called liberals, disciples of Danton and Robespierre, French revolutionaries.[74] We chose the latter, which was not made for us and which has led us into the abyss.)[75]

Mercier's language is significant for a number of reasons. First, he is clearly tapping into the language of Dessalinean independence and the early post-independence *guerre de plume*, recasting it within the context of the US occupation and Haiti's national revolution. Recall that the Acte de l'indépendance called upon Haitians to choose a different path than the French: "Marchons sur d'autres traces," those of Haiti's first inhabitants who preferred to die rather than live unfree. Furthermore, Dessalinean and Christophean language wrote constantly of the threat of the *abîme* (abyss) and the treachery of the French—and later Pétion—that threatened to lead the country back into slavery. Here, like Werleigh's "Défilée-la-folle" poem, Mercier situates the US occupation as the consequence of these historical "mistakes": the assassination of Dessalines and the imposition of a liberal ("pseudo") republic—a phrasing that echoes Mercier's position that the nation should have had a strong leader following the revolution, someone who could have guided the nation's new citizens to make these hard choices for the survival of the nation, to ensure its strength and independence. Instead, Haiti followed the path offered by these "pseudo-libéraux," Alexandre Pétion and André Rigaud and other liberal republican leaders—a path that Mercier argued had led the nation to destruction.[76] Finally, Mercier expresses the seeds of an antidemocratic, authoritarian idea that is a fixture in twentieth-century Haiti, even today: that the liberal path "was not made for us." It is this same kind of thinking that informs Haiti's detractors, inside and outside the country, to proclaim that democracy "was not made" for Haiti. Indeed, Mercier is expressing a variant of what Lyonel Trouillot has called the "modèle Dessalines"—the idea that a possible future or path forward for the country was cut short in 1806.[77]

Mercier thus returns to the immediate aftermath of the Haitian Revolution and the revolutionaries' failure to follow the path traced by Dessalines—indeed, to follow the very orders that Dessalines gave in 1804. As Mercier saw it, Dessalines's and later Christophe's policies were just as pertinent to the nationalist crisis of the 1920s as they had been nearly a century before. In order to solve the crisis of the occupation and Haiti's national decline, Mercier proposed the path not taken in the nineteenth century—that of labor, order, and discipline. The failure to follow Dessalines's example, according to Mercier, was at the root of Haiti's early twentieth-century national crisis—a crack in the foundation of the nation that only weakened further during the nineteenth century and ultimately led the country into the "abîme," of foreign occupation (again recalling the language of early post-independence writing that Mercier was steeped in). Mercier depicted nineteenth-century Haiti as an extended period of revolution, which ended with the loss of the nation's sovereignty: "revolts, revolutions, executions, anarchy, tyranny and, finally, the invasion of a foreign power in our internal affairs."[78] In this way, Mercier cast the US occupation of Haiti as merely the symptom of a greater ill that one could trace all the way back to the founding of the nation and the Haitian Revolution. This kind of reasoning had a profound effect on the way he conceived of Haiti's future, and what he envisioned for a newly independent nation. Indeed, Mercier conceived of the end of the occupation as something far more radical than the mere reestablishment of national sovereignty. Rather, Mercier proposed a cultural nationalist project that attempted to reconceive of the nation, to rethink the project of Haiti as it was established in 1804.

* * *

The commitment among Capois intellectuals to Maurrassisme and Action Française was evident not just to an insider like Gérard de Catalogne. Others noticed it, too: in 1927 the French travel writer Paul Morand noted the Maurrassian orientation of Haiti's young intellectual class in his travel narrative *Hiver caraïbe*. While scholars have paid attention to Morand's interaction with the *Revue indigène* group in Port-au-Prince, none have remarked on the short trip he took to the northern city of Cap-Haïtien. While there only for a short time, Morand referred to northerners as Camelots du Roi, the youth league of Maurras's Action Française: "All the young people here are either Camelots du Roi or Reds."[79] Marc Péan's rarely cited three-volume history of Cap-Haïtien affirms that the French far right has long been a source of ideological inspiration for the northern region: "Since 1870, the northern intelligentsia has drawn its ideas almost exclusively from the journals, magazines and works of the French far right."[80] The intertextual, ideological, and intellectual connection between the anti-occupation sentiment professed in *Stella* and Maurrassian nationalism is clear. I have aimed in this chapter to present these shared ideological positions as more than just the circulation of far-right nationalist ideas throughout the Atlantic, and certainly as more than mimicry, which is often how scholars tend to position Haitian thought vis-à-vis French political and ideological movements. Instead, these were ideas shared by intellectuals in conversation, in intellectual circles, in periodicals, in France, Belgium, Switzerland, French Canada, but also in Martinique, in Guadeloupe, in Mauritius, and beyond.

There is nevertheless something even more specific about Haiti's relationship to the French authoritarian right that is essential for us to unpack. Haitian intellectuals recognized in Maurrassisme elements of the Dessalinean critique of Enlightenment liberalism, as well as nineteenth-century Haitian critiques of the 1806 republican revolution. Indeed, French and Haitian integral nationalists tapped into a shared revolutionary heritage that reveals a much deeper, structural connection between these two intellectual traditions and the way each conceptualized what they perceived as the failures of the long nineteenth century. French Maurrassisme and Haitian integral nationalism share a profound distrust of liberalism and the aftermath of both the French and Haitian Revolutions. Much in the way that Maurras and French thinkers of the far right advocated a counterrevolution that returned to some pre- or counter-Enlightenment order of the world, Haitian integral nationalists advocated a counter-1806 revolution and a return to the Dessalinean order—a position we see in their scathing rebukes of Pétion's liberal republicanism, a refusal of 1806, and an emphasis on regeneration through order, tradition, work, decentralization, and the peasantry.

And yet Haitian integral nationalists' early twentieth-century embrace of the Maurrassian counter-Enlightenment project to make the case for a return to some pre-1806 order of society demonstrates a profound misuse of Dessalinean critique. Recall that the practice of Dessalinean critique was not a refusal of the Enlightenment, nor was it a counterrevolutionary or anti-Enlightenment project. It is a practice of space-making to allow for alternative epistemologies and ontologies: to create the possibility of alternative futures of thinking, knowing, and existing. It created space for the instantiation of an anticolonial, antislavery state and a people that, in their very existence, challenged the progressive universalist claims of the Enlightenment as defined by—and limited to—the white, Western world. Dessalinean thought did not reject the Enlightenment; it challenged the Enlightenment's putatively universal self-framing by positing—and living—alternative epistemologies and ontologies. The Haitian Maurrassian integral nationalists of the 1920s and 1930s did not engage in this vital aspect of Dessalinean critique when they called for a return to the pre-1806 order. This is the danger of misuses of Dessalines's legacy and the "modèle Dessalines": if the fundamental practice of *critique* is obscured or removed, then Dessalines's heritage folds easily into antiliberal, fascist politics.

The shadow of the impending Duvalier dictatorship looms large here, though it would be an error to draw a line straight from the Maurrassian ideologues of the 1920s and 1930s to the ethno-nationalist, fascist Duvalier dictatorship in 1957. Indeed, the fever pitch of occupation-era Maurrassian integral nationalism momentarily died down in Haiti with the outbreak of the Second World War. In 1941 the newly elected president Elie Lescot aligned with the Allied forces and supported, at least outwardly, democracy and anti-totalitarianism. When a populist, urban revolution overturned the Lescot regime in 1946, it appeared that Haiti might even turn toward a sustained, radical leftist politics. This would not be the case. The social scientific ethno-nationalist doctrine that had emerged in the late 1930s in learned societies and magazines like *Les Griots* (which François Duvalier himself had cofounded) had gained ground and national purchase during the 1940s and 1950s. It is the intellectual, social, and political marriage of ethno-nationalism with the ever-present, if latent, antiliberal, Maurrassian integral nationalism that shaped the emergence of Duvalierism in the 1950s and 1960s, or what Leslie Péan has called "the elaboration of a creolized fascism adapted to Haitian conditions."[81] The hemispheric forces of anticommunism combined with the rise of populist nativism and the extant integral nationalist framework worked together to install a hereditary fascist dictatorship that would last for nearly thirty years.

Epilogue

On the eve of January 1, 1954, residents of Cap-Haïtien and the surrounding towns gathered in the Sans Souci palace to celebrate the 150th (*Tri-Cinquantenaire*) anniversary of Haitian independence planned at the request of President Paul Magloire. The early 1950s were full of development, tourism, and possibility in Haiti. Magloire, a general in the military and native Capois, had campaigned on a platform of decentralization, and made good on his promise by constructing new schools, modernizing provincial towns, and promoting agricultural exports.[1] His staunch anticommunism garnered him international support from the US government and the US press, which was at that point at the height of McCarthyism and its attendant propaganda. As a result, tourism was booming throughout Haiti, especially at the Sans Souci palace and the Citadelle.[2] The 1950s also marked the expansion of political rights for all Haitians: the government granted universal suffrage for males over the age of twenty-one, and after years of activism, women finally claimed their rightful place in the political and public spheres when they won the right to vote in 1950.[3] The feminist organization the Ligue féminine d'action sociale participated in the official 150th anniversary celebrations, putting together a volume of important women in Haitian history, which the government published as part of its commemorative collection.[4]

Dressed in their finest attire, the celebrants brought the palace back to life: "The palace, so long deserted, had for one night recaptured its long-lost splendor."[5] The ball ignited the imagination and activism of Luc Grimard, a prominent Capois lawyer and historian and a close supporter of the president. In June 1954, Grimard founded the Société des amis du roi Henry, a learned and historical society whose stated goal was to "magnify the Christophean undertaking, to praise the memory of the brilliant black monarch, to locate in his remembrance some grounds to better understand ourselves, to raise ourselves up."[6] Notable founding members of the society came from throughout the country, not just

Cap-Haïtien, including Ernst Trouillot (who served as general secretary), Francis Etienne and Kurt Fischer (vice presidents), J. B. Cinéas, and president Magloire ("grand protecteur de la société"), among many others. The most tangible initiative the Société des amis du roi Henry undertook was the construction and installation of a statue of Henry Christophe on the Place des Héros de l'indépendance on the Champ de Mars in downtown Port-au-Prince on December 6, 1954.

Ten years later, Michel Leiris, M. A. Perinette, and Nita Green incorporated an association called Les amis du roi Christophe in Paris.[7] The association was formed for legal purposes: to bring *La tragédie du roi Christophe*, the play that Aimé Césaire had penned in the early 1960s, to Paris.[8] Leiris, his lawyers, and his associates were attempting to work around the contract Césaire had previously signed with Europa Studio in Salzburg so that Jean-Marie Serreau's Compagnie de Toucan could play at the Théâtre de France (Odéon) in 1965.[9] In addition to Leiris and the lesser-known officers of the association, various historians and literary critics over the years have remarked on the more notable "members" of the French association: artists Pablo Picasso and Alberto Giacommetti, French writers Gaëtan Picon and Marguerite Duras, Cuban writer Alejo Carpentier, and Senegalese writer Alioune Diop, among others. The association's official documentation does not contain a record of their involvement, though it is likely that these above-mentioned supporters gradually signed on after the Paris premiere and helped to support the play's subsequent performances in Berlin, Brussels, Venice, Milan, Montréal, and Dakar. Similarly, there are no records of the participation of the Haitian Société des amis du roi Henry in the efforts of Leiris's legal association. Indeed, I have found no documentation—besides Michel-Rolph Trouillot's childhood recollection—that the 1965 French association was linked to the 1954 Haitian société.[10] In fact, the records of Leiris's association reveal no knowledge of the Haitian Société des amis du roi Henry that preceded it. This extraordinary and yet unremarked doubling of Christophean societies begins to make more sense when we distinguish between the two *uses* of Christophe in each case. I would argue that the difference is between the society of the friends of the man, Henry Christophe, and the association of the friends of the play, *La tragédie du roi Christophe*. That is: the Haitian society was inaugurated to celebrate the memory and legacy of Henry

Christophe, while the French association was created in support of Césaire and his play.

I insist here on this strange doubling of Christophean societies because it reveals something about the conflicting *uses* of Christophe and his legacy—and more broadly the uses of the Haitian Revolution—inside and outside Haiti in the mid-twentieth century. In Haiti in the 1950s, intellectuals and statesmen (primarily but not exclusively northerners) lauded Christophe as an anticolonial, antislavery icon whose memory deserved celebration not just among the other heroes of national independence, but on the world's stage. Alongside Toussaint and Dessalines, he was proof of Haiti's groundbreaking anticolonial revolution and the establishment of a modern postcolonial state that defiantly held its own among the Atlantic world powers of the era. To be sure, they were instrumentalizing Christophe and his memory to glorify Haiti's 150th anniversary of independence and to justify and legitimate Magloire's military-authoritarian leadership. Yet there was nothing *tragic* in their memorialization of Christophe. Or rather, if pushed to identify the tragic element, it was that his legacy had been denigrated for so long. In Césaire's play, on the other hand, Christophe and his legacy are cast within the tragic mode, and of a specific kind. Césaire's Christophe is not doomed by a tragedy of circumstances—say, of a pro-slavery Atlantic world that refused to recognize an anticolonial, antislavery monarch— but by his own authoritarian impulses. Césaire's Christophe possesses a tragic fatal flaw that is his undoing. He thus serves Césaire's tragic rescripting of early postrevolutionary Haiti as a cautionary tale: a fierce, absurd military dictator whose regime of forced labor and inability to effectively govern his own people brought about his downfall. The contemporary 1950s Haitian uses of Christophe, the recuperation of his historical memory, is all but lost in Césaire's play. Undoubtedly Duvalier's rise to power in 1957 and the installation of his violent, fascist dictatorship between 1957 and 1962 contributed to Césaire's tragic recasting of his earlier narrative of Haiti's anticolonial heritage in *Cahier d'un retour au pays natal* (1939).[11]

But I am getting off topic. Césaire's or any other mid-twentieth-century uses of Haiti and its revolutionary heritage are outside the scope of my intervention here because they ultimately tell us very little about Haiti.[12] To be clear, this is not an indictment of Césaire or any other work that represents and rescripts the Haitian Revolution and its radical anticolonial project—these are key sources for understanding anticolonial Black Atlantic thought and its trajectory in the mid-twentieth century. My objection is that these mid-twentieth-century works tend to stand in for, and sometimes take the place of, engagement with *Haiti* and with *Haitians*—especially in scholarship on "Haiti."[13] Again, I am not saying that we shouldn't engage *La tragédie du roi Christophe* or any other representation of the Haitian Revolution, but we have to be clear about what engaging these texts tells us—and what it does not.Engaging these texts does not tell us much about Haiti's long postcolonial nineteenth century, Haitian writers and historians, Haiti's literature, and Haiti's own *uses*, varied and antagonistic as they are, of the revolution and the fraught heritage of 1804/1806. In sum, I am asking scholars to think more deeply about the distinction between the *uses* of Haiti and Haiti itself when they write and think about "Haiti."

Haiti has served many purposes for many different groups across time and space. As the great black republic, it was a beacon of hope and promise of future liberation for enslaved black people in the US South, Cuba, and the wider Atlantic world throughout the early nineteenth century.[14] In the twentieth century, it became central to black radical thought, as intellectuals, writers, and playwrights allegorized Haiti's radical antislavery revolution and its leaders in order to emplot the origins of their own radical struggle for freedom and self-determination. But Haiti was also used by slaveholders in the United States, who instrumentalized Haiti as a warning, creating an image of a violent, horror-filled abyss—a dangerous foil against which a continental, slave-based American polity defined itself.[15] In early twentieth-century US popular culture, Haiti was portrayed as a premodern cannibal nation through salacious, sensationalized depictions of "voodoo" and "black magic." It is this same discursive creation that underwrites contemporary punditry and news coverage of the country. We specialists of Haiti and the Haitian Revolution have had uses for Haiti, too. We instrumentalize it to some degree when we privilege our own agendas, perhaps even our own *desires*, in the way we write about Haitian independence.

It is precisely against the notion of any singular "idea" or *use* of Haiti—celebratory, derogatory, redemptive—that I have endeavored to write this book.[16] Yet this book is its own use of Haiti; of this I am well aware. I have done my best to make it one that is not extractive, obscuring, or monolithic. The "Haiti" that this book has engaged is its archive, the accumulation of a long nineteenth century of postcolonial critique: of the Enlightenment and its limits, of the meaning of liberty, civilization, and the West. Haiti was always already a critique, its very existence a reminder of the limits and possibilities of these concepts.

This is the vital heritage of Dessalines and Dessalinean thought in Haiti: the critique of the systems of oppression that underwrote Enlightenment colonialism that independent, sovereign Haiti, by its very existence, activates. This radical Dessalinean critique was silenced early in Haitian "national" history: internally by those Haitians committed to casting the nation within the dominant norms of civilization and humanism, and externally by those foreign powers whose own systems of oppression depended upon the silencing of Haiti's radical critique of them. And yet, as I hope to have shown in this book, this discursive, imagistic, and embodied radical critique persists, and pierces through, continually throughout the nineteenth and twentieth centuries. The legacy of Dessalinean critique is especially urgent today. Outside Haiti, the structural roots of white supremacy and ethno-nationalism are laid bare. In Haiti, a new generation of grassroots Haitian activists mobilizing against government corruption are forced to contend with the common refrain that the country was not, is not, "ready for democracy" (*pa pre pou demokrasi*). Dessalinean critique reminds us that it was the West that was not ready for Haiti. This is, in the end, the most powerful "use" of Haiti: to continually critique the narrow confines of white, Western normativity and assert the inherent dignity and humanity of all beings. In the words of Emile Nau: *Posterity must know this. Posterity will admire this island too, I hope.*

ACKNOWLEDGMENTS

Time. More time, uninterrupted time, other people's time. Without it this book would not have been possible. I am grateful to the institutions and individuals who afforded me this luxury: my departmental colleagues at the Catholic University of America for juggling extra duties to make my fellowship leave possible; the John W. Kluge Center at the Library of Congress for facilitating a year of uninterrupted access to its collection; the truly wonderful Interlibrary Loan staff at the Catholic University of America Libraries for finding me *all* the things; my research cohort for generously giving their time on chapter drafts, conference feedback, and invaluable advice; all of the Fred caregivers, paid and unpaid, for showing such patience and love for both of us; and my family and friends, for always making the most of the time we had together and never asking me to choose. It is my hope that in naming them below, I might honor their role in this work. It is, in the end, as much theirs as it is mine.

Thank you to my professors and mentors on both sides of 19 University Place: Judy Miller, Denis Hollier, John Moran, Stephane Gerson, Frédéric Viguier, Herrick Chapman, and most of all Michael Dash. I regret deeply that he will not read these words, and hope that they serve as a testament to the presence and power of his work.

I am indebted to the pathbreaking work of scholars before me, and even more grateful for the mentorship that they have provided. Chris Bongie generously offered advice and feedback on this project in its early stages and has been a major voice for me to think alongside ever since. Doris Garraway and Sibylle Fischer are paragons of the field who showed me strength in the face of unexpected hazard. Marlene Daut's knowledge is matched only by her commitment to equity and justice. I am honored to call her a friend. At various stages Kate Ramsey, Charles Forsdick, Jean François (A20), Kamau Brathwaite, Ada Ferrer, Maurice Etienne, Emile Eyma, Martin Munro, Olivier Compagnon, Guillemette

Martin, Olivier Dard, Daniel Desormeaux, John Walsh, Miléna Santoro, Nadève Ménard, Kaiama Glover, Alex Gil, Kelly Baker Josephs, Ted Vallance, Madeline Dobie, Zahia Rahmani, Ana Lucia Arajuo, Watson Denis, and Pierre Buteau have offered a warm welcome and invaluable intellectual support. Patrick Weil has been there since the very beginning—I am grateful for his trust and encouragement.

I am awed by the brilliance and generosity of so many colleagues and friends, and humbled to think and work alongside them: Claire Payton, and Jonathan too, Dasha Chapman, Grégory Pierrot, Tabitha McIntosh, Julia Gaffield, Délide Joseph, Vanessa Mongey, Laura Wagner, Nathan Dize, Erin Zavitz, Rob Taber, Hadassah St. Hubert, Adam Silvia (who was the only one who really knew how long this would take), Paul Clammer, Charlotte Maus, Sophonie Joseph, Michael Reyes, Alex Lenoble, Steven Crumb, Emily Teising, Yasser Elhariry, Katie LaPorta, Paul Descloitres, Laurie Lambert, Nathalie Pierre, Anne Eller, Vanessa Agard Jones, Travis Hensley and the amazing John W. Kluge Center staff at the Library of Congress, Loubna El Amine, Humberto Cucchetti, Carole Sargent, Kathryn Kleppinger, Anne O'Neil-Henry, Masha Belenky, Erin Twohig, Anne Nguyen, Fan Yang, Vivi MacManus, Dixa Ramirez, Maria Cecilia Ulrickson, Raj Chetty, April Mayes, Ginetta Candelario, Kyrstin Mallon Andrews, Maja Horn, Rodrigo Bulamah, Benjamin Fagan, Alyssa Sepinwall, Régine Joseph, Ben Cowan, Brandon Byrd, and all of the new and wonderful people I have surely forgotten or have yet to meet.

None of this would have been possible if not for some formative experiences made possible by Pierre Joanis, Gina Cunningham Eves, and Odonel Pierre-Louis. They each steered me toward the political and social lives of this work and patiently helped me to see what they already knew. I am certain that this book would not be what it is, or where it is today without Ashley Cohen. I am humbled and truly grateful for her friendship.

Thanks to David Kazanjian, Elizabeth McHenry, Priscilla Wald, Eric Zinner, Dolma Ombadykow, the anonymous readers, and everyone else at New York University Press for believing in this book and making it a reality.

I shudder to think what the last six years might have been without my DC crew: Julia Young, Josh Shepperd, Lev Weitz, Jonathan Monaghan, and David Sartorius. Thank you for your beautiful minds and even better taste in cocktails. Thank you to my dearest friend Dane Stalcup for loving me and my family. Thank you to Ama Ahofe for caring for me and my family. Thank you to my longest, oldest friends for waiting patiently as I worked many long years on this: Kate Snyder, Greg Stender, Laura Blackburn, Maggie Porter, Sophie Ward, Jane and Julia Fairorth, Vicki Janeski.

Thank you to my in-laws, Jerry and Sandy, for their unwavering support. And to my brilliant, beautiful sisters Erin Stieber, Lindsey Stieber, and Molly Stieber, who know me so well. And to Diane Stieber, who is so strong. And to Scott Stieber, who didn't just survive in time to see this, but thrived and grew. He is a miracle and an inspiration.

Thank you, finally, to Frederick Stieber Lewis and Michael Lewis: Fred, who may have to settle for a dog and a book for siblings, and Michael, my expert proofreader (all errors are his, not mine!) and source of unwavering, unconditional love and support whom I love so much.

NOTES

INTRODUCTION

1. On scholars' various reparative, redemptive, and utopian analyses of the revolution, see Garraway, "Empire of Freedom." David Scott speaks of C. L. R. James's *longing* and romanticism in his narrative of the Haitian Revolution in *Conscripts of Modernity*. Scott identifies what he terms the tragedy of colonial Enlightenment in James's 1963 tragic rescripting of his earlier romantic anticolonial narrative: the inevitable, fated tragic end that awaited hopeful "anticolonial imagining." Scott, *Conscripts of Modernity*, 1. Nevertheless, I am not so sure that Toussaint's own writing and political action exemplify the romantic anticolonial imagining that James ascribes to him in 1938. See Deborah Jenson's description of Toussaint Louverture as a "spin doctor" in *Slave Narrative*. On Louverture's clever use of the "black Spartacus" trope, see Pierrot, *Black Avenger*. Rachel Douglas challenges Scott's interpretation of James's 1938 text as solely romantic in her new work, *Making the Black Jacobins*. On Haiti, the Enlightenment, and (re)visions of modernity, see Dayan, *Haiti, History*; Fischer, *Modernity Disavowed*; Nesbitt, *Universal Emancipation*; and Buck-Morss, *Hegel, Haiti*.
2. Gaffield, *Haitian Connections*; Ferrer, *Freedom's Mirror*; Clavin, *Toussaint Louverture*; Dun, *Dangerous Neighbors*.
3. Chris Bongie suggests that North Atlantic scholars have avoided this early post-independence period precisely because it offers only a "disappointing vista that fails to match the transformative expectations raised by 'the idea of 1804.'" Bongie, Introduction, 2 Bongie is citing Nesbitt, "Idea of 1804." For an example of this scholarly commitment to the idea of 1804 as the instantiation of radical Enlightenment, see Nesbitt, *Universal Emancipation*. See also Miller, *Elusive Origins*.
4. On this notion of plurality, I am following Nadève Ménard's imperative for scholarship on Haiti to move beyond the "image of Haiti and Haitians that fosters the denial of Haitian plurality." Ménard, "Myth of the Monolingual Haitian Reader," 53.
5. David Geggus points to the "truly remarkable . . . frequency with which historians of all persuasion have written of the founding in 1804 of the 'Haitian Republic.'" Geggus, "Haiti's Declaration," 30. From this perspective, even the idea of a singular Haitian Revolution begins to look problematic. Geggus has long maintained that the Haitian Revolution was "several revolutions in one," marked by highly contested, fractious divisions between revolutionary factions that periodically

broke out into civil war. Geggus, "Haitian Revolution in Atlantic Perspective," 535. The War of Knives or War of the South pitted Toussaint Louverture's northern, independentist army against André Rigaud's southern, French republican troops in 1799–1800, and saw Toussaint and the North victorious and Rigaud briefly exiled in France. The arrival of the Leclerc expedition in 1802 antagonized old factions and created new conflicts. Rebel insurgent leaders like Jean-Baptiste Sans Souci wielded considerable power, threatening the unity of Dessalines's Armée Indigène. Meanwhile, the southern peninsula remained consistently out of Dessalines's reach. These threats were largely put to rest when Dessalines's generals assassinated the main insurgent leaders during the final phase of the War of Independence (what Michel-Rolph Trouillot calls a "war within a war"), and the South finally recognized Dessalines's authority in July 1803. Trouillot, *Silencing the Past*, 37; Garrigus, *Before Haiti*, 308.

6 The term *guerre de plume* was used by Haitians during the early post-independence civil wars and after. See, for example, the *Gazette royale*'s polemical response to Hérard Dumesle's newspaper (*L'Observateur*) reprinted in Madiou, *Histoire*, t. 6, 50. Beaubrun Ardouin also refers to the period as a *guerre de plume* in *Etudes*. I translate *guerre de plume* as "paper war" (instead of the more literal "pen war") to more readily anchor post-independence Haitian print within a larger tradition of polemical pamphlets and wars of words waged in civil wars and between nations that shaped the early modern print culture of the Atlantic world.

7 On Toussaint's use of *liberté générale*, see Ghachem, "Law, Atlantic Revolutionary Exceptionalism"; and Moïse, *Le projet national de Toussaint Louverture*. On the meanings of *liberté* cultivated by maroons and ex-slaves outside the print public sphere, see René, *Haïti après l'esclavage*; and Gonzalez, *Maroon Nation*.

8 I define Dessalinean critique not as evaluative or taste-based judgment, but as a *practice*. It is a practice of space-making to allow for alternative epistemologies and ontologies, to create the *possibility* of alternative futures of thinking, knowing, and existing. I use "critique" here in the sense that Michel Foucault establishes in "What Is Critique?" and "What Is Enlightenment?," which is distinct from—and indeed critical of—the narrow, actively ideological concept of "criticism" that Raymond Williams argues is a socio-historical development of writing and taste in the bourgeois public sphere (see my discussion below). As Judith Butler has elaborated on Foucault's idea of "critique," the task of critique is not "to evaluate whether its objects—social conditions, practices, forms of knowledge, power, and discourse—are good, or bad, valued highly or demeaned, but to bring into relief the very framework of evaluation itself." Butler, "What Is Critique?," 214. See also Butler, "Critique, Dissent, Disciplinarity." To be sure, Foucault (and Butler) are putting words to a praxis of critique (space-making, challenging the terms of evaluation, and supporting alternative possibilities for structuring the world) that Dessalinean critique was already doing at the turn of the nineteenth century. It is precisely this kind of Dessalinean (Foucauldian) critique that Achille Mbembe activates—founding alternative genealogies and new futures of structuring the

world—in *Critique of Black Reason*. Crucially, as I argue throughout this book, these two notions of critique (space-making praxis and taste-based criticism) are in conflict in Haiti: the republican faction pursued this modern, normative Enlightenment notion of "criticism" as evaluative or taste-based judgment, while Dessalineans (and their intellectual heirs) would continue to return to and deploy this praxis of space-making and alternative possibilities of ordering.

9 Daut, *Baron de Vastey*, xviii.
10 Peter Beaumont, "Sick of Corruption, Haiti Looks Back to Its Revolutionary Hero for Hope," *Guardian*, December 7, 2019, www.theguardian.com/world/2019/dec/07/haiti-looks-to-revolutionary-hero-dessalines. In the same article, historian Pierre Buteau notes that Dessalines's mythic status has become indistinguishable from historical truth. On the recent appeals to Dessalines's memory in the current 2019 *peyi lòk* (lockdown) protests in Haiti, see Julia Gaffield, "Haiti Protests Summon Spirit of the Haitian Revolution to Condemn a President Tainted by Scandal," *Conversation* (blog), November 15, 2019, http://theconversation.com/haiti-protests-summon-spirit-of-the-haitian-revolution-to-condemn-a-president-tainted-by-scandal-126315.
11 I see two strands of black radical thought at work in postcolonial Haiti, which I think are illuminating for further complicating our understanding of black radical thought as only Marxist. See, for example, Robinson, *Black Marxism*. On challenges to Robinson's conception of radicalism, see Gilroy, "Black Fascism"; and Thompson, *Black Fascisms*.
12 Bogues, *Black Heretics*, 1. In addition to Bogues, my intervention on the limits of Western episteme, its archive, its discourses, and its categories is enriched by the writings of Frantz Fanon, Achille Mbembe, and Paul Gilroy. See Fanon, *Peau noire, masques blancs*; Mbembe, *Critique of Black Reason*; and Gilroy, *Between Camps*.
13 Pierrot, *Black Avenger*, 126.
14 Janvier, *Les constitutions*, 32.
15 Fischer, *Modernity Disavowed*, 233.
16 Bogues, *Black Heretics*, 13.
17 Jenson, *Slave Narrative*, 82. Here, my reading of Dessalinean thought challenges—and perhaps answers—Bogues's wariness of a genealogy of black radical intellectual production; see Bogues, *Black Heretics*, 3.
18 My reading of vindicationism departs from David Scott's narrow use of the term as an emplotted narrative structure in chivalric romance by resituating it in the dominant practice of pamphlet writing in Haiti's early post-independence period: in rhetoric and refutation. That is, while Scott focuses on (the problem with) romantic narratives of overcoming in (his)stories of the Haitian Revolution, I look to the fifteenth-century origins of the word *vindication* (and its link to refutation): meaning "act of avenging, revenge," from the Latin *vindication*, "act of claiming or avenging," and *vindicare*, "lay claim to, assert; claim for freedom, set free; protect, defend; avenge." Written refutation is intimately linked to the Renaissance and

early modern uses of *vindication*: from the 1640s *vindication* is used to denote written "justification by proof, defense against censure." See Online Etymology Dictionary, "Vindication (n.)," www.etymonline.com/word/vindication. In these terms, then, I see vindicationism in Haiti's radical anticolonial independence and massacre of the French *colons* on the island, and written vindicationism—or refutation—in its legitimate claims to independence through printed texts. On vindicationism in the twentieth-century black intellectual tradition specifically, see Drake, "Anthropology and the Black Experience"; and Robert A. Hill, "C. L. R. James." Hill offers a reading of James's vindicationism that is more akin to refutation and rhetoric than romantic overcoming—a reading that Scott does not take up.

19 See Jonassaint, "Césaire et Haïti"; and Daut, *Baron de Vastey*.
20 On Haitian thought as "prophetic," see Dash, "Nineteenth-Century Haiti"; Bongie, Introduction; and Daut, *Baron de Vastey*.
21 On postcolonialism's enterprise of "attacks" on the Enlightenment project, see Scott, *Conscripts of Modernity*, 177–81.
22 On the other hand, I am not saying that Haitian radical intellectuals invented deconstruction: as I argue below, they were activating protocols of radical polemical pamphleteering with roots as far back as the sixteenth century.
23 Dessalinean thought offers a possible resolution to the unease with which some radical and anticolonial black thought deploys poststructuralism and postmodernism, rooted as they are in the conceptual protocols of Western episteme. As Bogues points out, "When the Western tradition is unmasked, deconstructed, and decentered," we too often call upon "the thinkers who critiqued the modern project but who themselves are an integral part of the canon" (i.e., Derrida et al.). Bogues, *Black Heretics*, 3.
24 It is not worth committing to print a list of two hundred years' worth of these *written in blood* narratives; suffice it to say that they were initiated the moment Haiti proclaimed its independence to "prove" that the first anticolonial, antislavery black state was incapable of self-governance.
25 Bogues, *Black Heretics*, 13.
26 Garraway has pointed out the degree to which recent scholarship on the Haitian Revolution fails to take into account the "contradictions of freedom, autonomy, and the universal that were manifested from the moment of the nation's founding" because it relies solely on the "idiom of Western political modernity." Garraway, "Empire of Freedom," 3.
27 On the performance and visibility of power in Christophe's kingdom, see Fischer, *Modernity Disavowed*, 252.
28 Fatton, "Authoritarian 'Habitus.'"
29 Williams, *Marxism and Literature*, 44–45.
30 Ibid., 46.
31 Ibid., 49–50. See also Wellek and Warren, *Theory of Literature* and the distinction of "imaginative literature" that they make.

32 Williams, *Marxism and Literature*, 49. See also Bongie's presentation of criticism as the "Romantic-era consolidation of the ideology of the aesthetic in which (good) Art becomes the supposed antidote to (bad) factionalism." Bongie, *Friends and Enemies*, 91.
33 Bongie's work raises crucial questions about Francophone postcolonial studies' treatment of politics, popular culture, and "hierarchies of aesthetic value" that I see as central to reevaluating the field and moving it forward. Bongie, *Friends and Enemies*, 12. Bongie's work on Vastey further develops this critique, especially his reflection on the "scribal" politics of postcolonial literature. He exposes a central assumption in contemporary literary criticism that situates artists relative to an arc of progress toward autonomous (non-"scribal") aesthetic production, and encourages scholars to rethink their own investment in early post-independence Haitian texts, "precisely by *not* subjecting them to our own understandable, if historically conditioned, desire for 'autonomous' literary and cultural production." Bongie, Introduction, 5.
34 See in particular Jenson, *Slave Narrative*. For a recent, excellent discussion of the problem of the discourse of literacy as it relates to Dessalines, see Pierrot, *Black Avenger*.
35 David Scott's insistence on the work of the postcolonial critic in formulating the kinds of questions we ask is germane here: "It is our postcolonial *questions* and not our answers that demand our critical attention, ... identifying the *difference* between the questions that animated former presents and those that animate our own." Scott, *Conscripts of Modernity*, 3.
36 Many thanks to the co-organizers of our ACLA 2019 panel "How to Do Things with Literature," Osman Nemli, Mukasa Mubirumusoke, and Katie LaPorta, as well as my fellow panelist Christophe Schuwey and participants. Thanks especially to Erin Greer for her discussion of the many other kinds of reading beyond Habermas, and her recommendations for further exploration.
37 Habermas, *Public Sphere*.
38 On the proletarian public sphere as a "counterconcept" to the dominant liberal, male, property-owning public, see Negt and Kluge, *Public Sphere*. See Nancy Fraser's feminist critique and proposal of "alternative counterpublics" or "subaltern counterpublics" in Fraser, "Rethinking the Public Sphere." More recently, Joanna Brooks has theorized a distinctive black counterpublic in early African American literary studies in order to account for the "distinctly black tradition of publication informed by black experiences of slavery and post-slavery, premised on principles of self-determination and structured by black criticisms of white political and economic dominance." Brooks, "Early American Public Sphere," 68.
39 Though Fraser announces the existence of "explicitly anti-democratic and anti-egalitarian" counterpublics in her work, she leaves them largely unaddressed in favor of studying antibourgeois discourse. Fraser, "Rethinking the Public Sphere," 67.
40 Allan, *Shadow of World Literature*. See also Zerelli, *Theory of Judgment*.

41 Allan, *Shadow of World Literature*, 4.
42 Garrigus, *Before Haiti*.
43 On the creation of counterhegemonic texts, see Bogues, *Black Heretics*.
44 Chris Bongie's assertion that Baron de Vastey's writing "adopts and adapts, revises and resists, generic conventions that were available to it at that time" is central to my thinking here. Bongie, Introduction, 66. I also rely on Judith Butler's explorations of strategies of reiteration, radical reappropriation, and innovative reuse to disrupt and displace established discourses of authority. See Butler, "Restaging the Universal." On the practice of borrowing, recycling, and "plagiarism" in early African American print culture, see Cohen and Stein, *Print Culture*; Daut, *Tropics*; and McGill, *American Literature*.
45 Doris Garraway's work on Christophean writing is foundational to my understanding of the politics of post-independence Haitian print culture and the centrality of performativity to claims of equality and subjecthood. See Garraway, "Print, Publics," and Garraway, "Abolition, Sentiment."
46 LaPorta, *Performative Polemic*.
47 Butler, "Restaging the Universal."
48 See the work of Michel Wieviorka, in particular his introduction to Wieviorka, *Une société fragmentée?* See also Stovall, "Liberatory Republic"; and Wilder, *French Imperial Nation State*.
49 Martin, *Contre-révolution*, 9.
50 Armitage, *Civil War*, 147.
51 For nearly fifty years after its publication, Haitians had access only to Madiou's first three volumes. The fourth volume was published posthumously in 1904, and the remaining four in 1989.
52 See Dayan, *Haiti, History*. See also Zavitz, "Revolutionary Narrations."
53 Dayan, *Haiti, History*, 288n13. While there are occasional passages in Madiou that read as partisan or propagandistic, I do not agree with Jenson's dismissal of Madiou in *Slave Narrative*. I nevertheless approach Madiou's historical account of Haiti just as critically, and textually, as all of my other sources. Readers will see that I mostly draw upon the reproductions of original texts that he includes, or the oral interviews he references. If I choose to cite a more editorial comment, I include his name ("Madiou notes" or "Madiou suggests").
54 See Stieber, "Beyond Mentions." On the need for comparative studies that center Haiti, see Daut, "Daring to Be Free." See also Seigel, "Beyond Compare."
55 On locally produced periodicals, see Stieber, "Haitian Literary Magazine."
56 Michel-Rolph Trouillot, *Les racines historiques*, 239.
57 Casanova, *World Republic*.
58 On the ex-slaves who fought to own and cultivate their own land, see Gonzalez, *Maroon Nation*. On the counter-plantation system, see Casimir, *Une lecture décoloniale*. Jean Alix René's work on popular political practices reveals that, though they were rendered passive citizens by Jean-Pierre Boyer's 1826 Code Rural, peasants and former slaves accessed the state through petitions and other forms of written protest. His work is a much-needed post-independence continuation of

Carolyn Fick's method of working "from below." See René, *Haïti après l'esclavage*. On Boyer's Code Rural, see chapter 3. On African political ideology in the Haitian Revolution, see Thornton, "'I Am the Subject'"; and Desch-Obi, "'Koup Tet.'" Vincent Brown's new book *Tacky's Revolt* insists on the politics of the enslaved and sheds important light on sources and methodologies beyond print production. Christina Mobley's current book project, *Vodou History: The Kongo History of the Haitian Revolution*, is sure to add crucial insight into this question.

59 There exist many non-print archives that warrant further research to deepen our understanding of Haiti's long nineteenth century: archives of Vodou, song, foodways, popular art, popular song, agricultural practices, and oral history. On manuscript culture and diasporic poetry in the Haitian literary tradition, see Jenson, *Slave Narrative*. There is undoubtedly a vibrant manuscript culture produced by literate women in the nineteenth century that warrants further study. Marc Péan notes the existence of a decades-long personal diary written by Elida Blain, an educated woman who lived in Cap-Haïtien at the turn of the twentieth century. Péan, *Vingt-cinq ans*, t. 3, 41. For an exploration of meanings of liberty in the manuscript culture of nineteenth-century Liberia and the Yucatán Peninsula, see Kazanjian, *Brink of Freedom*.

60 For a recent groundbreaking take on "region" in Latin America and the Caribbean, see Bassi, *Aqueous Territory*. On translocal exchange within the Caribbean, see Puri, *Marginal Migrations*; and Putnam, *Radical Moves*. On the transnationalism of minority cultural formations, see Lionnet and Shih, *Minor Transnationalism*.

61 As Michel-Rolph Trouillot and Georges Anglade have argued, Port-au-Prince was one of eleven major provincial capitals that functioned largely independently of one another throughout the nineteenth century, including Cap-Haïtien, Port-de-Paix, Gonaïves, and Saint-Marc in the North, and Jérémie and Les Cayes in the South. Trouillot, *State against Nation*; Anglade, *Atlas critique*.

CHAPTER 1. DESSALINES'S EMPIRE OF LIBERTY

1 One of the rare instances where the post-independence Haitian state is referred to as a republic occurs in a translated address dated May 2, 1804, and published in the *Times of London*. Addressing the "Inhabitants of the Universe," Dessalines proclaims that "the Republic of Hayti wishes to live in peace with all mankind, except with the White slaves of Buonaparte." "Proclamation of Dessalines," *Times of London*, September 26, 1804. Dessalines's use of the term "republic" here is designed to highlight Haiti's black anticolonial, antislavery freedom in contrast with white Frenchmen's servitude to Napoleonic imperial rule. On the May 2 address as it relates to Dessalines's massacre of the remaining French on the island, see Gaffield, *Haitian Connections*. On the May 2 address as it relates to British imperial discourses of political slavery and oriental despotism, see Cohen, *New History of the Two Indies*.

2 Madiou, *Histoire*, t. 3, 108–9. Madiou incorrectly dismisses the November 29, 1803, declaration as apocryphal or forged. Recent documentary evidence, includ-

ing translations of the proclamation in Philadelphia newspapers, such as the *Aurora General Advisor* on January 5, 1804, confirm its authenticity. See Jenson, *Slave Narrative*.

3 "N'allons pas, boutes-feu révolutionnaires, nous érigeant en législateur des Antilles, faire consister notre gloire à troubler le repos des Isles qui nous avoisinent." Haitian Declaration of Independence, 1804, transcript available in Gaffield, *Haitian Declaration of Independence*, 239–47, and at Julia Gaffield's blog, *Haiti and the Atlantic World*, https://haitidoi.com/doi/. Dessalines's words here are as much for his countrymen as they are a performance for the colonial powers of the Atlantic world: he is seeking to carve out a space for Haiti's legitimate existence, not necessarily to instigate a world historical event.

4 In addition to the primary sources I cite throughout, to answer these questions I rely on the historical documents reproduced in Madiou's *Histoire*, t. 3, Julia Gaffield's extraordinary primary source collection the Dessalines Reader, https://haitidoi.com/dessalines-reader/; and Gaétan Mentor's documentation of the 1806 republican revolution in *Histoire d'un crime*.

5 "Barbare[s] contre la barbarie colonial." Madiou, *Histoire*, t. 3, 329.

6 Garraway, "'Légitime Défense,'" 78.

7 My approach here differs importantly from that of Doris Y. Kadish, Deborah Jenson, and Norman R. Shapiro, who give the civil war remarkably short shrift in their *Poetry of Haitian Independence*.

8 For the Dessalineans, Mentor proposes the terms "irréductibles," "contre-révolutionnaires," "patriotes," and "inconditionnels." Thomas Madiou refers to Dessalineans as "ultra-révolutionnaires" or the "zélés partisans du système de Dessalines." Mentor refers to the republicans as the "révolutionnaires," while Madiou refers to them as the "modérés" and "constitutionalistes." During the 1804–1806 period, both Dessalineans and republicans launched the term "factieux" against the other group. There was not a monopoly on the word "tyrannie," either: the republicans named their movement "la campagne haïtienne contre la tyrannie," while Dessalineans called out Pétion's actions as the "tyrannie des parricides."

9 Madiou, *Histoire*, t. 3, 168.

10 Ibid., 243.

11 "Il importait peu que le chef de l'état s'appelât roi, empereur, ou president." Ibid., 169.

12 As early as June 1803, Dessalines was thinking about the independent state. See Gaffield, *Haitian Declaration*. By that point, England had declared war on France and the French army in Saint-Domingue had been decimated by sickness. The ranks of the Armée Indigène swelled, with free people of color switching sides, especially in the southern peninsula.

13 On Boisrond Tonnerre's biography, see Garrigus, "'Victims of Our Own Credulity.'"

14 Madiou, *Histoire*, t. 3, 49.

15 Mentor, *Histoire d'un crime*, 29. Dessalines even offered money to American ship captains who would agree to offer passage to members of the Saint-Dominguan diaspora back to Haiti: "blacks and men of color from Haiti taking refuge in other countries to return to their fatherland" (*les noirs et les hommes de couleur d'Haïti réfugié dans les autres pays à revenir dans leur patrie*). Madiou, *Histoire*, t. 3, 121.
16 Juste Chanlatte is the most important writer in Haiti's early postcolonial existence, yet there is remarkably little scholarly engagement with his life and work—inside and outside Haiti. It is only in the last five years that scholars have begun to engage substantively with his life and work. See Grégory Pierrot's new biography of Chanlatte in Pierrot, "Juste Chanlatte." See also Pierrot and Tabitha McIntosh's website dedicated to Chanlatte and his oeuvre: https://kingdomofobjects.wordpress.com/the-author-bis/. There is still little consensus and a lot of confusion about the other "Chanlattes" and "Chanlatts" from this period in history. The proliferation of other Chanlattes that Madiou cites ("Desruisseau" Chanlatte, "Desravines" Chanlatte, "Desroches" Chanlatte) all appear to be punny pseudonyms used by the younger François Desrivières Chanlatte.
17 See Tardieu, "Pierre Roux et Leméry." See chapter 2 for a more in-depth discussion of the history of the press as it relates specifically to the civil war in Haiti.
18 Jenson, *Slave Narrative*, 5.
19 Madiou describes the multilingual process by which the January 1, 1804, independence proclamation took place: Dessalines spoke first, recounting in Kreyòl "the compendium of cruelties that the French had visited upon the *indigènes*" (*l'historique des cruautés que les Français avait exercées sur les indigènes*), after which Dessalines ordered Boisrond Tonnerre to read aloud (in French) Dessalines's own words proclaiming independence. Madiou, *Histoire*, t. 3, 121. On Dessalines as a non-Western author, see Pierrot, *Black Avenger*.
20 Jenson, *Slave Narrative*, 96.
21 On deconstruction in Baron de Vastey's later writing, see Doris Garraway, Chris Bongie, Marlene Daut, and Nick Nesbitt's contributions to Vastey, *Colonial System*. The connection between Dessalinean writing and sixteenth- and seventeenth-century Protestant and anti-absolutist pamphlets is further suggested in the language of anti-idolatry that Dessalines uses. See Jenson, *Slave Narrative*, 96–97.
22 Haitian Declaration of Independence, 1804. On the structure of the Acte de l'indépendance, see Geggus, "Haiti's Declaration," 26.
23 "Victimes pendant quatorze ans de notre crédulité et de notre indulgence; vaincus, non par des armées françaises, mais par la pipeuse éloquence des proclamations de leurs agens." Haitian Declaration of Independence, 1804.
24 A pro-slavery plantation owner in Saint-Domingue. For more on Malouet, see chapter 2. This notion of deceptive eloquence resonates with Boisrond Tonnerre's condemnation in his *Mémoires* of the French forces' use of a "nouveau vocabulaire" to describe their genocide of insurgent slaves and free men of color. Boisrond Tonnerre, *Mémoires*, 75.

25 Centre national de ressources textuelles et lexicales, *Trésor de la langue française informatisé*, s.v. "pipeur," accessed April 11, 2018, www.cnrtl.fr/definition/pipeuse. Garrigus, *Before Haiti*, Dubois and Garrigus, *Slave Revolution*, Garraway, "'Légitime Défense'"; and Jenson, *Slave Narrative*, all translate *pipeuse* as "piteous," either incorrectly transcribing or mistranslating the word. Importantly, the adjective "pipeuse" creates a much more compelling connection to Robert Stepto's African American narrative practice of "distrust" that Jenson posits in *Slave Narrative*. See Stepto, *From Behind the Veil*.

26 See the introduction for a discussion of Dessalinean critique as the *practice* of space-making.

27 This is not to say small mistakes did not occur, such as the missing agreement on the past participle *vu* with the direct object pronoun *nous* in the passage cited in the epigraph above.

28 This inward focus on Haiti's struggles is an important piece of Dessalinean political culture that will be evoked at various times throughout Haiti's history to confront the challenges of civil war and external intervention.

29 See Centre national de ressources textuelles et lexicales, *Trésor de la langue française informatisé*, s.v. "ravir," accessed April 11, 2018, www.cnrtl.fr/definition/ravir; and Haitian Declaration of Independence, 1804, 3.

30 "Sachez que vous n'avez rien fait, si vous ne donnez aux nations un exemple terrible, mais juste, de la vengeance que doit exercer un peuple fier d'avoir recouvré sa liberté, et jaloux de la maintenir; effrayons tous ceux qui oserait tenter de nous la ravir encore." Haitian Declaration of Independence, 1804.

31 For a reading of Dessalinean vengeance as a systematic political decision, see Pierrot, *Black Avenger*.

32 Geggus, "Haiti's Declaration," 33.

33 Ibid., 32.

34 Ibid.

35 On Dessalines's specific use of the phrase in relation to Jefferson's, there has been surprisingly little scholarly attention. Jenson considers Dessalines's possible "anticolonial imperialism" in the context of Jefferson's expansionist ideals, but not Jefferson's use of the phrase itself. On Jefferson's use of the phrase, see Boyd, "Thomas Jefferson's 'Empire of Liberty.'" Boyd argues that Jefferson wrote this phrase for the first time in 1779 in the context of Lewis and Clark's western explorations. See also Tucker and Hendrickson, *Empire of Liberty*.

36 Bogues, *Empire of Liberty*, 5.

37 Jenson, *Slave Narrative*, 106.

38 "Le nom français lugubre encore nos contrées. Toute y retrace le souvenir des cruautés de ce peuple barbare; nos lois, nos mœurs, nos villes, tout encore porte l'empreinte Française; que dis-je, il existe des français dans notre Isle, et vous vous croyez libres et indépendans de cette République qui a combattu toutes les nations, il est vrai; mais qui n'a jamais vaincu celles qui ont voulu être libres." Haitian Declaration of Independence, 1804. On the term "lugubrer," see Fischer, *Moder-*

nity Disavowed; Garraway, "'Légitime Défense'"; and Daut, "'Nothing in Nature Is Mute.'"

39 "S'il pouvait exister parmi nous un cœur tiède, qu'il s'éloigne et tremble de prononcer le serment qui doit nous unir." Haitian Declaration of Independence, 1804.

40 This is an early iteration of the "génie de la patrie" or "spirit of the nation" that we will see throughout nineteenth-century Haitian writing, most notably in Ignace Nau (chapter 4) and Emeric Bergeaud (chapter 5).

41 "Et si jamais tu refusais ou recevais en murmurant les lois que le génie qui veille à tes destins me dictera pour ton bonheur, tu mériterais le sort des peuples ingrats." Haitian Declaration of Independence, 1804.

42 We see a variation on this same theme in his April 1804 address, threatening the Haitian who would refuse to engage in the massacre against the French: "Who is this lowly Haitian, so unworthy of his regeneration. . . . If there be one, may he go away from here; may nature, indignant, repel him from our midst; may he go and hide his shame far from here." (*Quel est ce vil haïtien, si peu digne de sa régénération. . . . S'il en est un, qu'il s'éloigne; la nature indignée le repousse de notre sein; qu'il aille cacher sa honte loin de ces lieux*). Julia Gaffield, "Dessalines Reader, 28 April 1804," *Haiti and the Atlantic World* (blog), October 30, 2015, https://haitidoi.com/2015/10/30/dessalines-reader-28-april-1804/.

43 Madiou, *Histoire*, t. 3, 168.

44 Michel-Rolph Trouillot, *Silencing the Past*, 37.

45 Madiou, *Histoire*, t. 3, 58. See also Geggus, "Haiti's Declaration"; and Mentor, *Histoire d'un crime*.

46 Madiou, *Histoire*, t. 3, 113.

47 Boisrond Tonnerre famously proclaimed to Dessalines, "All that has been done is not in harmony with our current frame of mind; to draw up the declaration of independence, we need the skin of a white man for parchment, his skull for an inkwell, his blood for ink, and a sword for a pen!" (*Tout ce qui a été fait n'est pas en harmonie avec nos dispositions actuelles; pour dresser l'acte de l'Indépendance, il nous faut la peau d'un blanc pour parchemin, son crâne pour écritoire, son sang pour encre, et une baïonnette pour plume!*) As Geggus notes, Charéron's was "supposedly very literary and based on the US Declaration of Independence." Geggus, "Haiti's Declaration," 33–34. See also Mentor, *Histoire d'un crime*; and Mentor, *Les fils noirs de la veuve*. Jenson calls into question the veracity of Boisrond Tonnerre's "authorship" altogether. See *Slave Narrative*, 87–89. Though I cannot develop it further here, I have long believed that the language of this (apocryphal) story of Boisrond Tonnerre's draft—and perhaps the language of Dessalinean vengeance more broadly—is inscribed in the specific discourse of an early modern Caribbean phenomenon: piracy. And why not? What extant discourse is Boisrond Tonnerre activating with his imagery (skulls, blood, parchment made of skin)? There is, I think, a tendency to associate it with some vague African notion when it fits more clearly, and more logically, within the discourse of Caribbean piracy: written in blood, the prevalence of the skull imagery, the idea of "liberté ou la mort," and

the recourse to vengeance and other forms of justice and legitimacy in an Atlantic world system dominated by Old World order and privilege. It is entirely logical to suggest that Boisrond Tonnerre's famous phrase draws upon the discursive font of violence, vengeance, and liberty that was purely Caribbean in origin.
48   Geggus, "Haiti's Declaration," 30.
49   He was the author of at least one revolutionary published text, an impressive, violent call to arms entitled "Appel des hommes de couleur de l'Ouest." The November 1791 call rallies free men of color as "avengers of perfidy and betrayal" (*vengeurs du parjure et de la perfidie*), encouraging them to rise up, to "plunge our blood-stained arms . . . into the breasts of these monsters from Europe" (*plongeons nos bras ensanglantés . . . dans le sein de ces monstres d'Europe*) who have treated free people of color as "playthings of their passions and their insidious maneuvering" (*jouet à leur passions et à leurs manœuvres insidieuses*). The tropes and vocabulary in Chanlatte's call to arms—vengeance, perfidy, insidious maneuvering—are deployed throughout subsequent revolutionary and early post-independence writing. Translation from Geggus, *Haitian Revolution*, 70–71. The original text of "Appel" is reproduced in Ardouin, *Etudes*, t. 1, 314–15. See also Pierrot, "Juste Chanlatte."
50   Juste Chanlatte, "Hymne haytiène," reproduction of archival copy available at Julia Gaffield, *Haiti and the Atlantic World* (blog), March 23, 2013, https://haiti-doi.com/2013/03/23/hymne-haitiene/. Though the dating of texts during 1804 is a complicated affair (see below), this text is almost certainly from January 1804. It is archived along with the earlier papers and proclamations that date from January 1804, including the Acte de l'indépendance. What is more, the poem itself does not include a date; it does, however, include an annotation in English that states that the poem was "composed & sung, I believe for the first time upon the 21st of January, Dessalines being present" (TNA CO 137/111). See also Tardieu, "Debate."
51   "Quoi? tu te tais Peuple Indigène! / Quand un Héros, par ses exploits, / Vengeant ton nom, brisant ta chaine, / A jamais assure tes droits?" Chanlatte, "Hymne haytiène." Readers will note that I have chosen to translate Chanlatte's hymn, as well as other poetry throughout this study, into unmetered, unrhymed verse. Though I have sacrificed form, I believe I have better captured meaning.
52   Many thanks to Henry Stoll for drawing my attention to the importance of contrafacta in the *songs* of Haitian independence. Henry Stoll, "The Songs of Haitian Independence" (paper presented at the annual meeting of the Haitian Studies Association, Gainesville, Florida, October 17–19, 2019).
53   Bibliothèque nationale de France, "La marseillaise," http://data.bnf.fr/11938165/claude_joseph_rouget_de_lisle_la_marseillaise/#work.rejected_forms.
54   "La Marseillaise" lyrics available at the office of the president of France, www.elysee.fr/la-presidence/la-marseillaise-de-rouget-de-lisle.
55   Chanlatte, "Hymne haytiène."
56   Ibid.

57 Norman Shapiro makes this assumption, which leads him to suggest, wrongly, that Chanlatte's use of the third-person imperative "may be an error." Kadish, Jenson, and Shapiro, *Poetry of Haitian Independence*, 257n6.
58 On figurative slavery, see Nyquist, *Arbitrary Rule*. For a discussion of figurative slavery specifically in the colonial context of the Global Indies, see Cohen, *New History of the Two Indies*.
59 "Pour lever nos fronts abattus, / Jacque paraît, ils ne sont plus." Chanlatte, "Hymne haytiène."
60 The capitalization of "Tonnerre" is not a personification; rather, I interpret it as an appeal to the Vodou god (*lwa*) of thunder, Agaou Tonnerre. See Marcelin, *Mythologie vodou*. Chanlatte's formulation here does offer another possible reading: that he is referring to his brother in Dessalinean writing, Boisrond Tonnerre, suggesting that he might step in and expiate this sin.
61 "Désormais, Jacque est le Patron / De qui repousse l'esclavage." Chanlatte, "Hymne haytiène."
62 "Sous ce bon Père, unis / A jamais réunis / Vivons, mourons, ses vrais Enfants (*bis*) / Libres, indépendants." Ibid.
63 "Nomination de l'empereur d'Hayti, J. J. Dessalines."
64 Madiou argues that Dessalines's counselors "backdated his appointment as Emperor and his proclamation to the people" (*antidatèrent l'acte de sa nomination au titre d'Empereur et sa proclamation au peuple*). Madiou, *Histoire*, t. 3, 170. On the backdating of documents specifically related to Dessalines's nomination, see Madiou, *Histoire*, t. 3; and Jenson, *Slave Narrative*.
65 According to Madiou. This is further confirmed in the National Archive, which has catalogued these texts according to their date of receipt, along with other texts from late 1804. Moreover, there is a handwritten note with the date "15 December," suggesting that George Nugent (Governor of Jamaica) received the documents on December 15, 1804, which is logical timing for their arrival in Jamaica. As further evidence of this date, Madiou notes that in a letter dated September 1, the day before the snap decision to hold the nomination ceremony, Dessalines had written to Pétion under the title of "gouverneur general," and in a subsequent letter dated September 4, he signed it as emperor of Haiti. See Madiou, *Histoire*, t. 3, 170, 175. Jenson's own research on the circulation of these documents confirms the late 1804 date, noting that both texts do not appear in North American newspapers until early October. Jenson, *Slave Narrative*, 105.
66 Madiou, *Histoire*, t. 3, 169.
67 Ibid., 170.
68 Ibid.
69 Ibid.
70 Ibid., 171.
71 Ibid., 179. These sung couplets are also published in the second issue of the *Gazette politique et commerciale d'Haïti* (November 22, 1804), indicated as "C. Cezar Télémaque, contrôleur du department du Nord."

72 Thomas Madiou reproduces lengthy excerpts from this early document of Haitian independence. For a recent scholarly engagement with the text, see Bongie, "Cry of History." The pamphlet does not indicate a precise date, though the original is archived alongside the nomination documents in the British National Archives, which suggests that it was circulated along with them in September 1804. Gaffield's Dessalines Reader shows this clearly: Julia Gaffield, "Dessalines Reader, Nomination as Emperor," *Haiti and the Atlantic World* (blog), November 18, 2015, https://haitidoi.com/2015/11/18/dessalines-reader-nomination-as-emperor/.

73 Bongie, "Cry of History."

74 "Il va fixer plus particulièrement l'attention du Vieux Monde sur le Nouveau." Chanlatte, *A mes concitoyens*, 1.

75 This is a revolutionary term, used both in France and Saint-Domingue, that translates roughly as "the right of revolution," and Chanlatte uses it here as just that—a *right* to overthrow an arbitrary or oppressive government. The term was first used in the colony in November 1793 in the coalition between free men of color and white planters against the French commissioners Sonthonax and Polvérel, in opposition to the "liberté générale" the French agents had proclaimed. Madiou, *Histoire*, t. 1, 158–59. Thus, Chanlatte used the term in the Dessalinean fashion of reversal: justifying Haiti's right to expel the tyrannical French colonists and calling into question the legitimacy of the rights and liberty practiced by the French. Chanlatte was reappropriating and rescripting a term used by French colonists—a tactic he and other Dessalinean writers (especially Vastey) would continue under Christophe.

76 "Grâce à l'Etre-suprême qui ne veut pas que l'innocent périsse, nos bourreaux ont disparu devant les Phalanges Indigènes, comme on voit une vapeur impure s'évanouir aux rayons du soleil." Chanlatte, *A mes concitoyens*, 1. This image of evaporating dew will be used again by Chanlatte in *Cri*. See Bongie, "Cry of History."

77 "Sur-tout, fidèles aux loix de la discipline et de la subordination, vivons ou mourons sous les ordres du chef intrépide et précieux que le ciel nous destinait." Chanlatte, *A mes concitoyens*, 5.

78 Ibid.

79 "Malheur à l'insensé qui tenterait de troubler l'ensemble et l'harmonie qui doivent régner parmi nous! qu'au moment même il soit extirpé de la société, comme on déracine avec la serpe une plante parasite et venimeuse." Ibid.

80 "Loin de ces lieux cet esprit de discorde et de division qui prépare sourdement et opère enfin la chute des Etats les mieux consolidés!" Ibid.

81 On Dessalines's failed march on the East, see Sara E. Johnson, *Fear of French Negroes*. See also Mentor, *Histoire d'un crime*.

82 Madiou, *Histoire*, t. 3, 228.

83 On the 1805 imperial constitution, see Janvier, *Les constitutions*; see also Moïse, *Constitutions*. On the importance of Article 14, which dictated that all Haitians

be known under the generic denomination of blacks, see Fischer, *Modernity Disavowed*; Jenson, *Slave Narrative*; and Girard, "Jean-Jacques Dessalines."
84 The text of the ceremony is reproduced in Madiou, *Histoire*, t. 3, 217.
85 Ibid., 218.
86 Ibid., 217.
87 "En même temps que vos bras victorieux fertilisaient ce sol imbibé d'une rosée salutaire et expiatoire, vos regards se sont tournés vers une constitution qui assied vos droits sur des bases invariables, et vous fait prendre place au rang des nations civilisées." Ibid.
88 "Honneur aux généraux dont la plume n'a pas dédaigné de stipuler les intérêts du peuple, après les avoir conquis à la pointe de l'épée." Ibid.
89 Ibid., 217–18.
90 "Depuis que je parcours le cercle des vicissitudes dans lequel m'ont lancé les mouvemens révolutionnaires; ce serment est mon arrêt." Ibid.
91 "Ils sont donc connus, ces secrets pleins d'horreurs." Madiou, *Histoire*, t. 3, 309. I adapted my translation from Bongie's translation of Vastey's iteration of the phrase in Vastey, *Colonial System*.
92 Madiou, *Histoire*, t. 3, 344. It is important to note the republicans' use of language here in response to Dessalines's empire. Dessalines's June 16, 1805, speech had lauded the Haitian people for their efforts "against tyranny" (*contre la tyrannie*). Here, of course, he was speaking of the tyranny of French colonial rule. Ibid., 217.
93 Ibid., 322.
94 Mentor, *Histoire d'un crime*, 121–22.
95 For a narrative account of the assassination, see Madiou, *Histoire*, t. 3, 322–25. See also Brutus, *L'homme d'airain*. Mentor's more recent study is one of the few histories that recount the event as a republican-Dessalinean or revolutionary-counterrevolutionary story, though he clearly draws upon the language and arguments of turn-of-the-century writers like Massillon Coicou and Joseph Jérémie (see chapter 6).
96 The many Haitian theatrical representations of Dessalines's assassination include Hénock Trouillot, *Dessalines, ou Le sang du Pont-Rouge*; Liautaud Ethéart, *Essais dramatiques de Liautaud Ethéart*, 3e série, *La Fille de l'empereur, drame historique en 3 actes* (Paris: Moquet, 1860); Coicou, *L'empereur Dessalines*; Jean Métellus, *Le pont rouge* (Paris: Nouvelles du Sud, 1991); and Dominique Hippolyte, *Le torrent: Drame historique en 3 actes* (Port-au-Prince: Presses nationales d'Haïti, 1965), among many others. On Dessalines's legacy in Haitian theater, see Hénock Trouillot, *Dessalines, ou La tragédie post-coloniale*; and Coates, "Dessalines: History in the Theater." To date, there remain remarkably few book-length biographical studies of Dessalines's life and assassination—from scholars in Haiti or in the Atlantic world. This is all the more troubling given how many scholarly works have been written on the other leaders of the Haitian Revolution, especially Toussaint Louverture. See Brutus, *L'homme d'airain*, t. 1 and 2; Jean-Baptiste, *Le fondateur*;

and Mentor, *Dessalines*. Julia Gaffield is currently working on a biography of Dessalines in English to address this gap.

97 Christophe assumed the mantle of "vengeur de Dessalines" (Dessalines's avenger), though only after his attempts to secure sufficient executive power as the president of the republic failed in late 1806, as we shall see below. When Christophe was still attempting to curry favor with the republican faction, he referred to Dessalines and his government as *l'arbitraire*—a slightly less provocative term for despotism. Madiou, *Histoire*, t. 3, 349.

98 Ibid., 262.

99 Dun, *Dangerous Neighbors*, 223. On the embargo and Haitian diplomacy, see Gaffield, *Haitian Connections*. On Dessalines's commercial duties, David Geggus does note that Dessalines rejected a British trade treaty. Geggus, "Haiti's Declaration," 40n44.

100 "Sous cet homme stupide." Madiou, *Histoire*, t. 3, 314. Both Pétion's republic and Christophe's rival state-turned-monarchy emphasized international commerce and the promotion of trade in their respective governments.

101 Ibid., 276.

102 Ibid.

103 "Mais la liberté, grand Dieu! est un vain nom dans ce pays, qu'on n'ose plus prononcer ouvertement, quoiqu'il soit placé à la tête des actes; mais elle n'existe que là." Ibid., 308.

104 Ibid.

105 Madiou suggests that Guy Joseph Bonnet—a staunch southern republican and Rigaudin—had long maintained that the rumor was fabricated. Ibid., 315. At the time, Dessalines referred to the rumor as a "trame des factieux." Mentor, *Histoire d'un crime*, 115.

106 Translation from Bongie, Introduction, 50. Malouet's original phrase is "Le voilà donc connu ce secret plein d'horreur: la liberté des noirs, c'est leur domination! c'est le massacre ou l'esclavage des blancs, c'est l'incendie de nos champs, de nos cités." Malouet, *Collection de mémoires*, 46. Malouet italicizes the original, either for emphasis or because he is quoting it from another (unnamed) source. Indeed, it is unlikely that Malouet coined the phrase; instead, his phrasing captures the sentiments that the slave uprising evoked for the rest of the slaveholding Atlantic world: horror and fear in the face of the ontological threat posed to plantation society and to white supremacy.

107 One key text that draws on the Atlantic world circulation of the "horror" that related to the uprising in the colony is Lenora Sansay's 1808 *Secret History; Or, The Horrors of St. Domingo*. See Accilien, "Secret History." On the importance of Malouet's text to Baron de Vastey, as well as Vastey's own variation on Malouet's phrase, see Bongie, Introduction; and Daut, "Monstrous Testimony."

108 I am using the reproduction of this document in Madiou, *Histoire*, t. 3. For more on this document, see Hénock Trouillot, *Les origines*. Trouillot argues that it was written by André Dominique Sabourin.

109 Madiou, *Histoire*, t. 3, 316.
110 Déclaration des droits de l'homme et du citoyen de 1789, Legifrance, accessed April 13, 2018, www.legifrance.gouv.fr/Droit-francais/Constitution/Declaration-des-Droits-de-l-Homme-et-du-Citoyen-de-1789.
111 It is important to underline the republicans' use of the phrase as purely within its earlier French revolutionary context, rather than—and likely in response to—Chanlatte's subversive, anti-French use of the term in *A mes concitoyens* discussed above.
112 "Aucun frein enfin n'arrêtait la férocité de ce tigre altéré du sang de ses semblables." Madiou, *Histoire*, t. 3, 315.
113 Ibid.
114 "Aucune loi protectrice ne garantissait le peuple contre la barbarie du souverain; sa volonté suprême." Ibid.
115 Dun, *Dangerous Neighbors*, 230.
116 Ibid., 225.
117 Ibid., 225–26. The US language that denounced Dessalines as a "tiger" is in keeping with language from the British empire that associated despotism with "tigers." Ashley Cohen's work on "oriental despotism" is illustrative here: the English denounce their most formidable enemy in India, Tipu Sultan, as the Tiger (sometimes "Tyger") of Mysore. See Cohen, *New History of the Two Indies*. On Faustin Soulouque's critique of this trope of despotism, see chapter 5.
118 Madiou, *Histoire*, t. 3, 316.
119 Ibid.
120 "Le peuple, ainsi que l'armée, lassé du joug odieux qu'on lui imposait, rappelant son courage et son énergie, vient enfin, par un mouvement spontané, de le briser. Oui, nous avons rompu nos fers!" Ibid.
121 Ibid., 314.
122 Mentor, *Histoire d'un crime*, 116.
123 "Vengeur de Dessalines." Madiou, *Histoire*, t. 3, 384.
124 Mentor, *Histoire d'un crime*, 125. The 1805 imperial constitution refers to Dessalines as "le vengeur et le libérateur."
125 Ibid., 121, 127.
126 Ibid., 127. Mentor notes that Corneille Brelle proposed the idea of officiating a funeral mass in Dessalines's honor, an offer Chanlatte communicated to Dessalines's widow, Marie-Claire Heureuse Félicité Bonheur, in a letter that was also read aloud to the remaining Dessalinean troops. Mentor, *Histoire d'un crime*, 136.
127 Mentor, *Histoire d'un crime*, 135. It was Pétion who apparently intervened to save his life, as Chanlatte later described it in a letter to Dessalines's widow.
128 "Vous avez toujours dit et je me plais à vous répéter que, le premier bien d'un Peuple, la première condition de la vie civile, c'est la liberté." Ibid., 135.
129 Ibid.
130 "Combien d'entre nous, ne sont pas restés fidèles à vos idées, vos opinions, combien d'entre nous n'ont pas subi l'influence de votre pensée, de votre langage?" Ibid.

131 Pétion would name Chanlatte's younger brother secretary of the Senate in March 1807, perhaps as an intentional provocation of the elder Chanlatte. Madiou, *Histoire*, t. 3, 415.
132 "Une grande amitié me liait avec votre illustre mari, une amitié fondée sur plusieurs années de luttes communes et sur les idéaux les plus nobles." Mentor, *Histoire d'un crime*, 137.
133 "A protéger sa vénérable mémoire; "les rêves grandioses qu'il nourrissait pour ses frères, et qui lui ont coûté la vie." Ibid., 136.
134 "Loin de me porter à me faire changer d'avis, ils ne font que me maintenir dans mes résolutions. Je reste donc en armes, jurant de disparaître plutôt que d'entériner un crime aussi odieux." Ibid., 137.
135 Madiou, *Histoire*, t. 3, 317.
136 Ibid., 349–50.
137 Ibid., 350.
138 "La nécessité d'une rigoureuse obéissance aux lois"; "s'il est au milieu de vous des agitateurs, des stipendiés de nos ennemis, . . . sachez les connaître." Ibid.
139 "Le peuple veut la liberté, et je le seconderai de tous mes efforts." Ibid., 358. Madiou notes that Pétion's reply is quoted from a work entitled "La réponse de Pétion aux calomnies du général Christophe."
140 Ibid., 372.
141 Ibid.
142 "Viennent de lever le masque; ils ont mis au jour leurs projets . . . ils veulent établir une Constitution qui mettra le pouvoir entre leurs mains." Ibid., 372–73.

CHAPTER 2. CIVIL WAR, *GUERRE DE PLUME*

1 Chanlatte, *Réflexions*. His signature on the pamphlet also identifies him as "Rédacteur de la Gazette Officielle de l'Etat d'Haïti," having replaced Rouanez in this important position in Christophe's new government.
2 Chanlatte was also, undoubtedly, writing for a multiplicity of other audiences: he was writing to power, performing within Christophe's northern state, and rallying the subjects of the monarchy against the southern republic. He was also writing to an international audience to legitimize Christophe's claims to statehood in the North, and to rally supporters, especially British abolitionists, to the northern government. For an in-depth discussion of audience in Christophean writing in particular, see Garraway, "Print, Publics."
3 "Rectifier l'opinion de mes concitoyens ou les éclairer sur l'existence illégitime de ce sénat, sur sa composition illégale et sur ses injustes usurpations, voilà le précieux objet de cet écrit." Chanlatte, *Réflexions*, 1.
4 "[Le] Sénat de Port-aux-Crimes ou, plutôt [le] Sénat de Pétion, dont il est tout à la fois le meneur, le régulateur, le président et demi-Dieu." Ibid., 7. On Chanlatte's use of the term "Port-aux-Crimes" in the 1791 "Appel des hommes de couleur de l'Ouest," see Pierrot, "Juste Chanlatte."

5 Theater and performativity were central to all of Chanlatte's writing, but especially his final three pieces of writing from Christophe's monarchy: two *opéras comiques*, *L'entrée du roi en sa capitale* (1818) and *La partie de chasse du roi* (1820), and his three-act *tragédie*, *Néhri, chef des Haytiens* (1819). See McIntosh and Pierrot, *Néhri*.
6 Chanlatte, *Réflexions*, 2.
7 Ibid., 7, 5.
8 Richard Sieburth defines the *physiologie* as "the inventory of contemporary social types ... of different studies of manners that became very popular with the growing urban readership." Sieburth, "Une idéologie du lisible." Though physiologies became wildly popular in France in the 1840s with, for example, *Les Français peints par eux-mêmes*, Sieburth notes the importance of late eighteenth-century precursors, which Chanlatte clearly draws upon here. For a recent analysis of physiologies as popular literature, see O'Neil-Henry, *Mastering the Marketplace*.
9 "Ne reconnaissez-vous pas par son ampleur et sa rotondité le faux, l'ingrat Télémaque?" Chanlatte, *Réflexions*, 13.
10 "Ancien satellite du roitelet Rigaud." Ibid., 19.
11 "N'en doutons pas; c'est lui, c'est l'infernal Pétion qui s'approche." Ibid., 28.
12 "Une violente contraction de nerfs l'a tout-à-coup arrêté, ses traits sont renversés, une fureur farouche étincelle dans ses yeux." Ibid., 31.
13 "N'est-ce pas en ces lieux que les furies de l'enfer ont fait siffler sur ma tête leur serpens odieux? ... Oui c'est bien ici; je vois, je reconnais ce marais fangeux." Ibid.
14 "Faibles efforts," "prétendu sénat du Port-au-Prince," "l'opinion publique de la juste indignation." Ibid., 33.
15 Madiou, *Histoire*, t. 3, 436.
16 Laurent Dubois notes that by 1810, there were only five senators left in the legislature. Dubois, *Aftershocks*, 60. For more on Pétion's republicanism, see chapters 3 and 4.
17 Madiou, *Histoire*, t. 3, 417.
18 Ibid., 413.
19 Ibid., 409. The choice of these specific Catholic holidays undoubtedly aimed to associate Henry Christophe with the revolutionary heritage of Toussaint Louverture and Jean-Jacques Dessalines.
20 Janvier, *Les constitutions*, 89. Juste Chanlatte is notably absent from the list of signatories on the northern constitution; he may have been in hiding or in transit to the northern state, as he did not officially appear in northern print until May 1807 (see above).
21 Castera, *Bref coup d'œil*, Desquiron, *Haïti à la une*; Bissainthe, *Dictionnaire*.
22 The 1820 Almanach lists Buon as the "imprimeur" of the kingdom, and he is likely the printer who took over from Roux. Esterquest, "L'imprimerie royale." After 1816, Roux's name does not appear on any document published in Cap-Henry. The circumstances of his removal remain unknown. With Roux's departure we see a more drastic shift in the typeset and a decrease in the quality of the printing, not only of the *Gazette royale*, but of all texts published for the new royal press under the direction of Buon.

23 Two issues of the *Sentinelle* from 1808 and two issues of the *Bulletin officiel* from 1809 are held at the BNF.

24 For more on Rigaud's separatist government, see chapter 3. See also Hall, *La péninsule républicaine*.

25 Though I do not have specific biographic information for this printer, the Fourcand family remained prominent in southern Haiti. See Pascal-Trouillot and Trouillot, *Encyclopédie*.

26 F. D. Chanlatte is later listed as the "Directeur de l'Imprimerie du Gouvernment" (as well as "Interprète des Langues Etrangèrs") in the *Almanach républicain pour l'année commune 1818*, for which he is also listed as the main author. He was likely an interpreter of English, having lived in Baltimore for a period of time with his older brother. Chanlatte, *Almanach républicain*, 83.

27 Girard provides an example of letterhead used in 1802 by the French general Pierre Quantin during the Leclerc expedition. Girard, "Birth of a Nation." See Julia Gaffield's site for a discussion of early examples of the Haitian coat of arms: https://haitidoi.com/2013/09/15/the-haitian-coat-of-arms/.

28 It is possible that the French expeditionary forces surrendered templates along with their printing presses, which would have included some similar letterhead engraving. It does indeed appear as though the banner at the head of the *Bulletin officiel* was a modification of some other original.

29 *Le Télégraphe* ran for twenty-nine years, through 1843. Jean Alix René's research on the finances of Pétion's republic confirms 1814 as a decisive date in the southern republic and the increased stability in print production. The early years of the civil war had bankrupted the state but by 1814, Pétion was finally beginning to see some financial gains from his 1809 land reform policy. See René, *Haïti après l'esclavage*.

30 On the other hand, we do know that there was a vibrant theater culture in the early southern republican public sphere. As Thomas Madiou notes, the works of Antoine Dupré, a poet and playwright, "drew the whole town to the show every night" (*attiraient chaque soir toute la population au spectacle*). Madiou, *Histoire*, t. 4, 253. Dupré did also publish a few poems in *Le Télégraphe*. The newspaper also published fables written under the pseudonym "Florian," almost certainly Jules Solime Milscent, who continued to publish similar texts in *L'Abeille* (see chapter 3). On Dupré, see Fouchard, *Le théâtre à Saint-Domingue*.

31 A French national, journalist, and political exile, Peltier (occasionally "Lepellier" or "Pelletier" in Madiou) founded a number of newspapers while in exile, including *L'Ambigu*, which ran from 1802 to 1818. Madiou notes that Chanlatte sent his own writing for Peltier to publish in *L'Ambigu* for a fee, which Madiou says Chanlatte paid in sugar, coffee, and cotton. Madiou, *Histoire*, t. 4, 120, 201.

32 The archival afterlives of publications from the North and South during the *guerre de plume* reveal the networks of influence and print publics that each side of the civil war sought to cultivate. The southern republican publications are almost uniquely held in France at the BNF and resulted in many fewer archived copies.

The publications from the northern monarchy, on the other hand, are decidedly more voluminous and traveled much further; they are spread far and wide in Europe, North America, South America, and the Caribbean. For or an ever-growing digital archive of the North's early print culture, see Daut, *La Gazette royale d'Hayti* (blog). For an interactive map and bibliography of surviving editions of works published in the Kingdom of Haiti between 1811 and 1820, see Tabitha McIntosh's "Mapping the Kingdom" (www.google.com/maps/d/u/o/viewer?mid=1faonhoazgXxa2lFsom_6HCfkge5lOF69&ll=0%2C0&z=3) and "Mapping the Library" (https://docs.google.com/spreadsheets/d/1MPSH1U4seVZlO4-kujSUXM7krvsleIDvxRZmmTryXQA/edit#gid=0) projects.

33 Jenson, *Slave Narrative*, 6.
34 One early example of a North-South paper war exchange can be found in the southern *Bulletin officiel*: Antoine Dupré wrote a scathing rebuke, in epigram form, of an "invitation pastorale" (ministry invitation) sent by the northern priest Corneille Brelle, dated December 7, 1808, which implored the republicans to put down their arms and participate in the efforts of Christophe's northern state. Hénock Trouillot notes a third "contre-réplique" to Dupré's epigram from a northern writer in the private Edmond Mangonez collection, "Brochure en réplique à une attaque contre S. E. le préfet Apostolique de l'Etat d'Hayti." Hénock Trouillot, *Les origines*, 26.
35 Madiou conveys the republicans' lamentations that Dessalines's widow, Marie-Claire Heureuse, did not join them when they evacuated to the South after Christophe's troops retook Gonaïves: "It would have been a great victory for the Republic to have in its midst the widow of Emperor Dessalines who would have voluntarily taken refuge there." (*C'eût été pour la République une grande victoire que d'avoir dans son sein la veuve de l'Empereur Dessalines qui s'y serait réfugiée volontairement.*) Madiou, *Histoire*, t. 3, 429–30.
36 The men whose lives were spared included Antoine Dupré, Hérard Dumesle, and Faustin Soulouque, who were then serving as aides-de-camp for Lamarre. Madiou, *Histoire*, t., 215.
37 On Goman's peasant state, see Madiou, *Histoire*, t. 3 and t. 4. See also Nicholls, *Caribbean Context*; and Hector and Lissade, "Echos et nouvelles." Goman was a member of Christophe's nobility, named in 1811 as the Comte de Jérémie. Cheesman, Vendryes, and Jean, *Armorial of Haiti*. Crystal Eddins's forthcoming work on Goman is sure to shed new light on his separatist peasant state.
38 Madiou, *Histoire*, t. 5, 438.
39 On the Malouet affair, see Bongie, Introduction; and Madiou, *Histoire*, t. 5. On the Malouet affair in British public opinion specifically, see McIntosh and Pierrot, "Capturing."
40 Not Pompée-Valentin Vastey, as has been erroneously repeated by critics and historians for over a century, present author included. Among the excellent recent scholarship on Vastey's life and works, see Daut, *Baron de Vastey*; and Bongie, Introduction. See also Daut, *Tropics*; and Laurent Quevilly, *Baron de*

Vastey (Paris: Books on Demand, 2014); on Christophe's regime, see Hector, "Une autre voie."

41 Malouet participated in the May 1791 debates in France in which he argued against free people of color gaining rights and in 1802 published his memoirs based in his time in the colony (1767–1774) with an updated introduction designed to coincide with Napoléon's ambitions to end racial equality and abolition in the Caribbean colonies.

42 General Jérôme Maximilien Borgella was an important southern military general. He had fought alongside Rigaud (and against Toussaint) in the War of the South before joining the Armée Indigène under Dessalines. He had served as a general in the southern peninsula after 1804 and had helped reintegrate southern secessionists back into Pétion's republic in 1812.

43 "[Sa Majesté] a résolu de ne déployer sa puissance pour faire rentrer les insurgés des Saint-Domingue dans le devoir, qu'après avoir épuisé toutes les mesures que lui inspire sa clémence." Qtd. in Prévost, *Le machiavélisme*, 11.

44 Madiou, *Histoire*, t. 3, 209–10. On Dessalines's 1805 expedition, see Johnson, *Fear of French Negroes*.

45 Given Lavaysse's rogue activities, it is worth speculating whether he deliberately dismissed Draverneau in order to consolidate his own negotiating power with Pétion and avoid an uprising in the South.

46 "Les souverains de l'Europe, quoiqu'ils aient fait la paix, ils n'ont pas encore remis l'épée dans le fourreau." Qtd. in *Procès verbal*, 7.

47 Christophe likely intended to arrest Médina the moment he stepped into the northern department. See Madiou, *Histoire*, t. 5; Vastey, *Colonial System*; Daut, *Baron de Vastey*.

48 Vastey, *Colonial System*, 61. For more on Pétion and his attitude toward Lavaysse and the possibility of French "restauration" versus "rapprochement," see Nicholls, "Race, couleur"; and Manigat, "Le délicat problème."

49 Griggs and Prator, *Correspondence*, 59. The idea of an indemnity has precedent in the 1783 Treaty of Paris, which included provisions for reimbursement to British loyalists for loss of property during the American Revolutionary War.

50 "Nous ne traitons avec le Gouvernement français que sur le même pied de puissance à puissance, de souverain à souverain." Qtd. in Price-Mars, "Le sentiment de la valeur." On Christophe's approach to international recognition and monarchy, see Garraway, "Empire of Freedom"; and Bongie, Introduction, 60–61. Pétion's negotiations with Lavaysse became the central example upon which the northern government built its critique of Pétion's republic and underwrote the monarch's attempts to invade and conquer the southern government. Moreover, as we will see in subsequent chapters, critics would return to this early example of Christophe's refusal of indemnity negotiations as a rallying cry against elites in the capital seeking to "sell the country to the French."

51 Juste Chanlatte, now Comte de Rosiers, is not listed among the officers, nor is he one of the signatories of the resolution they drafted. Indeed, he is conspicuously

absent from virtually all meetings, negotiations, and textual production from this period in Christophe's kingdom. His name does not reappear until 1818 with the publication of some of his *opéras comiques* written for the court.
52 The minutes indicate that Julien Prévost, Comte de Limonade, secretary of state and minister of foreign affairs, was selected to read aloud for the room the documents under review: Lavaysse's October 1 letter to Christophe; the copy of Lavaysse's September 6 letter to Pétion; and a pro-colonial pamphlet published in Jamaica by a certain H. Henry entitled "Considérations offertes aux Habitans de Saint-Domingue, sur leur sort actuel et sur le sort présumé qui les attend." Baron de Dupuy published two separate refutations of the H. Henry pamphlet.
53 Vastey revisits the October 1814 General Council meeting in detail in *Essai*. For a detailed analysis, see Bongie, Introduction, 53. On the importance of the voices of unlettered former slaves to testimonial and collective memory in Christophean writing, see Daut, "Monstrous Testimony."
54 "Haytiens! méditez ces écrits avec calme et sagesse, tel qu'il convient à des hommes libres, qui ont conquis leur indépendance au prix de leur sang. Méditez-les tel qu'il convient enfin à des mandataires qui représentent la nation, et qui . . . ont à prononcer sur leur sort et les intérêts les plus chers de leurs concitoyens!" *Procès verbal*, 1–2.
55 See chapter 1.
56 *Procès verbal*, 20. The fact that Malouet was already dead, unbeknownst to the northern writers, creates a somewhat absurd effect: their fearful and passionate addresses are made to a man who is no longer alive.
57 Henceforth, *Notes à Malouet*. Vastey's title transposes Malouet's initials.
58 Like Chanlatte, Boisrond Tonnerre, and countless other free men in the colony, Vastey went to France to live with relatives after the outbreak of the revolution in the colony. Vastey did not frequent the best Parisian schools or society, however, spending most of his time between Rouen and the small town of Bacqueville. He returned to the colony in 1796. For a bibliography of works from Christophe's entire secretarial corps, see McIntosh, "Mapping the Library."
59 See the introduction for a discussion of the displacement of authority in print. I draw especially here on Butler, "Restaging the Universal," Garraway, "Print, Publics," and Bongie, Introduction. Jean Jonassaint suggests that Aimé Césaire's use of an alternating citation and rebuttal structure in *Discours sur le colonialisme* (1950) relies on Vastey's *Notes à Malouet* pamphlet as a model. Jonassaint, "Césaire et Haïti."
60 Garraway has referred to Vastey's work as an "antislavery tract" in the genre of the "antislavery polemic." Garraway, "Abolition, Sentiment." Bongie has elsewhere discussed Cyrille-Charles-Auguste Bisette's "book-length *Réfutations*" of Victor Schoelcher's works in the 1840s. Bongie, *Islands and Exiles*, 279.
61 One pre-independence refutation pamphlet, André Rigaud's 1797 *Mémoire du général de brigade André Rigaud en réfutation des écrits calomnieux contre les citoyens de couleur de Saint-Domingue*, is an important precursor to the Christophean refutation pamphlets and likely served as a model for them. Rigaud penned his pamphlet in refutation of a proclamation from Léger-Félicité

Sonthonax denouncing the actions of free people of color in Saint-Domingue (including Rigaud himself) during the 1796 Affaire Villatte, in which free men of color rose up against the acting governor general, Etienne Laveaux. In his proclamation, Sonthonax accused the free men of color of "excessive ambition" (*ambition démesurée*) and "worn-out tyranny" (*tyrannie abattue*) and of trying to sow discord in the colony among free men of color, ex-slaves, and colonial administrators using "lies and slander" (*le mensonge et la calomnie*), which Sonthonax dismisses as the "everyday weapons of dissidents" (*les armes ordinaires des factieux*). Rigaud's pamphlet set out to disprove and ultimately negate Sonthonax's proclamation by reproducing Sonthonax's original text in full, and then providing a side-by-side evidentiary "development and refutation" of it. Visually, this has the effect of breaking apart the erstwhile coherence, legitimacy, and sovereignty of Sonthonax's original text, visually and rhetorically overwhelming it.

62 Bongie, Introduction, 66.
63 Vastey and his fellow Christophean writers, great supporters of Grégoire, were undoubtedly familiar with his 1808 work and de Tussac's 1810 refutation of it. According to a letter that Prévost penned to Grégoire, Christophe ordered fifty copies of Grégoire's *De la littérature des Nègres* and asked that large excerpts be reprinted in the *Gazette*. Sepinwall, "Grégoire et Haïti," 112. On Grégoire and Christophe, see also Sepinwall, *Abbé Grégoire*; and Bénot, "Grégoire contre Christophe."
64 Vastey, *Notes à Malouet*, iv.
65 Ibid., 10.
66 Ibid., 14.
67 "Echanger ces droits éternels et imprescriptibles, contre des substitutions de mots, des cocardes, des babioles propres tout au plus à amuser des enfants." Ibid., 23.
68 "Ce peuple n'est plus celui que vous avec connu jadis; nous nous appelons maintenant *Monsieur*, nous avons un grand Roi que nous chérissons; des Princes, des Ducs, des Comtes, . . . etc." Ibid., 23–24.
69 "Ce peuple . . . vous le trouverez toujours inaccessible à la séduction." Ibid.
70 Ibid. (emphasis original). Vastey recycles this language in his 1819 *Essai*.
71 See Cheesman, Vendryes, and Jean, *Armorial of Haiti*.
72 Garraway, "Abolition, Sentiment," 239.
73 Daut, *Tropics*, 113. On Vastey's deconstructive reading practices, see Bongie, Introduction.
74 See the introduction for a discussion of the limits of the bourgeois public sphere, especially when it comes to the importance of sixteenth- and seventeenth-century traditions of anti-absolutist polemics. I suggest that these early modern polemics informed the strategies of vindicationist writing and postcolonial refutation.
75 Malouet's successor, Jacques Claude Beugnot, may well have tried to retake the colony if Napoléon hadn't returned for his hundred days in March 1815, and, to curry favor among critics of the Restoration, outlawed slavery. In 1816, after the Restoration government returned, they tried a new approach, and sent the lieutenant Vicomte de Fontanges and a state council member, Esmangart. Though

their approach was markedly less maverick than Lavaysse's, there would be no negotiations; Pétion politely but sternly refused to treat with them in the light of his indemnity debacle, while Christophe simply returned their letters unopened. Griggs and Prator, *Correspondence*, 60; Madiou, *Histoire*, t. 5.
76 Madiou, *Histoire*, t. 5, 283.
77 Prévost, "Copie de la lettre du Secrétaire d'Etat."
78 The monarchy's olive branch strategy seems to adapt and redeploy Lavaysse's approach in the Malouet affair. Christophean writers criticized Lavaysse's threatening letter as a false "olivier de la paix" in their refutations of him. See Prézeau, "Réfutation."
79 "Se ranger sous la bannière de l'autorité Royale." Royaume d'Hayti, *L'olivier de la paix*.
80 "Il est constant que depuis le commencement de la révolution, les haytiens de couleur ont toujours tergiversés tantôt pour les noirs, tantôt pour les blancs, et qu'ils ont toujours été victimes de leur inconstance. Ô vous à qui je m'adresse maintenant! revenez donc au véritable point de fixité, à votre propre cause, à celle des noirs, à celle des haytiens." Vastey, *A mes concitoyens*, 21.
81 Madiou reprints Pétion's written rejection in full in *Histoire*, t. 5, 283–88.
82 "Avec les mots de république, égalité, liberté, Pétion et les blancs français voudraient nous enchaîner." Vastey, *Le cri de la patrie*, 21.
83 Vastey, *Le cri de la conscience*, 39.
84 Vastey, *Le cri de la patrie*, 11.
85 "Rien ne peint mieux le caractère diabolique de Pétion, que cet amalgame de principes hétérogènes qui se repoussent mutuellement. . . . C'est vraiment un prodigue extraordinaire d'hypocrisie." Ibid., 27.
86 Daut, *Tropics*, 133.

CHAPTER 3. SOUTHERN REPUBLIC OF LETTERS
1 Sainte-Claire, "Régénération et élitisme."
2 See the introduction for a discussion of the bourgeois public sphere and Raymond Williams's historicization of the concept of literature.
3 Berrou and Pompilus, *Histoire*; Castera, *Bref coup d'œil*.
4 On the importance of small-scale, bourgeois publishing in the elaboration of the print public sphere, see Habermas, *Public Sphere*. On the history of *revues littéraires*, see Martin and Chartier, *Histoire de l'édition française*, t.3. See also Portebois and Speirs, *Entre le livre et le journal*, t. 1.
5 Bongie, *Friends and Enemies*.
6 "Une littérature de combat, et aussi de partis." Hénock Trouillot, *Les origines*, 15.
7 I am placing quotes around the term "refugee" here following recent vital critiques from activists and scholars in American studies that have troubled the use of this term as it relates to the flight of colonial planters and their enslaved. Tao Leigh Goffe is working on a new project that further theorizes the term and its limits.

8   On the lives and livelihoods of these republican "refugees," see Mongey, "Two Brothers"; Mongey, "Going Home"; Mongey, *Rogue Revolutionaries*; and Joseph, *L'état haïtien*. On republicans in Spanish America, see Fischer, "Bolívar in Haiti"; Verna, *Bolívar y los emigrados*; and Lasso, *Myths of Harmony*.
9   On these Jacobins and abolitionists in Haiti, see Madiou, *Histoire*, t. 6; Ardouin, *Etudes*, t. 8; Joseph, *L'état haïtien*; and Joseph, "Genèse d'une idée avantageuse d'Haïti." See also Lerebours, *Haïti et ses peintres* on the case of French artist Barincou fils, who arrived in Haiti in 1816 and linked up with the editors of *L'Abeille*, Milscent and Colombel. For biographical details on Milscent, Laprée, and Colombel, see Joseph, *L'état haïtien*. Milscent, a native of Grande-Rivière-du-Nord, returned in 1816. Madiou describes Milscent as an "island-born [man] from the North" (indigène du Nord) who had the "good instinct not to go to Christophe's Kingdom" (*bon instinct de ne pas aller dans le Royaume de Christophe*) when he returned. Madiou, Histoire, t. 5, 454. Colombel, a native of the southern town of Miragoâne, returned in 1815 after studying in France. According to Beaubrun Ardouin, the French colonial agent Lavaysse actually recommended that Colombel return to work for Pétion: "Having had the chance to see D. Lavaysse in Paris, the latter [Lavaysse] spoke very highly of the president to him [Colombel], enlisting him to go and serve for the Republic. This young man had been born in Miragoâne to respectable parents; he had received an excellent education in France." (*Ayant eu l'occasion de voir D. Lavaysse à Paris, ce dernier lui fit les plus grands éloges du président en l'engageant à aller servir la République. Ce jeune homme était né à Miragoâne, de parents respectables; il avait reçu une brillante instruction en France.*) Beaubrun Ardouin, *Etudes*, t. 8, 154.
10 Milscent, *Ode*. On Milscent père, see Popkin, "Colonial Media." On the decline and threat to people of color in Europe during the Napoleonic era, see Crosby-Arnold, "Disintegration and Destruction."
11 Mongey, "Two Brothers," 46–47. The paper's liberalism was clear in the couplet cited in the epigraph on the first page: "Despotism is an impossibility, / As long as there is a free press." (*L'Arbitraire est de toute impossibilité, / Tant qu'il existera libre publicité.*) *Feuille du Commerce*, April 20, 1834.
12 Mongey, "Two Brothers." Mongey notes as many as two hundred departures from Bordeaux to Haiti and Saint Thomas in late 1816 alone.
13 Mongey, "Two Brothers," 48.
14 Fischer, "Bolívar in Haiti," 25.
15 Bolívar qtd. and trans. in Fischer, "Bolívar in Haiti," 38.
16 Mongey, "Two Brothers." Mongey astutely describes the "central contradiction of the Age of Revolutions between desire for universal freedom and reliance on human oppression" at work in these various republican projects in the Atlantic (56).
17 On Bolívar's 1826 constitution, see Helg, "Simón Bolívar's Republic"; and Fischer, "Bolívar in Haiti." Bolívar's letter to Pétion congratulating the Haitian leader on his appointment as president-for-life is fascinating in this regard. Bolívar compares Pétion to the other great republican leader, George Washington, and admits that Pétion's road to power was much more arduous: "the hero of the

North only had to defeat enemy soldiers and his major triumph was that of his ambition. Your Excellency has to defeat everything and everybody, enemies and friends, foreigners and citizens, the fathers of the fatherland and even the virtues of his brothers." Qtd. and trans. in Fischer, "Bolívar in Haiti," 47. In listing all of those whom Pétion had to defeat in order to secure the republic, Bolívar seems to be pointing here not only to the 1804 massacre of the remaining French colonists ("los padres de la patria" or "fathers of the fatherland") but also to Pétion's assassination of Dessalines ("hasta las virtudes de sus hermanos" or "even the virtues of his brothers"). Verna, *Petión y Bolívar*, 491.
18 Fischer, "Bolívar in Haiti," 45.
19 Janvier, *Les constitutions*, 109.
20 The circumstances of Rigaud's return in 1810 remain opaque and certainly warrant further exploration. Thomas Madiou notes that Rigaud traveled to Philadelphia first before making his way south to Les Cayes. Madiou speculates that Napoléon wanted to send him back to "prepare a pro-French reaction" and that Rigaud intended to place the southern department "under French protectorate" and begin to counteract the majority of black peasants with white immigration from neighboring colonies. Madiou, *Histoire*, t. 4, 271, 280.
21 Ibid.
22 Madiou, *Histoire*, t. 5, 291; Fischer, "Bolívar in Haiti," 46. The 1816 constitution did also codify new checks on Pétion's presidential power by institutionalizing a new democratically elected Chamber of Representatives.
23 Ferrer, "Free Soil." It bears noting that these same principles of free soil and sovereignty would underwrite Jean-Pierre Boyer's invasion of the east in 1822, and the unified, imperial republic of the island of Haiti just a few years later. See chapter 4.
24 On the limits of color-blind republicanism specifically, see chapter 4.
25 On education under Pétion, see Sainte-Claire, "Régénération et élitisme."
26 Preston, *Bee*. Many thanks to Nelly Schmidt for her suggestions on the apian imagery in *L'Abeille* during a lively discussion following my presentation of this material at France's Institut national d'histoire de l'art (INHA) in June 2017.
27 "A l'aspect naissant des beaux jours d'Haïti, quelques amis des arts ont désiré seconder les intentions libérales du gouvernement." *L'Abeille*, no. 1 (July 7, 1817).
28 "Dans l'intérêt commun"; "que l'élégance du discours doit ajouter au lustre de vos productions littéraires." Ibid.
29 "Celui qui fait profession du talent littéraire." *L'Abeille*, no. 11 (January 1, 1818).
30 Ibid.
31 "Qui ont été suscitées . . . par le Roi théâtral de la partie du nord de notre patrie." Ibid.
32 "Si tous nos compatriotes du nord étaient instruits de la libéralité du Gouvernement de la République; ou, disons mieux, s'il leur était permis de suivre le mouvement de leurs cœurs, ils viendraient goûter avec nous les douceurs de la liberté." Ibid.
33 "Où les idées républicaines ont formé le réseau de l'opinion." Dumesle, *Voyage*, 4–5.

34 Pascal-Trouillot and Trouillot, *Encyclopédie*, 345.
35 "Durant la longue oppression sous laquelle nos têtes courbaient . . . Les individus de notre classe dans lesquels on remarquait les étincelles du génie furent les plus persécutés, et pour jouir de la paix n'en faisait plus parade, contens de rendre un culte secret aux beaux-arts." *L'Observateur*, no. 6 (July 15, 1819).
36 "Il est avantageux aux progrès des lumières que dans l'origine des peoples, ils conservent avec une sorte de vénération, les ouvrages de leurs premiers écrivains, et placent leurs noms à côté de ceux des héros qui ont illustré la Patrie." *L'Observateur*, no. 3 (June 1, 1819).
37 Ibid. On Pierre Pinchinat, see Geggus, *Revolutionary Studies*. On the Braquehais family, see Geggus and Fiering, *Haitian Revolution*.
38 "Il est non moins utile pour former l'esprit public, qu'intéressant à l'histoire des progrès de la littérature et des belles-lettres, de rassembler avec soin les productions de nos premiers écrivains. C'est un bien qui appartient à la nation: sa gloire est intéressée à le conserver." *L'Observateur*, no. 3 (June 1, 1819).
39 "A l'idée de ce féroce usurpateur qui opprime une portion intéressante de ma chère patrie, mon âme éprouve une cruelle agitation: il faut que je prenne haleine avant de continuer." *L'Observateur*, no. 6 (July 15, 1819).
40 "L'état de langueur et de désolation où la férocité de Christophe a réduit la belle contrée qu'il a usurpée, et qui ne sera vraisemblablement bientôt qu'un vaste désert, car depuis long-temps Sa majesté a prouvé que son cœur paternel ne veut régner que sur des tombeaux." *L'Observateur*, no. 15 (December 1, 1819). Emphasis original. *Le Constitutionnel* newspaper became a space in which surrogates of each regime vied for legitimacy. An anonymous French reader appeared in a subsequent issue in response to the letter Dumesle referenced, disagreeing with the negative characterization of Christophe's monarchy.
41 Translation adapted from Chris Bongie in Vastey, *Colonial System*, 84.
42 Lyon-Caen and Ribard, *L'historien et la littérature*. See also Darnton, *Edition et sédition*.
43 "Ecrase les autres écrivains du poids de sa science et de son érudition; avec sa plume méchante et badine, il fait sourire de plaisir ses amis les ex-colons, répand l'ironie la plus amère sur les productions des haytiens." Vastey, *Essai*, 301.
44 "Arretons-nous ici un instant, et contemplons"; "Je reprends mon sujet." Ibid., 118, 158.
45 Ibid., 222, emphasis added.
46 On the distinctive nature of northern Kreyòl, see Valdman, "Haitian Creole"; and Hyppolite, *Les origines*.
47 "Tableau hideux de la situation du Cap-Henry." Reproduced in Madiou, *Histoire*, t. 6, 50. He published his response to Dumesle in *La Gazette royale* (which is reproduced in Madiou). The first issues of Dumesle's paper reached Cap-Henry in October 1819, possibly via their English agents in Europe. The Cayenne paper was available only by subscription in the main cities of the southern republic—Jérémie, Les Cayes, Jacmel, and Port-au-Prince—and Vastey claims in the intro-

duction to his *Essai* that southern writing reached the Cap by "un détour de deux mille lieues." Vastey, *Essai*, xxi.
48 "Messieurs les écrivains du Sud-Ouest croient-ils qu'il n'y a que dans leur République seulement où les hommes sont libres? . . . dans les monarchies bien organisées, on jouit de la vraie liberté, de la garantie des personnes et des propriétés qui sont le but de toutes les communautés sagement administrées?" Reproduced in Madiou, *Histoire*, t. 6, 51.
49 "Du fond de son cabinet des Cayes." Ibid.
50 "Qu'ils n'ont pas écrit dans le sens de M. Hérard Dumesle et que ces écrivains patriotes se sont attachés à défendre la cause générale des Haytiens qui est, nous le voyons bien, très éloignée d'être la sienne." Ibid., 52.
51 "[Ils] ont rivalisé avec les guerriers qui combattaient nos oppresseurs, ils ont détruit l'échafaudage du système colonial et terrassé l'hydre de l'esclavage." Ibid.
52 "J'ai suivi spontanément l'impulsion de mon cœur, c'est le Cri de ma Conscience! Je vous écris en homme libre, en vous dévoilant la turpitude, l'hypocrisie et la trahison d'un traître . . . s'il en était autrement, si je ne pouvais exprimer librement mes sentiments dans mes écrits personnels, je déposerai la plume et je garderai le silence." Vastey, *Le cri de la conscience*, 85. Vastey is responding to a pamphlet from André Dominique Sabourin, *Le peuple de la république d'Hayti, à Messieurs Vastey et Limonade* (Port-au-Prince: Imprimerie du gouvernement, 1815).
53 "Que ce scribe mercenaire, aux gages du plus farouche comme du plus sanguinaire des despotes, nous injurie, nous calomnie, vomisse contre nous tout le fiel et tout le venin dont son cœur est infecté, entasse mensonges sur mensonges pour faire naître dans l'esprit de nos compatriotes des soupçons défavorables sur notre compte, il ne fait que son métier; il se sert de ses armes habituelles et favorites; il gagne son infâme salaire." Colombel, *Examen*, 7–8.
54 "Nous nous exprimerons sur son compte et sur le compte de ses productions littéraires" and "notre opinion sur le mérite littéraire de ses productions avec la même franchise que nous l'avons énoncée sur ses qualités morales." Ibid., 5, 13.
55 "Il n'a ni souplesse, ni élégance, mais en revanche il a passablement de dureté; sa diction est incorrecte, souvent diffuse, toujours prolixe et monotone." Ibid., 15, 16.
56 "Il se traine sans cesse sur des lieux communs; ressasse avec une puérile complaisance, et dans un flux de mots, des idées avortées qu'il a délayées vingt fois dans vingt pamphlets différens." Ibid., 16.
57 In the introduction to *Essai*, Vastey accuses Colombel, Milscent, and others of having formed a *ligue* to spread misinformation about Christophe's kingdom throughout Europe at Pétion's behest.
58 Colombel, *Examen*, 7.
59 Accounts vary as to the exact circumstances of his suicide. See Griggs and Prator, *Correspondence*.
60 "Qu'il n'existe plus aujourd'hui à Haïti qu'un seul gouvernement et qu'une seule Constitution." Madiou, *Histoire*, t. 6, 142.
61 Hénock Trouillot, *Les origines*, 91.

62 Griggs and Prator, *Correspondence*, 211.
63 Qtd. in Bongie, "Cry of History," 812n7.
64 Hodgson, "'Internal Harmony.'"
65 Not until Demesvar Delorme's *L'Avenir* appeared in 1859. The 1842 earthquake in Cap-Haïtien undoubtedly contributed to this continued textual silence from the North.
66 A footnote indicates that the date of his voyage was "L'an 17e de l'Indépendance d'Haïti," or 1820, and not 1824 as most scholars have indicated.
67 We must consider Dumesle's extended performance of his voyage north in the context of Vastey's 1819 refutation of Dumesle, discussed above, in which Vastey criticizes the southern writer for making observations "from his armchair in Les Cayes."
68 For more on Dupré and the Guerre du Môle, see chapter 2. The site was of personal importance to Dumesle, who had served under General Lamarre in Môle Saint-Nicolas during the republic's military expedition to the Northwest between 1807 and 1810.
69 Chris Bongie has argued that Dumesle wrote *Voyage* to enact the "symbolic unification of the country to match the political events of 1820." Bongie, *Friends and Enemies*, 26.
70 Sommer, *Foundational Fictions*.
71 "Cette contrée qui retentit encore du nom de Christophe." Dumesle, *Voyage*, 2.
72 Middelanis, "Les mémoires."
73 The subject of ruin poetry is vast, as are its interpretations. See Cammagre, "Ruines et retraite."
74 "N'offre plus à l'œil consterné du voyageur que des ruines, des décombres, des tronçons des piliers ensevelis sous des lianes . . . tout a disparu." Dumesle, *Voyage*, 9.
75 The emptiness and ruins of the North are set into further relief against the plenitude and vibrancy of the South that Dumesle depicts. One of the final scenes in *Voyage* depicts a group of farmers in the small southwestern coastal town of Anse-d'Hainault engaged in a form of collective labor that brings together men and women from around the rural community. Though Dumesle does not use the term, it is unmistakably a *konbit*, the most important peasant agricultural practice in Haiti, which we can identify by the music, playful competition, and collective labor of this gathering. The ludic, *productive* communal labor of the *konbit* in the South is juxtaposed with the desolate ruins and infecund dust of Christophe's regime that Dumesle depicts in *Voyage*. We are seeing in Dumesle, then, one of the first instances of symbolic cultural nationalist appropriation of the *konbit*—what will later become arguably the most identifiable trope in Haitian national writing.
76 Dumesle, *Voyage*, 252.
77 On the hybrid nature of Dumesle's text, see Chemla, "*Voyage*"; and Daut, "'Nothing in Nature.'"

78 Prévost, *Relation*. Doris Garraway is preparing a book-length study of Christophe's coronation. Doris Garraway, "Performance and Theatricality in the Kingdom of Henry Christophe" (paper presented at the annual meeting of the Haitian Studies Association, Cap-Haïtien, Haiti, November 10–13, 2016).
79 "Les bienfaits de la civilisation"; "assemblage monstreux de despotisme." Dumesle, *Voyage*, 43, 49.
80 "L'ombrageux gouvernement de Christophe. . . . Cette puissance épouvantable qui couvrit le nord d'un crêpe lugubre; marchant toujours dans l'ombre; sous le voile du secret." Dumesle, *Voyage*, 11, 13–14, 36, 51.
81 Ibid., 224.
82 "Partout où les idées libérales avaient pénétré la République trouvait des partisans." Ibid., 46.
83 "Je me pénétrai de plus en plus . . . de cette vérité impérissable, la Liberté est le phare des sciences, elle est l'âme de l'agriculture, du commerce, et des arts; tandis que le despotisme abrutit l'homme; ses étreintes oppressives éteignent la pensée, privent les âmes de ces émotions fortes qui tendent vers le grand, le beau et l'utile." Ibid., 62.
84 "Vouloir la contester serait vouloir faire reculer le siècle, et les partisans des ténèbres mêmes sont obligés de contenir que les principes libéraux ne rétrogradent jamais." Ibid., 45.
85 "Je me suis donc occupé et par goût, et par le désir de connaître toutes les productions littéraires de mes concitoyens, des différens ouvrages qui ont apparu dans le Nord." Ibid., 263.
86 Dumesle returns to—indeed, recycles—arguments he previously made in *L'Observateur*. He reiterates that the only good writing that came out of the North was from writers who had been educated long before the creation of the northern monarchy. Dumesle thus wants to show that real education—progress from ignorance to enlightenment in the most literal sense—did not exist in the North, or that northern education had failed to achieve this progress because it was not founded on liberal principles.
87 "Son cœur ne guidait pas sa plume." Ibid., 265.
88 "Ecrivant sous la férule d'un tyran dont toutes les sciences et tous les arts étaient tributaires, son ouvrage se ressent de cette influence qui, assignant des bornes à la pensée, prive le génie de cette heureuse indépendance indispensable au développement de son essor créateur." Ibid., 264.
89 "Echappées pour ainsi dire de sa plume." Ibid., 268.
90 "Occuper un haut rang dans notre littérature." Ibid., 267.
91 "Sa muse célébrera . . . la naissance des arts sous le beau ciel d'Haïti." Ibid., 268. See Kadish, Jenson, and Shapiro, *Poetry of Haitian Independence*; and Daut, "'Nothing in Nature'" for a discussion of "La Haïciade" (sometimes spelled "La Haïtiade") and Chanlatte's authorship. Still, there remains much more to say about Chanlatte's authorship in the context of the post-1820 republican unification,

given that the text also tells the story of the Haitian Revolution in an epic poem and from the perspective of republican hegemony.

92 "Combien les ouvrages tracés par la plume du favori d'un despote, et dans les vues de plaire à son maître, sont indignes de figurer parmi les productions qui font juger l'esprit d'un peuple naissant et de ses progrès dans les connaissances." Dumesle, *Voyage*, 268.

93 Ibid., 266–67.

94 "Et c'est à côté des dégoûtantes platitudes de la flatterie que se trouvent des beautés de cet ordre!!!" Ibid., 383–84n.L.

95 Vastey, *Le système colonial*, 3–4. The passage clearly draws upon the Acte de l'indépendance and other first texts of the post-independence period, with its references to "ossemens humains . . . blanchis par le temps."

96 Translation from Chris Bongie in Vastey, *Colonial System*, 86–87.

97 Métral, "De la littérature haïtienne," 533. Métral does mistake Vastey's essay as a refutation of Claude Pierre Joseph Leborgne de Boigne's *Nouveau système de colonization pour Saint-Domingue* (1817) rather than of Malouet's 1802 text. However, Métral never refers to Vastey's text with the erroneous title *Réfutation de Leborgne de Boigne* that Dumesle conjures in his footnote. For a reading of Métral's larger oeuvre, see Daut, *Tropics*.

98 "La nature et les progrès de l'esprit." Dumesle, *Voyage*, 269.

99 "L'impulsion que lui donna la libre faculté de penser." Ibid., 270–71.

100 "Essentiellement un livre de combat." Hénock Trouillot, *Les origines*, 46.

CHAPTER 4. THE MYTH OF THE UNIVERSAL HAITIAN REPUBLIC OR *DEUX NATIONS DANS LA NATION*

1 See chapter 1. Dessalines's unsuccessful attempt resulted in numerous casualties, leading some Dominicans to point to the violent debacle as the origin story of Haitian-Dominican enmity. Interestingly, however, Dessalines's invading army gained a number of new troops in his retreat from the East: many slaves "abandoned" their posts fighting for their masters against the invading forces and returned to the western side of the island to join the ranks of Dessalines's army as free men. One such man, José Campos Tavares (or Thabares and occasionally Tabarrès in the Haitian spelling), offers important insight into northern transborder connections that warrant more attention in historical studies of Haiti and the Dominican Republic, specifically the affinities going back to Amerindian times in the Cibao or *banda norte* region that continued well into the postcolonial era. On Tavares-Thabares during Dessalines's expedition to the East, see Johnson, *Fear of French Negroes* (note: Johnson spells his name Taváres). In fact, after Dessalines's assassination, Tavares-Thabares served Christophe and became Baron de Thabares, serving as commander of the Cibao region. He undoubtedly played a role in the apprehension of Malouet's emissary, Médina, who would have been known to Tavares-Thabares during the French occupation of the eastern side of the island. Tavares-Thabares appears elsewhere in the historical record: he signed

Christophe's 1807 constitution and the 1814 General Council declaration discussed in chapter 2.
2 On the Boba period, see Eller, "'All Would Be Equal.'" See also Maria Cecilia Ulrickson, "'Esclavos que fueron' in Santo Domingo, 1768–1844" (PhD diss., Notre Dame University, 2018).
3 Madiou, *Histoire*, t. 6, 249.
4 See Fraginals, Moya Pons, and Engerman, *Slavery and Free Labor*. Andrew Walker's recent work is beginning to address the dearth of scholarship on the 1822–1844 unification period from the East. See Walker, "All Spirits." There remains work to be done from the western side. Thomas Madiou's *Histoire* is an indispensable but underutilized resource for the period and transcribes in full many original historical documents, including, for example, both independence proclamations from the rival factions in the East. Still more work remains on the island-wide newspapers coming out of the East during the unification period, such as the *La Sentinelle de l'Est* and *L'Etoile*. There is also the question of cultural and artistic exchange; Michel Lerebours suggests that "cultural exchanges occurred between the two sides of the island" which he traces in shared painting styles and interest in religious syncretism. Lerebours, *Haïti et ses peintres*, t. 1, 100.
5 The term "creole" has specific meaning in the eastern context in the 1820s: it refers primarily to light mixed-race and white males of European descent.
6 "Un Etat séparé de la République ne pouvait exister sur notre territoire." Madiou, *Histoire*, t. 6, 273. Article 40 of the 1816 constitution stated, "L'Ile d'Haïti (ci-devant appelée Saint-Domingue) avec les îles adjacentes qui en dépendent, forment le territoire de la République."
7 See Dumesle's *L'Observateur* for rumors of invasion.
8 As Gary Wilder puts it, "republican France was never not an imperial nation-state." Wilder, *French Imperial Nation-State*, 3.
9 Geggus, "Rights, Resistance," 167. This is not unlike what British abolitionists were attempting in the Caribbean during the same period. See Huzzey, *Freedom Burning*.
10 Eller, *We Dream Together*, 6.
11 From a Dominican perspective, Boyer's invasion of the East is referred to as an occupation or an annexation. See Walker, "All Spirits."
12 On *concorde*, see Hodgson, "'Internal Harmony.'" While I am most interested in this chapter in attempts to create *concorde* through written, printed narratives of Haiti's republican unity and universalism under Boyer, it is worth noting here that republicans also pursued this propaganda by other means. In painting, for example, the work of Thimoléon Déjoie commemorated (and narrated) Boyer's unification of the North and the South of Haiti, in historical paintings depicting "l'entrée de Boyer au Cap-Haïtien" and "la clémence de Boyer envers le fils de Goman." Lerebours, *Haïti et ses peintres*, t. 1, 102. Guillaume Guillon-Lethière's painting *Le serment des ancêtres* (painted in Guadeloupe in 1822) certainly belongs to this tradition of unity-creating, and was likely painted expressly for that purpose,

and to be given to Boyer. For more on the painting and on Lethière (or Le Thière), see Lerebours, *Haïti et ses peintres*. Lethière also painted another mythic tableau, *Faustulus découvrant Romulus et Rémus allaités par la louve*, in 1822.

13 The work is rarely cited in scholarship on Haiti's nineteenth century. Nevertheless, Marlene Daut has pointed out that the text served as "the standard geography textbook throughout nineteenth-century Haiti." Daut, *Tropics*, 533.

14 Though Pétion had the right to choose his successor, he had not yet named one at the time of his death. The Senate chose Boyer to replace him. Boyer had fought alongside André Rigaud in the civil war against Toussaint, and fled to France with Rigaud, Pétion, and other southern generals after Toussaint's victory. He returned in 1802 with the Leclerc expedition. He returned to Cap-Haïtien once independence had been proclaimed to pay his respects to Dessalines, who allowed him to serve as Pétion's secretary. Pascal-Trouillot and Trouillot, *Encyclopédie*, 153.

15 See Sainte-Claire, "Régénération et élitisme."

16 Wong, "Shadow of Haiti."

17 Territorial unity (though not under a republic) had also been the goal of Dessalines, and Toussaint before him. Sara Johnson has argued that we must consider Boyer's integration of the eastern side of the island as part of a "historical arc that stretches from 1801 through 1840." Johnson, *Fear of French Negroes*, 57, 209n12.

18 Madiou, *Histoire*, t. 6, 173.

19 Ramsey, *Spirits and the Law*, 57.

20 Payton, "City and the State." Dayan calls this "essentially slave status." See Dayan, *Haiti, History*, 14.

21 "Dans un pays qu'on prétendait égalitaire deux nations dans la nation." Janvier, *Les constitutions*, 152.

22 Payton, "City and the State," 24, 17. On Haiti's rural codes and their impact on Haiti's administrative and social divisions, see also Girard, "Making Freedom Work."

23 Many have noted that this sum was roughly ten times Haiti's annual revenues. As such, the indemnity also involved a loan of 30 million francs from France to pay the first installment. Madiou, *Histoire*, t. 6, 497. On the indemnity, see Blancpain, *Un siècle de relations*; Brière, "L'emprunt de 1825"; and Forsdick, "Haiti and France." The indemnity has been the subject of calls for reparations, such as by Angela Davis in a speech at the Caribbean Studies Association meeting in Port-au-Prince in June 2016 and most recently by economist Thomas Piketty in an interview published in the Haitian newspaper *Le Nouvelliste*. See Thomas Lalime, "'Au minimum, la France devrait rembourser plus de 28 milliards de dollars américains à Haïti aujourd'hui', soutient le célèbre économiste français Thomas Piketty," *Le Nouvelliste*, January 20, 2020, https://lenouvelliste.com/article/211316/au-minimum-la-france-devrait-rembourser-plus-de-28-milliards-de-dollars-americains-a-haiti-aujourdhui-soutient-le-celebre-economiste-francais-thomas-piketty.

24 Qtd. in Madiou, *Histoire*, t. 6, 341.

25 *Christophistes* in French. This is the term used to designate opposition actors (mostly military generals) from the North who remained favorable to Christophe's legacy and leadership.
26 *Histoire*, t. 6, 477. In the heritage of Dessalines's 1805 Constitution, *blanc* uttered in this context means "white" and "(French) foreigner" interchangeably.
27 Reproduced in Madiou, *Histoire*, t. 6, 490.
28 We can translate *éclaireur* as "scout" or "pathfinder."
29 For more on Darfour, see Joseph, *L'état haïtien*; and Madiou, *Histoire*, t. 6.
30 "Pour gouverner les hommes et décider de leur sort, il suffit communément d'être né, ou de descendre d'une race particulière." Qtd. in Castera, *Bref coup d'œil*, 49.
31 He was not the first Haitian to be assassinated under Boyer for having fomented "des troubles" by bringing up race. In 1821 Boyer assassinated General Romain, a Christophist who was highly critical of the republican government on the question of foreign commerce, for having accused Boyer of planning to hand the country over to the French (*les blancs*). Boyer brushed off the accusation as ridiculous (this is four years before he signed the indemnity agreement with France), and dismissed Romain as a would-be despot: "To do this he used the tired and absurd method of spreading rumors that the country had been sold to the French. . . . Such was the end of the man who, because he had fought like so many others for his country, convinced himself that he could subjugate it to his own law and whims." (*On employa pour cela le moyen devenu vieux et ridicule de faire colporter partout que le pays était vendu aux Français. . . . Telle a été la fin de l'homme qui, parce qu'il avait combattu comme tant d'autres pour son pays, s'était persuadé qu'il pouvait l'asservir à sa loi et à ses caprices.*) Darfour was accused of leveling the same "tired" accusations against Boyer, and for them, was sentenced to death. Boyer qtd. in Madiou, *Histoire*, t. 6, 328–29.
32 Madiou, *Histoire*, t. 6, 331–32.
33 Joseph, *L'état haïtien*, 278.
34 Madiou, *Histoire*, t. 6, 331.
35 Pascal-Trouillot and Trouillot, *Encyclopédie*, 270.
36 Joseph, *L'état haïtien*, 282.
37 To be sure, previous 1806 and 1816 republican constitutions referred to race or "blood" in some capacity: the 1806 and 1816 constitutions restricted the right of white French foreigners to own land or property, and the 1816 constitution declared that Africans and Indians (or those of their "sang") could become naturalized Haitian citizens after a year of residence: "Tout Africain, Indien et ceux issus de leur sang, nés dans les colonies ou en pays étrangers, qui viendraient résider dans la République seront reconnus Haïtiens." Janvier, *Les constitutions*, 117. On Article 44 of the 1816 constitution, see also Fischer, *Modernity Disavowed*; and Ferrer, "Free Soil."
38 Lasso, *Myths of Harmony*, 137; Fischer, "Bolívar in Haiti," 29.
39 On color-blind republicanism in the French perspective, see Frader and Chapman, *Race in France*; and Noriel, "French and Foreigners." On race and citizenship in the revolutionary Caribbean, see Dubois, "Republican Anti-Racism."

40 On Boyer's control of the press and repression of dissent from reformers like Darfour, see Sheller, *Democracy after Slavery*.
41 Ardouin's massive multi-volume *Etudes*, which he published in exile in the 1850s, expands many of the themes he explored first in *Géographie* but from a position of embattled republicanism (see chapter 5). For more on Ardouin's *Géographie* as it relates to David Nicholls's "legends" thesis, see Stieber, "Myths of the Haitian Republic."
42 In addition to Saint-Méry's earlier text, Ardouin uses research from the national archives in Santo Domingo. Beaubrun Ardouin, *Géographie*, 178n11.
43 Ibid., 19.
44 Ibid.
45 "Le général Dessalines ne vit bientôt dans ses concitoyens que des esclaves faits pour obéir aveuglement à ses caprices." Ibid., 23.
46 "Elle vint de nouveau diviser les enfans d'une même famille et porter la désolation dans un pays qui renaissait à peine de ses ruines." Ibid.
47 "Ses mœurs douces, ses vertus publiques et privées, sa modération exemplaire, son courage et ses talens militaires." Ibid., 26.
48 "La supériorité du régime légal sur le despotisme, de la justice sur la tyrannie." Ibid., 29.
49 "Un gouvernement fondé sur des principes si contraires à ceux de l'ordre social devait infailliblement s'écrouler au moindre choc: il ne fallut en effet qu'un instant pour renverser le formidable Empereur qui, une minute auparavant, menaçait de tout écraser sous le poids de son sceptre de fer." Ibid., 24.
50 For a thick, layered, and masterful analysis of Dessalines in Haitian Vodou, see Dayan, *Haiti, History*.
51 On opposition to Boyer during the 1830s in particular, see Sheller, *Democracy after Slavery*. On Boyer's repressive criminalization of peasants during this period, especially practitioners of Vodou, see Gonzalez, *Maroon Nation*.
52 Madiou, *Histoire*, t. 7, 218, 226.
53 Eller, *We Dream Together*, 24.
54 Berrou and Pompilus, *Histoire*, 187. On the naming of Haiti and indigenism, see Geggus, "Naming of Haiti"; and Perry, "Becoming Indigenous."
55 Castera, *Bref coup d'œil*, 62.
56 Hénock Trouillot, *Les origines*, 126.
57 See chapter 5. Nau's interest in Haiti's Amerindian history was not new: Dessalines named the island in honor of Haiti's Amerindian predecessors, while Prévost mentions the history of the Cacique Henry in *Relation* and Vastey refers to their massacre in *Le système colonial* and *Essai*. Still, Nau's early sketches of the caciques and Taino history predate Spanish American interest in their stories, by about twenty years. Alejandro Tapia y Rivera penned *La palma del cacique* in 1852 and an opera libretto, *Guarionex*, in 1854—both based on the history of Ayti and the cacique Guarionex. Arias, "Reconstituting the Archive." In addition to Tapia y Rivera's work, Anne Eller also notes the appearance of the cacique Guarionex in Eugenio María de Hostos's *Bayoán* in 1863. Eller, "Let's Show the World," 420n53; Ramírez, *Colonial Phantoms*, 42.

58 *Le Républicain*, no. 16 (April 1, 1837); no. 17 (April 15, 1837).
59 Under Boyer's rule, the university had closed. *L'Union*, September 6, 1838; September 20, 1838; March 3, 1839. These texts were published in French translation. It is important to note that Boyer did communicate with the eastern side of the island in bilingual French-Spanish texts. See, for example, a speech given by Borgella to the residents of Santo Domingo on November 16, 1828 (Bencomo Collection, Library of Congress, https://lccn.loc.gov/mm82082416).
60 *L'Union*, April 26, 1838; May 10, 1838; November 20, 1838.
61 On the other hand, under Christophe's reign, Juste Chanlatte's operas celebrated the Kreyòl language and the African traditions of the peasant population.
62 *Le Républicain*, no. 11 (January 15, 1837).
63 *Le Républicain*, no. 10 (January 1, 1837).
64 *L'Union*, November 20, 1838; December 13, 1838.
65 *L'Union*, August 9, 1838.
66 *L'Union*, December 13, 1838; December 20, 1838.
67 Dayan, *Haiti, History*, 29.
68 Consider the following passage, for example: "It was midday. Not a breath of air to ease the scorching heat. Hummingbirds flitted swiftly to the bottom of the ravines, searching for shelter from the sun's heat under the forest canopies." (*Il était midi. Pas un souffle d'air ne tempérait par sa fraicheur la brulante atmosphère. Les colibris voltigeaient avec rapidité au fond des ravines, et cherchaient un abri sous le feuillage des fôrets contre les ardeurs du soleil.*) *L'Union*, October 4, 1838.
69 "Avant de fermer les yeux à la lumière, il maudit la France, et demanda à Dieu un vengeur. Nous savons que sa prière monta au ciel." October 11, 1838.
70 Coriolan Ardouin, *Poésies*, 57–58. Coriolan Ardouin was one of three Ardouin brothers who were active adherents of Boyer's regime. He died of illness in 1835, but his friends (the Nau brothers among them) published many of his poems posthumously in their newspapers. This poem was written in the early 1830s and posthumously published in 1881.
71 Given that this poem was likely still in draft form, I have chosen to translate the verb "fesaient" (as it appears in the published text) as "pesaient" (to weigh on, to trouble). Ardouin may have been deciding in the draft between "lui pesaient" and "pesaient à lui."
72 *L'Union*, January 3, 1839. On the dismal financial situation in the late 1830s, see René, *Haïti après l'esclavage*.
73 Ibid.
74 This is a common trope in *indigéniste* poetry of the early twentieth century.
75 See Dayan, *Haiti, History*. It is possible here that Nau is rescripting the idea of Haitians' having "trembled" (*tressaillir*) under Dessalines's rule. Dayan notes that Yayou is said to have proclaimed over Dessalines's body after his assassination: "Who would have said that this little wretch, only twenty minutes ago, made all

of Haiti tremble!" *Haiti, History,* 39. The mountains, personified in Nau's poem, "tremble" in their revolutionary fervor.
76 Deren, *Divine Horsemen.*
77 In her excellent reading of this poem, Amy Reinsel has argued that the "Demain" of Nau's final stanza refers not only to the January 1, 1839, celebration, but "to a future time which will rejoin these past accomplishments." Reinsel, "Poetry of Revolution," 94.
78 Centre national de ressources textuelles et lexicales, "Génie," www.cnrtl.fr/definition/génie. Nau wrote a separate poem dedicated "Au génie de la patrie" in *L'Union* (April 14, 1839).
79 *Le Manifeste* was founded in 1841 and run by Dumai Lespinasse and E. Heurtelou. The paper eschewed the line-toeing that previous opposition papers had attempted, proclaiming in the first issue, "Point de journal sans politique" (No newspapers without politics). *Le Patriote* was also founded in 1841 as an even more radical opposition paper. It was subtitled "presse indépendante" to distance itself from pro-Boyer state-run papers, and included writing from Ignace Nau, E. Heurtelou, and Thomas Madiou. Castera, *Bref coup d'œil,* 66.
80 On the influence of European socialist writing in Haiti, see Sheller, *Democracy after Slavery,* 118–19.
81 Castera, *Bref coup d'œil,* 65.
82 Sheller, *Democracy after Slavery,* 120.
83 Smith, *Liberty*; Madiou, *Histoire,* t. 7. For a first-person account of the earthquake, see Delorme, "Le séisme de 1842."
84 Smith, *Liberty,* 49. Janvier argues that Boyer's Code Rural was the root cause behind the post-earthquake looting in the North. Janvier, *Les constitutions,* 153.
85 "La ville du Cap-Haïtien, qui, après avoir tant souffert sous le régime de la tyrannie, commençait à renaître à la prospérité, a été détruite de fond en comble."*Télégraphe,* May 22, 1842; Smith, *Liberty,* 49.
86 Madiou, *Histoire,* t. 7, 407–22. Note that the Liberal Revolution is also sometimes known as the Praslin Revolt/Revolution because the revolutionaries assembled at Rivière Hérard's habitation, named Praslin, to draft a list of their grievances and a call to arms. Sheller, *Democracy after Slavery,* 121–23.
87 Garrigus, *Before Haiti,* 268.
88 See Furet and Ozouf, *Dictionary.*
89 Madiou, *Histoire,* t. 7, 442.
90 Sheller, *Democracy after Slavery,* 131–32.
91 Madiou, *Histoire,* t. 7, 486.
92 Madiou, *Histoire,* t. 8, 90; Eller, *We Dream Together.*
93 Sheller, *Democracy after Slavery,* 135; Madiou, *Histoire,* t. 8, 121–36.
94 "Le peuple du Département du Nord, fatigué de se voir le jouet d'un Gouvernement sans principe, s'est détaché du Gouvernement de Rivière Hérard pour le motif suivant: L'ex-Président Boyer, appelé en 1820 à sympathiser avec nous, nous enleva nos trésors, nos arsenaux, et en retour nous légua la division dans la Société et la

corruption dans nos vertus politiques, après avoir, pendant sa présidence, exilé l'élite du Cap et l'avoir plongée dans l'humiliation." Madiou, *Histoire*, t. 8, 149.
95 Pierrot was the brother-in-law of Queen Marie-Louise, and served as Baron, then Comte de Valière under Christophe. Guerrier was formerly Comte du Mirebalais, then Duc de l'Avancé. Cheesman, Vendryes, and Jean, *Armorial of Haiti*.
96 Madiou, *Histoire*, t. 8, 148–52; Edner Brutus, *Instruction publique*.
97 Madiou, *Histoire*, t. 8, 139.
98 *Le Moniteur*, May 10, 1845.
99 *Le Moniteur*, August 2, 1845; August 23, 1845.
100 *Le Moniteur*, November 8, 1845.
101 Madiou, *Histoire*, t. 8, 326.
102 *Le Moniteur*, January 24, 1846.
103 Madiou, *Histoire*, t. 8, 346. Their uprising echoes the 1820 Saint-Marc uprising against Christophe.
104 "Toutes les anciennes traditions de Pétion contre Christophe s'étaient reveillées en eux." Ibid., 348.
105 Ibid., 356.
106 *Le Moniteur*, June 13, 1846. During this period the government paper, *Le Moniteur*, also began to take a form that was more representative of the executive and bicameral legislature: beginning with a proclamation from the president and a long section from the vice-president of the Senate.
107 Soulouque was not the front-runner. His name was apparently put forward by Beaubrun Ardouin.
108 *Le Moniteur*, March 6, 1847.
109 Thomas Madiou's brief personal account, published in his posthumous *Autobiographie*, reveals that he was a member of the uprising in Port-au-Prince and that they were easily defeated by Soulouque's troops. Madiou, *Autobiographie*, 21. On the racialist presentations of Soulouque's repression of the uprising, see MacLeod, "Soulouque Regime"; and Smith, *Liberty*. For a retrospective analysis, see Frédéric Marcelin's family accounts of the 1848 uprising in *Au gré du souvenir* (1913).
110 Daut, *Tropics*, 547.
111 On the world of 1848, see Thomson, *Revolutions of 1848*.
112 *Le Moniteur*, March 17, 1849.
113 *Le Moniteur* had the benefit of hindsight in recounting these events: the paper had ceased publication between April 15 and July 8 during Soulouque's campaign against the 1848 liberal uprising . The July 8 issue of the paper reprints in chronological order all of the official decrees and government proclamations issued during the uprising, giving the reader a sense of how the events unfolded. The proclamations also reveal the degree to which Soulouque inscribed his actions within the discourse of civil war that had preceded him. He lamented the "fratricidal struggles" (*luttes fratricides*) and decried the "shadowy reasoning" (*démarches ténébreuses*) of a "perverse" minority who "plotted" (*tramait*) against the people and their "true interests" (*ses véritables intérêts*). Their mask fell (*le masque*

était tombé) and the people saw these traitors for what they were. *Le Moniteur*, July 8, 1848.
114 Smith, *Liberty*, 82.
115 As Soulouque proclaimed of these "traitors," "The Homeland casts them out, the Homeland disinherits them!!!" (*La Patrie les réprouve, la Patrie les déshérite!!!*) *Le Moniteur*, July 8, 1848.
116 *Le Moniteur*, July 22, 1848.
117 "Renversement de l'ordre établi, pour y substituer l'anarchie et la guerre civile." *Le Moniteur*, July 29, 1848. Their list includes the names of over fifty men from the Grand'Anse region.
118 "La France ne nous paralyserait-elle pas dans nos efforts légitimes pour ramener cette partie de la République à l'obéissance du gouvernement légal, et ne nous placerait-elle pas dans l'impossibilité de payer l'indemnité à laquelle nous avons consenti que parce que nous comptions sur les ressource que nous offrait l'île entière, et notamment la partie de l'Est?" *Le Moniteur*, March 17, 1849.
119 "J'ai juré de maintenir l'indivisibilité du territoire. Je serai fidèle à ce serment." *Le Moniteur*, March 31, 1849; April 21, 1849; May 5, 1849. For accounts of Soulouque's 1849 campaign from the perspective of the Dominican Republic, see Eller, *We Dream Together*.
120 Throughout the course of the 1850s, *Le Moniteur* published a number of bilingual Spanish-French addresses that Soulouque made to "los habitantes del Este," lamenting the separation and urging them to rejoin the Haitian territory. He is careful in his address to distinguish between his addressees ("caros compatriotas") and those pro-independence republican forces in power ("y vosotros que tenéis la autoridad en el Este"), whom he accuses of maintaining a separation that was not in the interests of humanity or their shared future (dated May 14, 1851, published in *Le Moniteur* on May 24, 1851). Soulouque made an unsuccessful attempt in 1855 to retake the East, and also tried to maneuver politically to bring the territory under his empire when opposition leaders rebelled within the Dominican government in 1857. Dominican accounts of the 1855 attempt insist that they easily retook the territory that Soulouque had captured and that his attempts were "piratic and impotent" (quoted in Eller, *We Dream Together*, 261n239). On the 1857 rebellion, Janvier argues that the towns of Dajabón (Laxavon) and Monte Christi (Monte-Christ) were on the verge of coming over to him when his empire fell. Janvier, *Les constitutions*, 267–68.
121 As reported in a French newspaper. Smith, *Liberty*, 77.
122 "Haïtiens! Que la nouvelle ère qui s'ouvre pour nous soit marquée par la plus complète fusion des cœurs; qu'elle fasse taire les passions, s'il en existe encore parmi nous et tous, serrons-nous la main de la réconciliation sur l'autel sacré de la patrie." *Le Moniteur*, September 1, 1849.
123 Ignace Nau died in 1845, but he and his brothers Emile and Laurore-Auguste were staunch critics of Boyerism and early supporters of Soulouque. Emile likely penned the words to Soulouque's 1849 address using his brother's earlier call to unity, infusing it with the hope for a new era of unity that had colored his

brothers Independence Day poem celebrating Dessalines. On Emile Nau during Soulouque's regime, see chapter 5.

CHAPTER 5. THE SECOND EMPIRE OF HAITI AND THE EXILED REPUBLIC

1 "Faustin Soulouque pass[e] à l'histoire comme un symbole 'd'ignorance et de cruauté.'" Lerebours, *Haïti et ses peintres*, t. 1, 127. *L'empereur Soulouque et son empire* (1856) offers the quintessential caricature of the cruel and ignorant Soulouque. The work, first published in serial by the French consul general in Haiti, Maxime Raybaud, under the pseudonym Gustave d'Alaux, is a highly fictionalized, sensationalized, and racist description of life in Haiti under Soulouque.

2 According to education historian Edner Brutus, the December 29, 1848, law sought to make education accessible to all genders, regions, and classes. Brutus argues that it was the most revolutionary and most democratic education reform in Haiti's first 150 years of independence: "la plus complète et démocratique prise depuis l'indépendance, et, dans ses lignes essentielles, inspiratrice de celles prises jusqu'à present [1945]." Brutus, *Instruction publique*, 156.

3 Lerebours, *Haïti et ses peintres*, t. 1, 128.

4 Edner Brutus, *Instruction publique*, 172–74. These changes were spearheaded by Soulouque's minister of education, Francisque (Duc du Limbé). Despite his commitment to Soulouque's government and to the reformist, populist government program, Francisque fell victim to palace intrigue: he was falsely accused of conspiracy against the Soulouque government and sentenced to death in 1851. See Madiou, *Autobiographie*. We see small modifications (such as the punishment for families that did not send their children to school) made to the 1848 law throughout the 1850s, especially in 1853.

5 Williams, *Marxism and Literature*, 13.

6 Ramsey, *Spirits and the Law*, 55. Julia Gaffield's new research on Haitian national sovereignty in the nineteenth century reveals how the concept of "civilization" was an ever-shifting and increasingly narrowly demarcated target (as defined by North Atlantic jurists) throughout the century: toward an exclusively racial (white), Western, Christian notion of "civilization." "The Racialization of International Law in the Aftermath of the Haitian Revolution: The Holy See and National Sovereignty," Alessandro Crisafulli Lecture, Catholic University of America (April 3, 2019).

7 Gaétan Mentor's current project on Soulouque is sure to repair this gap. For now, the best study of Soulouque is MacLeod, "Soulouque Regime." See also Etienne, "La diplomatie."

8 Lerebours, *Haïti et ses peintres*, t. 1, 131; Ramsey, *Spirits and the Law*, 55. As with his approach to memorialization of Dessalines and his broader populist rhetoric, Soulouque was drawing on examples set by previous opposition regimes: Guerrier and Pierrot's regimes had softened Boyer's draconian categorization and criminalization of *sortilèges*.

9 Ramsey, *Spirits and the Law*, 79. The popular Haitian memory of Soulouque's empire stands in stark opposition to the Atlantic world's caricatural image of Soulouque, typified in French consul general Maxime Raybaud's sensationalist, racist portrait of the emperor. Raybaud pointed to Vodou as evidence of the violent debauchery and barbarism of the black emperor.

10 Ibid., 80.

11 Lerebours, *Haïti et ses peintres*, t. 1, 131; Célius, "L'imagerie chrétienne."

12 Madiou says that after the failed uprising, he stepped down as director of the Lycée national (where he had been named under Riché) and planned to enter private life. Much to his surprise, Soulouque asked him to serve as the director of *Le Moniteur*. Madiou, *Autobiographie*, 23. See also Lescouflair, *Thomas Madiou*.

13 *Le Moniteur*, February 25, 1854.

14 The translation by Léon Pilatte as *La case de l'oncle Tom, ou Vie des noirs au sud des Etats-Unis* first appeared in the French paper *La Presse* with a preface by the British abolitionist John Lemoinne, which *Le Moniteur* reproduces in full (*Le Moniteur*, January 29, 1853, and February 5, 1853).

15 Brickhouse, *Transamerican Literary Relations*. For a reading of Stowe's novel, its reception in the press, and slavery in Brazil, see Castilho, "Brazilian Narratives."

16 Albanese, "Uncle Tom," 762.

17 Ibid., 760.

18 Hoffmann and Middelanis, *Faustin Soulouque*. Even Karl Marx and Victor Hugo used Soulouque's image and reputation to criticize the French emperor. Honoré Daumier, France's most popular caricaturist of the time, produced numerous racist caricatures of Soulouque throughout the 1850s. Second only to Daumier was Cham (Amédée de Noé). Not incidentally, Noé descended from a prominent French planting family in Saint-Domingue: Pantaléon de Bréda, on whose plantation Toussaint Louverture (formerly Toussaint Bréda) is said to have been born into slavery. See the sixteen-page pamphlet of Soulouque caricatures in Cham, *Soulouque et sa cour* (Paris: Le Charivari, 1850).

19 These developments were well known in Haiti: Soulouque's official newspaper, *Le Moniteur haïtien*, reproduced excerpts of *Le Moniteur de France* recounting the events.

20 Quillenbois's anti-republicanism makes sense in this context: the short-lived and relatively little-known satirical magazine *Le Caricaturiste* positioned itself as the conservative, legitimist-leaning counterpoint to Charles Philipon's much better-known anti-monarchist satirical publication *Le Charivari*.

21 See Childs, *Daumier and Exoticism*.

22 Many thanks to Erica Moiah James for drawing this engraving to my attention. See James, "Decolonizing Time." Edouard Duval-Carrié is preparing a new work based on the Torchiana engraving entitled *Le Roi Henry et sa cour*. He presented a charcoal preparation for what will eventual be an engraving on plexiglass at the

annual meeting of the Haitian Studies Association, Gainesville, Florida, October 17–19, 2019.
23 McIntosh and Pierrot, "Capturing," 139.
24 Ibid., 128.
25 For a discussion of this little-studied series, see Draper, "Thirty Famous People."
26 McIntosh and Pierrot, "Capturing," 137.
27 Dubroca, *Vida de J. J. Dessalines*.
28 Jenson, "Jean-Jacques Dessalines," 624.
29 Dayan, *Haiti, History*, 13.
30 *Le Moniteur* published the "programme" for the coronation events on March 27, two weeks before the ceremony was to take place on April 11. The written program draws heavily upon Christophe and Napoléon I's written coronation ceremonies.
31 MacLeod, "Soulouque Regime"; Smith, *Liberty*. Both historians draw from consular records for the majority of their primary source material. MacLeod notes that the pope did send an "ecclesiastical superior," Cossens, to Soulouque and that the emperor "obtained the services of the Abbé at his coronation, without papal authorization!" MacLeod, "Soulouque Regime," 45. Cossens is not named in the program for the coronation ceremony, published in *Le Moniteur*. Instead, a "vicaire general" is indicated for the church ceremony, suggesting that the ceremony program was drafted and sent to print before the name of the church official was known.
32 The British consul in Port-au-Prince, Ussher, noted that Soulouque's quarters even included wallpaper of gilded bees. Soulouque's crown, held today in Haiti's Musée du pantheon national haïtien, was created by the jeweler Rouvenat in Paris for 50,000 francs. Joseph, *L'état haïtien*, 150.
33 Many thanks to Jonathan Dusenbury for introducing me to this piece from Soulouque's empire. Thanks also to Adam Silvia and the staff at the Prints and Photographs Division at the Library of Congress for sharing their expertise on this item.
34 Célius, "L'imagerie chrétienne," 36.
35 On the circulation and politics of Soulouque's *Album Impérial*, see Salt, "Black Body Politic."
36 The symbolism included in Soulouque's imperial crest enacts many of these same critiques of Napoleonic power, as I have argued elsewhere. See "Haiti's Paper War: Post-Independence Writing and the Making of the Republic," Kluge Café Series, Library of Congress, August 31, 2017, https://youtu.be/gnnKhmouXGI?t=3317.
37 Jenson, "Toussaint Louverture."
38 Wiley gave his sitters the option of various Old Masters to choose from. Ice-T selected Ingres and his 1806 portrait of Napoléon I. Logan Hill, "Kehinde Wiley."
39 Carrington, "Cultural Politics."
40 Pascal-Trouillot and Trouillot, *Encyclopédie*, 31–33.
41 See Hénock Trouillot, *Beaubrun Ardouin*.

42 Daut, *Tropics*; Brickhouse, *Transamerican Literary Relations*; Bergeaud, *Stella* (Mucher and Curtis edition).
43 Madiou, *Histoire*, t. 7, 534, and t. 8, 77.
44 *Le Moniteur*, November 1, 1845. It was on this occasion and in the midst of the popular peasant uprisings in the South that Lysius Salomon gave a well-known and fiery speech in Les Cayes honoring "the avenger of the black race, the liberator of Haiti, a hero of Independence, the famous Jean Jacques Dessalines." Zavitz, "Revolutionary Commemorations," 228. See also Hodgson, "Haiti's *Fête Nationale*."
45 *Le Moniteur*, December 23, 1848. The law represents only a small sliver of the numerous ideas debated in parliament (and reproduced in *Le Moniteur*) for ways to commemorate the "reconnaissance nationale à la mémoire des fondateurs de l'indépendance." For example, there were proposals to make different churches for leaders in regionally significant locations (Pétionville for Pétion, his daughter, and Riché; Saint-Marc for Guerrier); to construct a monument in Dessalines-Marchand that would eventually hold the national archives; and to build a column in Gonaïves upon which the Acte de l'indépendance and its signatories would be inscribed.
46 Madiou, *Histoire*, t. 3, 142–43.
47 Ibid., 329. For a reading of Dessaliness's systematic, political use of vengeance in relation to the "public vengeance" of the Terror, see Pierrot, *Black Avenger*.
48 Daut, *Tropics*, 598.
49 On Faubert's biography and larger oeuvre, including *Ogé*, see Daut, *Tropics*; and Brickhouse, *Transamerican Literary Relations*.
50 Daut, *Tropics*, 598.
51 Faubert, *Ogé*, 81–82.
52 Albert's prescient concern for Haiti's future standing among the Western family of nations must also be read alongside Dessaliness's concern for posterity and Haiti's future in the Acte de l'indépendance (discussed below). Albert's forward-looking concern is juxtaposed with Dessaliness's turn back to the past, to the island's pre-Columbian inhabitants.
53 See chapter 1. As we shall see, writers will continue to evoke the metaphor of "solid ground" in debates about 1804/1806 well into the twentieth century.
54 Saint-Rémy, preface to Boisrond Tonnerre, *Mémoires*.
55 "Odieuses paroles, qui répondaient parfaitement aux sentiments de vengeance sauvage qui lui gonflaient le cœur." Ibid., x.
56 "Il aimait le sang et il faisait sentir à son maître l'avant-goût de ce breuvage infernal." Ibid.
57 In the preface to the novel, Bergeaud describes his use of allegory and symbolism, adorning historical fact with "ornements de la fiction" as a strategy to attract foreign readers who might not otherwise study Haitian history in detail. Bergeaud, *Stella* (Ardouin edition), v.
58 Bergeaud spent most of his exile in Saint Thomas, traveling to Paris in 1857 to seek medical treatment. There, he met with Beaubrun Ardouin, with whom he left

the manuscript for *Stella*. Ardouin brought Bergeaud's text to the Paris publisher Dentu in 1859, adding his own note "au lecteur" describing the circumstances under which he had acquired the novel. Bergeaud, *Stella* (Ardouin edition). Ardouin's "Au lecteur" message is not included in Dentu's 1887 reprint of the novel. Emeric Bergeaud, *Stella* (Paris: E. Dentu, 1887). Ardouin's central role in the publication of Bergeaud's text has led many to speculate on the historian's influence on the text, and even the veracity of his claim to authorship. See Daut, *Tropics*; and Bergeaud, *Stella* (Mucher and Curtis edition). At the very least, Ardouin did edit Bergeaud's text and add pertinent historical context, including, likely, the entire last chapter of the book (a historical overview of the origins of Haiti from pre-Columbian times to the contemporary inhabitants of the western part of the island). Given that these writers came from the same political tribe and a similar regional-social background, it stands to reason that they would share many of the same ideas they expressed in their writing. That is to say, if Ardouin did alter sections of Bergeaud's book, it was a logical fit: they were both committed to countering the violent image of Dessalinean vengeance in Haitian history—and the present violent image of Soulouque's empire—by reimagining the Haitian Revolution outside of Dessalinean violence.
59 Bergeaud describes the mother's life in Africa as one of joy and abundance. Her journey to the New World resembles closely the story Coriolan Ardouin told in his poem "Les Betjouanes."
60 One need only look to Victor Hugo, the great republican in exile, and his poem "Stella" in *Les châtiments*, which he wrote *also* in exile during the Second Empire of Napoléon III and published in 1853. The final lines exalt the guiding light of "l'ange Liberté": "Debout, vous qui dormez!—car celui qui me suit, / Car celui qui m'envoie en avant la première, / C'est l'ange Liberté, c'est le géant Lumière!" Hugo, *Les châtiments*.
61 "Les Romains se délient de Romulus parce qu'il était devenu tyran, mais ils le placèrent au ciel." Madiou, *Histoire*, t. 3, 330.
62 In the Vodou pantheon he is Ogou Desalin, a *lwa* associated with liberty and combat. See Dayan, *Haiti, History*.
63 On Bergeaud's use of the Roman myth, see Daut, *Tropics*.
64 "Jeune homme, . . . tu es nécessaire à l'accomplissement de mon dessein." Bergeaud, *Stella* (Ardouin edition), 150.
65 Ibid., 203.
66 On the question of parricidal violence in the novel, see Perry, "Becoming Indigenous."
67 Bergeaud, *Stella* (Ardouin edition), 319–20.
68 Ardouin's antipopulism here remains unchanged from his earlier Boyerist political manifestations (see chapter 4): leadership by a select, "capable" elite.
69 Madiou, *Histoire*, t. 3. See also Popkin, *Racial Revolution*.
70 "Le génie de l'humanité s'étaient sincèrement mises à l'œuvre; et, malgré cet immense concours d'intelligences et de vertus, la première pierre de l'édifice fut posée dans le sang." Bergeaud, *Stella* (Ardouin edition), 299.

71 Ibid., 58.
72 "On se battait, on se tuait, on s'égorgeait en mon nom." Ibid. Other more subtle hints to her identity as liberty incarnate abound, such as her self-proclaimed inability to live in confined spaces or with any limitations on her ability to move and be *free*. She explains that she is injured grievously "par la plus légère contrainte," and says that life in a prison cell would undoubtedly snuff out her life force.
73 Though I do not attend to religion here, Jonas Ross Kjærgård's recent analysis of religious references in Bergeaud's novel suggests that the question of Haitian "civilization" Bergeaud was presenting also touched on Haiti's Catholic faith. Kjærgård, "Narratives and Fortresses: Building Haiti in a World of Geopolitical Interests" (paper presented at the annual meeting of the Haitian Studies Association, Gainesville, Florida, October 17–19, 2019).
74 "Les aînés de la révolution s'étaient fait connaître dans les années 1790 et 1791; leurs brevets dataient de l'ère de la république française: aussi avaient-ils été longtemps des républicains enthousiastes, des patriotes exaltés: ils ne songèrent à être indépendants que quand on leur apprit à ne plus avoir foi en la métropole." Bergeaud, *Stella* (Ardouin edition), 282–83.
75 Nau, *Histoire des caciques*. Nau had published an anonymous excerpt of the work "de la langue et de la literature des Aborigènes d'Haïti" in 1851 in *Le Moniteur* under the title "Histoire inédite des caciques." By 1853 he published an excerpt from the preface in *Le Moniteur*. See also Liautaud Ethéart's *Les miscellenées* (1855), cited in Daut, *Tropics*. Otherwise, the only other publications are *Abécédaires français*, which appear to have been published in France and sold in Haiti.
76 To avoid temporal confusion, I refer to the island as Ayti in the Amerindian (pre-Columbian) period, Saint-Domingue in the colonial period, and Haiti in the post-independence period.
77 See chapter 1.
78 In his preface to the work, Nau argues that by studying the period of Columbian contact, he is filling a hole in Haitian history. Once a Haitian undertakes an in-depth historical study of the period of French colonization, Haitians will be in possession of "toute l'histoire d'Haïti édifiée par des mains haïtiennes." Nau, *Histoire des caciques*, 12.
79 "Marchons sur d'autres traces; imitons ces peuples qui, portant leur sollicitude jusques sur l'avenir, et appréhendant de laisser à la postérité l'exemple de la lâcheté, ont préféré être exterminés que rayés du nombre des peuples libres." Haitian Declaration of Independence, 1804.
80 "C'est en me plaçant au milieu d'eux, et de ce point de vue, que j'ai raconté la découverte et la conquête de l'île." Nau, *Histoire des caciques*, 14–15.
81 "Depuis la découverte jusqu'à nos jours, que de souffrances, que de meurtres, que d'héroïsme et de martyres!" Ibid., 12–13.
82 "L'Africain et l'Indien se sont donné la main dans les chaînes. Voilà par quelle confraternité de malheur, par quelle communauté de souffrances, leurs destinées se sont trouvées mêlées." Ibid., 14.

83 Fischer, *Modernity Disavowed*, 242–43. See also Michael Reyes, "The Gravity of Revolution: The Legacy of Anticolonial Discourse in Postcolonial Haitian Writing, 1804–1934" (PhD diss., Cornell University, 2018).
84 Nau, *Histoire des caciques*, 14.
85 Ibid., 13.
86 "O terre de mon pays! en est-il une sur le globe qui ait été plus imbibée de sang humain? En est-il une où les malheureux habitans aient éprouvés plus d'infortunes?" Translation from Chris Bongie in Vastey, *Colonial System*, 86. See chapter 3 for a discussion of Vastey's text. Vastey and Nau's use of the superlative appears to draw here upon the language and structure used by Claude-Corentin Tanguy de la Boissière to describe the unrest that followed European contact: "No country has ever experienced more physical, moral and political revolutions than the island of St. Domingo." Tanguy de la Boissière, *Proposals for Printing a Journal of the Revolutions in the French Part of St. Domingo*, qtd. in Jenson, *Slave Narrative*, 236.
87 "Quel crime en effet d'avoir égorgé tout un peuple! Oui, mais d'un autre côté, quelle gloire d'avoir découvert un monde nouveau à la civilisation, à la science et à la religion! Ce qui est regrettable, c'est que cette gloire soit entachée de meurtre, de torture et de sang." Nau, *Histoire des caciques*, 15.
88 Scott, *Conscripts of Modernity*, 175.
89 Nau, *Histoire des caciques*, 15.
90 Ibid.
91 "Les annales d'Haïti, malgré le peu de place qu'elles paraissent encore tenir dans celles du monde, abondent en enseignements utiles pour l'étude et l'instruction de l'humanité." Ibid., 15–16.

CHAPTER 6. NATIONALS AND LIBERALS, 1904/1906

1 Janvier, *Les constitutions*, 268. On exiled republicans' return to Haiti, see Smith, *Liberty*. The South in particular saw an influx of republican returnees, many of whom set to work founding a new newspaper in Les Cayes, *L'Union*. The paper was dedicated to the region's reawakening after years of Soulouque's imperial rule. The editors inflected their reawakening with particularly religious terms (*assoupissement*—often linked to a religious lapse that precedes a reawakening) in their inaugural issue, which coincides with Geffrard's courting of the Catholic Church and a concordat with the Holy See: "The *South* will awaken thus from its long slumber [*assoupissement*]! Like so many of the Republic's other departments, it will make its voice heard, for where is the place that has suffered more, in every respect, from the misfortunes that have plagued the country?" (*Le Sud va donc se réveiller de son long assoupissement! comme les autres départements de la République, il fera entendre sa voix, car quel est le point qui plus que lui a souffert, à tous égards, des malheurs qui ont affligé le pays?*) *L'Union*, March 22, 1860.

2 Ramsey, *Spirits and the Law*, 81. See Julia Gaffield's forthcoming project on the concordat, *The Abandoned Faithful: Sovereignty, Diplomacy, and Religious Dominion in the Aftermath of the Haitian Revolution*.
3 Qtd. in Nicholls, *Dessalines*, 84.
4 Ramsey, *Spirits and the Law*, 84.
5 Smith, *Liberty*, 111.
6 Ibid., 113.
7 Roger Gaillard takes 1870 as the starting point of his historical series on the brutal political repressions in the Haitian Republic, entitled "La république exterminatrice."
8 As Matthew Smith has recently shown in his gripping study of the 1865 civil war, it was the British government's decision to intervene through military force (what Smith deems "extraordinary" interference) that brought Salnave's separatist government to an end. Smith, *Liberty*. On Salnave, see Adam, *Une crise haïtienne*; and Gaillard, Gaillard-Pourchet, and Viard, *Le cacoïsme bourgeois*. See also the eight-part series on Salnave in the *Revue de la Société haïtienne d'histoire, de géographie et de géologie*.
9 Delorme was initially a champion of Geffrard's republican government in his newspaper, *L'Avenir*, the first to appear in the North after years of silence in northern presses. He quickly became disillusioned with Geffrard's antidemocratic, anti-peasant repressive actions and aligned with Salnave's 1865 movement, hoping to establish "progress and liberty, not just in words but in practice, in things, in all of the good that there was to be done" (*le progrès et la liberté, pas seulement dans les mots mais dans les faits, dans les choses, dans tout le bien qu'il y avait à faire*). Delorme, *La reconnaissance*, 5. See Watson Denis, "Les 100 ans de 'Monsieur Roosevelt en Haïti,'" *Revue de la Société haïtienne d'histoire, de géographie et de géologie*, no. 226 (2006): 1–41. On Delorme's decision to commit to the National cause, see the polemical exchange between Anténor Firmin and Nemours Auguste's newspaper, *Le Messager du Nord* (a Liberal Party outpost), and Delorme's *Le National*. According to Ertha-Pascal Trouillot and Ernst Trouillot, "Delorme became the heart and soul of it, while Salnave was only the muscle" (*Delorme en devint l'âme, alors que Salnave n'en était que le bras*). Pascal-Trouillot and Trouillot, *Encyclopédie*, 293. Salnave's very public falling-out with Delorme in 1868 is laid bare in Delorme's passionate text *La reconnaissance du général Salnave*, which reveals the nature of Salnave's regime, his unorthodox style of governing, and the ultimate source of their falling-out.
10 Salnave followed much of the same populist agenda as Lysius Salomon. He nevertheless still considered the southern populist leader a threat to his own power, and shrewdly placed him in a diplomatic post in Europe. Smith, *Liberty*, 173, 179. See also Adam, *Une crise haïtienne*.
11 Janvier, *Les constitutions*, 341.

12 Smith, *Liberty*; Nicholls, *Caribbean Context*. See also Delorme, *La reconnaissance*. The separatist states created their own flags and separate currency. On Michel Domingue and the separatist Etat Méridional, see Hall, *La péninsule républicaine*.
13 Janvier, *Les constitutions*, 345.
14 Smith, *Liberty*, 176. See also Adam, *Une crise haïtienne*.
15 "Tout fût à réorganiser après la crise de 1868–1869." Janvier, *Les constitutions*, 351.
16 Michel-Rolph Trouillot, *State against Nation*, 98.
17 On the Liberal Party, see Auguste, "Réflexions." See also Smith, *Liberty*.
18 Rameau was the nephew of the southern military leader Domingue. See Nicolas, "Anténor Firmin." The letter written to proclaim the foundation of the Liberal Party, by Paul and Bazelais, is reproduced in Price-Mars, *Anténor Firmin*. Demesvar Delorme may have co-founded the National Party with Rameau from the North, though it is not clear. A date for the founding of the National Party is hard to identify. It emerged sometime during Nissage Saget's presidency (1869–1874) and after the founding of the Liberal Party.
19 See Auguste, "Réflexions" on the Liberal Party fracture between Bazelais (*bazelaisistes*) and Boisrond-Canal (*canalistes*). See also Wesner, "Le courant libéral"; and Marc Péan, *Vingt-cinq ans*.
20 Louis Joseph Janvier devotes considerable attention to the 1883 civil war in his work, especially in *Les affaires d'Haïti*. On the events of 1883 from a Liberal Party perspective, see Paul, *Œuvres posthumes*; Price-Mars, *Jean-Pierre Boyer Bazelais*; and Turnier, *Mérisier Jeannis*.
21 On the divisions between Nationals, Liberals, and Firministes, see Marc Péan, *Vingt-cinq ans*; Nicolas, "Anténor Firmin"; and Acacia, "Firmin et Janvier."
22 Nicholls, *Dessalines*, 113, 119. For an excellent critique of Nicholls's color-based analysis of Haitian historiography, see Daut, *Tropics*. See also essays collected in Kate Quinn and Paul Sutton, eds., *Politics and Power in Haiti* (New York: Palgrave Macmillan, 2013). In particular, see Dupuy, "François Duvalier." For a critique of Nicholls's reading of the Liberal/National divide specifically, see Auguste, "Réflexions," 17. To be sure, I am not advocating that we dismiss Nicholls's book wholesale. It covers an impressive span of time and relies on a massive corpus of nineteenth-century newspapers that are difficult to find today. My hope here is that by fully fleshing out the problems with Nicholls's approach, we might be able to further develop the important interventions he makes.
23 There is perhaps nowhere in Nicholls's work that he imposes his rigid color-legend argument more than in his attempt to make sense of the emergence of the National and Liberal political parties, and in his analysis of Louis Joseph Janvier in particular. The color question that Nicholls identifies as the genesis of the National/Liberal debate becomes central to his larger methodological approach to *all* of Haitian history—his color-based approach to Haitian ideology, and Haitian action, from Dessalines to Duvalier.

24 Janvier remains woefully understudied in Anglophone scholarship on Haiti, perhaps in part due to Nicholls's dismissal of his oeuvre. A forthcoming series of essays and critical translation of Janvier's work, *Haïti aux Haïtiens*, seeks to remedy this gap. See Brandon Byrd, Chelsea Stieber, and Nathan Dize, eds., *Haiti for the Haitians* (Liverpool University Press, forthcoming).

25 Janvier explained that Chancy, a young Haitian legal scholar who shared his own interest in legislation, had conceived of the idea to respond to the "noble goal" of Janvier's social reform project, and Janvier helped him implement it. Janvier, *L'égalité*, 12.

26 See Chemla, "Louis-Joseph Janvier"; and Daut, "Caribbean 'Race Men.'"

27 Janvier, *L'égalité*, 8; Janvier, "Le vieux piquet," n.p.

28 Pascal-Trouillot and Trouillot note the National Party slogan as the following: "Le plus grand bien au plus grand nombre." *Encyclopédie*, 83. As Aldrich Nicolas points out, Marquis de Condorcet's phrase "plus grand bonheur au plus grand nombre" is the origin of their slogan. Nicolas, "Anténor Firmin," 206.

29 Janvier, *L'égalité*, 23, 29, 37.

30 "Aura droit à une mise en possession de trois à cinq carreaux de terre du domaine public." Janvier, *Les constitutions*, 496.

31 "La grande réforme, la primordiale . . . La terre au paysan, c'est la clef de voûte de l'édifice de reconstruction, le ciment du système général, l'assise de granit sur laquelle on pourra tout bâtir, tout construire, tout échafauder." Janvier, *L'égalité*, 11. On the history of land reform in nineteenth-century Haiti, see René, *Haïti après l'esclavage*; and Gonzalez, *Maroon Nation*.

32 Nicholls, *Dessalines*, 112–14.

33 Nicholls, *Dessalines*, 116.

34 Janvier, *Les détracteurs*; Janvier, *La République d'Haïti*.

35 Pressoir, Trouillot, and Trouillot, *Historiographie*, 259.

36 "Qu'est-ce que c'est que la civilisation, d'ailleurs? Pastiche ou copie." Janvier, *La République d'Haïti*, 511.

37 "L'homme se reflète dans son style . . . par ces lignes, je me prémunis contre les préjugés de ceux qui ne peuvent jamais exposer leurs sentiments au grand jour; je me précautionne contre les manœuvres occultes de ceux qui n'osent jamais ouvrir des avis en langage clair." Janvier, *Les constitutions*, 622.

38 "Pourquoi montrer nos plaies à découvert? Faut-il soulever le voile qui les couvre? eh! comment pourrions-nous les guérir si nous n'osons en sonder la profondeur?" Vastey, *Essai*, 106. Vastey undoubtedly borrowed this turn of phrase from Chanlatte's 1810 *Le cri de la nature*, in which he describes the horrors of slavery in apostrophe: "Quelle plaie horrible de l'humanité je viens de découvrir?" Chanlatte, *Le cri*, 9. What is more, in *Slave Narrative*, Deborah Jenson notes the similarity between Chanlatte's turn of phrase and the Dessalinean secretary B. Aimé's language in the November 1803 proclamation. Janvier's writing thus activates a long nineteenth-century heritage of Dessalinean writing with his insistence on writing in a frank, clear style.

39 Janvier, *L'égalité*, 5. His work in *Les constitutions d'Haïti* is most notable in this regard for the new possible future it puts forth in the last hundred pages.
40 "Je vois si souvent confier le soin de le représenter à l'étranger, soit à des personnes qui l'ont quitté depuis 1848, alors qu'il était de bon ton de le renier, soit à d'autres qui se vantent tout haut de ne jamais lire les écrits que publient les Haïtiens." Janvier, *Les constitutions*, 619.
41 On the *lodyans* as a Haitian genre, see Anglade, "Les lodyanseurs du soir."
42 Sheller, *Democracy after Slavery*, 135; Madiou, *Histoire*, t. 8, 121–36.
43 "Dès 1809, l'indépendance personnelle, qui est la vraie liberté, assise sur la propriété du sol, est l'objet des vœux constants du paysan; les cultivateurs ne visent qu'à une chose: se soustraire de la dépendance des propriétaires ou fermiers pour jouir de leur liberté naturelle; dès lors, ils n'entendent plus n'être que des instruments à récolter des denrées." Janvier, *Les constitutions*, 490.
44 "Ecoute, mon petit, et retenez bien ceci, vous tous." Janvier, "Le vieux piquet," 12.
45 Jonassaint, "Conflits langagiers," 41.
46 See Fleischmann, *Ecrivain et société*.
47 Literary critics and historians have largely excluded his 1889 novel *Une chercheuse* (as well as Demesvar Delorme's two novels *Francesca* and *Le Damné*) from the history of the modern Haitian novel because the works were published abroad and included characters and settings that were not Haitian. But even Janvier and Delorme's "European" novels address Haitian concerns, and are far from the escapist Francophilic productions that they are made out to be, as Yves Chemla has pointed out. Chemla, "Louis-Joseph Janvier." Janvier used the exotic setting of Europe, with characters such as Mimose Carminier, a rich divorcée, and Edriss Gazy, an intelligent Egyptian student who had come to Paris to study medicine (and a stand-in for Janvier), in order to explore the perfectly Haitian problems of political strife, exile, and otherness.
48 Janvier, "Le vieux piquet," 20.
49 Ibid.
50 Ibid., 28.
51 "Une Constitution sur le papier. Toute la Révolution s'arrêtait là pour eux." Ibid., 22.
52 On the peasant's recourse to petition and other forms of paper-based reclamations of rights, see René, *Haïti après l'esclavage*.
53 "Vous saurez tous que les constitutions, ils les font pour nous brider, mais que, eux, ils n'y obéissent jamais, ils se croient trop nobles pour cela." Janvier, "Le vieux piquet," 30–31.
54 Ibid., 29; Janvier, *Les constitutions*, 266.
55 "Amis de leur liberté propre, amis ennemis acharnés des nôtres . . . nos chefs furent fusillés. C'était dans l'ordre. Le libéralisme de nos ennemis le voulait ainsi." Janvier, "Le vieux piquet," 31.
56 "C'est notre bien-être à nous qui fait le bien-être de tous." Ibid., 41.

57 "La plainte de la nation trop souvent trahie depuis 1806 par ceux en qui elle avait mis tout son espoir." Janvier, *Les constitutions*, 620.
58 "En histoire, la vérité perce toujours, quelque précaution qu'on ait pris de la cacher, quelque soin qu'on mette à la travestir." Ibid., 3.
59 "Il est le seul dispensateur des apothéoses définitives." Ibid., 153.
60 See Marc Péan, *Vingt-cinq ans*.
61 On Firminisme, see especially Marc Péan, *Vingt-cinq ans*, t. 2; and Price-Mars, *Anténor Firmin*. See also Smith, *Liberty*.
62 Pascal-Trouillot and Trouillot, *Encyclopédie*, 402.
63 Fluehr-Lobban, "Anténor Firmin"; Firmin, *Equality*. It is important to note that the Société d'anthropologie was still relying primarily on the science of biological racism. Firmin was responding as much to the Société's approach to anthropology as he was to Gobineau's text in his essay. It is also important to note that Janvier's short pamphlet *L'égalité des races* preceded Firmin's by a few years. Janvier's 1884 essay (published in Paris in the "Jeune Haiti" collection he'd started for the "Bibliothèque démocratique haïtienne" series) was actually a reprint of an article he had originally published in 1883 in the *Revue de la Jeune France* in refutation of Ernest Renan's *Dialogues philosophiques*, in which the French civic nationalist proclaimed, "Les hommes ne sont pas égaux, les races ne sont pas égales" (quoted in Janvier, *L'égalité*, 19).
64 Dash, "Nineteenth-Century Haiti," 49, 48.
65 While many scholars read Firmin's successful navigation of the negotiations with the United States as evidence of his savvy and patriotism, at the time he received harsh criticism for negotiating at all. See Asselin Charles, "Race and Geopolitics." The Nationalist accusation that Firmin was "selling Haiti to the United States" undoubtedly echoes earlier nineteenth-century nationalist critiques of Pétion and Boyer.
66 See Péan, *Vingt-cinq ans*, t. 2.
67 See, for example, Michel Acacia's rethinking of Firmin and Janvier as more closely aligned than historians have traditionally allowed for. Acacia, "Firmin et Janvier."
68 Marc Péan, *Vingt-cinq ans*, t. 2, 50. Prior to the 1902 constitution, the head of state was elected by the bicameral National Assembly, composed of deputies and senators.
69 Ibid., 55.
70 Marc Péan, *Vingt-cinq ans*, t. 2; Smith, *Liberty*, 303–4. See also Desquiron, "Ecrire l'histoire."
71 On Firministe exiles, see Smith, *Liberty*; and Marc Péan, *Vingt-cinq ans*. Péan notes that many members of the Capois elite, including members of the de Catalogne family (whom we shall meet in the next chapter) accompanied Firmin.
72 Lhérisson, *Pour Dessalines*. For a comprehensive presentation of the Association du centenaire de l'indépendance nationale and its documentation, see Zavitz, "Revolutionary Commemorations."
73 See chapter 5.

74 "Entre tous les héros de l'indépendance, J. J. Dessalines s'est distingué par son courage et la noble direction qu'il a donnée à l'immortelle révolution qui a commencé pour nous une ère nouvelle. Les fautes du grand homme sont effacées par l'immensité des services rendus à la patrie." *Le Moniteur*, May 8, 1847. Linstant argued vehemently that the Haitian leaders be placed together in one mausoleum. Though Linstant's idea was not taken up under Soulouque, the Musée du panthéon national haïtien (MUPANAH) must be seen as the end point of these 1845–1847 discussions. The building was conceived in 1975 as a mausoleum for all of Haiti's founding fathers before becoming the national museum in 1983.
75 Lhérisson, *Pour Dessalines*, 9; Zavitz, "Revolutionary Commemorations."
76 Jérémie, *Haïti indépendante*, v.
77 Jolibois, *Frères Coicou*, 8.
78 Marc Péan, *Vingt-cinq ans*, t. 3, 32; *Stella: Organe de la bibliophile*, 858; Jérémie, *Haïti indépendante*, vi. As for those in the South, they too had their own communal committee for the centennial. The Comité du Centenaire des Cayes even published its own *revue* in Les Cayes, *La Revue du Centenaire de l'Indépendance*, directed by Duraciné Vaval. The committee and the review proved equally supportive of Dessalines and his legacy, exalting his memory as the hero and glorious founder of the nation. See, for example, a speech given by Vaval and reproduced in the review. Duraciné Vaval, "Dessalines devant l'histoire," *La Revue du Centenaire de l'Indépendance*, no. 3 (1903). The communal committee of Les Cayes also planned to inaugurate a monument to Toussaint Louverture as part of the centennial festivities.
79 "Ce crime qui a fait à la patrie un mal incalculable, un mal vraiment fécond, car nous l'expions encore." Coicou, *L'empereur Dessalines*, iii.
80 Jérémie, *Haïti indépendante*; Zavitz, "Revolutionary Commemorations."
81 Pascal-Trouillot and Trouillot, *Encyclopédie*, 241.
82 Coicou had recently taken the helm of the Petit Théâtre (sometimes referred to as the Théâtre Sylvain, for its earlier director Michel Sylvain). Antoine Innocent was one of its most notable members—he originated the role of Dessalines in Coicou's play, and his relative, Sylvia, originated the role of Défilé. Ibid., 242.
83 Coicou, *L'empereur Dessalines*. Liautaud Ethéart's 1860 play *La fille de l'empereur* had put violence on stage (the suicide of Dessalines's daughter's lover, Chancy), but not Dessalines's assassination.
84 Timoléon Brutus's biography of Dessalines includes an excerpt from the unpublished second act (act II, scène XVIII) that he cited from the manuscript copy lent to him by Victor Coicou, the author's son. Brutus, *L'homme d'airain*, t. 2, 245. See Dayan, *Haiti, History*, 293n90. Coicou self-published the first act of the play with the Bibliothèque Amica imprint, which Coicou had founded (and named for his mother) in 1902. Pascal-Trouillot and Trouillot, *Encyclopédie*, 242.
85 "L'heure sonne où la postérité opère son œuvre de révision, son travail d'élimination, son devoir de justice enfin." Coicou, *L'empereur Dessalines*, v.
86 Ibid., vi.

87 Louis Carius Lhérisson was a respected senator, educator, and pedagogue about whom even less has been written. For a portrait of Lhérisson's life and activism in education, see Chrisphonte, *Noces d'or*. See also Lélia J. Lhérisson, *Manuel de Littérature*.
88 "La Révolution de 1806 . . . fut une œuvre ambitieuse et inféconde, injuste et barbare." Lhérisson, *Pour Dessalines*, 8. Coicou engages a similar Dessalinean-style reversal of the idea of the liberator as a monster in his 1892 poem depicting Dessalines's assassination in "Une voix sur le Pont-Rouge." Coicou, *Poésies nationales*. Nathan Dize's forthcoming doctoral dissertation includes exciting new analysis of Coicou's life, work, and assassination.
89 "On ne tue pas impunément un chef d'Etat, voire un libérateur d'esclaves! C'est un crime irrémissible qui pèse lourdement sur la destinée d'une nation." Lhérisson, *Pour Dessalines*, 11.
90 Coicou and Lhérisson spell her name with one *e*, "Défilé."
91 Dédée Bazile was born in Cap-Français to slave parents and was a camp follower of Dessalines's army. After Dessalines's assassination, Bazile collected the fallen hero's body parts and carried them to the cemetery for burial. She earned the nickname "Défilée-la-folle" because many suspected that she either went mad from the trauma of Dessalines's death, or was already insane. Dayan suggests that she had been raped by her master, and that her brother and sons had died in battle during the revolution, which may have also caused her mourning and descent into grief. On Dédée Bazile, see Dayan, *Haiti, History*; Braziel, "Re-membering Défilée."
92 Colin Dayan's analysis of Défilée remains to this day some of the best analysis of the historical figure and her role in Haiti's national (his)stories. It is notable here that much of the information Dayan gleans from historical sources originates from Joseph Jérémie. Jérémie gave interviews to Jean Fouchard in the 1950s about Défilée, which Fouchard published in *La méringue*. Fouchard's documentation of Haiti's "oldest song," apparently sung by Défilée, comes from Jérémie and, I would argue, reflects the spirit of national commemoration and Défilée's importance to it that dominated in 1906.
93 "N'est-il pas vrai que, lorsque Défilé traversait Port-au-Prince, faisant d'un sac fangeux un linceul à l'empereur, bravant les huées . . . que la plus belle incarnation de la conscience nationale c'est elle, cette folle qui s'en allait ainsi au milieu de ces fous qui se croyaient des sages?" Coicou, *L'empereur Dessalines*, iv–v.
94 In other lore she is said to have used her own dress. Though beyond the scope of this book, it is worth noting that Etzer Vilaire engages a similar imagery and lexicon to critique Haiti's century of civil war and Dessalines's assassination in his 1903 epic poem *Le flibustier*.
95 Smith, *Liberty*, 307–8. Marc Péan recounts Firministe agitation in the North and Artibonite throughout 1906 and 1907, including several failed plots to bring Firmin back to power. This precedent undoubtedly contributed to Nord Alexis's swift and deadly rebuke of the Firministe uprising in 1908 and his

execution of the Coicou brothers and their associates. Péan, *Vingt-cinq ans*, t. 3, 50–61.
96 Jolibois, *Frères Coicou*, 17–18.
97 Smith, *Liberty*, 317.

CHAPTER 7. HAITI'S NATIONAL REVOLUTION

1 *Le palais national*. On Baussan, see the series of articles in the *Revue de la Société haïtienne d'histoire, de géographie et de géologie*.
2 Haitian president Jovenel Moïse announced plans to rebuild the palace and laid the first stone for the new structure in an official ceremony on January 12, 2018. "Reconstruction du Palais national: Jovenel Moïse fera d'une pierre deux coups," *Le Nouvelliste*, http://lenouvelliste.com/article/181554/reconstruction-du-palais-national-jovenel-moise-fera-dune-pierre-deux-coups.
3 "Nous ne demandons certes pas des palais." Luc Fouché, "Une administration communale," *Stella: Organe de la bibliophile*, no. 31 (1929).
4 "Divisions, haine, ambitions, préjugés, tueries, délations, trahisons, abominations, soif du pouvoir, cupidité, blancomanie, ignorance, lâcheté, faiblesse, fausseté, les mauvais haïtiens ... voilà le serpent qui a mordu notre mère Haïti! Il est encore vivant et continue son œuvre criminelle, jusqu'à ce qu'il ne reste plus pierre sur pierre de l'édifice National. Eh bien! que cela soit! La maison est à reconstruire sur des bases nouvelles, solides, éternelles. Nous ne voulons pas qu'elle soit simplement restaurée, qu'elle n'ait que la façade, un beau dôme avec des soubassements boueux, une charpente pourrie, vermoulue ... O sépulcre blanchi!!! —Poursuis ton œuvre infernale, serpent maudit par Dieu. Achève de détruire et de balayer le terrain pour que nous venions édifier dans le roc un ordre de choses nouveau auquel tes crochets acérés s'attaquent en vain." J. F. Magny, "1804-1915-1930," *Stella: Organe de la bibliophile*, no. 41 (1930).
5 Gaillard, *Les blancs débarquent*; McPherson, *Invaded*.
6 My approach to Maurrassisme and integral nationalism draws mainly upon Joly, *Action française*; Sternhell, *Ni droite ni gauche*; Weber, *Action Française*; and the essays and analysis in Jenkins, *Era of Fascism*.
7 I have explored these links in depth in Stieber, "Gérard de Catalogne"; and Stieber, "'Camelots du roi ou rouges.'"
8 The United States had already intervened in Cuba, Mexico, Panama, Puerto Rico, and Honduras, and would occupy Nicaragua in 1912 and the Dominican Republic in 1916. McPherson, *Invaded*.
9 For a substantive engagement with the *Revue indigène*, see Stieber, "Vocation of the Indigènes."
10 *Stella* writers were indeed fond of the northern heritage of paper wars, engaging in a number of polemicals with Haitian and foreign writers in the pages of their magazine. See, for example, Cinéas, "Les populations abruties du Nord," which he wrote in refutation of an article that Eugène de Lespinasse published in *Le Temps*. Jean-Baptiste Cinéas, "Les populations abruties du Nord," *Stella: Organe de la bibliophile*, no. 28 (1928).

11 On the 1930s press in Haiti, especially the polarization between these intellectual factions, see Stieber, "'Camelots du roi ou rouges.'"
12 "Ces mots de Barrès, voilà le dur granit fondamental sur lequel nous édifions la forteresse nationaliste." Roumain, "La terre et les morts" (qtd. in Roumain, Œuvres complètes, 447). He also celebrated his Breton ancestry in the pages of La Revue indigène. For more on Roumain's brief but intense engagement with Haitian nationalists in the late 1920s and early 1930s, see Stieber, "'Camelots du roi ou rouges.'"
13 See Stieber, "Vocation of the Indigènes."
14 Appiah, "Cosmopolitan Patriots."
15 The group's relationship to Valery Larbaud, especially the correspondence with Emile Roumer, Philippe-Thoby Marcelin, and Jacques Roumain, sheds additional light on this dynamic. Indeed, there is a full run of the Revue indigène (and some multiples) in Larbaud's private library, sent to him directly by the young poets. These original issues confirm that the Revue indigène never included subscription information and suggests to me that its creators intended it almost uniquely for an international audience—a calling card of sorts for entry into the cosmopolitan world of letters brokered by men like Larbaud. Stieber, "Vocation of the Indigènes."
16 The only scholarly work to engage these links at length, beyond my own, is Nérée, Duvalier; and Leslie J. R. Péan, Entre savoir et démocratie. Michael Dash has long footnoted the presence of Charles Maurras and Maurice Barrès's thought among Haitian nationalist thinkers of the 1920s and 1930s, most recently in Dash, "True Dechoukaj." David Nicholls has noted Sténio Vincent's affinity for Maurrassisme; see Nicholls, Dessalines.
17 One of the few scholars to have engaged the revue, J. Michael Dash laments the "quality of bathos and pity" produced by Stella writers' structured alexandrines and poetic non-innovation. He expresses relief that these poets' "self-conscious melancholy" and "grandiose clichés" were "discontinued by the younger writers of the Indigenous movement." Dash, Literature and Ideology, 55–57. See also Dominique, Esquisses critiques.
18 See the introduction for my discussion of Bongie's assessment of the problems of Francophone literary criticism and the "hierarchies of aesthetic value" that structure the cosmopolitan republic of letters.
19 "Ce désarroi moral et intellectuel constaté dans la société mondaine et littéraire." Guizot Mompoint, "L'étude de l'histoire," Stella: Organe de la bibliophile, no. 15 (1927).
20 Christian Werleigh, "Méditation: In memoriam," Stella: Organe de la bibliophile, no. 18 (1927).
21 Hippolyte, La route ensoleillée. The quote is taken from Maurras's 1918 poem, La bataille de la Marne: Ode historique. See Dash, Literature and Ideology.
22 "Le poète ignore à dessin les révolutions des verslibristes et des symbolistes—et à plus forte raison les anarchies des dadaïstes et des cubistes." Lector, "La route

ensoleillée," *Stella: Organe de la bibliophile*, no. 18 (1927). *Stella* published a number of Hippolyte's poems, which it celebrated for their rootedness in an ancestral *terre* and reverence of *les morts*. Citing Maurice Barrès, the *Stella* critic proclaims of Hippolyte's work, "Our Lords, the Dead! According to Barrès's fine expression. Mr. Hippolyte is careful not to forget them. He is not ashamed of his origins, like so many others." (*Nos Seigneurs les Morts! Selon la belle expression de Barrès. Mr. Hippolyte se garde bien de les oublier. Il ne rougit pas de son origine, comme tant d'autres.*) Ibid.
23 See chapter 6.
24 "Rendre hommage à ces grands bâtisseurs de Nation dont la mémoire est salie par des historiens bouffis de haine, de préjugés et de bêtise." Louis Mercier, "Nous écrirons l'histoire," *Stella: Organe de la bibliophile*, no. 22 (1928).
25 Werleigh, *Défilée-la-folle*.
26 "Il était mort . . . l'horrible chose s'était faite, / Et les grands chefs, la populace étaient en fête." Ibid, 1.
27 Ibid., 4.
28 "Elle prend seule le chemin du cimetière, / Assurant le destin de la Patrie entière." Ibid., 5.
29 "En entendant le nom de ce héros qu'on hue, / Soudain un clair rayon, dans ses yeux vagues, luit." Ibid, 6.
30 Ibid., 7.
31 We see a similar joining of the feminine and the patriotic in poems on Anacaona and Haiti's pre-Columbian past, with Werleigh's "Anacaona" and Burr-Reynaud's "Eloge funèbre d'Anacaona." On the woman-as-earth metaphor in Latin American literature, see Sommer, *Foundational Fictions*.
32 Werleigh, *Défilée-la-folle*. It was not just men who were pointing out the importance of Haiti's heroines during this period; female feminist activists were organizing and agitating for women's rights. Haiti's first official women's organization, the Ligue féminine d'action sociale, was founded a short time later, in 1934. See Verna, "The Ligue Féminine d'Action Sociale." On women's intellectual and political activism during this period, see Sanders Johnson, "Burial Rites"; and Byrd, "Moral Elevation."
33 "On les verra au travail, on les observera dans leurs frustres amours, on étudiera leurs besoins, on assistera aux injustices journalières dont ils sont l'objet." Campagnard (Jean-Baptiste Cinéas), "Le paysan au travail: Le coumbite," *Stella: Organe de la bibliophile*, no. 16 (1927).
34 For readings of these short stories in *Stella*, see Stieber, "Northern *Récit Paysan*."
35 On the *homme du nord*, see Gérard Laurent, preface to Marc Péan, *Vingt-cinq ans*, t. 1.
36 "Relever aux yeux du peuple haïtien la valeur de son folk-lore"; "ramener l'opinion." Price-Mars, *Ainsi parla*, 7; Campagnard (Cinéas), "Le coumbite."
37 While the southern poet Emile Roumer claimed that no one in Port-au-Prince had any idea who Price-Mars was in the 1920s, northerners considered Price-

Mars to be a respected and trusted fellow northern writer. Christophe Charles, *Dialogue avec Emile Roumer*, 11.

38 "L'écrivain s'est identifié à ses personnages avec une aisance telle, qu'on ne sait plus du tout si c'est un conteur qui a découpé une tranche du réel . . . ou si son œuvre est la transcription d'un de ces longs bavardages auxquels se complaisaient les vieux d'autrefois." Cinéas, *Le drame de la terre*, ii.

39 "Mon savant, très cher et grand Ami . . . l'homme qui m'aime le plus et que j'aime le plus au monde." Cinéas, *La vengeance de la terre*, n.p.

40 Roumain published a first, shorter version of *Gouverneurs* as a *récit* in 1938 in the Parisian weekly *Regards* during his European exile. The post-occupation Vincent government, anticommunist and far-right nationalist, had twice jailed Roumain and outlawed his PCH. For background and commentary on Roumain's short story and novel, as well as a comprehensive list of translations, adaptations, and editions of the novel, see Roumain, *Œuvres complètes*. His short story "La montagne ensorcelée," which appeared in serial in the newspaper *Haïti-Journal* in early 1931, was not based in ethnographic research.

41 Philippe Thoby-Marcelin likely based his adolescent coming-of-age short story (published in serial in *La Revue indigène*) on Valery Larbaud's novel *Fermina Marquez* (1911); see Stieber, "Vocation of the Indigènes."

42 J. Michael Dash links Manuel's machete to "his own mark left on the deflowered body of Annaïse" and the image of the "lame" of water cutting through the earth at the end of the novel. Dash, *Other America*, 78.

43 "La houe et la machette brillaient au soleil, telles de flamboyantes épées"; "les houes longuement emmanchées, couronnées d'éclairs." Cinéas, *Le drame de la terre*, 7; Roumain, *Œuvres complètes*, 271.

44 Cinéas, *Le drame de la terre*, 74. Faustulus, one of the main characters in the Roman myth of Romulus and Remus, was the shepherd who discovered the twin boys and raised them with his wife.

45 Ibid., 151.

46 Dalencour, *Le sauvetage national*. The *Stella* writers engaged in spirited refutations of Dalencour's 1923 essay in the pages of their magazine. Not only was Dalencour highly critical of the North, but his championing of land distribution in the North directly challenged the social structures of large-scale landownership that organized the northern department and the intertwined interdependence of life there.

47 "C'est beau de demander, de prêcher le retour à la terre"; "la confiance de la masse, la reconquête de son âme . . . Mais qui donc étudie sérieusement ce problème? Qui donc l'aborde d'un esprit résolu et lucide? Qui même l'envisage?" Cinéas, *Le drame de la terre*, 167.

48 Deslys and Flosel reappear in the next novel in the cycle, *La vengeance de la terre*, which, though written in a very different style from the previous novel, continues to probe the same themes of agriculture, the earth, the city and the country, social order, and the misery of the peasant.

49 Weber, *Action Française*.

50 See Dard and Grunewald, *Charles Maurras et l'étranger*; Dard, *Doctrinaires, vulgarisateurs et passeurs*; Jennings, *Vichy in the Tropics*; and Bowd, "Maurras and Colonial Madagascar." Indeed, Maurras considered the global adherents to the Action Française movement to be a kind of moral "greater France" (*plus grande France*) as opposed to the Third Republican empire based in language, civilization, and centralization. Charles Maurras, "La plus grande France," *Almanach de L'Action française pour l'année 1935* (Paris, 1935). Among Maurras's personal letters at the Archives nationales in Paris are indeed letters from throughout the Francophone world, including a few letters from a Haitian adherent, Prosper Chrisphonte.

51 "Actuellement sous la poussée irrésistible du nationalisme intégral chassant les émanations pestilentielles du pacifisme et de l'internationalisme cruels et sanguinaires, tous les peuples se forgent des âmes de héros en cultivant l'amour et la vénération des plus grands ... de leurs enfants." Louis Mercier, "L'année jubilaire," *Stella: Organe de la bibliophile*, no. 10 (1927).

52 Contributors bemoaned the ostracism and asphyxiation of Haiti's provinces by those in Port-au-Prince, which created a general sense of decadence and decline evidenced in articles such as Bossuet Mathieu, "La campagne se vide," *Stella: Organe de la bibliophile*, no. 11 (1927).

53 See Sternhell, *Les anti-Lumières*.

54 Stieber, "Gérard de Catalogne." See also Stieber, "'*Camelots du roi ou rouges*.'"

55 Stieber, "Gérard de Catalogne," 242. Other members included Antonio Vieux, André Liautaud, and Maurice Ethéart.

56 Duvalier, *Œuvres essentielles*, t. 2.

57 Contemporary observers refer to him as the "white bear." See Heinl and Heinl, *Written in Blood*; also see Bernard Diederich Collection, file "Haiti, 1949–1970," box 18, Florida International University, https://archives.fiu.edu/repositories/2/archival_objects/62689. See also Gerry L'Etang and Dominique Batraville's new novel *Fillette Lalo*, which depicts a thinly veiled version of Catalogne named Gérard d'Andalousie.

58 Gérard de Catalogne, "L'influence française en Haïti," *L'Action française*, November 17, 1927.

59 Ibid.

60 See Stieber, "Gérard de Catalogne," on his decision to return to Haiti, fleeing a bankrupt literary magazine that he had started in France and generally leaving a trail of frustration and ire behind him.

61 Catalogne would eventually work his way back into the publishing industry, first with *La Lanterne*, which he founded with his cousins in Cap-Haïtien, then as director of *La Phalange*, the Catholic weekly in Port-au-Prince, then back to his own press organs: *Le Soir*, *Le Jour*, and most notably, *Le Nouveau monde*, while also serving as Duvalier's director of tourism.

62 Luc Fouché, "Une revue est nécessaire," *Stella: Organe de la bibliophile*, no. 2 (1926). Given the short-lived nature of so many reviews in this era, the lead

article was of critical importance to the success of the review. Inaugural lead articles resemble manifestos, though they are rarely titled as such, in order to avoid an overtly political stance.

63 "Nous sommes à une période singulière de notre vie nationale: suivant la direction que nous aurons donné à notre esprit, elle sera un prélude de réhabilitation ou un acheminement définitif vers la décadence . . . C'est donc le moment, ou jamais, de nous ressaisir pour former l'âme nationale, j'entends une communauté d'idées, de sentiments, d'aspirations qui fait . . . toutes les énergies qui tendent vers un même but: *la régénération du pays.*" Ibid.

64 "Il a fallu 1915 pour nous aider à comprendre Dessalines, à l'admirer encore d'avantage et l'aimer de toute le ferveur de notre âme." Jean-Baptiste Cinéas, "L'imperator," *Stella: Organe de la bibliophile*, no. 39 (1930).

65 "Aucun historien sensé n'écrira maintenant que le fondateur de la Patrie haïtienne est tombé au Pont-Rouge, victime de sa tyrannie." Louis Mercier, "La vérité qui parle," *Stella: Organe de la bibliophile*, no. 33 (1929).

66 One of his descendants recently published a short work based on his personal papers: Apollon, *Louis Mercier*.

67 "Défenseur farouche de Christophe, campé sur la gloire immarcescible du Monarque comme sur une citadelle inexpugnable pour repousser l'attaque de quelque côté qu'elle vienne." Price-Mars, *Une étape*, 89.

68 Apollon, *Louis Mercier*, 1.

69 "Plus grand des hommes d'action du siècle." Louis Mercier, "Au seuil d'une vie novelle," *Stella: Organe de la bibliophile*, no. 6 (1926). Unlike most black nationalists in the 1930s, some members of *Les Griots* (though certainly not all) continued to express their support for Mussolini even after he invaded Abyssinia in 1935.

70 Mercier, "Au seuil d'une vie nouvelle."

71 See chapter 2.

72 "Ce baron de Vastey que les historiens croient pouvoir flétrir parce qu'il fut un grand fonctionnaire de Christophe." "Comment on défend un pays," *Stella: Organe de la bibliophile*, no. 31 (1929).

73 "Les écrivains du Nord, indignés de voir que la population du Sud-Ouest avait été abusée et entraînée dans des démarches honteuses par leur gouvernement, faisait gémir les presses de leurs productions pour éclairer l'esprit public de cette partie de contraindre Pétion à changer de système." Ibid.

74 That Mercier cites the more centrist Danton and the radical Robespierre is a commentary, perhaps, on the kinds of revolutionary republicanism in tension in Saint-Domingue/Haiti, or a dismissal of all liberal republicanism, no matter where it fell on the spectrum.

75 Mercier, "La vérité qui parle." Mercier appears to be quoting here from some unattributed original.

76 Here, Mercier also echoes Louis Joseph Janvier's Nationalist critiques of the "pseudo-libéraux" and the "antinationaux" in the Liberal Party (see chapter 6).

Stella considered Louis Joseph Janvier to be an "illustrious historian" and occasionally cited his work.
77 See the introduction for a discussion of the "modèle Dessalines."
78 "Les révoltes, les révolutions, les fusillades, l'anarchie, la tyrannie et finalement l'intrusion d'une puissance étrangère dans nos affaires intérieures." Mercier, "Nous écrirons l'histoire." Mercier did not only draw parallels between the French Revolution and Haiti's failures after its own revolution. He also saw connections between France's loss in 1870 and the US occupation of Haiti in 1915: ""The 'Wounded One' that France was in 1870 got back on its feet thanks to the unparalleled devotion of its sons. Haiti, no less unfortunate, expects the same sacrifices from all of you." (*La 'Grande Blessée' que fut la France de 1870 s'est relevée, grâce au dévouement sans pareil de ses fils. Haïti, non moins malheureuse attend de vous tous, les mêmes sacrifices.*) Ibid.
79 "Tous les jeunes gens d'ici sont camelots du roi ou rouges." Morand, *Hiver caraïbe*, 138. The Camelots du Roi were the far-right nationalist youth league of Action Française, Charles Maurras's far-right "nationalisme intégral" movement, who got their start as the paper boys for the movement's press organ, *L'Action française*. See Stieber, "'Camelots du roi ou rouges.'"
80 Marc Péan, *Vingt-cinq ans*, 130.
81 Leslie J. R. Péan, *Entre savoir et démocratie*, 19. On the role of Gérard de Catalogne in the fusing of doctrinal Maurrassian integral nationalism with *Les Griots* nativist ethno-nationalism in François Duvalier's dictatorship, see Stieber, "'Camelots du roi ou rouges.'"

EPILOGUE
1 On the 1950s as a moment of "possibility," see Smith, *Red and Black*; and Smith, "Jamaica Needs Haiti."
2 Gérard de Catalogne, our Maurrassian *passeur*, was at this point serving the Magloire government as the national director of tourism and churning out glossy pamphlets as head of the Haiti Tourist Information Bureau in New York City.
3 On male suffrage, see Smith, *Red and Black*, 151. On women's fight for gender equality in Haiti and especially the work of the feminist organization the Ligue féminine d'action sociale, see N'Zengou-Tayo, "'Fanm Se Poto Mitan'"; and Sanders Johnson, "Burial Rites."
4 See Ligue féminine d'action sociale, *Femmes haïtiennes*. Régine Joseph's forthcoming book project on culture and Duvalierism will shed new feminist light on this period in Haitian history.
5 Georges Marc qtd. in Ernst Trouillot, *Hommage à Luc Grimard*, 37. This 1954 event, or at least the memory of it, likely informed Charles Najman's 2002 film *Royal Bonbon*.
6 Ernst Trouillot, *Hommage à Luc Grimard.*, 57. On his childhood memories of his father (Ernst) and uncle (Hénock) and the Société des amis du roi Henry, see Michel-Rolph Trouillot, *Silencing the Past*.

7 *Le amis du roi Christophe*, AJ/55/163, Archives Nationales, Pierrefitte-sur-Seine, France. It is also referred to in its official documentation as the Association des amis du roi Christophe.
8 See Jonassaint, "Un Christophe ignore des Césairiens"; and Arthéron, *Le théâtre révolutionnaire*. For a reading of Césaire's play from a "Haitian point of view," see Laroche, *L'image comme écho*.
9 *Le amis du roi Christophe*, AJ/55/163, Archives Nationales, Pierrefitte-sur-Seine, France.
10 Michel-Rolph Trouillot, *Silencing the Past*.
11 The parallels between C. L. R. James's and Césaire's 1960s tragic rescriptings of the Haitian Revolution are compelling: both had previously represented Haiti's revolution as a radical example of triumphant black anticolonialism in the interwar period: James, in the first edition of *Black Jacobins: Toussaint L'Ouverture and the San Domingo Revolution* (1938), and Césaire in *Cahier d'un retour au pays natal* (1939), in which Césaire famously proclaimed Haiti the ground upon which "Négritude stood up for the first time."
12 In addition Césaire's *La tragédie du roi Christophe*, see Langston Hughes, *Emperor of Haiti* (1936); Alejo Carpentier, *El reino de este mundo* (1949); and Edouard Glissant, *Monsieur Toussaint* (1961), to name only a few.
13 Walsh, "Césaire Reads Toussaint Louverture." See also Walsh, *Free and French*; Kaisary, *Haitian Revolution*; and Figueroa, *Prophetic Visions*.
14 Byrd, *Black Republic*.
15 Dun, *Dangerous Neighbors*; Clavin, *Toussaint Louverture*; White, *Encountering Revolution*.
16 Farmer, *Uses of Haiti*; Polyné, *Idea of Haiti*.

BIBLIOGRAPHY

ARCHIVAL NEWSPAPERS AND MAGAZINES CONSULTED
L'Abeille haytienne (Port-au-Prince)
L'Avenir (Cap-Haïtien)
L'Avertisseur haytien (Port-au-Prince)
Le Bulletin officiel (Port-au-Prince)
La Concorde (Cap-Haytien)
L'Eclaireur haytien ou Le Parfait patriote (Port-au-Prince)
Feuille du commerce (Port-au-Prince)
Gazette officielle de l'état d'Hayti (Cap-Haïtien)
Gazette politique et commerciale d'Haïti (Cap-Haïtien)
Gazette royale d'Hayti (Cap- Henry)
Les Griots (Port-au-Prince)
L'Information (Cap-Haïtien)
La Lanterne (Cap-Haïtien)
Le Moniteur (Port-au-Prince)
L'Observateur (Les Cayes)
La Phalange (Port-au-Prince)
Le Républicain (Port-au-Prince)
La Revue du Centenaire de l'Indépendance (Les Cayes)
Le Revue indigène (Port-au-Prince)
La Sentinelle d'Haïti (Port-au-Prince)
Stella: Organe de la bibliophile (Cap-Haïtien)
Le Télégraphe (Port-au-Prince)
Le Temps (Port-au-Prince)
L'Union (Les Cayes)
L'Union (Port-au-Prince)

OTHER SOURCES
Acacia, Michel. "Firmin et Janvier, entre convergence et divergence." *Le Nouvelliste* (Port-au-Prince, Haiti), December 28, 2011.
Accilien, Cécile. "Secret History: or, The Horrors of St. Domingo in a Series of Letters . . . (Philadelphia, 1808): Saint-Domingue through the Lens of an American Woman on the Eve of Haitian Independence." *Journal of Haitian Studies* 25, no. 1 (2019): 66–89.

Adam, André-Georges. *Une crise haïtienne, 1867–1869: Sylvain Salnave*. Port-au-Prince: H. Deschamps, 1982.
d'Alaux, Gustave (Maxime Raybaud). *L'empereur Soulouque et son empire*. Paris: Michel Lévy, 1856.
Albanese, Mary Grace. "Uncle Tom across the Sea (and Back): Pierre Faubert and the Haitian Response to Harriet Beecher Stowe." *American Literature* 88, no. 4 (2016): 755–86.
Allan, Michael. *In the Shadow of World Literature: Sites of Reading in Colonial Egypt*. Princeton: Princeton University Press, 2016.
Anglade, Georges. *Atlas critique d'Haïti*. Montreal: ERCE & CRC, 1982.
———. "Les lodyanseurs du soir: Il y a 100 ans, le passage a l'ecrit." In *Ecrire en pays assiégé: Haïti*, ed. Marie-Agnès Sourieau and Kathleen M. Balutansky. Amsterdam: Rodopi, 2004.
Apollon, Marlène Rigaud. *Louis Mercier: A la reconquête de l'idéal haïtien*. Self-published, 2008.
Appiah, Kwame Anthony. "Cosmopolitan Patriots." *Critical Inquiry* 23, no. 3 (1997): 617–39.
Ardouin, Beaubrun. *Etudes sur l'histoire d'Haïti: Suivies de la vie du Général J.-M. Borgella*. T. 1–11. Paris: Dezobry et E. Magdeleine, 1853–1860.
———. *Géographie de l'Ile d'Haïti*. Port-au-Prince, 1832.
Ardouin, Coriolan. *Poésies de Coriolan Ardouin*. Port-au-Prince: R. Ethéart, 1881.
Arias, Santa. "Reconstituting the Archive: The Ancient Indigenous World." In *The Cambridge History of Latin American Women's Literature*, ed. Ileana Rodríguez and Mónica Szurmuk. New York: Cambridge University Press, 2016.
Armitage, David. *Civil War: A History in Ideas*. New Haven: Yale University Press, 2017.
Arthéron, Axel. *Le théâtre révolutionnaire afro-caribéen au XXe siècle*. Paris: Honoré Champion, 2018.
Auguste, Claude B. "Réflexions sur l'histoire mouvementée et combien dramatique du Parti Libéral." *Revue de la Société haïtienne d'histoire, de géographie et de géologie*, no. 237 (2009): 5–37.
Auguste, Jules, Arthur Bowler, Clément Denis, Justin Dévost, and Louis Joseph Janvier. *Les détracteurs de la race noire et de la République d'Haïti: Réponses à Léo Quesnel*. Paris: Marpon et Flammarion, 1882.
Bassi, Ernesto. *An Aqueous Territory: Sailor Geographies and New Granada's Transimperial Greater Caribbean World*. Durham: Duke University Press, 2016.
Beckman, Ericka. *Capital Fictions: The Literature of Latin America's Export Age*. Minneapolis: University of Minnesota Press, 2013.
Bénot, Yves. "Grégoire contre Christophe: Un manuscrit inédit." *Outre-Mers: Revue d'histoire* 87, no. 328 (2000): 143–48.
Bergeaud, Emeric. *Stella*. Ed. Beaubrun Ardouin. Paris: E. Dentu, 1859.
———. *Stella: A Novel of the Haitian Revolution*. Ed. and trans. Christen Mucher and Lesley S. Curtis. New York: New York University Press, 2015.
Berrou, Raphaël, and Pradel Pompilus. *Histoire de la littérature haïtienne*. Port-au-Prince: Editions Caraïbes, 1975.

Bissainthe, Max. *Dictionnaire de bibliographie haitienne*. Washington: Scarecrow Press, 1951.
Blancpain, François. *Un siècle de relations financières entre Haïti et la France (1825–1922)*. Paris: L'Harmattan, 2001.
Brown, Vincent. *Tacky's Revolt: The Story of an Atlantic Slave War*. Cambridge: Belknap, 2020.
Bogues, Anthony. *Black Heretics, Black Prophets: Radical Political Intellectuals*. New York: Routledge, 2003.
———. *Empire of Liberty: Power, Desire, Freedom*. Hanover: Dartmouth College Press, 2010.
Boisrond Tonnerre, Louis Félix. *Mémoires pour servir à l'histoire d'Haïti*. Paris: France Libraire, 1851.
Bongie, Chris. "The Cry of History: Juste Chanlatte and the Unsettling (Presence) of Race in Early Haitian Literature." *MLN* 130, no. 4 (2016): 807–35.
———. *Friends and Enemies: The Scribal Politics of Post/Colonial Literature*. Liverpool: Liverpool University Press, 2008.
———. Introduction to *The Colonial System Unveiled*, by Baron de Vastey. Liverpool: Liverpool University Press, 2014.
———. *Islands and Exiles: The Creole Identities of Post/Colonial Literature*. Stanford: Stanford University Press, 1998.
Bowd, Gavin. "Jean-Joseph Rabearivelo, Charles Maurras and Colonial Madagascar." *Modern and Contemporary France* 24, no. 1 (2016): 1–14.
Boyd, Julian P. "Thomas Jefferson's 'Empire of Liberty.'" *Virginia Quarterly Review* 24, no. 4 (1948): 538–54.
Braziel, J. E. "Re-membering Défilée: Dédée Bazile as Revolutionary *Lieu de Mémoire*." *Small Axe* 9, no. 2 (2005): 57–85.
Brickhouse, Anna. *Transamerican Literary Relations and the Nineteenth-Century Public Sphere*. Cambridge: Cambridge University Press, 2004.
Brière, Jean-François. "L'emprunt de 1825 dans la dette de l'indépendance haïtienne envers la France." *Journal of Haitian Studies* 12, no. 2 (2006): 126–34.
Brooks, Joanna. "The Early American Public Sphere and the Emergence of a Black Print Counterpublic." *William and Mary Quarterly* 62, no. 1 (2005): 67–92.
Brutus, Edner. *Instruction publique en Haïti, 1492–1945*. Port-au-Prince: Editions Panorama, 1948.
Brutus, Timoléon. *L'homme d'airain*. T. 1–2. Port-au-Prince: N. A. Théodore, 1946.
Buck-Morss, Susan. *Hegel, Haiti, and Universal History*. Pittsburgh: University of Pittsburgh Press, 2012.
Butler, Judith. "Critique, Dissent, Disciplinarity." *Critical Inquiry* 35, no. 4 (2009): 773–95.
———. "Restaging the Universal: Hegemony and the Limits of Formalism." In *Contingency, Hegemony, Universality*, by Judith Butler, Ernesto Laclau, and Slavoj Žižek. London: Verso, 2000.
———. "What Is Critique? An Essay on Foucault's Virtue." In *The Political*, ed. David Ingram. Boston: Blackwell, 2002.

Byrd, Brandon R. *The Black Republic: African Americans and the Fate of Haiti*. Philadelphia: University of Pennsylvania Press, 2019.

———. "The Transnational Work of Moral Elevation: African American Women and the Reformation of Haiti, 1874–1950." *Palimpsest: A Journal on Women, Gender, and the Black International* 5, no. 2 (2016): 128–50.

Cammagre, Geneviève. "Ruines et retraite, de Diderot à Volney." *Dix-huitième siècle*, no. 48 (2016): 181–95.

Carrington, André M. "The Cultural Politics of Worldmaking Practice: Kehinde Wiley's Cosmopolitanism." *African and Black Diaspora* 8, no. 2 (2015): 245–57.

Casanova, Pascale. *The World Republic of Letters*. Trans. M. B. Debevoise. Cambridge: Harvard University Press, 2004.

Casimir, Jean. *Une lecture décoloniale de l'histoire des Haïtiens: Du Traité de Ryswick à l'occupation américaine (1697–1915)*. Port-au-Prince: Imp. SA, 2018.

Castera, Justin Emmanuel. *Bref coup d'œil sur les origines de la presse haïtienne, 1764–1850*. Port-au-Prince: H. Deschamps, 1986.

Castilho, Celso Thomas. "The Press and Brazilian Narratives of Uncle Tom's Cabin: Slavery and the Public Sphere in Rio De Janeiro, Ca. 1855." *Americas* 76, no. 1 (2019): 77–106.

Célius, Carlo. "L'imagerie chrétienne dans la création plastique d'Haïti." *Histoire, monde et cultures religieuses* 29, no. 1 (2014): 143–72.

Césaire, Aimé. *Discours sur le colonialisme*. Nanterre, Impr. des Editions Réclame, 1950.

———. *La tragédie du roi Christophe*. Paris: Présence Africaine, 1963.

Chanlatte, F. D. *Almanach républicain pour l'année commune 1818*. Port-au-Prince: Impr. du Gouvernement, 1818.

Chanlatte, Juste (Comte de Rosiers). *A mes concitoyens*. Port-au-Prince: Imprimerie du Gouvernement, 1804.

———. *Le cri de la nature, ou Hommage haytien, Au très-vénérable abbé H. Grégoire, auteur d'un Ouvrage nouveau, intitulé: De la littérature des nègres*. Cap Haïtien: P. Roux, imprimeur de l'Etat, 1810.

———. *Réflexions sur le prétendu Sénat de Port-au-Prince*. Cap Haïtien: Roux, imprimeur de l'Etat, 1807.

Charles, Asselin. "Race and Geopolitics in the Work of Anténor Firmin." *Journal of Pan African Studies* 7, no. 2 (2014): 68–88.

Charles, Christophe. *Dialogue avec Emile Roumer*. Port-au-Prince: Christophe, 1992.

Cheesman, Clive, Marie-Lucie Vendryes, and Michaëlle Jean. *The Armorial of Haiti: Symbols of Nobility in the Reign of Henry Christophe*. College of Arms Manuscript JP 177. London: College of Arms, 2007.

Chemla, Yves. "Louis-Joseph Janvier, écrivain national." *Francofonia*, no. 49 (2005): 7–36.

———. "*Voyage dans le Nord d'Hayti, ou Révélations des lieux et des monuments historiques*, d'Hérard Dumesle (1824), un hypotexte fondateur." *Continents manuscrits*, no. 11 (2018): 1–11.

Childs, Elizabeth. *Daumier and Exoticism: Satirizing the French and the Foreign*. New York: Peter Lang, 2004.

Chrisphonte, Prosper. *Noces d'or de Monsieur L.C. Lhérisson (portrait-essai-critique)*. Port-au-Prince, 1939.
Cinéas, Jean-Baptiste. *Le drame de la terre*. Port-au-Prince: Fardin, 1981.
———. *La vengeance de la terre*. Port-au-Prince: Imp. du Collège Vertières, 1934.
Clavin, Matthew J. *Toussaint Louverture and the American Civil War: The Promise and Peril of a Second Haitian Revolution*. Philadelphia: University of Pennsylvania Press, 2009.
Coates, Carrol F. "Dessalines: History in the Theater." *Journal of Haitian Studies* 2, no. 2 (1996): 167–78.
Cohen, Ashley. *A New History of the Two Indies: British Imperialism and the Reshaping of the World*. New Haven: Yale University Press, forthcoming.
Cohen, Lara Langer, and Jordan Alexander Stein, eds. *Early African American Print Culture*. Philadelphia: University of Pennsylvania Press, 2012.
Coicou, Massillon. *L'empereur Dessalines: Drame en deux actes, en vers*. Port-au-Prince: Chenet, n.d.
———. *Poésies nationales*. Paris: Imprimerie V. Goupy et Jourdan, 1892.
Colombel, Noël. *Examen d'un pamphlet, ayant pour titre: Essai sur les causes de la révolution et des guerres civiles d'Haïti, etc*. Port-au-Prince, 1819.
Crosby-Arnold, Margaret B. "A Case of Hidden Genocide? Disintegration and Destruction of People of Color in Napoleonic Europe, 1799–1815." *Atlantic Studies* 14, no. 3 (2017): 354–81.
Dalencour, François. *Le sauvetage national par le retour à la terre*. Port-au-Prince: Imp. Pierre-Noel, 1923.
Dard, Olivier, ed. *Doctrinaires, vulgarisateurs et passeurs des droites radicales au XXe siècle, Europe-Amériques*. Bern: Peter Lang, 2012.
Dard, Olivier, and Michel Grunewald, eds. *Charles Maurras et l'étranger: L'étranger et Charles Maurras: L'action française, culture, politique, société* 2. Bern: Peter Lang, 2009.
Darnton, Robert. *Edition et sédition: L'univers de la littérature clandestine au XVIIIe siècle*. Paris: Gallimard, 1991.
Dash, J. Michael. *Literature and Ideology in Haiti: 1915–1961*. Basingstoke, Hampshire: Macmillan, 1981.
———. "Nineteenth-Century Haiti and the Archipelago of the Americas: Anténor Firmin's Letters from St. Thomas." *Research in African Literature* 35, no. 2 (2004): 44–53.
———. *The Other America: Caribbean Literature in a New World Context*. Charlottesville: University Press of Virginia, 1998.
———. "True *Dechoukaj*: Uprooting *Bovarysme* in Post-Duvalier Haiti." In *Politics and Power in Haiti*, ed. Kate Quinn and Paul Sutton. New York: Palgrave Macmillan, 2013.
Daut, Marlene. *Baron de Vastey and the Origins of Black Atlantic Humanism*. New York: Palgrave Macmillan, 2017.
———. "Caribbean 'Race Men': Louis Joseph Janvier, Demesvar Delorme, and the Haitian Atlantic." *L'Esprit créateur* 56, no. 1 (2016): 9–23.

———. "Daring to Be Free/Dying to Be Free: Toward a Dialogic Haitian-U.S. Studies." *American Quarterly* 63, no. 2 (2011): 375–89.

———. *La Gazette royale d'Hayti* (blog). https://lagazetteroyale.com/.

———. "Monstrous Testimony: Baron de Vastey and the Politics of Black Memory." In *The Colonial System Unveiled*, by Baron de Vastey, ed. and trans. Chris Bongie. Liverpool: Liverpool University Press, 2014.

———. "'Nothing in Nature Is Mute': Reading Revolutionary Romanticism in *L'Haïtiade* and Hérard Dumesle's *Voyage dans le Nord d'Hayti* (1824)." *New Literary History*, no. 49 (2018): 493–520.

———. *Tropics of Haiti: Race and the Literary History of the Haitian Revolution in the Atlantic World, 1789–1865*. Liverpool: Liverpool University Press, 2015.

Dayan, Colin (Joan). *Haiti, History, and the Gods*. Berkeley: University of California Press, 1995.

Delorme, Demesvar. *La reconnaissance du général Salnave, par M. Delorme*. Paris: A. Chaix, 1868.

———. "Le séisme de 1842 au Cap-Haïtien, raconté par un témoin oculaire: Demesvar Delorme." *Revue de la Société haïtienne d'histoire, de géographie et de géologie* 46, no. 160 (1988): 43–52.

Deren, Maya. *Divine Horsemen: Voodoo Gods of Haiti*. London: Thames and Hudson, 1953.

Desch-Obi, Thomas J. "'Koup Tet': A Machete Wielding View of the Haitian Revolution." In *Activating the Past: History and Memory in the Black Atlantic World*, ed. Andrew Apter and Lauren Derby. Newcastle: Cambridge Scholars Publishing, 2010.

Desquiron, Jean. "Ecrire l'histoire est difficile: Cinq récits différents de la geste de l'Amiral Killick." *Revue de la Société haïtienne d'histoire, de géographie et de géologie* 45, no. 154 (1987): 69–80.

———. *Haïti à la une: Une anthologie de la presse haïtienne de 1724 à 1934*. Port-au-Prince: 1993–1997.

Dominique, Max. *Esquisses critiques*. Port-au-Prince: Editions du CIDIHCA, 1999.

Donnadieu, Jean-Louis. *Un grand seigneur et ses esclaves: Le comte de Noé entre Antilles et Gascogne, 1728–1816*. Toulouse: Presses Universitaires du Mirail, 2009.

Douglas, Rachel. *Making "The Black Jacobins": C. L. R. James and the Drama of History*. Durham: Duke University Press, 2019.

Drake, St. Clair. "Anthropology and the Black Experience." *Black Scholar* 11, no. 7 (1980): 2–31.

Draper, James David. "Thirty Famous People: Drawings by Sergent-Marceau and Bosio, Milan, 1815–1818." *Metropolitan Museum Journal* 13 (1978): 113–30.

Dubois, Laurent. *Avengers of the New World: The Story of the Haitian Revolution*. Cambridge: Harvard University Press, 2009.

———. *Haiti: The Aftershocks of History*. New York: Metropolitan Books, 2012.

———. "Republican Anti-Racism and Racism: A Caribbean Genealogy." In *Race in France: Interdisciplinary Perspectives on the Politics of Difference*, ed. Laura Frader and Herrick Chapman. New York: Berghahn, 2004.

Dubois, Laurent, Julia Gaffield, and Michel Acacia. *Documents constitutionnels d'Haïti, 1790–1860*. New York: De Gruyter, 2013.
Dubois, Laurent, and John D. Garrigus. *Slave Revolution in the Caribbean, 1789–1804*. New York: St. Martin's, 2006.
Dubroca, Louis. *Vida de J. J. Dessalines, gefe de los negros de Santo Domingo*. Ed. Juan Lopez Cancelada, trans. D.M.G.C. Mexico, 1806.
Dumesle, Hérard. *Voyage dans le Nord d'Hayti, ou Révélations des lieux et des monuments historiques*. Les Cayes: Impr. du gouvernement, 1824.
Dun, James Alexander. *Dangerous Neighbors: Making the Haitian Revolution in Early America*. Philadelphia: University of Pennsylvania Press, 2016.
Dupuy, Alex. "From François Duvalier to Jean-Bertrand Aristide: The Declining Significance of Color Politics in Haiti." In *Politics and Power in Haiti*, ed. Kate Quinn and Paul Sutton. New York: Palgrave Macmillan, 2013.
Duvalier, François. *Œuvres essentielles*. T. 1–4. Port-au-Prince: Presses nationales d'Haiti, 1966–1967.
Eller, Anne. "'All Would Be Equal in the Effort': Santo Domingo's 'Italian Revolution,' Independence, and Haiti, 1809–1822." *Journal of Early American History* 1, no. 2 (2011): 105–41.
———. "Let's Show the World We Are Brothers: The Dominican *Guerra de Restauración* and the Nineteenth-Century Caribbean." PhD dissertation, New York University, 2011.
———. *We Dream Together: Dominican Independence, Haiti, and the Fight for Caribbean Freedom*. Durham: Duke University Press, 2016.
Esterquest, Ralph T. "L'imprimerie royale d'Hayti (1817–1819)." *Bibliographical Society of America* 34 (1940): 171–84.
L'Etang, Gerry, and Dominique Batraville. *Fillette Lalo*. Paris: HC Editions, 2018.
Etienne, Eddy V. "La diplomatie agissante de Faustin Soulouque (Mars 1847–Janv. 1859)." *Revue de la Société haïtienne d'histoire, de géographie et de géologie* 42, no. 145 (1984): 79–93.
Fanon, Frantz. *Peau noire, masques blancs*. Paris: Editions Points, (1952) 2015.
Farmer, Paul. *The Uses of Haiti*. Monroe, ME: Common Courage, 1994.
Fatton, Robert. "The Haitian Authoritarian 'Habitus' and the Contradictory Legacy of 1804." *Journal of Haitian Studies* 10, no. 1 (2004): 22–43.
Faubert, Pierre. *Ogé, ou Le préjugé de couleur: Drame historique*. Paris: C. Maillet-Schmitz, 1856.
Ferrer, Ada. *Freedom's Mirror: Cuba and Haiti in the Age of Revolution*. New York: Cambridge University Press, 2014.
———. "Haiti, Free Soil, and Antislavery in the Revolutionary Atlantic." *American Historical Review* 117, no. 1 (2012): 40–66.
Fetterley, Judith, and Marjorie Pryse. *Writing out of Place: Regionalism, Women, and American Literary Culture*. Urbana: University of Illinois Press, 2003.
Figueroa, Víctor. *Prophetic Visions of the Past: Pan-Caribbean Representations of the Haitian Revolution*. Columbus: Ohio State University Press, 2015.

Firmin, Anténor. *De l'égalité des races humaines (anthropologie positive)*. Paris: F. Pichon, 1885.
———. *The Equality of the Human Races*. Trans. Asselin Charles. Chicago: University of Illinois Press, 2002.
Fischer, Sibylle. "Bolívar in Haiti: Republicanism in the Revolutionary Atlantic." In *Haiti and the Americas*, ed. C. Calargé, R. Dalleo, L. Duno-Gottberg, and C. Headley. Jackson: University of Mississippi Press, 2013.
———. *Modernity Disavowed: Haiti and the Cultures of Slavery in the Age of Revolution*. Durham: Duke University Press, 2004.
Fleischmann, Ulrich. *Ecrivain et société en Haïti*. Chicoutimi: J.-M. Tremblay, 2015.
Fluehr-Lobban, Carolyn. "Anténor Firmin and Haiti's Contribution to Anthropology." *Gradhiva*, no. 1 (2005): 95–108.
Forsdick, Charles. "Haiti and France: Settling the Debts of the Past." In *Politics and Power in Haiti*, ed. Kate Quinn and Paul Sutton. New York: Palgrave Macmillan, 2013.
Foucault, Michel. "What Is Critique?" Trans. Lysa Hochroth. In *The Political*, ed. David Ingram. Boston: Blackwell, 2002.
Fouchard, Jean. *La méringue, danse nationale d'Haïti*. Montréal: Leméac, 1973.
———. *Le théâtre à Saint-Domingue*. Port-au-Prince: H. Deschamps, 1988.
Frader, Laura, and Herrick Chapman, eds. *Race in France: Interdisciplinary Perspectives on the Politics of Difference*. New York: Berghahn, 2004.
Fraginals, Manuel Moreno, Frank Moya Pons, and Stanley L. Engerman, Eds. *Between Slavery and Free Labor: The Spanish-Speaking Caribbean in the Nineteenth Century*. Baltimore: Johns Hopkins University Press, 1985.
Fraser, Nancy. "Rethinking the Public Sphere: A Contribution to the Critique of Actually Existing Democracy." *Social Text*, no. 25/26 (1990): 56–80.
Furet, François, and Mona Ozouf, eds. *A Critical Dictionary of the French Revolution*. Cambridge: Belknap, 1989.
Gaffield, Julia. *Haiti and the Atlantic World* (blog). https://haitidoi.com/.
———. *Haitian Connections in the Atlantic World: Recognition after Revolution*. Chapel Hill: University of North Carolina Press, 2015.
———, ed. *The Haitian Declaration of Independence: Creation, Context, and Legacy*. Charlottesville: University of Virginia Press, 2016.
Gaillard, Roger. *Les blancs débarquent*. T. 1–7. Port-au-Prince: Impr. Le Natal, 1973–1983.
———. *La république exterminatrice*. T. 1–6. Port-au-Prince: Impr. Le Natal, 1984–1998.
Gaillard, Roger, Gusti-Klara Gaillard-Pourchet, and Ducis Viard. *Le cacoïsme bourgeois contre Salnave, 1867–1870: Inclus le récit commenté de Ducis Viard: La dernière étape*. Port-au-Prince: Fondation Roger Gaillard, 2003.
Garraway, Doris L. "Abolition, Sentiment, and the Problem of Agency." In *The Colonial System Unveiled*, by Baron de Vastey, ed. Chris Bongie. Liverpool: Liverpool University Press, 2014.
———. "Empire of Freedom, Kingdom of Civilization: Henry Christophe, the Baron de Vastey, and the Paradoxes of Universalism in Postrevolutionary Haiti." *Small Axe* 16, no. 3 (2012): 1–21.

———. "'Légitime Défense': Universalism and Nationalism in the Discourse of the Haitian Revolution." In *Tree of Liberty: Cultural Legacies of the Haitian Revolution in the Atlantic World*, ed. Doris L. Garraway. Charlottesville: University of Virginia Press, 2008.

———. "Print, Publics, and the Scene of Universal Equality in the Kingdom of Henry Christophe." *L'Esprit créateur* 56, no. 1 (2016): 82–100.

Garrigus, John D. *Before Haiti: Race and Citizenship in French Saint-Domingue*. New York: Palgrave Macmillan, 2006.

———. "'Victims of Our Own Credulity and Indulgence': The Life of Louis Félix Boisrond-Tonnerre." In *The Haitian Declaration of Independence: Creation, Context, and Legacy*, ed. Julia Gaffield. Charlottesville: University of Virginia Press, 2016.

Geggus, David Patrick. "The Haitian Revolution in Atlantic Perspective." In *The Oxford Handbook of the Atlantic World: 1450–1850*, ed. Nicholas Canny and Philip Morgan. Oxford: Oxford University Press, 2011.

———, ed. and trans. *The Haitian Revolution: A Documentary History*. Indianapolis: Hackett, 2014.

———. *Haitian Revolutionary Studies*. Bloomington: Indiana University Press, 2002.

———. "Haiti's Declaration of Independence." In *The Haitian Declaration of Independence: Creation, Context, and Legacy*, ed. Julia Gaffield. Charlottesville: University of Virginia Press, 2016.

———. "The Naming of Haiti." *NWIG: New West Indian Guide / Nieuwe West-Indische Gids* 71, nos. 1–2 (1997): 43–68.

———. "Rights, Resistance and Emancipation: A Response to Robin Blackburn." In *Self-Evident Truths? Human Rights and the Enlightenment*, ed. Kate E. Tunstall. New York: Bloomsbury Academic, 2012.

Geggus, David Patrick, and Norman Fiering, eds. *The World of the Haitian Revolution*. Bloomington: Indiana University Press, 2009.

Ghachem, Malick. "Law, Atlantic Revolutionary Exceptionalism, and the Haitian Declaration of Independence." In *The Haitian Declaration of Independence: Creation, Context, and Legacy*, ed. Julia Gaffield. Charlottesville: University of Virginia Press, 2016.

Gilroy, Paul. *Between Camps: Race, Identity and Nationalism at the End of the Colour Line*. London: Allen Lane, 2000.

———. *The Black Atlantic: Modernity and Double Consciousness*. London: Verso, 2007.

———. "Black Fascism." *Transition*, nos. 81–82 (2000): 70–91.

Girard, Philippe R. "Birth of a Nation: The Creation of the Haitian Flag and Haiti's French Revolutionary Heritage." *Journal of Haitian Studies* 15, nos. 1–2 (2009): 135–50.

———. "Jean-Jacques Dessalines and the Atlantic System: A Reappraisal." *William and Mary Quarterly* 69, no. 3 (2012): 549–82.

———. "Making Freedom Work: The Long Transition from Slavery to Freedom during the Haitian Revolution." *Slavery & Abolition* 40, no. 1 (2019): 87–108.

Glissant, Edouard. *Poétique de la relation*. Paris: Gallimard, 1990.

Gonzalez, Johnhenry. *Maroon Nation: A History of Revolutionary Haiti*. New Haven: Yale University Press, 2019.

Grégoire, Henri (Abbé). *De la littérature des nègres, ou Recherches sur leurs facultés intellectuelles, leurs qualités morales et leur littérature*. Paris: Chez Maradan, 1808.

Griggs, Leslie Earl, and Clifford H. Prator, eds. *Henry Christophe, Thomas Clarkson: A Correspondence*. New York: Greenwood, 1968.

Habermas, Jürgen. *The Structural Transformation of the Public Sphere: An Inquiry into a Category of Bourgeois Society*. Trans. Thomas Burger. Cambridge: MIT Press, 1989.

Hall, Alin Louis. *La péninsule républicaine*. Port-au-Prince: C3 Editions, 2014.

Hector, Michel. "Une autre voie de construction de l'état-nation: L'expérience christophienne (1806–1820)." In *Genèse de l'Etat haïtienne*, ed. Michel Hector and Laënnec Hurbon. Paris: Editions de la Maison des sciences de l'homme, 2009.

Hector, Michel, and Guerdy Lissade. "Echos et nouvelles: Sur les traces de Goman." *Revue de la Société haïtienne d'histoire, de géographie et de géologie*, nos. 257–58 (2015): 180–81.

Heinl, Robert Debs, and Nancy Gordon Heinl. *Written in Blood: The Story of the Haitian People, 1492–1971*. Boston: Houghton Mifflin, 1978.

Helg, Aline. "Simón Bolívar's Republic: A Bulwark against the 'Tyranny' of the Majority." *Revista de Sociologia e Política* 20, no. 42 (2012): 21–37.

Hill, Logan. "Hot Artist: Kehinde Wiley." *Rolling Stone*, no. 10011 (2006): 112.

Hill, Robert A. "C. L. R. James: The Myth of Western Civilization." In *Enterprise of the Indies*, ed. George Lamming. Port-of-Spain: Trinidad and Tobago Institute of the West Indies, 1999.

Hippolyte, Dominique. *La route ensoleillée*. Paris: Editions de la Pensée latine, 1927.

Hodgson, Kate. "Haiti's *Fête Nationale*: A Revolutionary Site of Memory." In *Remembering Early Modern Revolutions*, ed. Edward Vallance. London: Routledge, 2018.

———. "'Internal Harmony, Peace to the Outside World': Imagining Community in Nineteenth-Century Haiti." *Paragraph* 37, no. 2 (2014): 178–92.

Hoffmann, Léon-François, and Carl Hermann Middelanis. *Faustin Soulouque d'Haïti: Dans l'histoire et la littérature*. Paris: L'Harmattan, 2007.

Hugo, Victor. *Les châtiments*. Paris: Lévy, 1875.

Huzzey, Richard. *Freedom Burning: Anti-Slavery and Empire in Victorian Britain*. Ithaca: Cornell University Press, 2012.

Hyppolite, Michelson P. *Les origines des variations du créole haïtien*. Port-au-Prince: Imprimerie de l'Etat, 1949.

James, C. L. R. *The Black Jacobins: Toussaint L'Ouverture and the San Domingo Revolution*. New York: Vintage, (1963) 1989.

James, Erica Moiah. "Decolonizing Time: Nineteenth-Century Haitian Portraiture and the Critique of Anachronism in Caribbean Art." *NKA: Journal of Contemporary African Art*, no. 44 (2019): 8–23.

Janvier, Louis Joseph. *Les affaires d'Haïti*. Paris: C. Marpon et E. Flammarion, 1885.

———. *Les antinationaux: Actes et principes*. Paris: Imprimerie G. Rougier et Cie, 1884.

———, ed. *Les constitutions d'Haïti (1801–1885)*. Paris: C. Marpon et E. Flammarion, 1886.
———, ed. *Les détracteurs de la race noire et de la république d'Haïti*. Paris: C. Marpon et E. Flammarion, 1882.
———. *L'égalité des races*. Paris: Imprimerie G. Rougier et Cie, 1884.
———. *Haïti aux Haïtiens*. Paris: Imprimerie A. Davy, 1884.
———. *La République d'Haïti et ses visiteurs (1840–1882): Réponse à M. Victor Cochinat de la Petite presse et à quelques autres écrivains*. Paris: C. Marpon et E. Flammarion, 1883.
———. "Le vieux piquet: Scène de la vie haïtienne." Paris: Imprimerie A. Davy, 1884.
Jean-Baptiste, St. Victor. *Le fondateur devant l'histoire*. Port-au-Prince: Imprimerie Eben-Ezer, 1954.
Jean-Jacques, Stephen. *Les cendres du passé*. Port-au-Prince: Les Presses Libres, 1953.
Jenkins, Brian, ed. *France in the Era of Fascism: Essays on the French Authoritarian Right*. Oxford: Berghahn, 2007.
Jennings, Eric. *Vichy in the Tropics: Pétain's National Revolution in Madagascar, Guadeloupe, and Indochina, 1940–1944*. Stanford: Stanford University Press, 2002.
Jenson, Deborah. *Beyond the Slave Narrative: Politics, Sex, and Manuscripts in the Haitian Revolution*. Liverpool: Liverpool University Press, 2011.
———. "Jean-Jacques Dessalines and the African Character of the Haitian Revolution." *William and Mary Quarterly* 69, no. 3 (2012): 615–38.
———. "Toussaint Louverture, Spin Doctor?" In *Tree of Liberty: Cultural Legacies of the Haitian Revolution in the Atlantic World*, ed. Doris L. Garraway. Charlottesville: University of Virginia Press, 2008.
Jérémie, Joseph. *Haïti indépendante*. Port-au-Prince: Chéraquit, 1929.
Johnson, Grace Sanders. "Burial Rites, Women's Rights: Death and Feminism in Haiti, 1925–1938." *Caribbean Review of Gender Studies*, no. 12 (2018): 121–42.
Johnson, Sara E. *The Fear of French Negroes: Transcolonial Collaboration in the Revolutionary Americas*. Berkeley: University of California Press, 2012.
Jolibois, Gérard. *L'exécution des Frères Coicou*. Port-au-Prince: Le Natal, 1986.
Joly, Laurent. *Naissance de l'Action française: Maurice Barrès, Charles Maurras et l'extrême droite nationaliste au tournant du XXe siècle*. Paris: Grasset, 2015.
Jonassaint, Jean. "Césaire et Haïti, des apports à évaluer." *Francophonies d'Amérique*, no. 36 (2013): 135–65.
———. "Un Christophe ignore des Césairiens." *Il Tolomeo* 19 (2017): 133–63.
———. "Des conflits langagiers dans quelques romans haïtiens." *Etudes françaises* 28, nos. 2–3 (1992): 39–48.
Joseph, Délide. *L'état haïtien et ses intellectuels: Socio-histoire d'un engagement politique (1801–1860)*. Port-au-Prince: Editions Le Natal, 2017.
———. "Genèse d' 'une idée avantageuse d'Haïti': Socio-histoire de l'engagement des intellectuels haïtiens, 1801–1860." PhD dissertation, Ecole des hautes études en sciences sociales, 2014.
Kadish, Doris Y., Deborah Jenson, and Norman R. Shapiro, eds. *Poetry of Haitian Independence*. New Haven: Yale University Press, 2015.

Kaisary, Philip. *The Haitian Revolution in the Literary Imagination: Radical Horizons, Conservative Constraints*. Charlottesville: University of Virginia Press, 2014.

Kaussen, Valerie. *Migrant Revolutions: Haitian Literature, Globalization, and US Imperialism*. Lanham, MD: Lexington Books, 2008.

Kazanjian, David. *The Brink of Freedom: Improvising Life in the Nineteenth-Century Atlantic World*. Durham: Duke University Press, 2016.

LaPorta, Kathrina. *Performative Polemic: Anti-Absolutist Pamphlets and Their Readers in Late Seventeenth-Century France (1667–1715)*. Newark: University of Delaware Press, forthcoming.

Largey, Michael. *Vodou Nation: Haitian Art, Music, and Cultural Nationalism*. Chicago: University of Chicago Press, 2006.

Laroche, Maximilien. *L'image comme écho*. Montréal: Editions Nouvelle Optique, 1978.

———. "La tragédie du roi Christophe du point de vue de l'histoire d'Haïti." *Etudes littéraires* 6, no. 1 (1973): 35–47.

Lasso, Marixa. *Myths of Harmony: Race and Republicanism during the Age of Revolution: Colombia, 1795–1831*. Pittsburgh: University of Pittsburgh Press, 2007.

Leconte, Vergniaud. *Henri Christophe dans l'histoire d'Haiti*. Paris: Berger-Levrault, 1931.

Lerebours, Michel Philippe. *Haïti et ses peintres de 1804 à 1980: Souffrances et espoirs d'un peuple*. T. 1–2. Port-au-Prince: Bibliothèque nationale d'Haïti, 1989.

Lescouflair, Arthur. *Thomas Madiou: Homme d'état et historien haïtien*. Port-au-Prince: Instituto panamericano de geografía e historia, 1950.

Lhérisson, L. C. *Pour Dessalines: 17 octobre 1806, 17 octobre 1906*. Port-au-Prince: A. Héraux, 1906.

Lhérisson, Lélia J. *Manuel de littérature haïtienne*. Port-au-Prince: Département de l'Education Nationale, 1955.

Ligue féminine d'action sociale. *Femmes haïtiennes*. Port-au-Prince: H. Deschamps, 1953.

Lionnet, Françoise, and Shu-Mei Shih, eds. *Minor Transnationalism*. Durham: Duke University Press, 2005.

Lutz, Tom. *Cosmopolitan Vistas: American Regionalism and Literary Value*. Ithaca: Cornell University Press, 2004.

Lyon-Caen, Judith, and Dinah Ribard. *L'historien et la littérature*. Paris: La Découverte, 2010.

MacLeod, Murdo J. "The Soulouque Regime in Haiti, 1847–1859: A Reevaluation." *Caribbean Studies* 10, no. 3 (1970): 35–48.

Madiou, Thomas. *Autobiographie*. Port-au-Prince: H. Deschamps, 2017.

———. *Histoire d'Haïti*. T. 1–3. Port-au-Prince: J. Courtois, 1848–1849.

———. *Histoire d'Haïti*. T. 1–8. Port-au-Prince: H. Deschamps, 1989–1991.

Malouet, Pierre Victor. *Collection de mémoires sur les colonies, et particulièrement sur Saint-Domingue*. T. 2. Paris: Baudouin, 1802.

Manigat, Leslie F. "Le délicat problème de la critique historique." *Revue de la Société haïtienne d'histoire, de géographie et de géologie* 25–26, nos. 95–96 (1954–1955): 19–60.

Marcelin, Milo. *Mythologie vodou (rite arada)*. Port-au-Prince: Editions haïtiennes, 1949.
Martin, Henri-Jean, and Roger Chartier. *Histoire de l'édition française*. T. 3. Paris: Promodis, 1985.
Martin, Jean-Clément. *Contre-révolution, révolution et nation en France (1789–1799)*. Paris: Seuil, 1998.
Mbembe, Achille. *Critique of Black Reason*. Trans. Laurent Dubois. Durham: Duke University Press, 2017.
McGill, Meredith L. *American Literature and the Culture of Reprinting, 1834–1854*. Philadelphia: University of Pennsylvania Press, 2003.
McIntosh, Tabitha, and Grégory Pierrot. "Capturing the Likeness of Henry I of Haiti (1805–1822)." *Atlantic Studies* 14, no. 2 (2017): 127–51.
———. *Néhri, chef des Haytiens: Tragédie en 3 actes et en vers par son Excellence M. le Comte de Rosiers* (blog). https://kingdomofobjects.wordpress.com/.
McPherson, Alan. *The Invaded: How Latin Americans and Their Allies Fought and Ended US Occupations*. New York: Oxford University Press, 2014.
Ménard, Nadève. "The Myth of the Monolingual Haitian Reader: Linguistic Rights and Choices in the Haitian Literary Context." *Small Axe* 45 (2014): 52–63.
Mentor, Gaétan. *Dessalines: L'esclave devenu empereur*. Pétionville: Self-published, 2003.
———. *Les fils noirs de la veuve: Histoire de la franc-maçonnerie en Haïti*. Pétionville: Self-published, 2003.
———. *Histoire d'un crime politique: Le géneral Etienne Victor Mentor*. Port-au-Prince: Editions Le Natal, 1999.
Métral, Antoine. "De la littérature haïtienne." *Revue encyclopédique*. T. 1 (1819), 524–37.
Middelanis, Carl Hermann. "Les mémoires fleurissent dans les lieux ruinés: *Le voyage dans le Nord d'Hayti*, ou Les paradoxes de l'historiographie d'une jeune nation." *Ethnologies* 28, no. 1 (2006): 99–118.
Mignolo, Walter. *Local Histories/Global Designs: Coloniality, Subaltern Knowledges, and Border Thinking*. Princeton: Princeton University Press, 2000.
Miller, Paul B. *Elusive Origins: The Enlightenment in the Modern Caribbean Historical Imagination*. Charlottesville: University of Virginia Press, 2010.
Milscent, Jules S. *Ode sur l'avènement de Napoléon au trône; Suivie d'Une épitre à un jeune militaire*. Paris: Imp. des frères C., 1805.
Moïse, Claude. *Constitutions et luttes de pouvoir en Haïti (1804–1987)*. Vols. 1–2. Montréal, Québec: Editions du CIDIHCA, 1997.
———. *Le projet national de Toussaint Louverture et la constitution de 1801*. Montréal, Québec: Editions du CIDIHCA, 2001.
Mongey, Vanessa. "Going Home: The Back-to-Haiti Movement in the Early Nineteenth Century." *Atlantic Studies*, 2018, 1–19.
———. *Rogue Revolutionaries: The Fight for Legitimacy in the Greater Caribbean*. Philadelphia: University of Pennsylvania Press, forthcoming.
———. "A Tale of Two Brothers: Haiti's Other Revolutions." *Americas* 69, no. 1 (2012): 37–60.

Morand, Paul. *Hiver caraïbe*. Paris: Flammarion, 1929.
Nau, Emile. *Histoire des caciques d'Haïti*. Port-au-Prince: T. Bouchereau, 1855.
Negt, Oskar, and Alexander Kluge. *Public Sphere and Experience: Toward an Analysis of the Bourgeois and Proletarian Public Sphere*. New York: Verso, 2016.
Nérée, Bob. *Duvalier: Le pouvoir sur les autres, de père en fils*. Port-au-Prince: H. Deschamps, 1988.
Nesbitt, Nick. "The Idea of 1804." *Yale French Studies*, no. 107 (2005): 6–38.
———. *Universal Emancipation: The Haitian Revolution and the Radical Enlightenment*. Charlottesville: University of Virginia Press, 2008.
Nicholls, David. *From Dessalines to Duvalier: Race, Colour and National Independence in Haiti*. New Brunswick: Rutgers University Press, 1996.
———. *Haiti in Caribbean Context: Ethnicity, Economy and Revolt*. New York: St. Martin's, 1985.
———. "Race, couleur et indépendance en Haïti (1804–1825)." *Revue d'histoire moderne et contemporaine* 25, no. 2 (1978): 177–212.
Nicolas, Aldrich. "Anténor Firmin, le libéralisme et la pensée sociale en Haïti." In *Genèse de l'etat haïtien (1804–1859)*, ed. Michel Hector and Laënnec Hurbon. Paris: Maison des sciences de l'homme, 2009.
Noriel, Gérard. "French and Foreigners." In *Realms of Memory: The Construction of the French Past*, vol. 1, ed. Pierre Nora, trans. Arthur Goldhammer. New York: Columbia University Press, 1996.
Nyquist, Mary. *Arbitrary Rule: Slavery, Tyranny and the Power of Life and Death*. Chicago: University of Chicago Press, 2013.
N'Zengou-Tayo, Marie-José. "'Fanm Se Poto Mitan': Haitian Woman, the Pillar of Society." *Feminist Review* 59, no. 1 (1998): 118–42.
O'Neil-Henry, Anne. *Mastering the Marketplace: Popular Literature in Nineteenth-Century France*. Lincoln: University of Nebraska Press, 2017.
Oriol, Jacques, Léonce Viaud, and Michel Aubourg. *Le mouvement folklorique en Haïti*. Port-au-Prince: Imprimerie de l'Etat, 1952.
Le palais national de la République de Haïti. Port-au-Prince: H. Deschamps, 2003.
Pascal-Trouillot, Ertha, and Ernst Trouillot. *Encyclopédie biographique d'Haïti*. Montréal: Editions SEMIS, 2001.
Paul, Edmond. *Œuvres posthumes*. Paris: Vve C. Dunod et P. Vicq, 1896.
Payton, Claire. "The City and the State: Construction and the Politics of Dictatorship in Haiti (1957–1986)." PhD dissertation, Duke University, 2018.
Péan, Leslie J. R. *Entre savoir et démocratie: Les luttes de l'Union nationale des étudiants haïtiens (UNEH) sous le gouvernement de François Duvalier*. Montréal: Mémoire d'encrier, 2010.
Péan, Marc. *Vingt-cinq ans de vie capoise (1890–1915)*. T. 1–3. Port-au-Prince: H. Deschamps, 1977–1993.
Perry, Amanda T. "Becoming Indigenous in Haiti, from Dessalines to *La Revue Indigène*." *Small Axe: A Caribbean Journal of Criticism* 21, no. 2 (53) (2017): 45–61.

Pierrot, Grégory. *The Black Avenger in Atlantic Culture*. Athens: University of Georgia Press, 2019.

———. "Juste Chanlatte: A Haitian Life." *Journal of Haitian Studies* 25, no. 1 (2019): 39–65.

Plummer, Brenda Gayle. *Haiti and the United States: The Psychological Moment*. Athens: University of Georgia Press, 1992.

Polyné, Millery, ed. *The Idea of Haiti: Rethinking Crisis and Development*. Minneapolis: University of Minnesota Press, 2013.

Popkin, Jeremy. "A Colonial Media Revolution: The Press in Saint-Domingue, 1789–1793." *Americas* 75, no. 1 (2018): 3–25.

———. *Facing Racial Revolution: Eyewitness Accounts of the Haitian Insurrection*. Chicago: University of Chicago Press, 2008.

Portebois, Yannick, and Dorothy E. Speirs. *Entre le livre et le journal*. T. 1. Lyon: ENS Editions, 2013.

Pressoir, Catts, Hénock Trouillot, and Ernst Trouillot. *Historiographie d'Haïti*. Mexico: Pan American Institute of Geography and History, 1953.

Preston, Claire. *Bee*. London: Reaktion Books, 2006.

Prévost, Julien (Comte de Limonade). *Copie de la lettre du Secrétaire d'Etat, Ministre des Affaires étrangères, Datée du Palais Royal de Sans-Souci, le 10 février 1815, l'an douze de l'indépendance, A S.E. Monsieur le Général de Division Pétion, etc. etc. ect.* [sic]. Cap-Henry: P. Roux, 1815.

———. *Le machiavélisme du cabinet français*. Cap-Henry: Impr. P. Roux, 1814.

———. *Relation des glorieux événemens qui ont porté leurs majestés royales sur le trône d'Hayti; Suivie de L'histoire du couronnement et du sacre du roi Henry Ier, et de la reine Marie-Louise*. Cap-Henry: P. Roux, imprimeur du Roi, 1811.

Prézeau, Sylvain (Chevalier de Prézeau). *Réfutation de la lettre du général française Dauxion Lavaysse*. Cap-Henry: P. Roux, 1814

Price-Mars, Jean. *Ainsi parla l'oncle, suivi de Revisiter l'oncle*. Montréal: Mémoire d'encrier, 2009.

———. *Une étape de l'évolution haïtienne*. Port-au-Prince: Imprimerie La Presse, 1929.

———. *Jean-Pierre Boyer Bazelais et le drame de Miragoâne: A propos d'un lot d'autographes, 1883–1884*. Port-au-Prince: Imprimerie de l'Etat, 1948.

———. *Joseph Anténor Firmin*. Port-au-Prince: Imprimerie Séminaire adventiste, 1964.

———. "Le sentiment de la valeur personnelle chez Henry Christophe en fonction de son rôle de chef: Psychologie d'un homme d'état." *Revue de la Société d'histoire et de géographie d'Haïti* 5, no. 13 (1934): 19–39.

Procès verbal des séances du Conseil général de la Nation. Cap-Henry: Imp. de P. Roux, 1814.

Puri, Shalini, ed. *Marginal Migrations: The Circulation of Cultures within the Caribbean*. Oxford: Macmillan Caribbean, 2003.

Putnam, Lara. *Radical Moves: Caribbean Migrants and the Politics of Race in the Jazz Age*. Chapel Hill: University of North Carolina Press, 2013.

Rainford, Marcus. *An Historical Account of the Black Empire of Hayti*. Ed. Paul Youngquist and Grégory Pierrot. Durham: Duke University Press, 2013.
Ramírez, Dixa. *Colonial Phantoms: Belonging and Refusal in the Dominican Americas, from the 19th Century to the Present*. New York: New York University Press, 2018.
Ramsey, Kate. *The Spirits and the Law: Vodou and Power in Haiti*. Chicago: University of Chicago Press, 2011.
Reinsel, Amy. "Poetry of Revolution: Romanticism and National Projects in Nineteenth-Century Haiti." PhD dissertation, University of Pittsburgh, 2008.
René, Jean Alix. *Haïti après l'esclavage: Formation de l'état et culture politique populaire (1804–1846)*. Port-au-Prince: Editions Le Natal, 2019.
Rigaud, André. *Mémoire du général de brigade André Rigaud en réfutation des écrits calomnieux contre les citoyens de couleur de Saint-Domingue*. Les Cayes: Imprimerie Leméry, 1797.
Robinson, Cedric. *Black Marxism: Making of the Black Radical Tradition*. Chapel Hill: University of North Carolina Press, 2015, 1983.
Roumain, Jacques. *Œuvres complètes*. Ed. Léon-François Hoffmann. Paris: Allca XX, 2003.
Royaume d'Hayti. *L'olivier de la paix*. Cap-Henry: P. Roux, 1815.
Sainte-Claire, Linsey. "Régénération et élitisme scolaire sous Alexandre Pétion et Jean-Pierre Boyer (1816–1843)." *L'Esprit créateur* 56, no. 1 (2016): 116–28.
Saint-Rémy, Joseph. Preface to *Mémoires du général Toussaint-L'Ouverture écrits par lui-même*. Paris: Pagnerre, 1853.
———. Preface to *Mémoires pour servir à l'histoire d'Haïti*, by Louis Boisrond Tonnerre. Paris: France Libraire, 1851.
Salt, Karen. "Migrating Images of the Black Body Politic and the Sovereign State: Haiti in the 1850s." In *Migrating the Black Body: The African Diaspora and Visual Culture*, ed. Heike Raphael-Hernandez and Leigh Raiford. Seattle: University of Washington Press, 2017.
Sansay, Leonora. *Secret History; or, The Horrors of St. Domingo and Laura*. Ed. Michael J. Drexler. Ontario, Canada: Broadview, 2007.
Scott, David. *Conscripts of Modernity: The Tragedy of Colonial Enlightenment*. Durham: Duke University Press, 2004.
Seigel, Micol. "Beyond Compare: Comparative Method after the Transnational Turn." *Radical History Review*, no. 91 (2005): 62–90.
Sepinwall, Alyssa Goldstein. *The Abbé Grégoire and the French Revolution: The Making of Modern Universalism*. Berkeley: University of California Press, 2005.
———. "Grégoire et Haïti: Un héritage compliqué." *Outre-Mers: Revue d'histoire* 87, no. 328 (2000): 107–28.
Serie di vite e ritratti de famosi personaggi, degli ultimi tempi. Milano: Ed. Batelli e Fanfani, 1815–1818.
Sheller, Mimi. *Democracy after Slavery: Black Publics and Peasant Rebels in Haiti and Jamaica*. Gainesville: University Press of Florida, 2000.
Sieburth, Richard. "Une idéologie du lisible: Le phénomène des physiologies." *Romantisme* 47 (1985): 39–60.

Smith, Matthew. "Jamaica Needs Haiti: Island Exchanges and Cultural Relations in the 1950s." *Caribbean Quarterly* 62, no. 1 (2016): 13–38.

———. *Liberty, Fraternity, Exile: Haiti and Jamaica after Emancipation*. Chapel Hill: University of North Carolina Press, 2014.

———. *Red and Black in Haiti: Radicalism, Conflict, and Political Change, 1934–1957*. Chapel Hill: University of North Carolina Press, 2009.

Sommer, Doris. *Foundational Fictions: The National Romances of Latin America*. Berkeley: University of California Press, 1991.

Stepto, Robert. *From Behind the Veil: A Study of Afro-American Narrative*. Urbana: University of Illinois Press, 1979.

Sternhell, Zeev. *Les anti-Lumières*. Paris: Gallimard, 2006.

———. *Ni droite ni gauche: L'idéologie fasciste en France*. Paris: Gallimard, 2012.

Stieber, Chelsea. "Beyond Mentions: New Approaches to Comparative Studies of Haiti." *Early American Literature* 53, no. 3 (2018): 961–75.

———. "'Camelots du roi ou rouges': Radicalism in Early Twentieth-Century Haitian Periodicals." *Contemporary French Civilization* 45, no. 1 (2020): 47–69.

———. "Gérard de Catalogne, passeur transatlantique du maurrassisme entre Haïti et la France." In *Doctrinaires, vulgarisateurs et passeurs des droites radicales au XXe siècle (Europe-Amériques)*, ed. Olivier Dard. Bern: Peter Lang, 2012.

———. "The Haitian Literary Magazine in Francophone Postcolonial Literary and Cultural Production." In *Beyond Tradition: French Cultural Studies (1800–2014)*, ed. Anne O'Neil-Henry, Kathryn Kleppinger, and Masha Belenky. Newark: University of Delaware Press, 2017.

———. "The Myths of the Haitian Republic." In *Remembering Early-Modern Revolutions*, ed. Edward Vallance. London: Routledge, 2018.

———. "The Northern *Récit Paysan*: Regional Variations of the Modern Peasant Novel in Haiti." *French Studies* 70, no. 1 (2016): 44–60.

———. "The Vocation of the Indigènes: Cosmopolitanism and Cultural Nationalism in *La Revue Indigène*." *Francosphères* 4, no. 1 (2015): 7–19.

Stovall, Tyler. "The Myth of the Liberatory Republic and the Political Culture of Freedom in Imperial France." *Yale French Studies*, no. 111 (2007): 89–103.

———. *Transnational France: The Modern History of a Universal Nation*. Boulder: Westview, 2015.

Tardieu, Patrick. "The Debate Surrounding the Printing of the Haitian Declaration of Independence: A Review of the Literature." In *The Haitian Declaration of Independence: Creation, Context, and Legacy*, ed. Julia Gaffield. Charlottesville: University of Virginia Press, 2016.

———. "Pierre Roux et Leméry, imprimeurs de Saint-Domingue à Haïti." *Revue de la Société haïtienne d'histoire, de géographie et de géologie*, no. 218 (2004): 1–30.

Thompson, Mark Christian. *Black Fascisms: African American Literature and Culture between the Wars*. Charlottesville: University of Virginia Press, 2007.

Thomson, Guy. *The European Revolutions of 1848 and the Americas*. London: Institute of Latin American Studies, 2002.

Thornton, John K. "'I Am the Subject of the King of Congo': African Political Ideology and the Haitian Revolution." *Journal of World History* 4, no. 2 (1993): 181–214.

Toussaint Louverture, François-Dominique. *Mémoires du général Toussaint-L'Ouverture écrits par lui-même*. Paris: Pagnerre, 1853.

Trouillot, Ernst, ed. *Hommage à Luc Grimard*. Port-au-Prince: Imp. de l'Etat, 1955.

Trouillot, Hénock. *Beaubrun Ardouin: L'homme politique et l'historien*. México: Instituto panamericano de geografía e historia, 1950.

———. *Dessalines, ou Le sang du Pont-Rouge*. Port-au-Prince: Impr. des Antilles, 1967.

———. *Dessalines, ou La tragédie post-coloniale*. Port-au-Prince: Panorama, 1966.

———. "Le gouvernement du roi Henri Christophe." *Revue de la Société haïtienne d'histoire, de géographie et de géologie* 35, no. 117 (1972): 1–170.

———. *Les origines sociales de la littérature haïtienne*. Port-au-Prince: Imprimerie N. A. Théodore, 1962.

Trouillot, Michel-Rolph. *Haiti: State against Nation*. New York: Monthly Review Press, 1990.

———. *Les racines historiques de l'état duvaliérien*. Port-au-Prince: H. Deschamps, 1986.

———. *Silencing the Past: Power and the Production of History*. Boston: Beacon, 1995.

Tucker, Robert W., and David Hendrickson. *Empire of Liberty: The Statecraft of Thomas Jefferson*. Oxford: Oxford University Press, 1990.

Turnier, Alain. *Avec Mérisier Jeannis: Une tranche de vie jacmélienne et nationale*. Port-au-Prince: Imp. Le Natal, 1982.

Valdman, Albert. "Haitian Creole at the Dawn of Independence." *Yale French Studies* 107 (2005): 146–61.

Vastey, Jean Louis (Baron de). *A mes concitoyens: Haytiens, qu'il ne soit qu'un parti parmi nous, celui du bien public et du salut de tous*. Cap-Henry: P. Roux, imprimeur du Roi, 1815.

———. *The Colonial System Unveiled*. Ed. and trans. Chris Bongie. Liverpool: Liverpool University Press, 2014.

———. *Le cri de la conscience, ou Réponse a un écrit, imprimé au Port-au-Prince, intitulé: Le peuple de la République d'Hayti, á Messieurs Vastey et Limonade*. Cap-Henry: P. Roux, imprimeur du Roi, 1815.

———. *Le cri de la patrie*. Cap-Henry: P. Roux, 1815.

———. *Essai sur les causes de la révolution et des guerres civiles d'Hayti*. Sans-Souci: Impr. royale, 1819.

———. *Notes à M. le baron V. P. Malouet, ministre de la marine et des colonies, de Sa Majesté Louis XVIII, et ancien administrateur des colonies de la marine, ex-colon de Saint-Domingue, etc., en réfutation du 4e volume de son ouvrage, intitulé: Collection de mémoires sur les colonies, et particulièrement sur Saint-Domingue, etc*. Cap-Henry: P. Roux, imprimeur du Roi, 1814.

———. *Réflexions politiques sur quelques ouvrages et journaux française concernant Hayti*. Sans-Souci: Imprimerie royale, 1817.

———. *Le système colonial dévoilé*. Cap-Henry: P. Roux, imprimeur du Roi, 1814.

———. *Le système colonial dévoilé*. Ed. and trans. Michel Hector and Jean Casimir. Port-au-Prince: Société haïtienne d'histoire, de géographie et de géologie, 2013.
Verna, Chantalle F., and Paulette Poujol Oriol. "The Ligue Feminine D'Action Sociale: An Interview with Paulette Poujol Oriol." *Journal of Haitian Studies* 17, no. 1 (2011): 246–57.
Verna, Paul. *Bolívar y los emigrados patriotas en el Caribe*. Caracas: INCE, 1983.
———. *Petión y Bolívar: Una etapa decisiva en la emancipación de Hispanoamérica (1790–1830)*. Caracas, Venezuela: Ediciones de la Presidencia de la República, 1980.
Vilaire, Etzer. *Le flibustier*. Port-au-Prince: F. Smith, 1902.
Walker, Andrew. "All Spirits Are Roused: The 1822 Antislavery Revolution in Haitian Santo Domingo." *Slavery and Abolition*, 40, no. 3 (2019): 583–605.
Walsh, John Patrick. "Césaire Reads Toussaint Louverture: The Haitian Revolution and the Problem of Departmentalization." *Small Axe* 15, no. 1 (2011): 110–24.
———. *Free and French in the Caribbean: Toussaint Louverture, Aimé Césaire, and Narratives of Loyal Opposition*. Bloomington: Indiana University Press, 2013
Weber, Eugen. *Action Française: Royalism and Reaction in Twentieth-Century France*. Stanford: Stanford University Press, 1962.
Wellek, René, and Austin Warren. *Theory of Literature*. New York: Harcourt, Brace, 1949.
Werleigh, Christian. *Défilée-la-folle*. Port-au-Prince: Cheraquit, 1927.
Wesner, Emmanuel. "Le courant libéral en Haïti au XIXe siècle." *Revue de la Société haïtienne d'histoire, de géographie et de géologie* 39, no. 131 (1981): 18–29.
White, Ashli. *Encountering Revolution: Haiti and the Making of the Early Republic*. Baltimore: Johns Hopkins University Press, 2010.
Wieviorka, Michel, ed. *Une société fragmentée? Le multiculturalisme en débat*. Paris: La Découverte, 1996.
Wilder, Gary. *The French Imperial Nation State: Negritude and Colonial Humanism between the Two World Wars*. Chicago: University of Chicago Press, 2005.
Williams, Raymond. *The Country and the City*. New York: Oxford University Press, 1973.
———. *Keywords: A Vocabulary of Culture and Society*. New York: Oxford University Press, 1985.
———. *Marxism and Literature*. Oxford: Oxford University Press, 2009.
Wong, Edlie. "In the Shadow of Haiti: The Negro Seamen Act, Counter-Revolutionary St. Domingue, and Black Emigration." In *The Haitian Revolution and the Early United States: Histories, Textualities, Geographies*, ed. Elizabeth Maddock Dillon and Michael J. Drexler. Philadelphia: University of Pennsylvania Press, 2016.
Zavitz, Erin. "Revolutionary Commemorations: Jean-Jacques Dessalines and Haitian Independence Day, 1804–1904." In *The Haitian Declaration of Independence: Creation, Context, and Legacy*, ed. Julia Gaffield. Charlottesville: University of Virginia Press, 2016.
———. "Revolutionary Narrations: Early Haitian Historiography and the Challenge of Writing Counter-History." *Atlantic Studies* 14, no. 3 (2017): 336–53.
Zerelli, Linda. *A Democratic Theory of Judgment*. Chicago: University of Chicago Press, 2016.

INDEX

L'Abeille haytienne (newspaper), 92–93, 98, 99, *100*, 102, 105, 134
Acaau, Jean-Jacques, 156, 157, 202, 212, 214
Acacia, Michel, 316n67
Acte de l'indépendance (1804), 6, 21, 30, 34, 40, 199
Action Française, 244–47, 252–53, 323n50, 325n79
L'Action française (newspaper), 246–47, 323n50, 325n79
Adélina (Empress), 166, *169*, 170
Age of Revolution, 1, 16, 80, 290n16
agricultural laborers (*cultivateurs*), 57, 132, 201, 212–13, 216, 315n43
Aigron, Lamothe, 62
Ainé, Brisson, 167
Ainsi parla l'oncle (Price-Mars), 240, 243
d'Alaux, Gustave. *See* Raybaud, Maxime
Albanese, Mary Grace, 168
Album impérial d'Haïti, *176*, 177–80
L'Ambigu (newspaper), 70, 284n31
American Revolutionary War, 286n49
Amerindian history, 141, 194, 196, 300n57
Anacaona, 141
"Anacaona" (Werleigh), 235, 321n31
Anglade, Georges, 213, 271n61
anticolonial: empire, 31–32; gesture (1804), 3, 14, 22; vengeance, 29–30, 33, 37, 182, 187–88, 195, 199
anticolonial critique, 37. *See also* Dessalinean critique
anticolonialism, 5, 23, 26–27; commitment to, 39; promotion of, 34–35; sacrifice for, 50–51; securing radical, 41; vengeance and, 29, 182, 184, 187–88, 195, 199; violence and, 13, 33, 184, 188, 192, 194
anticolonial rhetoric, 123. *See also* Dessalinean rhetoric
anticolonial violence, 43–44, 47, 184, 192, 194. *See also* Dessalinean violence
anticolonial writing, 25, 27, 77, 80, 111, 179. *See also* Dessalinean writing
Les antinationaux (Janvier), 207
antislavery empire, 1, 9, 32
Appiah, Kwame Anthony, 232
"Après le sacrilege" (Durand), 235
Ardouin, Beaubrun, 17, 130, 154, 181, 225, 300n41; Bergeaud and, 308n58, 309n58; on Dessalines, 144–45; with Manifesto of May 3, 1844, 157; with myth of universal Haitian republic, 135–38, 164
Ardouin, Céligny, 140, 158, 181
Ardouin, Coriolan, 140, 142–45, 225, 301n70, 309n59
Armée Indigène: Borgella and, 286n42; Dessalines and, 1, 23, 25, 33, 162, 221, 266n5, 272n12; in historical context, 195; "Liberté ou la mort" and, 191; natural law and, 44; rallying cry of, 40; secretarial corps of, 25
Armitage, David, 16
artistic production, 163, 165, 166–67
assassinations: of Boisrond Tonnerre, 56; of Cappoix, 57; of Dessalines, 2, 22, 49, 51–52, 59, 60, 62, 65, 96, 224–25, 279n96; war of Independence and, 266n5

Association des amis du roi Christophe, 256, 326n7
Auguste, Claude, 205–6
authority: adaptation, reiteration and displacement of, 79, 270n44; Christophe claiming, 58–59; colonial, 27; Dessalines usurping, 50; legitimacy, subjectivity and, 15, 270n45; mystique of, 12
authorship, 15, 295n91, 309n58; as autonomous, 107; of Boisrond Tonnerre, 275n47; literature and, 11, 26, 84
Autobiographie (Madiou), 303n109
L'Avertisseur haytien (newspaper), 134

bad books (*mauvais livres*), 15, 107
barbarism, 164, 201, 306n9
Barlatier, Louis, 62
Barrès, Maurice, 232, 320n16
La bataille de la Marne (Maurras), 234–35
Battle of Sibert, 58
Baussan, Georges, 227
Bazelais, Louis Laurent, 24, 46, 49, 313n18
Bazile, Dédée (Défilée-la-folle), 235; with Dessalines and dismembered body, 224–25, 318n91; as national conscience, symbol of, 237, 318n92; as national hero, 238–39, 248
Bergeaud, Emeric, 181, 184, 195; allegory and, 188, 308n57; Ardouin, Beaubrun, and, 308n58, 309n58; with Haitian Revolution and Stella, 188–94
Bernadotte, Ulysse, 163
Beugnot, Jacques Claude, 288n75
Les Bibliophiles group, 231, 249
Billaud-Varenne, Jean-Nicolas, 94
Black Atlantic thought, 3
black despotism, 159
Black Heretics, Black Prophets (Bogues), 267n12
Black Jacobins (James), 326n11
"black magic," 258
blackness, 8–9, 132

black radical critique, 31
black radical thought, 6, 7–8, 258, 267n11
black republic, 2, 59, 258
Blain, Elida, 271n59
Blanchet, Bruno, 23, 62
Bobo, Rosalvo, 226, 230
Bogues, Anthony, 6–7, 8, 31, 267n12, 267n17, 268n23
Boisrond-Canal, Pierre Théoma, 205
Boisrond Tonnerre, Louis Félix Mathurin, 84, 104, 114, 273n24, 277n60; assassination of, 56; authorship of, 275n47; counseil privé and, 24; Dessalines and, 22, 41, 48, 49, 54–55, 151, 181, 188, 273n19, 275n47; Saint-Rémy and, 187–88; in secretarial corps, 25, 34, 46; speech read by, 46–48; violence and, 197
Bolívar, Simón, 91, 129, 218, 290n17; asylum request from, 95; Píar and, 135; slavery abolishment and, 97; with two-tiered citizenship, 96
Bonaparte, Louis Napoléon (Napoléon III): criticism of, 169–70, 172; empire and, 158; rule of, 166, 170, 177, 178, 180; Second Empire of, 169, 182, 309n60
Bonaparte, Napoléon (Napoléon I), 41–42, 52, 175, 177; coronation of, 94, 172; criticism of, 171, 172, 173, 180; Ice-T, Wiley and, 307n38; imprisonment of, 199; power abdicated by, 73; return of, 288n75; symbolism and, 68–69
Bongie, Chris, 11, 51, 80, 92, 265n3, 269n33, 270n44, 278n72, 287n60, 294n69, 320n18
Bonnet, Guy Joseph, 23, 35, 58, 280n105
Borgella, Jérôme Maximilien, 74, 136, 214, 286n42, 301n59
Bosio, 172
Bourbon Restoration, 73, 91, 95, 182
bourgeois public sphere, 10–16, 92
Boyer, Jean-Pierre, 93, 102, 128, 170, 270n58, 291n23; Christophists and, 154;

civilization and, 164; *concorde* of, 131–39, 152, 181; despotism and, 139, 153; fall of, 181; fears of, 115; invasion of the East and "unification" of island Haiti and, 128–30; land reform and, 215; legacy of, 156; power of, 129–30; reunification and, 113; scribal complicity and, 121

Boyer Bazelais, Jean-Pierre, 205

Brelle, Corneille, 24, 43, 55, 65, 281n126, 285n34

Brissot, Jacques Pierre, 80

Brooks, Joanna, 269n38

Brutus, Edner, 305n2, 305n4

Brutus, Timoléon, 317n84

Le Bulletin officiel, Gazette du Port-au-Prince, 68, 69, 70, 284n23, 285n34

Buon, 66, 283n22

Burr-Reynaud, Frédéric, 235, 321n31

Buteau, Pierre, 267n10

Butler, Judith, 15, 266n8, 270n44

Cabral, José María, 203

caco rebels, 203, 230

Cahier d'un retour au pays natal (Césaire), 257, 326n11

Campos Tavares (Thabares), José, 65, 296n1

Caonabo, 141

Cappoix, François, 24, 54, 57

La Caricaturiste (newspaper), *169*, 169–70, 306n20

Carpentier, Alejo, 256

Carrington, André, 180

Casanova, Pascale, 12

Casimir, Jean, 270n58

Catalogne, Gérard de, 246–47, 252, 325n2

Catholicism, 201, 283n19, 310n73, 311n1

celebrations: centennial, 220, 221, 225, 237; Christophe's state with national, 65; historical events and, 167; national republican, 65

Célius, Carlo, 177–78

centennial celebrations, 220, 221, 225, 237

ceremonies: coronation, 94, 161, 170, 172, 175, 176, 177, 179, 307n30, 307n31; funeral, 167, 183, 281n126

Césaire, Aimé, 244, 256–58, 287n59, 326n11

Cham, 306n18

Chancy, Jean-Joseph, 207

Chanlatte, F. D., 284n26

Chanlatte, Juste, 22, 25–26, 250, 276n49, 276n50, 287n51; constitution read by, 46; as General, 114; Haiti returned to by, 94; influence of, 273n16; literary criticism for, 121–22; loyalty of, 54–57; Madiou on, 284n31; northern print culture dominated by, 73; operas and, 122, 287n51, 301n61; pamphlet from, 41, 43–47, 60–61; parricide and, 223–24; Pétion described by, 62–63; right of revolution and, 278n75; song by, 34–40; as wordsmith, 60; writing and, 282n2, 283n5; written portraits by, 61–62

Charéron, Jean-Jacques, 24–25, 34, 275n47

de Chateaubriand, François-René, 116

chattel slavery, 4, 7, 30, 38, 74, 104, 184

Chavannes, Jean-Baptiste, 185

Chemla, Yves, 315n47

Le choc en retour (Cinéas), 241

Chrisphonte, Prosper, 323n50

Christianity, 158, 198, 305n6

Christophe, Henry, 21, 33, 132, *171*, 172, 173, 280n97; attempts to retake South by, 71–73, 85–87; authority claimed by, 58–59; Catholicism and, 283n19; demands made to, 83; despotism of, 117, 119–20, 138; Dessalines's assassination and, 57; fall of, 93; General Council of, 76–77; labeled obscene, 115; legacy of, 256–57; Madiou on proclamation by, 58; monarchy of, 49; print culture under, 70–71, 89; with reign as aberration, 120; suicide of, 114–15; unity emphasized by, 85

Christophean sphere, 14, 64
Christophean writing: as creative, 118; critiques of, 93; disavowing heritage of, 126; discursive strategies of, 86; heritage of, 120; against liberalism, 113; opposition to, 90; political role of, 100–101; refutation of, 79; as reliant on previous practices, 84; significance of, 80; as sincere, 89; traditional, 122; Vastey and, 73
Christophists, 135, 139, 146, 157–58, 299n31; Boyer and, 154; Geffrard and, 201; indemnity agreement and, 133
Cinéas, Jean-Baptiste, 231, 239–44, 248, 256, 322n48
citadins (city dwellers), 132, 212, 214, 242
citizenship, 160, 164, 181, 208; residency and, 299n37; two-tiered system of, 96, 131
civility, 47, 132, 164, 194
civilization, 3, 18, 119, 182; Christianity and, 305n6; dominant norms in, 8; executions and, 201; freedom and, 19; nonviolent notion of, 165, 183–87; progress of, 164–65; vengeance and, 138, 183–87; Western, problem of, 194–200; Western notion of, 169, 170, 178, 180, 186
civil war, 1, 4; arguments deployed during, 119; in historical context, 201–3; myth of republicanism and, 16–19; with Nationals and Liberals, 204–11
Clarkson, Thomas, 76
Clerveaux, Augustin, 21
Code Rural (1826), 132–33, 207–8, 212, 270n58, 302n84
Cohen, Ashley, 281n117
Coicou, Massillon, 224–26, 235, 237, 279n95, 318n88; *L'empereur Dessalines* and, 221; execution of, 318n95; Firminisme and, 219; parricide and, 223; Petit Théâtre and, 317n82; *Poésies nationales* and, 222

Coicou, Victor, 317n84, 318n95
collective labor (*konbit*), 239, 241–42, 294n75
Colombel, Noël, 94, 98, 102, 112–13
colonialism, 1–2, 4, 27, 73–74; anticolonial gesture and, 3, 14, 22; decolonial thought and, 3; Dessalinean critique of, 87; language and, 209; postcolonial refutation and, 78–84; racism and, 5. *See also* anticolonialism
color-blind republicanism, 6, 133, 135, 178, 208
color prejudice, 185, 208–9
Columbus, Christopher, 194, 198, 199
Comité du Centenaire des Cayes, 317n78
Compagnie de Toucan, 256
concorde: of Boyer or myth of universal Haitian Republic, 131–39, 152, 181; Nau, Emile, and, 153, 162; paintings and, 297n12; territorial, 130; threats to, 164
La Concorde (newspaper), 115
Conscripts of Modernity (Scott), 265n1
Constituent Assembly, 58, 65, 98
Constitutional Army, 203
Le Constitutionnel (newspaper), 105
Les constitutions d'Haïti (Janvier), 165, 210, 315n39
contrafacta, 276n52
Corday, Charlotte, 172–73
Coronación de Juan Santiago Desalines primer emperador de Hayti (López López), *174*
coronation ceremonies: *Le Moniteur* and, 307n30, 307n31; Napoléon I and, 94, 172; Soulouque and, 161, 170, 175, *176*, 177, 179
"cosmopolitan patriotism," 232
counseil privé, 24
couplets, 71; in poetry, 235, 290n11; sung, 43, 277n71
Courtois, Joseph, 94–95, 98, 133
Courtois, Sévère, 94–95
creole (*créole*), 128, 141, 214, 297n5

Creole (*Créole*), 110
"La Crête-à-Pierrot" (Werleigh), 235
Critique of Black Reason (Mbembe), 267n8
Cuba, 242, 258, 319n8
cultivateurs (agricultural laborers), 57, 132, 201, 212–13, 216, 315n43
cultural production, 70, 167, 169, 211, 233, 269n33
culture: nonviolent notion of, 165; occupation-era cultural nationalism and, 230–39, 250; politics, identity and, 18; visual, 17, 165–67, 177, 181. See also print culture

daguerreotype, 177, 178, 179
Dalencour, François, 243, 322n46
Darfour, Félix, 133–34, 135
Dartiguenave, Jean-Baptiste, 58
Dash, J. Michael, 320n16, 320n17, 322n42
Daumier, Honoré, 306n18
Daut, Marlene, 5, 84, 88, 159, 184–85, 187, 298n13
Daut, Toussaint, 55, 65, 78–79
Davis, Angela, 298n23
Davy de la Pailleterie, Thomas-Alexandre, 168
Dayan, Colin, 17, 163, 175, 177, 270n53, 301n75, 318n91, 318n92
deceptive, dishonest (*pipeuse*), 27–28, 273n23
Declaration of Independence: Haitian, 14, 21, 151, 221, 272n3, 273n23, 274n38, 275n39, 275n41, 275n47, 297n4, 310n79; US, 34, 275n47
decolonial thought, 3
deconstruction, 27, 84, 268n22, 273n21
"Défilée" (Burr-Reynaud), 235, 318n92
Défilée-la-folle. See Bazile, Dédée
dehumanization, 5, 10, 21, 28–29, 200
Déjoie, Thimoléon, 297n12
De la littérature des Nègres (Grégoire), 288n63

De l'égalité des races humaines (Firmin), 218
Delille, Jacques, 116
Delorme, Demesvar, 202, 203, 218, 312n9, 313n18
Derrida, Jacques, 7, 15
Description topographique, physique, civile, politique et historique (Saint-Méry), 136
Desmoulins, Horace Camille, 94
despotism, 122–23, 129, 146, 280n97, 290n11; black, 159; Boyer and, 139, 153; of Christophe, 117, 119–20, 138; legalizing, 24; oriental, 271n1, 281n117; Quillenbois and, 173, 175; Toussaint Louverture and, 137
Desrivières Chanlatte, François, 68, 273n16
Dessalinean counter-revolution (*Venger l'empereur ou mourir*), 54–59
Dessalinean critique, 180, 253–54, 274n26; of colonialism, 87; defined, 266n8; silencing of, 259; of Western episteme, 4–10, 38
Dessalinean imagery, 37
Dessalineanism, 22–23, 24, 33, 50–51, 53, 65; battle between republicanism and, 49; resistance to, 48
Dessalinean rhetoric, 22–23, 26, 29, 31, 35, 40, 43, 44, 71, 77, 123, 133, 178
Dessalineans, 3, 5, 24, 32–33, 41; conspiracy against, 45–46; loyalty of, 54–57; Madiou on, 272n8
Dessalinean sphere, 92, 178, 181, 199, 210; in historical context, 28; influence of, 79, 84; Janvier and, 211; practices of, 13; refusal of, 118
Dessalinean thought, 6–8, 31, 254, 259, 267n17, 268n23
Dessalinean vengeance, 29–30, 32–33, 37, 142–43, 151, 182–88, 191–92, 194–97, 199, 275n47, 276n49, 308n47, 308n58
Dessalinean violence, 184, 187, 195, 309n58

Dessalinean writing, 25–32, 82; continuity in method of, 77; disavowing heritage of, 126; politics, poems and, 71; as reliant on previous practices, 84

Dessalines, Jean-Jacques, 5, 128, 132, 257, 273n15; address by, 32; with anticolonial violence, 43–44, 47, 184, 192, 194; Armée Indigène and, 1, 23, 25, 33, 162, 221, 266n5, 272n12; assassination of, 2, 22, 49, 51–52, 59, 60, 62, 65, 96, 224–25, 279n96; authority usurped by, 50; Boisrond Tonnerre and, 22, 41, 48, 49, 54–55, 151, 181, 188, 273n19, 275n47; commemorations, 170, 183; conspiracy against, 50; criticism of, 173; delegitimizing, 53; disavowal of, 63–64, 181–88; fall of, 237; as hero of Haitian Revolution, 61; independence declared by, 21; Jefferson and, 272n12, 274n35; as leader, 24; legacy of, 142–53, 220–21, 224; letter from, 277n65; loyalty to, 54–57; Madiou on, 41–43, 142–43, 190, 277n64; myth of, 267n10; nomination of, 41–42; post-independence role of, 26; power of, 52; as proclaimed emperor, 43; speech by, 46–48, 183–84; on threat of republicanism, 34; trade and, 272n12; transformation of original oath by, 54–55; US language denouncing, 281n117; vengeance and, 29–30, 32–33, 37, 142–43, 151, 182–88, 191–92, 194–97, 199, 275n47, 276n49, 308n47, 308n58; with warning to republicans, 39

"Dessalines, Christophe" (Burr-Reynaud), 235

Dessources, Cadet, 231

Diaquoi Aîné, Jean J. Dominique, 24–25, 46, 54–55

Diderot, Denis, 116

Diop, Alioune, 256

discourse: abolitionist, 187; analysis, 84; Christophean, 89, 210; Dessalinean, 26, 29, 222; integral nationalist, 229; performativity/power and, 27, 89, 266n8; pro-colonial, 13, 27–29, 79–84, 88, 108, 178; pro-slavery, 15; republican, 38, 53, 100, 106, 178

Discours sur le colonialisme (Césaire), 287n59

"Dix-huit cent quatre" (Werleigh), 235

documentation: dissemination en masse of, via printing press, 77–78; practices of, 76–77

dodecasyllabic verse, 234

Domingue, Michel, 203, 205

Dominican Republic, 130, 156, 160, 242, 296n1, 297n11, 304n119, 304n120, 319n8; Dominican border, 203; as "the East," 45–46, 72, 74, 103, 126, 128–33, 136–37, 139, 141, 154, 156–58, 160–61, 278n81, 291n23, 297n4, 297n5, 298n17, 301n59, 304n120; el Estado independiente de la parte española de Haití, 129; independence, 103, 155–56, 160–61; occupation ("unification") with Island Haiti, 128–30; rebels, 74–75; República Dominicana, 156. *See also* The East; Island Haiti; Stupid Spain (España Boba)

Douglas, Rachel, 265n1

Le drame de la terre (Cinéas), 240, 241, 242–44

Dridier, 171, 172, 173

drumming, 166

Du Bellay, Joachim, 116

Dubois, Laurent, 283n16

Dubois, Normil, 203

Dubroca, Louis, 173

Dumas, Alexandre, 168

Dumesle, Hérard, 102–6, 136, 155, 285n36, 292n47; literary criticism of Vastey by, 122–26; literary pantheon and, 105, 111, 120–23; in *L'Observateur*, 295n86; republican literary heritage and, 117; Vastey countering, 110–12; *Voyage dans*

le Nord d'Hayti by, 93–94, 115–16, 119, 294n69, 294n75
Dun, James, 50, 52–53
Dupré, Antoine, 72, 284n30, 285n34, 285n36
Dupuy, Alexis, 24, 54–55, 78, 121
Durand, Louis-Henry, 235
Duras, Marguerite, 256
Duval-Carrié, Edouard, 306n22
Duvalier, François, 9, 19, 254; fascism and, 9, 254; integral nationalism and, 246; with racism, critiques of, 10; rise of, 233, 257

earthquakes, 154, 227, 294n65, 302n84
The East, 45–46, 72, 74, 103, 126, 128–33, 136–37, 139, 141, 154, 156–58, 160–61, 278n81, 291n23, 297n4, 297n5, 298n17, 301n59, 304n120. *See also* Dominican Republic
L'Eclaireur haytien, ou Le parfait patriote (newspaper), 134
economy, 100, 207, 218, 230
education, 56, 110, 136, 204, 295n86; laws, 163, 305n2; promotion of, 153, 208, 209, 244, 305n2; respect for, 168
égalité (equality), 68, 87, 91, 99
L'égalité des races (Janvier), 207
"1804" (Burr-Reynaud), 235
"1804-1915-1930" (Magny, J. F.), 228–29, 319n4
Eller, Anne, 130, 300n57
"Eloge funèbre d'Anacaona" (Burr-Reynaud), 235, 321n31
l'éloquence républicaine (republican eloquence), 126
L'empereur Dessalines (Coicou, M.), 221
empire, 116, 158; antislavery, 1, 9, 32; freedom and, 30; of liberty, 30–31
Empire of Hayti, 41–48; proclamation of, 41
Enlightenment, 3, 80, 266n8; humanism, 5, 7; tragedy of colonial, 265n1

Enlightenment liberalism, 4, 91; challenges to, 9; hatred of, 53; hypocrisy of, 31; methodical language of, 52; radical critique of, 10; values of, 22
Enlightenment universalism, 4–6, 187; critique of, 37; debate set out by, 8–9; resistance to, 7
Enrico I. Re de Hayti (Dridier), *171*
equality (égalité), 68, 87, 91, 99
España Boba (Stupid Spain), 128
Une étape de l'évolution haïtienne (Price-Mars), 249
Etat Méridional, 203, 313n12
Etienne, Francis, 256
Etudes sur l'histoire d'Haïti (Ardouin, B.), 181, 300n41
executions, 160, 181, 201–2, 203, 318n95
expiation historique (historical atonement), 199, 221–24, 226

factionalism, 5, 17, 202–3, 205, 226, 230, 269n32
Fanon, Frantz, 267n12
fascism, 9, 254
Fatton, Robert, 10
Faubert, Pierre, 181, 184–87, 195
Faustin 1er, Emperor of Haiti, *176*
Fauxteint 1er, empereur d'Haïti, et son auguste famille (Quillenbois and Théo-Edo), *169*, 169–70
feminist activists, 321n32
Fermina Marquez (Larbaud), 322n41
Férou, Laurent, 23
La Feuille du commerce (trade journal), 95, 167
Fick, Carolyn, 270n58
Firmin, Anténor, 210, 312n9; anthropology and, 316n63, 316n65; Janvier, Louis Joseph, and, 218, 316n67; as leader, 217–20, 226; support for, 318n95
Firminisme, 218, 219, 226
Firministes: goal of, 219; Nordistes and, 217–26

First Republic (France), 4, 24
Fischer, Kurt, 256
Fischer, Sibylle, 95, 196
Le flibustier (Vilaire), 318n94
Foucault, Michel, 266n8
Fouchard, Calisthène, 217, 318n92
Fouché, Luc, 247–48
Fourier, Charles, 153
François, Jean-Louis, 23
Francophone, 3, 11, 13, 211, 233, 269n33
Fraser, Nancy, 269nn38, 39
fraternité, 130, 137, 188, 189, 193
freedom, 112; civilization and, 19; claiming, 29; empire and, 30; lack of guarantee for, 97; politics, literature and, 3; from slavery, 22; in *Stella*, 189, 190; surrendering, 30; of thought, 126. *See also* liberty
free men (*hommes libres*), 82, 96
free soil, 97, 134, 291n23
French colonists, massacre of, 23, 29
French Restoration, 64, 83
French Revolution, 98, 104, 165, 182, 192–93, 245, 325n78
Friends and Enemies (Bongie), 269n33
funeral ceremonies, 167, 183, 281n126

Gaffield, Julia, 272n12, 305n6
Gaillard, Roger, 312n7
Garraway, Doris, 268n26, 270n45, 287n60
de Gastine, Civique, 94
Gazette officielle de l'Etat d'Hayti, 66, 67
Gazette officielle de Saint-Domingue, 66
Gazette politique et commerciale d'Haïti, 34, 66, 67, 277n71
Geffrard, Nicolas, 23, 25, 311n1, 312n9; criticism of, 222; with executions, 201–2; rise of, 201
Geggus, David, 29–30, 129–30, 265n5, 275n47
gender, 180, 305n2; equality, 325n3
General Council, of Christophe, 76–78; text excerpts from Malouet presented to, 79

"Au génie de la patrie" (Nau, I.), 302n78
"génie de la patrie" (spirit of the nation), 153, 190–91, 275n40
genocide, 77, 273n24
Géographie de l'Ile d'Haïti (Ardouin, B.), 130, 135–36, 144–45, 164
George III (King of England), 172
Gérin, Elie, 23, 33, 35, 54; crimes committed by, 60, 63; insurgency led by, 51; for liberty, 53
Giacommetti, Alberto, 256
Gilroy, Paul, 267n12
Girard, Philippe, 68, 284n27
Global South, 3
Gobineau, Arthur de, 218, 316n63
Goffe, Tao Leigh, 289n7
Goman. *See* Perrier, Jean-Baptiste
Gorgues, Almonor de, 168
Gouverneurs de la rosée (Roumain), 240
Granville, Jonathas, 94, 98
Great Britain, 230
Green, Nita, 256
Grégoire, Abbé, 80, 288n63
Grimard, Luc, 231, 249, 255
Les Griots (magazine), 231, 244, 254, 324n69, 325n81
Groos, René, 246
guerre de plume (paper war), 3, 4, 19, 23, 92–93, 108, 119, 127; assassination of Dessalines and, 60; literary program during, 121; Malouet in context of civil war, 75–76; Mercier and, 251; pamphlets and, 118; print culture with civil war, 64–73; symbolism of civil war, 65–66; usage, 266n6
Guerre du Môle, 72
Guerrier, Philippe, 157, 181

Habermas, Jürgen, 11–12, 15–16, 107
Haiti: humanity and, 200; Island, 139–53; US occupation of, 226, 228–31, 234–38, 244, 246, 248–52, 325n78. *See also* Empire of Hayti; Second Empire, of

Haiti; universal Haitian Republic, myth of
Haiti, History, and the Gods (Dayan), 163, 270n53, 301n75, 318n91, 318n92
Haitian Declaration (Gaffield), 272n12
Haitian Revolution, 3, 182; Bergeaud with *Stella* and, 188–94; "1804-1915-1930" and, 228–29; end to, 48; goals of, 17; as "several in one," 265n5. *See also* War of Independence
Haïti et ses peintres (Lerebours), 163, 297n4, 297n12, 305n1
Hartmann, 177
haytian writing style (*tournure haytienne*), 109–10
Hérard, Rivière, 181, 183
L'héritage sacré (Cinéas), 241
Les héroïnes (Thoby-Marcelin), 241
Heureuse, Marie-Claire, 281n126, 285n35
Heurtelou, E., 302n79
Hibbert, Fernand, 213
Hill, Robert A., 268n18
Hippolyte, Dominique, 234–35, 279n96, 320n22
Histoire des caciques d'Haïti (Nau, Emile), 141, 194–200, 222
Histoire d'Haïti (Madiou), 17, 189–90, 272n4, 280n108, 297n4
historical atonement (*expiation historique*), 199, 221–24, 226
historiographic memory, 16
Hiver caraïbe (Morand), 252
hommes libres (free men), 82, 96
Honduras, 319n8
Hugo, Victor, 306n18, 309n60
humanism: Black Atlantic, 5, 7; Enlightenment, 5, 7
humanity: dignity and, 259; fundamental, 9; Nau, Emile, and Haitian, 200; sovereignty, legitimacy and, 15
human rights, 9, 41
Hyder Ali (Sultan of Mysore), 173

"Hymne à la famille impériale" (Gorgues), 168
"Hymne haytiène" (Chanlatte), 276n50
Hyppolite, Florvil, 217, 218, 221

Ice-T, 179, 180, 307n38
Ice T (Wiley), 179
identity: national, 19; politics, culture and, 18; of US, 50
illiteracy, 9, 14, 18, 37, 77, 163–64, 167
imagery: technology, 178; Vastey and use of, 83–84
imperial constitution, 6, 46–48
imperialism: Boyer, Jean-Pierre, with republican, 129; Dessalinean, 30–32; Napoleonic, 31; US hemispheric, 204
indemnity agreement (1825), 133, 160, 298n17, 299n31
indemnity payments, 75–76, 108
independence, 2, 10, 26, 28–31, 62; act and oath of, 27; from colonial rule, 4–5; commitment to, 108; Dessalines declaring, 21, 273n19; eternalizing, 32; events surrounding, 44; oath of, 48; production of writings for, 14; role of Dessalines, post, 26; sovereignty and, 76; survival and, 45
indigeneity (nativeness), 108
indigénisme, 130, 140, 196, 244
indigéniste poetry, 301n75
indigenous literature, of Island Haiti, 139–53
individual interests, protection of, 52
individual will, self-liberation and, 54
Inginac, Joseph Balthazar, 24, 54–55, 139
Ingres, Jean-Auguste-Dominique, 180, 307n38
Innocent, Sylvia, 225
Instruction publique (Brutus, E.), 305n4
integral nationalism, 9, 229, 233, 244–47, 253–54, 319n6, 325n81
Island Haiti (l'Ile d'Haïti), indigenous literature of, 139–53

James, C. L. R., 265n1, 326n11
Janvier, Louis Joseph, 9, 132, 241, 315n39; Dessalinean sphere and, 211; Firmin and, 218, 316n67; on land reform, 212–13; with Liberal Party as "pseudo-libéraux," 214, 324n76; with nationals, 203, 206–11, 216; on Soulouque, 165; Soulouque and, 175; *Stella* and, 232, 325n76; "Le vieux piquet" and, 207, 211–16
Jean-Louis Bon Dos, 211–16
Jefferson, Thomas: Dessalines and, 272n12, 274n35; liberty and, 30–31; trade suspended by, 50–53
Jenson, Deborah, 7, 26–27, 71, 173, 179, 265n1, 267n17, 270n53, 275n47, 277n65
Jérémie, Joseph, 223, 225
Johnson, Sara, 298n17
Jonassaint, Jean, 213, 287n59
Joseph, Délide, 135
Joseph, Régine, 325n4
Joséphine (Empress), *169*, 170
journalism, 94, 101, 134
J/P HRO, 227
Jumeau, Jean, 220

Killick, Hammerton, 220
Kjærgård, Jonas Ross, 310n73
konbit (collective labor), 239, 241–42, 294n75
Kreyòl, 14, 26, 28, 139, 141, 142, 216, 273n19, 301n61

Lacroix, Abel, 246
Laforest, Edmond, 230
Lamarre (General), 72, 285n36
land: distribution, 322n46; reform, 207–8, 212–13, 215, 284n29; rights for foreigners, 299n37
language, 14; colonialism and, 209; delegitimization through, 84; with Dessalines denounced by US, 281n117; dialects and regional, 110; as impenetrable, 81; inconsistent, ambiguous, 86–87; of Malouet as broken apart, 82–83; power of printed, 89; of republicans, 52; Vastey emphasis on certain, 82. *See also* Creole; discourse; Kreyòl
La Lanterne (magazine), 232, 323n61
LaPorta, Katie, 15
Laprée, Delille, 94, 98–99
Larbaud, Valery, 232, 320n15, 322n41
Laroche, Maximilien, 161
Lavaysse, Jean-Joseph Dauxion, 74–76, 83, 286n45, 286n48, 289n78, 290n9
Laveaux, Etienne, 288n61
laws, 47, 52; Armée Indigène and natural, 44; education, 163, 305n2; *hors la loi* or outlaws, 58; obedience to, 58; trade, 50; against Vodou, 201
Leclerc, Charles, 29, 42, 77, 88, 128, 266n5, 284n27, 298n14
Leconte, Charles, 221
Leconte, Cincinnatus, 227
Lefevre, Robert, 173
legal documentation, peasants and, 215
legitimacy: Haitian, 1; sovereignty, humanity and, 15; subjectivity, authority and, 15
Légitime, François, 217
Leiris, Michel, 256
Lemoinne, John, 306n14
Lerebours, Michel Philippe, 297n4, 297n12, 305n1; on Soulouque, 163–64; on visual culture and patronage, 166
Lescot, Elie, 254
Lespinasse, Dumai, 140, 302n79
Lespinasse, Massillon, 140
Lhérisson, Justin, 213
Lhérisson, Louis Carius, 221–22, 224, 226, 245, 317n87, 318n90
libelles (pasquinades), 80
liberalism: capacity of, 120; Christophean writing against, 113; literature, liberty and, 12; virtues of, 69. *See also* Enlightenment liberalism

Liberal Party, 205–8, 212, 214–15, 218, 313n18, 324n76
liberal republicanism, 127; Pétion and, 65, 69; threat to, 32, 34
Liberal Revolution, 103, 154–57, 302n86
Liberals: with Firministes and Nordistes, 216–26; Nationals and, 204–11
"Liberté ou la mort," 191
liberty (*liberté*), 4–5, 91, 266n7; compared to true liberty, 53; embracing, 107; empire of, 30–31; expression of, 121; freedom and, 3, 19, 22, 29–30, 97, 112, 126, 189, 190; Jefferson and, 30–31; liberalism, literature and, 12; meaning of, 18, 50, 52, 60; monarchy on meaning of, 76–77; monarchy stance on, 76; Pétion and Gérin for, 53; preserving, 34; from slavery, 35
liberty trees, 65
Ligue feminine d'action sociale, 255, 321n32, 325n3
l'Ile d'Haïti. *See* Island Haiti, indigenous literature of
Linstant, Pradine, 220–21, 317n74
de Lisle, Claude Joseph Rouget, 35, 37–39
literariness, 3, 28
literary and political journals (*revues*), 16, 91, 99
literary criticism, 10–12, 91, 104; for Chanlatte, 121–22; Colombel and, 112–13; by Dumesle for Vastey, 122–26
literature, 18; authorship and, 11, 26, 84; concept of, 10–12; criticism and, 92; freedom, politics and, 3; Island Haiti and indigenous, 139–53; knowledge of, 109; liberalism, liberty and, 12; limited possibility for, 99, 111; politics as separate from, 113; southern tradition, 107–8; value of, 121
Lochard, Colbert, 163
lodyans (short stories), 208, 212–14, 216, 240
Logan bill, 50

López López, Manuel, *174*
Louis XVIII, King, 74
Lycée national (Lycée Pétion), 91, 99, 185, 206, 306n12

Macaya, 18, 33
MacLeod, Murdo J., 307n31
Madiou, Thomas, 33, 194, 225, 271n2, 273n16, 277n65; *Autobiographie* and, 303n109; on Bonnet, 280n105; on Chanlatte, 284n31; on Christophe proclamation, 58; on Dessalineans, 272n8; on Dessalines, 41–43, 142–43, 190, 277n64; on Dupré, 284n30; on Heureuse, 285n35; with *Histoire d'Haïti*, 17, 189–90, 272n4, 280n108, 297n4; with historical research, 41–43, 45–46, 50, 57–58, 87, 129, 139, 278n72; on independence proclamation, 273n19; Jenson on, 270n53; legacy of, 140, 270n51; Lycée national and, 306n12; on Milscent, 290n9; *Le Moniteur* and, 167; on Pierrot, J.-L., 157; with poetry, 143; on republicans, 24, 32; on Rigaud, 291n20; secretarial corps and, 34; in *L'Union*, 142
Magloire, Paul, 255–56, 257, 325n2
Magny, Etienne, 54, 55, 65
Magny, J. F., 228–29, 237, 319n4
Maintenant (magazine), 232
Making the Black Jacobins (Douglas), 265n1
Malouet, Pierre Victor, 27, 51, 85, 89, 280n106; blasphemous characterizations by, 82; breaking apart language of, 82–83; as colonial minister, 73–74; in context of civil war, 75–76; published memoirs of, 78; text excerpts from, presented to General Council, 79
Malouet affair, 73, 75, 79, 85, 89, 289n78
Le Manifeste (newspaper), 153, 302n79
Manifesto of May 3, 1844, 157

Marcelin, Frédéric, 213
Marie-Louise (Queen), 303n95
Marines, US, 228–29
Martin, Jean-Clément, 16
Marx, Karl, 306n18
Marxism, 245
Marxism and Literature (Williams), 92
massacres, 23, 29–30, 47–48, 192
Maurras, Charles, 234–35, 244, 246, 252–53, 320n16
Maurrassisme, 229, 233, 245–46, 252–53, 319n6, 320n16
mauvais livres (bad books), 15, 107
Maxence, Jean-Pierre, 246
Mayobanex, 141
Mbembe, Achille, 266n8, 267n8, 267n112
McCarthyism, 255
McIntosh, Tabitha, 173
de Médina, Agoustine Franco, 74–75, 296n1
Mémoire du général de brigade André Rigaud en réfutation des écrits calomnieux contre les citoyens de couleur de Saint-Domingue (Rigaud), 287n61
Mémoires du général Toussaint-L'Ouverture écrits par lui-même (Toussaint Louverture), 181
Mémoires pour servir à l'histoire d'Haïti (Boisrond Tonnerre), 181, 187–88
men, 94, 160; with collective labor, 294n75; extermination of black, 29; massacres of, 192; with patronage and visual culture, 166; poetry and, 167; voting rights for, 255, 325n3
Ménard, Nadève, 265n4
Mentor, Etienne Victor, 24–26, 54, 55, 94
Mentor, Gaétan, 305n7
Mercier, Louis, 244, 246, 252, 324n74, 324n76; *guerre de plume* and, 251; *Stella* and, 231, 248–52; on US in Haiti and French Revolution, 325n78; Werleigh and, 235

La méringue, 318n92
Mes mémoires (Dumas), 168
Le Messager du Nord (newspaper), 218
Métral, Antoine, 125
Mexico, 319n8
Middelanis, Carl Hermann, 116
Milscent, Jules Solime, 94, 98–102, 108–9, 134, 284n30, 290n9
"Le miracle" (Werleigh), 235–38
misprinting, 27–28
modèle Dessalines, 6
modernity, 2; bourgeois liberal, 12; refusal of, 8; universalist claims of, 6
Moïse, Jovenel, 319n2
Môle Saint-Nicolas, 72, 218, 230, 294n68
Momplaisir Pierre, Sénèque, 205, 217
Mompoint, Guizot, 234
monarchism, 16
monarchy, 24, 54; inequality inherent to, 105; on meaning of *liberté*, 76–77
Mongey, Vanessa, 94–95
Le Moniteur (newspaper), 167–68, 175, 177, 303n113, 304n120, 307nn30, 31
monstrous hybridity, 88
Morand, Paul, 232, 252
La mort du Général Lamarre, 72
mouvement folklorique, 244
Musée du panthéon national haïtien (MUPANAH), 307n32, 317n74
music, 166, 294n75, 318n92
Mussolini, Benito, 249
myths: of Dessalines, 267n10; of republicanism and civil war, 16–19; of Rome, founding, 189–90, 322n44; of Romulus and Rémus, 188–90, 322n44; of singularity, 11; Voudou, 37. *See also* universal Haitian Republic, myth of

Najman, Charles, 325n5
Napoléon I. *See* Bonaparte, Napoléon
Napoléon III. *See* Bonaparte, Louis Napoléon
National Archive, 277n65, 278n72

nationalism: economic, 207; ethno-, 231, 244, 254, 259; integral, 9, 229, 233, 244–47, 253–54, 319n6, 325n81; occupation-era cultural, 230–39, 250
National Palace, 183, 227–29
National Party, 205–7, 219, 313n18, 314n28
National Portrait Gallery, 180
national revolution: in historical context, 227–29; with occupation-era cultural nationalism, 230–39, 250; peasant récits and, 239–44; Stella and, 244–54
Nationals: Firministes and Nordistes with, 217–26; Janvier and, 203, 206–11, 216; Liberals and, 204–11
nativeness (indigeneity), 108
natural law, Armée Indigène and, 44
natural obligation (devoir naturel), 44
Nau, Emile, 9, 140, 141, 222, 304n123; with Amerindian history, 194; concorde and, 153, 162; expiation historique and, 199, 224; humanity and, 200; on posterity, 259; with Western civilization, problem of, 194–200
Nau, Eugène, 140
Nau, Ignace, 140, 145–53, 187, 196, 302n78; with Amerindian history, 194; "conte créole" and, 142; death of, 304n123; poetry and, 143, 162, 198
Nau, Laurore-Auguste, 140, 304n123
Nérée, Bob, 320n16
neutrality, principle of, 43
Nicholls, David, 206, 209, 313n18, 313nn22, 23, 314n24
noiriste ideology, 206, 208
nomination documents, 43
nonviolence, civilization and, 165, 184
Nord Alexis, Pierre, 217, 219–21, 223, 226, 318n95
Nordistes, Firministes and, 217–26
North Atlantic scholarship, 2
northern kingdom: collective textual endeavor of, 77; dissemination of information in, 109; southern republic integration with, 114; southern republic negating legitimacy of, 98; wealth of, 110–11; writing of, 92
Nugent, George, 277n65
Núñez de Cáceres, José, 128–29, 141

Obama, Barack, 180
obedience: enforcing, 33; to laws, 58
L'Observateur, 92–93, 99, 119–20; Dumesle in, 295n86; front cover of, *103*; main subjects covered in, 104; style of, 102
L'Œuvre, 223
Ogé, ou Le préjugé de couleur (Faubert), 181, 184–87
Ogé, Vincent, 184
operas, 118, 122, 283n5, 287n51, 300n57, 301n61
oppression, 104; critiques of, 10; forms of, 9; systems of, 8
oral traditions, 143, 145, 150, 166, 237
oriental despotism, 271n1, 281n117
Orléans, Louis Philippe d', 172

La palma del cacique (Tapia y Rivera), 300n57
pamphlets, 224, 273n21, 278n72, 282n1, 287n61; *guerre de plume* and, 118; refutation, 79–84
Panama, 319n8
paper war (*guerre de plume*), 3, 4, 23
parricide, 55, 57, 191, 199, 222–24, 238, 272n8
parricide-regicide, 25, 50
pasquinades (*libelles*), 80
Le Patriote (newspaper), 153, 302n79
patronage, visual culture and, 166
Paul, Edmond, 205, 217, 313n18
Payton, Claire, 132
Péan, Leslie J. R., 254, 320n16, 325n81
Péan, Marc, 219, 271n59, 318n95
peasant *récits*, 141, 234, 239–41

peasants, 18; armed, 216; disenfranchised, 164; land reform and, 207–8, 212–13; legal documentation and, 215; lives of, 141–42; *récits*, 141, 234, 239–44; rights of, 166, 212; support of, 202; "Le vieux piquet" and, 211–16

Peltier, Jean-Gabriel, 70

pen, sword and, 47, 83–84

Penn, Sean, 227

Péralte, Charlemagne, 230

performativity, 15, 16, 62, 209, 270n45, 283n5; power and political, 9, 46–47, 62, 89, 101, 186; writing and, 12, 15, 34, 64, 84, 91, 93, 122, 130

Perinette, M. A., 256

Perrier, Jean-Baptiste (Goman), 18, 54–55, 57, 72, 285n36; armed insurgency of, 67; *lodyans* and, 214

Pétion, Alexandre, 23, 35, 42, 54, 85–87, 131, 136, 210; absolute power of, 64; Chanlatte description of, 62–63; consolidation by, 96–97; crimes committed by, 60; criticism of, 236, 237–38; expeditions sent by, 72; inauguration speech of, 61; land reform and, 212–13; legacy of, 138; liberal concepts of, 102; liberal republicanism and, 65, 69; for liberty, 53; new republicanism under, 94, 97–98; nomination for, 60; as outlaw, 58; personal secretary, 112; public image of, 73; reelection of, 91; returnees used by, 98–99; *Stella* and, 189; with successor, 298n14; suffering of, 56; symbolism adopted by, 68–69; transformations under, 93; Vastey depicting, 87–88

Pétion et Haïti (Saint-Rémy), 181

Petit Théâtre, 317n82

La Phalange (magazine), 232, 323n61

Philippe, Dalgé, 167

physiologie (written portrait), 61–62, 283n8

Píar, Manuel, 135

Picasso, Pablo, 256

Picon, Gaëtan, 256

Pierre, Louis Dumas, 250

Pierre, Sénèque Momplaisir, 217

Pierrot, Grégory, 6, 173, 273n16

Pierrot, Jean-Louis, 156, 157–58, 183

Pilatte, Léon, 306n14

pipeuse (deceptive, dishonest), 27–28, 273n23

piquet rebellions, 103

Pius IX (Pope), 177

plantation system, 96

Poésies nationales (Coicou, M.), 222

poetry, 119, 143, 162, 198, 301nn70, 71; anticolonialism promoted through, 34–35; couplets in, 235, 290n11; creole, 271n59; *indigéniste*, 301n75; politics, Dessalinean writing and, 71; ruin, 116–18, 294n73; silencing of, 124; women and, 167, 168

political liberalism, 4, 13, 16

political symbolism, 46

political uprooting (*déchoukaj*), 45

politics, 47; identity, culture and, 18; literature as separate from, 113

Polvérel, 278n75

"Le Pont Rouge" (Ardouin, C.), 143, 225

postcolonial refutation, 78–84

postcolonial state, 1–2

posterity, 196–97, 221–22, 224

Pour Dessalines (Lhérisson, L. C.), 221, 224

power: consolidation of, 114; of Dessalines, 52; mystique of, 13; people granting, 61; of Pétion, as absolute, 64; of printed language, 89; of printing presses, 85; sharing of democracy and, 34; usurpation of, 59; violence and, 32–33

Pressoir, Catts, 210

Prévost, Julien, 78, 80, 86, 121, 287n52

Prézeau, Sylvain, 78, 80, 85, 121

Price-Mars, Jean, 221, 231, 239–40, 243, 249, 321n37

INDEX | 361

print culture: Chanlatte dominating northern, 73; under Christophe, 70–71, 89; during civil war, 64–73; deconstruction of colonial, 84; performativity and, 9, 12, 15, 16, 34, 46–47, 62, 64, 84, 89, 91, 93, 101, 122, 130, 186, 209, 270n45, 283n5; in Saint Domingue, 66; tracing, 24
printing presses, 26; dissemination of documentation en masse via, 77–78; locations and control of, 65–66; power of, 85; quality of, 70
La proie et l'ombre (Roumain), 241
property titles, verifying, 50
Protestants, 15, 206, 207, 219, 273n21
"pseudo-libéraux," 214, 250, 251, 324n76
Psyché (magazine), 232
public performance, 12, 146, 166, 167
Puerto Rico, 319n8

Quantin, Pierre, 284n27
Quillenbois (Charles-Marie de Sarcus), 172, 178, 306n20; in *La Caricaturiste*, 169, 169–70; despotism and, 173, 175; Vodou and, 175

race, 88; color theory and, 206; exclusionary tactics based on, 13
racism: colonial, 5; Duvalier with critiques of, 10; Société d'anthropologie and, 316n63
Rameau, Septimus, 205, 206, 313n18
Ramsey, Kate, 132, 166
ravir (robbing), 29
Raybaud, Maxime (Gustave d'Alaux), 175, 305n1, 306n9
Raynal, Abbé, 172
récit de voyage genre, 116
recognition treaty, 76
reenslavement: threat of, 38; through violence, 30
Réflexions sur le prétendu Sénat de Port-au-Prince (Chanlatte), 224, 250

"refugees," Saint Dominguan, 94–98, 289n7
refutation (*réfutation*), 27, 79–80
refutation pamphlet, 79–84
regionalism, 18
Reinsel, Amy, 302n77
Rémus, 188–90, 322n44
René, Jean Alix, 270n58, 284n29
repli sur soi, 108, 248
Le Républicain (newspaper), 140, 141, 145, 153
republican eloquence (*l'éloquence républicaine*), 126
republicanism, 3, 4, 9, 13, 42; battle between Dessalineanism and, 49; civil war and myth of, 16–19; classical, 52; color-blind, 6, 133, 135, 178, 208; continuity in, 67; criticism of, 170; Dessalines on threat of, 34; Gérin role in, 51; illiberal nature of, 61; revolutionary, 31; role of, 131; symbolism of, 35, 50, 69; universal conception of, 95–96, 108
republican literary heritage, 117
republicans, 3; language of, 52; Madiou on, 24, 32; teleology, 16
République Septentrionale, 217
residency, citizenship and, 299n37
resistance: to Dessalineanism, 48; to Enlightenment universalism, 7; to oppression, 52; political journals as form of, 91; of republicans, 50
résistance à l'oppression (right of revolution), 44, 51, 52, 57, 278n75
revolution: Age of Revolution, 1, 16, 80, 290n16; concept of, 21; Dessalinean counter-revolution, 54–59; French Revolution, 98, 104, 165, 182, 192–93, 245, 325n78; as radical, liberal, universal, 1; republican, 2; right of, 44, 57, 278n75. *See also* Haitian Revolution; national revolution
La Revue indigène (literary magazine), 231–33, 240, 244, 252, 320n12, 320n15

revues (literary and political journals), 16, 91, 99
Riché, Jean-Baptiste, 158, 183
Rigaud, André, 67, 72, 189, 266n5, 287n61, 290n20
Rigaudins, 26
right of revolution (*la résistance à l'oppression*), 44, 51, 52, 57, 278n75
rights: foreigners and land, 299n37; human, 9, 41; of peasants, 166, 212; voting, 255, 325n3
Rivière Hérard, Charles, 103, 155, 157, 158, 183
Le Roi Henry et sa cour (Torchiana), 306n22
Romane, Jean-Baptiste, 167–68
Rome, founding myth, 189–90, 322n44
Romulus, 188–90, 322n44
Rouanez, Charles Victor, 24
Rougier et Cie, 207
Roumain, Jacques, 232, 233, 240, 241–42, 320n15, 322n40
Roumer, Emile, 320n15, 321n37
La route ensoleillée (Hippolyte), 234
Roux, Pierre, 66, 283n22
Royal Bonbon (film), 325n5
Les ruines, ou Méditations sur les révolutions des Empires (Volney), 116
ruin poetry, 116–18, 294n73

Saget, Nissage, 202–3, 205
Saib, Tippoo, 172
Saint Domingue, 23, 25–26, 28; print culture in, 66; refugees from, 94–98; Santo Domingo and, 128
Saint-Méry, Moreau de, 136
Saint-Rémy, Joseph, 17, 181, 184, 187–88, 195
Saint-Simon, Henri de, 153
Salnave, Sylvain, 202–3, 227, 312n9, 312n10
Salomon, Lysius, 156, 202, 205, 207, 216, 312n10
Sam, Tirésias Simon, 217, 219

Sam, Vilbrun Guillaume, 226, 230
Sánchez Ramírez, Juan, 141
Sansay, Lenora, 280n107
Sans Souci, Jean-Baptiste, 18, 33, 266n5
Sarcus, Charles-Marie de. *See* Quillenbois
Scission du Sud, 67, 72, 96–97
Scott, David, 198, 265n1, 268n18, 269n35
Second Empire, of Haiti: Bergeaud with *Stella* and, 188–94; with Dessalines, disavowal of, 181–88; in historical context, 163–65; Nau, Emile, and, 194–200; trolling Napoléon and, 165–80
Second Empire, of Napoléon III, 169, 182, 309n60
secretarial corps, 13, 25–26, 33–34, 46–47, 66, 77
Secret History (Sansay), 280n107
Séguy Villevaleix, Charles, 154
La Sentinelle d'Haïti, Gazette du Port-au-Prince, 67–68, 69, 284n23
Serie di vite e ritratti di famosi personaggi, degli ultimi tempi (Series of lives and portraits of famous characters of recent times), 172, 173
Serreau, Jean-Marie, 256
Shapiro, Norman, 277n57
short stories (*lodyans*), 208, 212–14, 216, 240
Sieburth, Richard, 283n8
Silencing the Past (Trouillot, M.), 1
Simpson, George Eaton, 239
Slave Narrative (Jenson), 265n1, 267n17, 270n53, 275n47
slavery, 37, 96, 270n58; abolishment of, 97, 128, 129, 168; antislavery empire, 1, 9, 32; chattel, 4, 7, 30, 38, 74, 104, 184; defending, 27; describing, 104; freedom from, 22; insurrection, 44; liberty from, 35
Smith, Matthew, 202, 226, 312n8
Société d'anthropologie, 218, 316n63
Société des amis du roi Henry, 255–56
songs, by Chanlatte, 34–40

Sonthonax, 25, 278n75, 287n61, 288n61
Soulouque, Faustin, 15, 285n36, 303n107, 304n115; *Album impérial d'Haïti* and, 176, 177–80; with artistic production, 163, 165, 166–67; caricature of, 169, 170, 176, 177; coronation ceremonies and, 161, 170, 175, 176, 177, 179; criticism of, 163–64, 175; crown of, 307n32; Dessalines and, 183; fall of, 201; imperial crest of, 307n36; with racism, 178; rise of, 158–62; rule of, 132, 165–80; as troll, 179–80; with Vodou, 166
southern literary tradition, 107–8
southern republic, 95; northern kingdom integration with, 114; northern kingdom legitimacy negated by, 98; opinions about, 110–11; returnees to, 97–98; turning point for, 91–92
southern republican writing, 89; tradition of, 93; Vastey on, 107–8
sovereignty, 61; acts of, 29; independence and, 76; legitimacy, humanity and, 15; post-independence, 1
Spanish American War of Independence, 91
spirit of the nation ("*génie de la patrie*"), 153, 190–91, 275n40
Stella (Bergeaud), 181, 188–94, 309n58
Stella (literary magazine), 309n58; Dalencour and, 322n46; Hippolyte and, 320n22; Janvier and, 232, 325n76; national revolution and, 244–54; occupation-era cultural nationalism and, 231–35; peasant *récits* and, 239–41; writers, 229, 232–33, 235, 239–40, 247, 319n10, 320n17, 322n46
Stowe, Harriet Beecher, 168, 306n14, 306n15
Stupid Spain (España Boba), 128
sung couplets, 43, 277n71
sword, pen and, 47, 83–84
symbolism: of Bazile, Dédée, as national conscience, 237, 318n92; Bonaparte and, 68–69; of civil war, 65–66; French republican, 99; of historic sites, 120; political, 46; of republicanism, 35, 50, 69; sword and pen, 47, 83–84

Taino Indians, 141, 195, 300n57
Tapia y Rivera, Alejandro, 300n57
Le Télégraphe (newspaper), 70, 99, 133, 144, 154, 284n29, 284n30
Le Temps (newspaper), 154
territorial *concorde*, 130
textual production, 13, 71, 77, 92; as performative, 93; practices of, 11–12; as valorized, 101; of Vastey, 82, 89
textual war, on south, 85–90
textual weaponry, 30, 60, 81
Théâtre Haïtien, 223
Théâtre Sylvain, 317n82
Thélémaque, Séide, 217
Théo-Edo, 169, 169–70, 306n20
"31 décembre 1838" (Nau, I.), 145–53
Thoby-Marcelin, Philippe, 241, 320n15, 322n41
Times of London (newspaper), 271n1
Torchiana, 172, 306n22
tourism, 255, 323n61, 325n2
tournure haytienne (haytian writing style), 109–10
Toussaint Louverture, 5, 181; arrest of, 199; despotism and, 137; legacy of, 142–43; with slavery, abolishment of, 128; as "spin doctor," 179, 265n1
trade: Dessalines and, 272n12; possibility of, 73; suspension of US and Haiti, 50–53
La tragédie du roi Christophe (Césaire), 244, 256, 258
transformations, 2–3; of Dessalines original oath, 54–55; under Pétion, 93
Treaty of Paris (1783), 286n49
Treaty of Ryswick (1967), 128
Trichet, Théodat, 62
Trois, David, 62

Trouillot, Ernst, 210, 256, 312n9, 325n6
Trouillot, Hénock, 93, 114, 126, 141, 210, 280n108
Trouillot, Lyonel, 6
Trouillot, Michel-Rolph, 1, 17, 33, 204, 256, 271n61
Troy, David, 23
true liberty (*vraie liberté*), 53–56
truth: masking, 28; unveiling of, 89
de Tussac, François Richard, 80
tyrannie des parricides ("tyranny of parricides"), 55, 272n8

Uncle Tom's Cabin (Stowe), 168, 306n14
L'Union (newspaper), 140, 141, 142, 145, 146, 153
United States (US): Haiti occupied by, 226, 228–31, 234–38, 244, 246, 248–52, 325n78; hemispheric imperialism, 204; identity of, 50; intervention by, 319n8; with language denouncing Dessalines, 281n117; Marines, 228–29; newspapers from, 52–53; Revolutionary War, 286n49
unity: Christophe emphasis on, 85; enforcing, 33
universal Haitian Republic, myth of: concorde of Boyer or, 131–39, 152, 181; in historical context, 128–31, 164; with indigenous literature of Island Haiti, 139–53; regionalism, world of 1848 and return to empire with, 153–62
universalism. *See* Enlightenment universalism
US. *See* United States

Vastey, Jean Louis, 49, 197, 210, 222; Bongie on, 80, 269n33, 270n44; Christophean writing and, 73; critiques by, 87; Dumesle countered by, 110–12; Dumesle literary criticism for, 122–26; imagery used by, 83–84; language emphasized by, 82; mode of expression, 109; Pétion depicted by, 87–88; published text of, 78; refutation and, 81; on southern republican writing, 107–8; textual production of, 82, 89; War of Independence and, 88
Vastey, Pompée-Valentin, 285n40
Vaval, Duraciné, 317n78
Vaval, Guillaume, 24, 35, 49, 51
vengeance, 55, 63, 105, 112, 182, 185–89, 194, 196–97; anticolonialism and, 29–30, 182, 184, 187–88, 195, 199; civilization and, 138, 183–87; Dessalines and, 29–30, 32–33, 37, 142–43, 151, 182–88, 191–92, 194–97, 199, 275n47, 276n49, 308n47, 308n58; violence and, 196
La vengeance de la terre (Cinéas), 240, 241, 322n48
Venger l'empereur ou mourir (Dessalinean counter-revolution), 54–59
verslibrisme, 231, 234
Vida de J. J. Dessalines (Dubroca), 173
La vie de Toussaint-L'Ouverture (Saint-Rémy), 181
"Le vieux piquet" (Janvier), 207, 211–16, 241
Vilaire, Etzer, 318n94
Vincent, Sténio, 228, 246, 320n16, 322n40
vindicationism, 27, 267n18, 268n18
violence: anticolonialism and, 13, 33, 184, 188, 192, 194; colonialism and, 27, 29, 77, 184, 192, 198; Dessalinean, 184, 187, 195, 309n58; as foundational, 197; and the French Revolution, 192; genocide and, 77, 273n24; human rights reclaimed through, 9; need for, 27; nonviolent notion of civilization, 165, 184; to order, 47; performance of, 22–23; power and, 32–33; reenslavement through, 30; republican, 49, 135; slavery and, 27, 77; transformed into metaphors, 44; vengeance and, 196; War of Independence and, 48

visual culture, 17, 165–67, 177, 181
Vodou, 271n59, 277n60, 309n61; laws against, 201; mythology, 37; practice of, 139, 166, 175, 248; traditions, 140, 146
Volney, Constantin-François, 116
Voltaire, 173
"voodoo," 258
voting rights, 255, 325n3
Voyage dans le Nord d'Hayti (Dumesle), 93–94, 115–16, 119, 294n69, 294n75
vraie liberté (true liberty), 53–56

Walker, Andrew, 297n4
War of Independence, 29, 33, 108, 142, 223; assassinations and, 266n5; with drownings, 192; Vastey and, 88; violence and, 48
War of Knives, 23, 266n5
War of the South, 33, 266n5, 286n42
Washington, George, 172
weapons: from forces of nature, 44; virtues of liberalism used as, 69; writing, pens as, 26–32, 62, 111–12, 125
Weber, Eugen, 244
Werleigh, Christian, 321n31, 321n32; national revolution and, 249, 251; occupation-era cultural nationalism and, 231, 235–38, 241, 244
Western civilization: Columbus and, 198; problem of, 194–200

Western episteme: Dessalinean critique of, 4–10; writers operating within, 38
Western notion of civilization, 169, 170, 178, 180, 186
"What Is Critique" (Foucault), 266n8
"What Is Enlightenment" (Foucault), 266n8
white supremacists, 8, 259
Wiley, Kehinde, 179, 180, 307n38
Williams, Raymond, 10, 92, 164
women, 18, 94, 160, 202, 238; with collective labor, 294n75; extermination of, 29; feminist activists, 321n32; gender equality and, 325n3; literate, 271n59; massacres of, 192; with patronage and visual culture, 166; poetry and, 167, 168; voting rights for, 255
writing, 3, 19; futility of contractual engagements in, 83; as good, 107; haytian writing style, 109–10; literary sense of, 64; militarized court, 93; of northern kingdom, 92; performativity and, 12, 15, 34, 64, 84, 91, 93, 122, 130; utilitarian, 101; as weapon, 26–32, 62, 111–12, 125. *See also* Christophean writing; Dessalinean writing; discourse; southern republican writing
written portrait (physiologie), 61–62

Yayou, 23, 35

ABOUT THE AUTHOR

CHELSEA STIEBER is Assistant Professor of French and Francophone Studies at Catholic University of America.

www.ingramcontent.com/pod-product-compliance
Lightning Source LLC
Chambersburg PA
CBHW020350080526
44584CB00014B/964